TIME OF CHANGE

TIME OF CHANGE

AN INSIDER'S VIEW OF RUSSIA'S TRANSFORMATION

Roy Medvedev and Giulietto Chiesa

Translated from the Italian by Michael Moore

PANTHEON BOOKS ☖ NEW YORK

The translator wishes to thank the individuals who carried this text the last leg of the journey into English. The sharp eyes and sharper pencils of Esther Allen, David Frederickson, and Fred Wiemer helped give the manuscript its final shape. Rosalie Kearns tackled the formidable problem of tracking down the names from the Italian text to the Russian originals, and rendering them in a form accessible to the English reader. And finally, special thanks to André Schiffrin for his continued support of this project.

—M.M.

Medvedev, Roy Aleksandrovich, 1925–
    [Rivoluzione di Gorbačev. English]
    Time of change : an insider's view of Russia's transformation / by
Roy Medvedev and Giulietto Chiesa.
        p.   cm.
    Translation of: Rivoluzione di Gorbačev.
    Includes bibliographical references.
    ISBN 0-394-58151-2
    1. Soviet Union—Politics and government—1985–   . 2. Perestroĭka.
I. Chiesa, Giulietto, 1940–   . II. Title.
DK288.M4313   1990—947.085'4—dc20   89-43246

Book design by Ronnie Ann Herman
Manufactured in the United States of America

First American Edition

Contents

PREFACE

When Roy Medvedev and I began this book, our second one together, he was still a dissident, as he had been ever since he was expelled from the Communist Party in 1969. But he was still a free agent, a source of independent analysis of Soviet society who could be counted on to be a severe but just critic. By the time this book went to press, Roy Medvedev was a member of the Congress of People's Deputies, elected by the citizens of a Moscow district, and he had just been readmitted to the party. I don't think you could find a more striking example of the changes that have taken place in the Soviet Union during the years surveyed in this chronicle.

There are various reasons why it is not superfluous to mention this fact now. Perestroika is still not complete: if anything, it's still taking its first and most dangerous steps. But it is indispensable to realize that it represents a process of extraordinary historical importance, which is destined to influence Soviet and international events for a long time to come. It has been correctly described as a revolution, not in the metaphorical, but in the literal sense of the word. The events we are analyzing prove this beyond a doubt. Yet— and here is the problem on which to focus—many Westerners have still not grasped how high the stakes are. We are in the presence of a comprehensive revision of the political, economic, and philosophical principles on which one of the two world powers has stood for the past seventy years. No one has failed to comprehend the weight of the influence the Soviet Union has exercised on the direction in which the world is moving. By the same token, no one should fail to comprehend that the extent of the revision promoted by Mikhail Gorbachev involves colossal problems and difficulties. The internal reassessment of such a giant can only result in powerful reverberations throughout the surrounding environment: the Chernobyl tragedy is the most appropriate negative metaphor. The international atmosphere will be affected in every way by the changes taking place in the Soviet Union. The facts prove this: the international climate has already changed appreciably, for the better, in every crucial area.

Conversely, a crisis or even a failure of perestroika could have a disruptive and perhaps a catastrophic effect on the network of international relations. Therefore, the West has a vital interest in a positive outcome to the reform efforts begun in April 1985. The concept of "interdependence," which was first presented by Gorbachev at the Twenty-Seventh Congress of the Communist Party of the Soviet Union, held from 25 February to 6 March 1986, represents both a startling theoretical shift and an open request for the concern and the active involvement of the rest of the world in the task of transforming the Soviet Union.

As has often been the case in the history of the formation of new societies (and in the history of great scientific discoveries), new ideas, and intuitions about new roads to take, are born in moments of crisis, at the difficult points where concepts hinge on reality. The crisis of the USSR is serious, epoch-making, and comprehensive. Gorbachev and the reform group, pressed by the untenable contradictions that have accumulated for decades, have been forced to elaborate a new way of thinking about international relations. "There is no other way," as the Soviet leader has said repeatedly since April 1985. But this does not mean that the only way possible was the road already taken; instead, this was the only one that would help the country out of its crisis, and help the world out of the stalemate created by the threat of nuclear war. But until perestroika has become an irreversible choice (and until the West has understood that it must join in as a protagonist, and not as a spectator), other options will remain open. This is not just our hypothesis. If we don't succeed, writes Aleksandr Yakovlev, a member of the current Soviet leadership's brain trust, then

> destructive tendencies in the economic, political, and moral spheres could reach levels that cannot be corrected. Then the danger we could be threatened by would not be a return to the past, to the times of a stagnant conscience, but to an aggressive and vindictive conservativism, that would celebrate its victory triumphally.[1]

Thus, the new way of thinking is not just an undertaking and a problem for the Soviet leadership. In my opinion it would be quite dangerous to leave the final tally up to the calculations of provisional opportunities, to maneuvers that leave little breathing space, and to attempts to exploit the Soviet crisis in order to dictate conditions to the USSR. It's true that the success of the reform project would give the Soviet Union more space and more ways to expand its huge economic and intellectual potential. But it is also true that the country would emerge from its distress in a new state, inserted into the world market, and freed from obsessions and separateness. It would become a partner in the network of commercial, political, technical, scientific, and cultural relations, rather than a military adversary in a stalemate with fewer and fewer reasons to survive.

I think that it would certainly be an illusion to expect the USSR to become a carbon copy of Western nations. A process of international integration of this dimension certainly helps mitigate many differences. But in a possible future scenario, unchangeable specifics will remain that are the legacy of the seventy post–October Revolution years, and of the millennia of history— of histories—of the Russian and Asian peoples.

In this sense no simplifications can be allowed, nor do they belong in the study of the events currently taking place. The present work is partly an attempt to provide a guided reading from inside the country. One of the factors that make these events mysterious and strewn with optical illusions is the Western observer's persistent habit of decodifying everything in Western terms. This approach loses sight of the fact that the political and social structure of the Soviet Union—however you may want to look at it—is the result of a unique experiment in history that aimed to create a form of society without precedents. Many accidents along the way from Marxist utopianism to real socialism may have upset the project, but that does not mean either that the experiment has gone back to the point where it started, or that it has ended up at the same point as Western societies. If you were to reduce Soviet history to a line diagram, it would look like a parabola, not a circle.

Studying the "laws" is thus a very complicated undertaking, partly because Soviet society has done everything in its power to hide its secrets from everyone, including itself. The beginning of glasnost and democratization, for example, clearly lowered the number of rituals that accompanied the exercise of power, but it did not eliminate them. The political struggle had become more explicit and public, but most of it was still behind closed doors.

One of the lines of questioning this work pursues most frequently regards the enemies of perestroika. They definitely exist, as we can clearly see in the chronicle of events, yet it has proven difficult to identify them for two main reasons. No thorough analysis of the structure of Soviet society exists. Soviet sociology has been impeded by the prohibitions of authority and clouded by ideology, and it has not been able to confront the question. Western research, which is definitely more precise, has run into great difficulty gaining access to even the most elementary data, so it has often been forced to proceed deductively, through analogies. During the April 1989 plenum Gorbachev repeated a sentence that Andropov had already said in 1983: "We realize that we know our country very little." For now, glasnost has allowed us to take a deep look only at those strata immediately beneath the surface.

This book does not aim to respond to such complex questions. Yet from the chronicle of events, the reader can appreciate the broad expansion of political and social forces set into motion by perestroika, and can grasp the evolution of the concept of adversaries within the Soviet leadership—from the repeated statement by Gorbachev and other Soviet leaders that "there is no political opposition to perestroika," to the more and more evident emergence, on the contrary, of antagonistic interests, and thus of opponents. Yet one cannot fault the political intelligence of the Soviet leaders; one cannot assume that they truly thought there was no political opposition to the revolution begun at the April 1985 plenum. The revolution was not against anybody. One of the many paradoxes is the fact that the revolution began in the party, but ran into its most relentless resistance from the party. Gorbachev could not tell the whole truth about this problem, first of all because at the beginning not even he could have determined the size of the opposition or of the support with any degree of precision, and secondly because, to tell the truth, he would have found it impossible to practice the tactics that had allowed him to conclude the Nineteenth Party Conference victoriously. Gorbachev assured the continuation of the party's leadership role—to a party (better yet, to an association of apparatchiks) that had always resisted change, or even been unwilling to understand its significance—at the same time as he created the conditions making the party accountable to public control for the first time. The 26 March elections dealt a solid blow to the apparatchiks, who had fooled themselves into thinking that they had substantially curbed the process of democratization within acceptable limits.

The tactics adopted by the Soviet leader during the years we survey reveal his proceeding by stages. He struck harsh blows against enemies who rarely came out into the open, and then stepped back long enough to let the latecomers catch up, to unite the uncertain, and to reassure the fearful. At the same time, he kept his positions surrounded by a broad circle of ambiguity, to prevent his adversaries from regrouping and an essential fact from being disclosed: that the promoters of the reform process were initially a minority in the party and in the country. From 1985 to 1989, Gorbachev succeeded in transforming this minority into a large-scale movement that is still heterogeneous and differentiated today, but which is quickly realizing its force.

I must beg the reader's indulgence. My accounts of the events were written while they were taking place. What was going on behind the scenes in many crucial moments was reconstructed from sources available during the writing of this book. This work is divided into two distinct parts: the "news" chapters, for which I take full responsibility, and the conversations with Roy Medvedev. The conversations serve a complementary function. They are meant to help the reader who wants a more thorough coverage of the subject, with explanations of controversial issues, historical background, and a comparison of different possible interpretations. This is exactly what we set out to do. The conversations also took place along the way, sometimes a few weeks, sometimes a few months after the events discussed. Roy Medvedev and I agreed in most cases, but, as you will see, there are also points of disagreement. We believe that this unusual format will allow two different levels of reading, by providing information that is essential for following the events, but also by suggesting critical variations on how events could be interpreted. In the years to come, new disclosures and developments in the battle will bring to light other factors that might correct or even disprove some of our interpretations. But this first systematization of the information and of the eyewitness accounts could be invaluable to future students of these events. Many of the things talked about here are appearing in print for the first time, and are pieces of a puzzle that could one day help to provide a complete and subtle picture of these years. In the future we will need to understand not only what has happened, but what could still happen. These years of change, however they may end, are destined to shake the world.

Moscow
July 1989

I am writing these final remarks from a new vantage point. After nine years in Moscow, where I witnessed all the convulsive phases of the end of an illusion, I have followed the earth-shaking events of recent months from farther away: Washington. Poland is led by Solidarity, and the Polish Communist Party has changed its name. Hungary has declared a multiparty system, changed the name of its Socialist Workers' Party, and opened the way to a market economy; the coming elections will likely result in a coalition government headed by a non-Communist. In East Germany, Erich Honecker's regime was swept away by public protests; now that the Berlin Wall has been torn down, East Germany is preparing to be reunited with West Germany. The people of Czechoslovakia elected as their new president a writer who six months earlier had been in prison as a dissident. They are moving toward a parliamentary democracy in which the Communists will probably be in the minority, if they are part of the government at all. In the public squares of Sofia, Todor Zhivkov is now described as a provincial Hitler, and Bulgaria is following in the footsteps of the other East European countries.

Each of these regimes collapsed like a house of cards, sometimes in a matter of days. The same parties that had boasted of their "indestructible unity with the people" were dissolved amid public scorn. All of this took place peacefully, without bloodshed, with the sole exception of the overthrow of Ceauşescu, where the dictator's folly exacted a horrifying tribute of victims from the country. The Warsaw Pact survived as an indistinctly shaped simulacrum. Comecon was not even salvaged as a formal fiction. The "empire" was dissolved, and all of this took place—who could have predicted it?—not despite or counter to Moscow's wishes, but rather with the Kremlin's encouragement.

The profundity of the changes and their rapidity took the West by surprise, and it does not know how to respond. There are many who realize that the security of the whole world—the United States included—is tied to the success of the revolutionary processes underway in the Soviet Union. But this realization coexists with the temptation to wait for the precipitation of a crisis that will finally bring the decades-old "great enemy" to its knees, and presumably extinguish the source of many past fears. Certainly, the task of setting up a new international order is vast and complex. The Europe on the horizon has different dimensions and borders than might have been imagined even a few months ago. Every military doctrine is now up for debate, as are the new shapes and functions of NATO and the military systems in the Western world. The processes of modernization and democatic development in Eastern Europe will most likely be slow and difficult. The question of reuniting the two Germanys opens up new political, economic, and psychological problems, and these will influence the speed and the structure of West European political and economic integration.

Now it has become clear that relations among the Western nations are destined to undergo profound changes. We are on the threshold of a world in which bipolarity will no longer exist, and the roles of the United States, Europe, Japan, the Soviet Union, and China will have to be redefined. Faced by this situation, the old categories of Sovietology can no longer explain what is happening or outline which strategies can be applied. Instead, there is an urgent need for a new, more long-term analysis. But we are still in the midst of extremely complex changes. Following in the footsteps of the great Roman warrior Quintus Fabius Maximus would be the worst tactic the West could choose at this watershed in world history. Delaying is possible and right when one thinks that letting events unwind by themselves is to one's own advantage. But by common judgment the situation is full of risks. Turning caution into passiveness means leaving things up to circumstance. The Soviet Union is undergoing transformations that are no less important than those produced by the October Revolution. And the West has the essential political, economic, and technical tools to influence these transformations.

Problems of such huge dimensions can only be dealt with by the Soviet Union; foreign interference would only complicate matters even further, weakening the reformer and providing the "Soviet Socialist Conservatives" with ammunition. But it is one thing to interfere, and another to take an active part, using the means one has available to assist processes deemed promising and positive. It must be understood that under current international and national conditions, Gorbachev has definite limits, and that the stream of events is rapidly approaching them. The two main doubts underlying the caution on the part of Western governments (and the hostility toward any concrete commitments on the part of conservative groups) concern Gorbachev's "true intentions" and his future. How far is the Soviet president willing to go? Toward which new economic and social system? And what would happen if the opposing conservative resistance were to force him into a retreat? These are legitimate doubts that this book can only partially answer. But it is essential that we not dwell on them.

How much further the Kremlin—whoever is in charge of it—can push itself (and how quickly) is a question that can only be answered in Moscow. The available options may either expand or shrink depending on the international context provided for them. Wisdom is often a gift provided by circumstance, and the greater the number of openings one can count on, the wiser and less desperate one is. In this way, for example, only a step-up in European détente, and a prompt and substantial commitment to conventional disarmament by NATO, can create the conditions for a progressive transformation of military blocs into predominantly political alliances, for an atmosphere of trust that would reduce the tensions of the new situation of some East European countries, favoring their interaction with the European Economic Community and the rest of the world. Even the ongoing movement for national independence inside Soviet borders (in particular, the future position of the three Baltic Republics) would take on an entirely new physiognomy in an atmosphere of mutual trust between NATO and the Warsaw Pact.

These are only a few examples concerning politics and disarmament. But still unexplored is the huge area that includes international economic cooperation, scientific and technical exchange, and the dismantling of barriers that have divided the world for the past fifty years. To say it in one word, interdependence. The time has come to make new decisions that only a few years ago would have been considered unthinkable and impossible. But first a fundamental question must be answered: what does the West stand to lose by the USSR's emerging from its crisis, and in a few decades renewing its presence on the international scene in more solid shape than it is in today, though certainly with different dimensions and another ideology? The answer is clear. If, as it seems justified to believe, the change is inevitable and irreversible, then a reformed Soviet Union will become a partner completely different from the one the world knew in the past. It will be integrated into the world market, immersed in a network of new economic, political, and military relations with other countries, and endowed with democratic institutions comparable to those of other constitutional democracies. In other words, it will no longer pose a threat. Once again, in the matter of security (not taking into consideration the prospect of a huge potential market being opened to international traffic), the West stands only to gain.

The conclusions that the venerable George Kennan presented to the United States Senate in January 1990 are therefore indisputable:

> Gorbachev has made a remarkable contribution to ending the cold war and to establishing a more stable and peaceful Europe. It is in your own interest and in the interest of world stability that he be able to move forward with his ideas and initiatives, at least as much as his energies and the patience of his associates will allow.

This truth is all the more pressing when one considers that the revolutionary year 1989 ended with new dangers and difficulties for the Soviet reformers. All the more so when the conservatives can still attempt to block the process of renewal. Gorbachev is faced by concentric pressures that are difficult to control, by desperate attempts at secession, and by a situation of general economic collapse. In the race against time, there are responsible forces on the move who realize that the only solution is a historical compromise between the national movements and the reform group in the Kremlin. In order to weather the storm, perestroika needs a new pact that regulates—as Gorbachev promised the Lithuanians—the "legal" secession from the Union by republics that request to do so. This pact could probably not prevent the separation of some republics. But it could facilitate a solution to unavoidable problems regarding the country's military security, the ethnic minorities that remain inside each state, and the forms of mutual support that must be created to avert other tragedies.

But there are forces that are moving in the opposite direction. Gorbachev tried to build a bridge between a hypothesis of socialism that had not worked, and a society whose outlines were yet to be defined. The final months of 1989 showed that one of the two shores on which that bridge was supposed to rest, the party, was beginning to collapse under the weight of the construction. The apparatchiks, lacking an alternative strategy, looked desperately for support in the enormous backwaters of cultural and political underdevelopment, in which Stalinist ideas, crude egalitarianism, nationalistic temptations, anti-Semitism, and Russian chauvinism still ferment. There are clearly those who cannot wait for the chance to blame Gorbachev and make him pay for all the difficulties, including the breakup of the country and the precipitation of the crisis. They are the same ones who were the first to boycott every real reform of the economy, who used up the party's last vestiges of credibility—comparable to Honecker, Zhivkov, and Ceaușescu—by belligerently defending their scandalous privileges. To their ranks should be added the people who just yesterday were pressing for even more radical reforms, demanding a multiparty system immediately, by decree, insisting on the crossover to capitalism tomorrow, likewise by decree. Both groups are incapable of understanding the true pace of history, for democracy cannot be introduced by decree, just as private ownership of the means of production cannot be abolished by decree.

Only an alliance between the Kremlin reformers and "Moscovia," which Aleksandr Zinoviev mentioned in one of his rare moments of clarity, can withstand the assaults of conservatives and reactionaries. But too large a percentage of the intelligentsia seems not to have fully grasped this. They are correct in realizing that the crisis is accelerating. They are also correct in realizing the growing intolerance of broad sectors of the public for a perestroika that has not produced results. But they do not see that radicalization moves in two directions: both to the right and to the left. Perhaps more to the right than to the left. And they do not seem to have realized—like Gorbachev—the great profundity of the national question. Thus, we are witnessing the incredible paradox of Gorbachev's popularity in decline in his own country while the entire world sings his praises. This would seem to confirm the old saying that no one is a prophet in his own country. Maybe perestroika is like a parachute that opened up too late. Or maybe the fall is so swift that no one could have stopped it. The irreversible fact remains—the indisputable achievement of Gorbachev's revolution—that politics has been given back to millions of Soviet citizens. No one, today or tomorrow, can lead the USSR without keeping the people in mind.

While I take sole responsibility for the opinions expressed in this book, every line was carefully scrutinized in often heated discussions with my colleague and lifetime companion, Fiammetta Cucurnia. This work could not have been completed were it not for the constant availability of her insight and for her extraordinary devotion.

I would also like to thank all those who contributed to this work through their suggestions and through their help, first and foremost Roy Aleksandrovich, who was not just the protagonist of the dialogues that accompany this chronicle, but an invaluable interlocutor, and a source of information whom I have frequently consulted both for this book and in my work as Moscow correspondent for L'Unità. I would like to express equal gratitude to all of my Soviet friends, with whom I have discussed the problems and the future of the USSR during my nine years in Moscow. If I have been able to understand anything, it is at least in part thanks to the contributions, advice, and criticism of Cecilia Kin, Yevgeni Ambartsumov, Len Karpinsky, Ilya Levin, Mikhail Geftner, Nikolai Shmelyov, and Yuri Karyakin. Equally helpful were my conversations with Shaun Byrnes and Jill Farrelly, who proved to be impartial and attentive observers of the Soviet scene.

Special thanks are due Paul Kozlov, for his dedicated assistance in searching for the documentary material, checking the translations from Russian, and organizing the whole. Arthur Burris's help was most efficient during the final revisions of the work in Washington.

G.C.
Washington, D.C.
January 1990

. . . I try to understand the pace of mankind, past and present, that I may keep step with it.

—Aleksandr Herzen

PART ONE
1986

CHAPTER 1

1986: FROM THE TWENTY-SEVENTH PARTY CONGRESS TO THE EIGHTH WRITERS' CONGRESS

•   •   •

The Twenty-Seventh Congress of the Communist Party of the Soviet Union (1986) carried all the signs of the political struggle that would dominate the months to come.[1] General Secretary Mikhail Gorbachev had planned the congress as a launching pad for the *radikalnaya reforma*. But his address to the party sent a powerful jolt through the leadership and through the other members of the audience, who listened in shock to his first harsh analysis of the crisis gripping Soviet society. Even the party leaders who had elected Gorbachev as general secretary in March 1985 were split in their reactions.[2] Gorbachev deliberately played on the tensions between the old and the new, but without letting them reach the breaking point. Although most of the cadres were unprepared to accept the idea of reform, Gorbachev's conclusion was unequivocal: there is no other way.

The eleven men in the Politburo all kept their places. The only new member was Lev Zaikov, who was now both a full member of the Politburo and a Central Committee secretary; this automatically made him the number-three man in the party hierarchy, next in line after Gorbachev and Yegor Ligachev. Gorbachev's three main opponents had been dealt with earlier: Grigori Romanov, Nikolai Tikhonov, and Viktor Grishin had been forced to resign between April 1985 and February 1986. Two new candidate members were named to the Politburo: Nikolai Slyunkov, the first secretary of Byelorussia, and Yuri Solovyov, the first secretary of Leningrad. Their election restored the time-honored procedure of seating the first secretaries of Leningrad and Byelorussia alongside the first secretaries of Moscow, the Ukraine, and Kazakhstan. The two octogenarian candidate members, Boris Ponomaryov and Vasili Kuznetsov, retired, ostensibly because of their age rather than their political positions. The greatest changes were in the Secretariat of the Central Committee, which grew from eight to eleven members with the departure of Ponomaryov and Ivan Kapitonov and the entrance

3

of Aleksandra Biryukova, Anatoli Dobrynin, Vadim Medvedev, Georgi Razumovsky, and Aleksandr Yakovlev.

The goals of the operation appeared clear: to avoid excessive turnover in the Politburo, in order to show its unity around the stated prospects of renewal, and at the same time to ensure the effective control of the party mechanism through a renewed Secretariat. The men who remained in the leadership were those who, as Gorbachev put it, "would like to improve things without changing anything."[3] However, the transition required a series of delicate, inevitable compromises. Even immediately below the tip of the hierarchical pyramid, the changes were considerable: more than half of the plenum emerging from the Twenty-Seventh Congress consisted of new members. Of its 559 members (full members, candidate members, and members of the Central Review Commission), a good 309, or 55.2 percent, were new. Of the 307 full members with the right to vote, 131 were new (42.6 percent). But this represented along process of rotations, which had already begun while Brezhnev was still alive, in the course of an underground struggle over choosing his successor. Yuri Andropov had accelerated the developments, and Konstantin Chernenko immediately put a stop to them, in a complex and contradictory transitional phase that inevitably led to the emergence of many compromise appointments. Soon enough it would become apparent that many of the appointees were cold, or even hostile, to the idea of change.

The Politburo's very first steps made it immediately clear that it was still taking a wholly traditional approach to the problems of economic reform. A reorganization of the Council of Ministers was begun with the creation of a coordinating bureau to supervise the country's energy policies. It was the third body of this kind, following the creation of the "agroindustrial complex" and the machine-tool industry bureau. But the discussion was clearly very intense. The shift from general formulations to concrete measures proved difficult, and not by accident. The party apparat, jealous of its traditional prerogative to command, saw a threat to its "guiding role" when it heard that the party should no longer directly manage social processes, but should instead guarantee a broad freedom of choice to labor collectives and to industrial cadres. The expression of a widespread and various resistance was inevitable. Gorbachev proved to be well aware of this and did not want to conceal the existence of the struggle in progress. In the middle of March he called a meeting of the editors of the most important newspapers and magazines and invited them to voice the "initiative of the masses." The situation was such that "it is necessary to fight, literally to fight, for every line of the decisions made by the party's congress."[4] And the battle could not be won only from within the apparat. The Soviet leader's logic pointed clearly to a vast social and political involvement, to the creation of "public opinion." The mass media was to perform a prominent role in these processes of "involvement" by voicing the workers' opinions. In the meantime, the Politburo passed certain measures designed to reorganize the agricultural and food industries that gave the kolkhozes and sovkhozes the right to sell "directly" on the free market those products that exceeded the quotas, and in the case of potatoes, fruit, and vegetables, "substantial percentages of the produce included in the plan" (20 March).[5] This uncertain and inadequate provision would produce only marginal results.

In the meantime, the economic figures for the first trimester of the year indicated a new dynamism. The press urged the leadership to forge ahead. Fyodor Burlatsky, the political commentator for *Literaturnaya Gazeta*, published a long article entitled "Lenin and the Strategy of Radical Change" that clearly advocated a return to the NEP.* In his speech to the congress, Gorbachev had made a significant allusion to the "tax on food."[6] Burlatsky explained the reference by extolling the "art of political change." Even Lenin, he said, had to fight against "strong prejudices." Even then the simple association of the words "socialism" and "reform" had provoked scandalized reactions. But the NEP; the abandonment of barracks communism; the replacement, in the relationship between city and country, of "administrative exchange with the exchange of equivalent goods"—did these not perhaps constitute a reform? Now it was necessary to dismantle many prejudices and proceed decisively toward autonomous kolkhozes and sovkhozes, and toward the allocation of the so-called family contracts. And it was necessary to reopen the discussion of cooperatives, not only in agriculture, but also in the cities: "There are those who think that the cooperative is a step backward with respect to state stores, state cafeterias, and state workshops. But who has ever proven this? Where is it written?" The policies of the Twenty-Seventh Congress opened up the problem of an explicit recognition of the "socialist market" and the "relationship between goods and money" (seeing that, as Burlatsky writes, "money is the measure of the costs and revenues of a business, and for now, no one has invented a better equivalent").[7]

The debate on the economy, however, was intertwined with a very interesting, though still highly circumspect, discussion of the themes of de-

---

* *Novaya Ekonomicheskaya Politika.* This is the name given to the new economic policies begun by the Soviet government in 1921 after the period of "barracks communism." Lenin advocated it after the sailors' revolt in Kronstadt (a more dramatic symptom than the peasants' resistance to the requisition of wheat) highlighted the impossibility of having a functioning economy based on centrally planned barter. The NEP introduced a mixed market and a planned economy. It was never formally rescinded, but Stalin gradually phased it out, replacing it with a planned system of "administrative command." By 1929 the NEP no longer existed.

mocracy. *Pravda*, for example, hosted a long theoretical article by Anatoli Lukyanov that, under the title "Socialist Self-Management of the People," repeated all the stereotypes of the past on the "perfecting of socialist democracy," while remaining within the formulations that Gorbachev had presented to the congress. Lukyanov extolled the "people who are united to their state through the soviets of people's deputies, mass assemblies of state power, in whose elections practically the entire adult population of the country participates."[8] The farcical election procedures, the "limited possibilities" of the soviets, the "excessive centralization," the very fact that the soviets' powers of intervention could be limited on a daily basis by the party's arbitrary decisions, and the consequent necessity to give them a "certainty of their own rights," through a new system of laws and regulations—all things which Gorbachev had suggested—were ignored by Lukyanov. The theme was clearly a delicate one. But other analyses and reports sending opposite signals also began to appear in the press. These fissures expressed a widespread aspiration to construct a system of formal legal guarantees that would defend not only the individual citizen from the abuse of power, but also the relationship between economic bodies, and between state and party organizations.

At the end of April 1986, the Chernobyl catastrophe proved a dramatic turning point for the political debate. The very fact of the accident seemed to symbolically summarize all of the problems that had accumulated in the long years of "stagnation." The reconstruction of events would prove that even in the most delicate mechanism of production—the nuclear sector—technological, organizational, and disciplinary disorders had reached intolerable levels. It seemed clear that Chernobyl was only the tip of an immense iceberg of problems. The serious delay with which information was given to both the Soviet and international public, and the heavy international repercussions of the tragedy, also had a powerful impact on the balance of power within the leadership, emphasizing the urgent need for radical measures of renewal. What immediately stood out was the absolute structural inadequacy of the country's information and communication systems. The systems' excessive secrecy had played a damaging role in blocking speedy measures to confront the emergency. The incident took place at 1:23 A.M. on Saturday, 26 April. The first reconstruction of the facts was not given until the 6 May press conference of Boris Shcherbin, deputy chairman of the Council of Ministers. And only on 14 May would Gorbachev appear on television with a dramatic eighteen-minute speech to say that "Chernobyl represents a lesson that cannot be avoided." This reflection helped Gorbachev enter a broader discourse, one that invited listeners not to forget the dangers of the "atom for war" alongside those of the atom for peace. But it also seemed addressed to the home front.[9]

The alarm demonstrated the need for reform and for a different relationship between state and citizen. The genuine acceleration of glasnost, which would register remarkable growth in the following months, was probably born from reflections on the serious shortcomings in the communication of information revealed by the tragedy. It was as if a profound shock had struck the entire mass media. The central organs began to publish news of events and problems that would have previously been concealed from the greater public and ignored. On 6 June the secretary of the Central Committee, Aleksandr Yakovlev, called a meeting of the members of the plenum of the Journalists' Union. Three days later Ligachev and Razumovsky called another meeting of the representatives of the mass media to push for an adjustment to the new situation not only by the central organs but also by the provincial organs, where the party's bureaucratic control stubbornly persisted in its tradition of censorship. Not only was there extensive newspaper coverage of the catastrophe, and an increase in the number of reports on the hard work of containing the damage and deactivating the radioactive area, but the press became involved in the public debate on the ecological safeguarding of the territory, setting off arguments over the diversion of the northern and Siberian rivers.[10]

More and more articles appeared in the newspapers urging people not to close their eyes to the reality of the country. In *Sovetskaya Kultura*, for example, Academician Georgi Morozov, director of the Central Institute of General and Criminal Psychology, raised the subject of drug dependency. We cannot repeat the mistake, Morozov wrote, of "being literally ashamed for years to declare out loud the countless tragedies that alcoholism has brought to the country, to the economy, and to morality."[11] But more numerous and diversified examples abounded. In *Pravda* Dmitri Lyubosvetov reported that the dissemination of information was too slow, and urged a more objective view of events in the rest of the world, including an end to the practice of representing the West as the place where the only thing that happens is anti-government demonstrations.[12] A few weeks later *Pravda* would dedicate an entire page to the "Sorrow and Lessons of Chernobyl," containing an interview with Academician Valeri Legasov, revealing that the newspapers were flooded with letters that "show a negative attitude toward nuclear power."[13]

The "Chernobyl effect" did not diminish; like a slow but powerful chain reaction, it influenced and stimulated different ideas. The investigation into Chernobyl would end on 19 July. The next day all the newspapers reported widely on the special meeting of the Politburo dedicated to the subject. Although the Soviet public was not presented with the whole truth, it heard a version that did not minimize the gravity of what had happened. When on 1 September the steamship *Admiral Nakhimov* sank in the Black Sea, Tass would immediately release news of this tragic incident. And on 22

7

September the Soviet people would learn in record time that a hijack attempt had been made at the Ufa airport. Public reaction oscillated between surprise, satisfaction, and dismay. So even in the Soviet Union there were airplane and train crashes, drug addicts and prostitutes. Subjects that had previously been taboo were now slowly filtering into the public sphere, as if the country were incredulously getting to know itself and freeing itself of old fears.

But every step was difficult and hard-won. On 28 May two resolutions (*postanovlenia*), one from the Central Committee and one from the Council of Ministers, were issued against "unearned income," in essence negating the reforms Gorbachev had proposed to the congress. The two provisions contained tough prohibitions that were allegedly aimed at the immense mass of "illegal" income, of "differential income," and of direct and indirect theft of government property. The measures ignored the fact that these "negative elements" were the unavoidable effects of imbalances that the existing economic mechanism had created. Rather than engaging in a structural analysis of the defects of centralized planning, the leadership was making tougher regulations, knowing full well that this would further encourage rather than check the growth of the bureaucracy. The conditioned reflexes of the apparats tended to proliferate and repeat themselves. The roots of the problem were left intact. The leadership expected to regulate a variety of objective economic and social problems as if they were questions of "moral rehabilitation," thereby confusing the causes with the effects. The compromise was to present a single package containing the two resolutions against "illegal" income and a law that authorized a series of "private" activities. In the end, this too fell through.

A close reading of Gorbachev's speech at the Central Committee's June plenum conveys the overall sensation that a perceivable slowing down was replacing the acceleration promoted by the Twenty-Seventh Congress. Perhaps this explains the decision to call the plenum only three months after the congress, in contrast with both the Twenty-Fifth and Twenty-Sixth congresses, after which no spring meeting was held. "We need an examination," Gorbachev said, in order to "derive lessons" from what was taking place. No one pretended that the changes affecting virtually every aspect of the country's life would be easy to make. But "more often the weight of inertia, of old habits," added to the objective "restraining elements." Among those who fought for the new, many "simply did not know what to do." But the greatest blows were inflicted against the state apparats, which "want to preserve their right to rule at any cost," and which make "troublesome the process of redistributing rights and responsibilities between departments and central ministries on the one hand, and firms, cooperatives, and labor partnerships on the other."[14]

The economic returns for the first five months of the year were anything but negative. But this was an effect of the change in leadership, obtained by emphasizing productive discipline. There had still been no structural change. Gorbachev and Nikolai Ryzhkov (a member of the Secretariat of the Central Committee who spoke at the 18 June meeting of the Supreme Soviet) did not hide this. Nor did they hide the fact that the plan itself "is not easily born." The first draft was turned down by the Politburo because it had been compiled in the old style. There would be no further modifications in the membership of the Politburo or of the Secretariat of the Central Committee.

On the next day, 19 June, Gorbachev held a meeting of a group of writers representing every tendency. The Eighth Congress of the Union was scheduled to open in a few days and the situation was tense. The old guard feared a repeat of the situation at the Fifth Congress of the Filmmakers' Union.[15] There was an air of protest. It was said that Georgi Markov, the incumbent first secretary, had handed in his resignation. The discussion lasted over four and a half hours. The next day *Pravda* would give an account of the meeting, limiting itself to a few sentences spoken by the Soviet leader that included an appeal to help "make irreversible" the process of profound changes taking place.[16] But some of the participants in the meeting, who may have been "authorized," immediately allowed indiscretions to filter out. Gorbachev's speech appeared to be of an unprecedented frankness; it was not meant for official publication, but a copy of the text reached *L'Unità*, which printed it at the beginning of October that same year.* "Every day that goes by," Gorbachev had begun, "brings new facts, one worse than the other, that demonstrate the difficulties facing those who assume responsibility and move along the lines of the Twenty-Seventh Congress." Those who "have in no way adapted to the existing system arouse the opposition of the surrounding environment, the resistance of every institution." Unbound by the constraints of official statements, the general secretary of the Communist Party spoke bluntly. And he returned to the episode that he had mentioned in his speech to the plenum:

> Take the story of Chabanov. I toned it down slightly, I did not tell it in full. But try to imagine. They blocked a letter to the congress of the party! This is how far things have gone! Here is a story just waiting for some author!

* *L'Unità* is a daily newspaper owned by the Italian Communist Party (PCI). It was the official PCI "organ"—an expression of the party line—until 27 March 1987, after which it assumed greater independence. Almost every political party in Italy has its own newspaper; of these, *L'Unità* has the largest circulation, and is ranked among the top ten Italian newspapers in terms of circulation.

Sure, if someone had written it there, on the spot, another story would have come out, because no one would have been able to represent it.

The episode had taken place in Cherkassy. The protagonist was Alim Chabanov, the director of a research institute who had been literally persecuted by the local party for trying to introduce more efficient systems of production in one of the Ministry of the Electrotechnic Industry's factories. He was slandered, prosecuted, and ousted from the party on the basis of anonymous accusations. When his friends tried to inform the party congress and the Central Committee and ask for justice, their letters and telegrams were blocked by the local police, on the express orders of Cherkassy's party officials. This episode was emblematic of the party committees' unrestrained abuse of power. But the example helped Gorbachev to introduce a general consideration:

A ruling stratum lies between the leadership of the country and the people, who wish for change, who dream of change—the apparat of the ministers, the apparat of the party, which does not want transformations, which does not intend to lose certain rights tied to privileges. [17]

This issue had already been raised by a collection of letters printed in *Pravda* a few days before the party congress, under the rubric "Purification" (*Ochishcheniye*), almost as a clue to Gorbachev's thought. [18] The letters complained about the "restraining role" of "inert strata" in the apparats, resistant to every change. The party paper was immediately forced to correct "the error," and during the congress it became clear where the pressures had come from. Yegor Ligachev himself had harshly criticized the complaints, with two first secretaries of regional committees following fast on his heels. Five months later Gorbachev let it be known that he shared the complaints. And he went further:

Everything begins in the party. The party should not have a double morality, a double law. This is a very serious situation. The whole society is in movement, the economy is upside down, and we find ourselves only at the beginning, right at the beginning of the journey. And whoever thinks that we can restructure ourselves in one or two months is truly naive! All of this has sedimented for years and years and now it requires a titanic effort. If we do not involve the people, nothing will come out of this.

He gave a list of the pockets of resistance:

Take Gosplan. To Gosplan no authority matters, no secretary-general matters. It does what it wants. . . . [19]

There was also an appeal to a social reality the mass media was only then beginning to illustrate:

> Let us take under consideration the nationwide tragedy of drunkenness, the so-called "drunken balance" (*pyany byudzhet*). . . . I know that threatening letters are arriving, but we will not surrender to these suggestions. We will save the people, especially the Slavic people. Because however much the phenomenon has struck the Moslems and the Caucasus, no other people of the USSR have been so struck as has the Slavic part of the population, i.e., the Russians, the Ukrainians, and the Byelorussians. I do not want to scare you, but we will not shy away from this task. We will fight.

Gorbachev, however, also addressed the question of democracy and glasnost: "A society cannot exist without glasnost . . . democracy without glasnost does not exist." But it is here that whenever a chance is opened in this direction, there are immediately those who "react with intolerance."[20] For example, what did the Fifth Filmmakers' Congress show?

> That, in the first place, there was restlessness; that there were no democratic methods to resolve disagreements. The leadership squinted upward. The congress proceeded democratically. There may have been some excesses. But the main questions were resolved and a new direction was chosen. All of this is right.

The proceedings of the writers' congress would show that the "excesses" would be toned down, but that the days of at least part of the old guard were numbered. This time, however, they would look for a compromise that prevented an obvious split. Gorbachev, in fact, added another invitation to caution on the subject of party history. This was one of the most delicate and explosive questions. While it gathered strength in the press, Gorbachev cautioned the intelligentsia on its most progressive views:

> If we begin worrying about the past, we will end up consuming all our energy. We would have divided the people, setting one against the other. Instead we have to move forward. We will come to terms with the past. We will put everything in its place. But now let us steer all our energy forward.

Disagreement sharpened in society as the real outlines of the reform took shape. And the disagreement was reflected, Gorbachev revealed, within the party's political leadership. Even at meetings of the Politburo:

> There are fights, arguments. We have been postponing for two, three years: now we want to act. The society is ripe for change. If we withdraw, the society

11

will not agree. We need to make the ongoing processes irreversible. If not us, who? If not now, when?

This speech did not convince everybody, but it was an invitation to open confrontation. Anatoli Ivanov, the editor in chief of *Molodaya Gvardia*, accepted this invitation, and in full battle gear started after the "negative influences" that would filter into literature and society.[21] Ivanov openly called for tighter party control and asked the Central Committee to set binding criteria that would act as a barrier against the penetration of extraneous ideologies of a Western stamp. The example he cited was no less significant: bring back the famous Zhdanovian resolutions of 1946 on music and literature that were used to put down Akhmatova and Zoshchenko.[22] Gorbachev replied negatively, but Ivanov's intervention proved that the conservatives still felt strong, and they did not intend to sit on the sidelines.

Thus, the climate leading up to the congress was tense. The discussion centered around three main subjects: the arguments against the literary bureaucracy; the clashes among critics and between critics and writers; and the relationships between man and nature and between man and society. On this last subject, the front for renewal was divided into two camps, showing how strong their currents were from within, sometimes ambiguously calling for a fight against wildcat industrialization, for the protection of cultural traditions, for the arguments against the diversion of the northern and Siberian rivers, for the defense of the "good old times" of the peasant villages. The moderate Vladimir Karpov was elected as the new first secretary. Men like Nikolai Fedorenko and Nikolai Oserov left the leadership, and writers of international fame such as Chingiz Aitmatov, Sergei Zalygin, Vasili Bykov, and Grigori Baklanov came in. But many of the "old men," such as Sergei Mikhalkov, remained. The "restraint" had had its effects, and the interests of the conflicting groups were still represented by the new secretary and by the new leaders.

FIRST CONVERSATION

CINEMA, LITERATURE, AND DIPLOMACY

•   •   •

G.C. The upheaval in the creative unions seems to have gone further than expected and the forces for renewal took the bit between their teeth—to such an extent that the writers' congress in June of the same year would follow more staid formulas and attempt more of a compromise between the old and the new, as compared to the Fifth Congress of the Filmmakers' Union in May, where the old guard of film directors had been eliminated (Lev Kulidzhanov, Vladimir Naumov, and Sergei Bondarchuk).

R.M. This was a very important moment, although it was overshadowed by the Chernobyl disaster. An understandable distraction, since Chernobyl also monopolized the general attention of the Soviet people. I recall that in the second half of May I was a guest in the home of a noted screen actor who had taken part in the filmmakers' congress by invitation. We talked about the state of the Soviet cinema for twenty minutes, but the conversation soon turned to the Chernobyl catastrophe and nuclear energy. In the months of May and June the same thing was happening everywhere.

But let us get back to the filmmakers' congress, which was truly a crucial event in Soviet cultural and political life. Soviet film studios produce from 150 to 170 films a year, but some years not a single work might appear worthy of attention for its artistic merits. Mediocre escapist films, mysteries, and films that distorted everyday life as well as history were the norm. Many films never made it through a vigilant and dogmatic censorship, while most of the projects of our many directors never made it off paper. Consequently, attendance figures at the cinemas started to go down, with a trend toward audiences comprised of a growing percentage of adolescents. For probably the first time in the history of Soviet cinema, domestically produced films ceased to turn a profit for the state. Our film studios became deficit enterprises and the only films that were profitable to release were Westerns or Indian films. Our directors were provided only low-grade technical equipment to

13

work with—there was even a shortage of film! Actors and directors were miserably paid. This painful list could go on at length. In the West they stopped buying our films, and one of our most important directors, Andrei Tarkovsky, decided to remain abroad after yet another quarrel with the leadership of the Filmmakers' Union. The elderly leaders of the union, of Goskino—the State Agency for the Cinema—and of the most important studios in Moscow and in the republics made it their practice to abuse power and to ostracize the more independent and talented actors, directors, and screenwriters. The members dissatisfied with the union began to greatly outnumber those who were pleased with the situation.

But the causes of the discontent went very deep. Before the filmmakers' congress, regional congresses had been held in Moscow, Leningrad, the Ukraine, and in other production centers starting in March—in other words, just after the party's Twenty-Seventh Congress. Regional leaders and delegates to the filmmakers' congress were elected in accordance with the union's bylaws. But this time both the debate and the voting procedures followed democratic procedures that had long been forgotten in all the creative unions. The members of the Filmmakers' Union took part in the meetings, where they could speak openly and nominate candidates. Voting was done by secret ballot, and on the lists there were more candidates than there were elective offices. All of this was quite different from the time-honored tradition of assemblies that were run like well-rehearsed spectacles. The party's Central Committee was clearly aware of these developments and approved of them. The party organs wanted to test the new and more democratic forms of running the creative unions. And, starting with the first meetings, the old leadership of the Filmmakers' Union was soundly criticized. Many office-holders, directors of big production studios, and certain well-known directors honored with awards and official prizes (such as Sergei Bondarchuk) were not even elected as delegates to the Fifth Congress.

The Fifth Filmmakers' Congress was a prominent event, with extremely tough interventions from the delegates. The union emerged from it with an almost completely renewed leadership. Yelem Klimov was elected first secretary, to the surprise of many. In the 1960s Klimov had directed a few successful comedies. His film *Sport, Sport, Sport* was interesting. Yet he was not Fortune's darling: many of his projects had remained unrealized or had been continuously delayed. And Klimov had experienced firsthand the drama suffered by all true artists who are not allowed to realize their ideas. His film on the German occupation of Byelorussia, *Idi i Smotri* (*Come and See*), was put into production twice. The film *Agony*, which told the story of the destiny of the last Russian monarch, Nicholas II, and of his favorite, Grigori Rasputin, was put into production a good three times and, when it was finally completed, it was not distributed for another seven years. It was no surprise, then, that the first meetings of the union's new leadership dealt with the fate of films that for various reasons had not reached audiences in the last twenty years. As it turned out, there were more than a few. We had to wait until 1986 to see a splendid film on the true reality of war: Aleksei German's *Proverka na Dorogakh* (*Control on the Streets*), which had been made in the late 1960s but gathered dust in the archives for more than fifteen years because of the absurd objections of film censors. Another example: only at the end of 1986 were tens of millions of television viewers able to see an interesting cycle of television films, entitled *Shtrikhi k Portrety V. I. Lenina* (*Brushstrokes for a Portrait of Lenin*), made by the playwright Mikhail Shatrov and the director Leonid Pchyolkin between 1965 and 1968. Even a film on Lenin could appear "suspect" to the leadership in that era. In this way it was possible to recover Kira Muratova's interesting films *Korotkiye Vstrechi* (*Brief Encounters*) and *Dolgoye Proshchaniye* (*The Long Good-bye*).

Other important films from the late fifties and early sixties returned to the screen. Soviet audiences began to be introduced to some of the best films from the West. We had been almost completely in the dark about the works of the most important Italian directors, such as Fellini, Pasolini, De Sica, and Antonioni. Klimov also worked hard to get Tengiz Abuladze's film *Pokayaniye* (*Repentance*) distributed. Its "opening night," in my opinion, represented the most important event in Soviet culture during the winter of 1986. It was an anti-Stalinist, antidictatorial, antitotalitarian film that had become the center of a bitter dispute, first to keep it from being made, and then to block its distribution. This dispute deserves particularly close scrutiny. The Fifth Filmmakers' Congress even ushered in new editors at the country's most popular film magazines, and new managers in the head offices of the most important production studios. I think, however, that the results of these democratic changes won't be seen for two to three years. You cannot improvise good films in just a few months, and in 1987–88 we would see many films that had been put into production between 1982 and 1984.

G.C. What about the Eighth Writers' Congress?

R.M. Most of the delegates to the Eighth Writers' Congress had been elected in 1985, when a true cultural perestroika had not yet begun. In Moscow, home to about two thousand writers, the preparatory conference was held in the fall of 1985, under the leadership of one of Grishin's closest collaborators. There was not even the smallest hint of democracy. The Writers'

15

Union is on the whole a rather conservative group, in which talented poets and writers figure in the minority. Even one of the union's most influential leaders, Sergei Mikhalkov, acknowledged in his speech to the congress the "widespread and triumphant mediocrity that has left its mark on an entire period of the history of our literature." Moreover, there are very few younger people in the union: in the Kremlin hall there were no writers younger than thirty; only three delegates were younger than thirty-five; only fifteen were younger than forty; the congress was guided and decided by 250 writers who were over sixty years old. Under these circumstances, neither great Russian poets like Lermontov and Yesenin, nor writers of the stature of Dobrolyubov or Pisarev, could have been elected delegates to or even become members of the union. It would have been difficult for Pushkin, Blok, or Mayakovsky to join.

The union leadership, under the dominating influence of Georgi Markov, Sergei Mikhalkov, Aleksandr Chakovsky, Yuri Bondarev, and others, frightened by the results of the filmmakers' congress, sharply restricted those allowed to attend, mainly to conservative writers. At the same time, attempts were made to curtail debate. I know that you, as the correspondent for *L'Unità*, were not able to follow the writers' congress, although you had been invited to the party's Twenty-Seventh Congress. Yet in spite of all this, the Seventh Writers' Congress as a whole proved to be more combative than the preceding congresses in the republics. Many of the speakers criticized the union's activities and its leadership. Daniil Granin said: "The Writers' Union has lost creative spirit. A position or an office often serves as protection from objective criticism. The winners are neither those who look for the truth, nor those who want to improve their talent, but rather those who are interested in vacuousness."

Andrei Voznesensky asked: "Why do readers give up on some of our books? There are many reasons, the main one being that the people want transparency. They know the truth about the terrible force of evil, of corruption, of embezzlement, of falsehood, of duplicity . . . they see the unfair distribution of goods. But instead books are forced on them that editors have purged and pruned: not *Dead Souls* but vaudeville shows."

Vasili Belov said: "We have transformed literature into a 'feeding trough.' Let us first of all acknowledge this openly, after which it will be easier to talk about all the rest." The congress, however, made substantial changes in the union leadership. Viktor Karpov was elected head of the Secretariat. This choice came as no surprise, for there had been speculation about such a move before the congress. Karpov was not in the circle of particularly popular writers. Nor was he tied to one of the groups of writers that had been formed in the past twenty years and at times took on the semblance of mafias.* Karpov has a military background, with twenty-five years in the army as a career man, retired with the rank of colonel. Before the war he was arrested and incarcerated for a period of time on charges that he had made "inappropriate" statements about Stalin. He was freed at the beginning of the war and sent to the front, where he distinguished himself as a daredevil and earned the award of Hero of the USSR. Among others who entered the Secretariat were Aitmatov, Baklanov, and Zalygin, all well known and recognized by Soviet readers, in part for their anti-Stalinist works in the 1960s. The members of the old leadership who remained in the Secretariat were Markov, Bondarev, and Yuri Verchenko: all three were tied to the union's conservative factions. However, it should be noted that the administrative structure of the union is huge, with more than forty secretaries and more than a hundred administrators. At the same time, the particularity of the writer's work allows the union members greater autonomy than film directors or artistic directors of theaters. The editorial boards of magazines have a big influence on literary life; 1986's biggest changes were in magazine editorships.

G.C. On the eve of the congress Gorbachev held a meeting with a group of the most influential writers. During that encounter, Anatoli Ivanov, director of the magazine *Molodaya Gvardia,* expressly asked the Central Committee to approve a detailed resolution on literature such as the one that the committee had issued in 1946 against the magazines *Zvezda* and *Leningrad,* resulting in the censure of Anna Akhmatova and Mikhail Zoshchenko. They tell me that Gorbachev turned down this proposal.

R.M. About thirty writers participated in that meeting, half of whom represented the progressive tendencies in the literary world, while the other half were conservative. Many of the conservatives had already begun to feel the earth shaking beneath their feet, and they were trying to obtain more solid

* The term "mafia" is used regularly in Soviet political commentary, especially after the eruption of the "Uzbek mafia" scandal in 1988. In many parts of the country, corruption exists in the form of organized crime, which in turn has established ties and contacts with political leaders, at times even placing its own men at the head of local party organizations. This use of "mafia" is thus perfectly appropriate, for like the Italian mafia, we are talking about organized crime with political connections.

A clan, on the other hand, is an informal association generally based on family ties or comembership in an ethnic group. In many cases the mafia organizations—in Soviet Central Asia, where family and tribal traditions remain strong—are intertwined with clans. In Kazakhstan the former first secretary of the party (and Politburo member) Dinmukhamed Kunayev organized a powerful family and Kazakh "clan," within which various jobs and benefits were distributed.

administrative support from the Central Committee. Ivanov was proposing that the Central Committee adopt a new resolution that would be a binding requirement for all writers. Gorbachev replied that he saw no need for such a resolution. Sergei Mikhalkov in turn claimed that the party leadership should beware lest the writers' congress get out of control, as had happened with the filmmakers. But Gorbachev answered that he did not agree with this appraisal and that the Central Committee had no objections to the filmmakers' congress. At the same time, Gorbachev showed great interest in the comments of Grigori Baklanov, who had criticized different aspects of the recent law against unearned income. Baklanov had claimed that some of the new rules proposed could worsen the living and working conditions of certain sectors of the farm population. Gorbachev disclosed that he had the same reservations and that he had presented them at a meeting of the Politburo.

All of this confirms the complexity of the cultural situation and the difficulty of the struggle in the early months of 1986. In that year no particularly significant literary works were published. Viktor Astafev's short but bitter novel *Pechalny Detektiv* (*Sad Detective Story*), published by *Oktyabr*, had attracted attention, as had Chingiz Aitmatov's long but uneven and hurriedly written novel *Plakha* (*The Executioner's Block*). In their books, both Astafev and Aitmatov treated a thorny subject that Valentin Rasputin had already introduced in 1985 in his *Pozhar* (*Fire*): the moral degradation not only of government officials and executives, but also of a considerable percentage of the population, including workers, farmers, office workers, and, especially, young people. However, while these writers raised very serious questions, they did not venture to offer an answer. As one critic perceptively put it, they expressed the discontent of the man on the street, of the "man without privileges," confronted with growing disorders; yet all they did was reproduce many of his thoughtless and not always praiseworthy reactions to society.

In the summer of 1986 a conspicuous group of well-known writers, including Veniamin Kaverin, Yevgeni Yevtushenko, Sergei Antonov, Bulat Okudzhava, and Andrei Voznesensky, addressed a letter to the Central Committee requesting a reexamination of the decision already taken on the fate of the great novel *Children of the Arbat* by the noted writer Anatoli Rybakov. The first part of this anti-Stalinist novel had been written before 1965 and was supposed to have been published by *Novy Mir*. But the novel, as they used to say, did not "pass." The second and third parts of the novel, which the author had continued to work on during the 1970s, the years of stagnation, were also "unpassable." With the support of Aleksandr Yakovlev, the new secretary of the Central Committee, the novel neared publication. But even

18

though the magazine *Druzbha Narodov* had prepared the printer's galleys, very few could believe that the novel would ever see the light of day in our country.

G.C. *Druzhba Narodov*, one of the few magazines whose director had not been replaced . . .

R.M. Exactly. For many years that editorial staff had been headed by Sergei Baruzdin, a noted writer of children's books. In the past he had refused to publish Rybakov's novel, but at this point he did a complete about-face. In the realm of culture, as in many other aspects of our life, it is possible today to observe different forms of behavior toward perestroika. In many situations perestroika began only with a change in the leadership, when new men came forth. This is the case of the weekly *Ogonyok*, which was radically transformed when the Kiev poet and writer Vitali Korotich was appointed to replace Anatoli Sofronov, an extremely conservative poet and playwright who had headed the magazine for thirty years. The policy shift of *Novy Mir* was likewise evident after Sergei Zalygin was appointed director. A similar development took place at the magazine *Znamya*, with the appointment of Grigori Baklanov as editor in chief and Vladimir Lakshin as deputy editor. The skilled publicist and writer Yegor Yakovlev revolutionized the weekly *Moskovskiye Novosti*.

However, many other magazines began to work in a new way even with old editorial boards. I have already mentioned the case of *Druzhba Narodov*. But let's take the case of *Oktyabr*, a magazine that had not distinguished itself at all in the 1970s. Anatoli Ananev has directed it for more than ten years. Yet even *Oktyabr* began to work in a new direction and today it is one of the most interesting magazines. For more than fifteen years the scholar and literary critic Albert Belyayev headed the literary sector of the Central Committee apparat, and he was generally considered a conservative and a "persecutor" of literature: it was under Belyayev that the 1970 purge of the editorial staff of *Novy Mir* took place and Tvardovsky was replaced. But in 1985 Belyayev was removed from the Central Committee's apparat and appointed editor in chief of *Sovetskaya Kultura*. The newspaper immediately began to improve, becoming one of the most active centers for the spread of perestroika.

On the other hand, some conservative voices in our literature—such as the magazine *Molodaya Gvardia*, headed by the writer Anatoli Ivanov— have taken even more extreme stands. The political and social positions of the magazine *Nash Sovremennik* have produced quite a few reactions; the magazine is directed by the poet Sergei Vikulov, and its editorial board is influenced by figures like Vasili Belov, Yuri Bondarev, Viktor Grachyov, and Valentin Rasputin. At the same time, it should be noted that the content of the popular press, periodicals such as *Znaniye—Sila, Nauka i Zhizn, Iskusstvo Kino, Nedelya*, and others, has changed for the better. These publications are read by tens of millions of people, most of them young.

G.C. On 23 May Gorbachev called a meeting of the entire Soviet diplomatic corps at the Ministry of Foreign Affairs, including all the ambassadors, and the officials of the ministry and of the Central Committee's Department of Foreign Affairs. How important was this meeting?

R.M. This meeting of diplomats was indeed a full-fledged affair. Neither Gorbachev's speech nor resolutions of any type were published. But the questions discussed and the essential points of Gorbachev's speech were no secret to most political observers, and they were confirmed by later events. A rapid renewal of all the most important diplomatic cadres would be noted starting in June 1986. Just before the meeting most of the deputy ministers for foreign affairs had been replaced. Immediately afterward, most of the department heads at the Ministry of Foreign Affairs were changed, as were many ambassadors, both to major and minor countries. Dozens of high-level officials at the Ministry of Foreign Affairs were sent into retirement; the party subjected more than a few to disciplinary proceedings, or even put them on trial. This was the case of Pyotr Abrasimov, ambassador at different times to France, East Germany, and Japan, who early in 1986 was caught in the act of illegally bringing contraband Japanese video equipment into the USSR.

Although the speech was not published, in Moscow it was immediately learned that Gorbachev had urged a decisive change in the style and substance of the work of the ministry, of its departments, and of the embassies. Soviet diplomats should no longer know only how to explain and argue the viewpoints of the Soviet leadership and defend the positions and interests of the Soviet Union; now they also had to know how to negotiate better, how to find reasonable compromises and an acceptable basis for agreements important to the USSR and its partners. They had to learn how to appreciate the fact that other countries also have their own legitimate interests to defend. Furthermore, they had to know how to listen to their interlocutor's arguments, for they may turn out to be not only authoritative, but fair. Gorbachev said, "We can no longer allow that, abroad, the Soviet minister of foreign affairs is nicknamed "Mr. Nyet." This label had been attached to both Molotov and Gromyko.

The other subject that Gorbachev addressed in his speech was the widespread corruption among ministry officials. Serious cases of smuggling, corruption, abuse of power, etc., were discovered both in the Ministry of Foreign Affairs and in the foreign trade apparat. Grave defects were also revealed in the training of the diplomatic cadres. The Moscow Institute for International Relations (MIMO) had been transformed into a center for the elite where students were accepted solely on the recommendation of high-ranking officials in the Ministry of Foreign Affairs. Before May 1986 the rector of MIMO had already been removed from his post and expelled from the party due to numerous irregularities. An inquiry was made into his activities. Many interpreted the diplomats' meeting of 23 May as a serious criticism of Gromyko, and that it was, even if Gorbachev never mentioned his name. But do not forget that the Soviet style of diplomacy took shape not only under the influence of Gromyko, but also under that of all those who preceded him.

CHAPTER 2

FROM JUNE TO DECEMBER 1986: PREPARING THE REFORM.

·　　　·　　　·

The June plenum had disclosed the "very troubled" progress of the reform, to use Gorbachev's words. Nikolai Ryzhkov had outlined the objectives of the new five-year plan to the Supreme Soviet.[1] The five-year plan predicted a 124-billion-ruble increase in the national income (as opposed to the 79 billion of the five-year plan that had just ended), to be created completely by an increase in productivity. To make this possible, a 25 percent increase in investments in manufacturing was projected, firmly giving priority to technological modernization. As Gorbachev put it at the plenum, the "ruin-ous insufficiencies" of the previous investment policy had to be overcome to enable the "passage into the intensive phase."[2] Several figures for the project, initially prepared by Gosplan, had been visibly corrected. There was a very tense debate between the "extensive" and the "intensive" hypotheses, and now the emphasis fell on the latter. Ryzhkov announced that 240 billion rubles would be set aside for the renovation of the machine depots (as opposed to the 110 billion of the preceding five-year plan). He acknowledged that "only 29 percent of the Soviet Union's equipment and mass-produced ma-chines meet international standards." This goal may have been grandiose, but so was the goal for a "multiplication in the growth rate of agricultural production by 2.6." But Ryzhkov warned that the "technical" choices were not enough. In this phase it was time to negotiate the political points, which he subdivided into two main goals: "to increase the efficiency of the cen-tralized leadership and to considerably expand the economic autonomy of the enterprises."

Yegor Ligachev made his way to the rostrum to announce a small re-shuffling: the first vice president of the Supreme Soviet, Vasili Kuznetsov, would retire. He would continue to be a member of the Central Committee, where he had served since 1952, and would be replaced as first vice president by Pyotr Demichev, who had just been freed from his duties as minister of culture. Both Boris Yeltsin, the new first secretary of Moscow, and Yuri Solovyov, first secretary of Leningrad and a candidate member of the Politburo since March 1985, entered the Presidium, while Viktor Grishin lost his post. Lev Zaikov left the Presidium in order to perform his duties in the Secretariat of the Central Committee. For the most part, these events were expected. But other news pointed to the existence of subtle maneuvers just beneath the surface. At the beginning of July the Brezhnev family was once again targeted: Yuri Brezhnev, son of the former general secretary, was no longer the first deputy minister of foreign trade. At the same time, the weekly *Moskovskiye Novosti* gave a surprise interview to the ninety-six-year-old Vyacheslav M. Skryabin, better known to the world by the pseudonym Molotov, in his dacha Zhukovka.[3] Two years earlier Chernenko had given him back his party membership, thereby sending out a definite conciliatory political signal to the Stalinists. Now it was opportune to exhume this figure for the second time, to have him express "enthusiasm" for the changes underway. The leadership wanted to calm some people down, to neutralize groups that had expressed their apprehension over the announced changes.

The torrent of dissonance continued into the following weeks. Academician Abel Aganbegyan gave an interview with Tass in which he stated in no uncertain terms that "the exclusively centralized management of an economic system that produces a fifth of the world's entire production has become impossible." A few days later, *Pravda* printed a long "theoretical" article dedicated entirely to defending central planning, in opposition to those proposals it scornfully defined as replacing the criteria of the plan with the "system of self-organization."[4]

One of the hypotheses used to explain the leadership's uncertain progress is the shock effect of Chernobyl. The assessment of its disastrous material, political, and psychological damages led to a harsh conflict of interests. Political responsibility for the disaster was assigned only vaguely and indirectly. Even if criminal investigations in various directions were announced, there was no indication of the responsibility borne by the party's organizations in the region and in the republic, nor was there an accounting for the delay in informing both the Soviet people and the rest of the world about the disaster. Both of these touched the highest levels of the *nomenklatura* and reached the Central Committee and the Politburo.

But the Chernobyl disaster did not just bring the process of renewal to a stop. It dramatically demonstrated the seriousness of the technical, organizational, and moral problems that fermented in the society's most delicate and vital areas. The catastrophe in relaying the news seemed just as great as the nuclear catastrophe itself. The barriers of secrecy magnified the tragedy and showed that Soviet society was paralyzed. Gorbachev learned the lesson of Chernobyl and used it to launch a new series of offensives against the conservative sectors of the apparat. On 22 July *Pravda* published an editorial dedicated to the "First Secretary," to the "number ones" who should "set the tone" for the changes, but who instead resisted and obstructed them. The party organ drew up a list of "culprits," including five first secretaries of the Kazakhstan Obkom (Regional Committee*)—in the republic headed by the already heavily criticized Dinmukhamed Kunayev—and two first secretaries of the Ukraine, whose chief was another Politburo member, Vladimir Shcherbitsky. Boris Yeltsin announced a relentless purging of cadres in the plenum of the Moscow Party Committee. Twenty-eight of the city's party officials had already been removed from their posts; others would follow. This extremely violent indictment appeared in *Moskovskaya Pravda* in all its severity, and it confirmed the numerous rumors of a growing opposition to Yeltsin in important sectors of the capital's apparat.[5] The announcement was made that the writer and political commentator Sergei Zalygin, one of the nonparty protagonists of renewal at the recent writers' congress, had been appointed editor in chief of *Novy Mir*, while Grigori Baklanov, from the same progressive group, would head the monthly *Znamya*.

It was in this fluid context that a manifesto-petition to the Soviet people appeared, signed by "a group of Soviet citizens who have access to objective information."[6] The document was circulated in Moscow and published in London by the *Guardian* on 22 July; an official spokesperson for the Soviet Ministry of Foreign Affairs immediately called it "a provocation to block the progress of perestroika."[7] But it deserves more attention than a first glance might indicate, especially when reread a few years later. While we cannot exclude the possibility that the original text had been tampered with, its authors present an analysis of the Soviet situation that is both "patriotic" and democratically inspired by Gorbachev's leadership. Moreover, its analysis of the causes of the crisis, which at that moment was far more "radical" than Gorbachev's official analysis at the Twenty-Seventh Congress, would resemble the official version in the following months. Thus, in retrospect, the hypothesis that the original document was prepared by a radical-reformist group situated immediately below the *nomenklatura* does not seem unfounded. The Movement for Socialist Renewal (as the promoting group called itself) must have sent the document to the Soviet newspapers starting

---

**Raikom, gorkom*, and *obkom* are acronyms used by the Soviet press to indicate the party committees at the district level (*raionny komitet partii*), at the city level (*gorodskoi komitet partii*), and at the regional level (*oblastnoi komitet partii*). A parallel structure exists for the corresponding governmental organizations, i.e., the administrative-executive bodies of the district, city, and regional soviets: *raiispolkom* (*raionny ispolnitelny komitet*), *gorispolkom* (*gorodskoi ispolnitelny komitet*), and *oblispolkom* (*oblastnoi ispolnitelny komitet*).

in November 1985, and finally decided to make it known to foreign correspondents. It presented a stinging analysis of the crisis in Soviet society, starting with the serious lag in technological development accumulated over the last decades, and supported a radical reform of the economy—the only way to prevent "tipping the current USSR-USA military balance in America's favor." The crisis, it said, is not just economic: it hits the family, the relationships between individuals, and the entire civil society. Alcoholism has become a national tragedy, and the waste and alienation at the workplace are symptoms of a more general and widespread malaise. The country continues to sink deeper into debt, and the Soviet people's standard of life is "one of the lowest in the industrially developed world." The Soviet Union's prestige had reached its lowest point in history.

Regarding the economy, the Movement asked for an expansion of the rights of enterprises, leading to complete autonomy in management: the "development of private initiative in the area of services and the manufacture of consumer goods"; the granting of citizens' rights to "lease farmlands and farming equipment, paying back the state with a part of their crops"; the creation of private plots in the country and the sale to city dwellers of lands unused by the state agricultural farms and cooperatives; the development of private commerce. Almost all of these demands were met by the reform laws that appeared in 1987. The political platform seemed much more radical: it went beyond the prospects that could be recognized by the Kremlin leadership during this phase of renewal. The petition asked for the creation of a press independent from the party and the state; an end to religious discrimination; the guarantee of the individual's basic freedoms; and the creation of "constitutional provisions for the formation of alternative political organizations." The manifesto was very different from a dissident samizdat, however. It worked from within the reform movement, but took more advanced positions; it constituted the first sign of the activation of "independent" forces and groups that pushed for radical changes.

The month of August, despite Gorbachev's vacation, saw a series of important new developments. Two months after Pyotr Demichev's dismissal from the Ministry of Culture, his place was taken by Vasili Zakharov, the former deputy manager in charge of propaganda for the Central Committee. Zakharov seemed closer to Ligachev and Zaikov than to the general secretary. In the meantime, the debate over conservation of the country's historical and artistic patrimony underwent a series of important changes. *Moskovskaya Pravda* made it known that a municipal commission had decided which names from the city's toponymy could no longer be modified, and at the same time had restored the original names to streets and squares that had been renamed in recent decades.[8] For example, the Lermontovskaya subway station would now be called by the historic name of the place where it was built, Krasnye Vorota. The Subway Builders Street would return to its old name, Ostozhenka. One of the five streets named after Mikhail Frunze, one of the fathers of the Red Army, would return to its eighteenth-century name, beloved by Tolstoy, Khamovnichesky Val. "The names of the streets and squares," the newspaper wrote, "tell the story of our old city," and have become "part of our national culture."

This was a small episode, but it took place within a larger cultural and political showdown. On 14 August the Politburo made a two-part decision that settled two public debates that had flared up in the press in the preceding months. First, they decided to cancel the project to divert the flow of northern and Siberian rivers toward the Central Asian regions. Second, "taking the findings of a broad investigation of the project and of the surveys into account, as well as the judgments and proposals put forward by public opinion," they decided to "announce an open competition for the principal monument for the Victory Memorial."[9] The first decision gave full approval to the requests of a huge movement, headed by leading writers such as Zalygin and Rasputin, and supported by a very solid group of academicians, scientists, and economists. The movement against the diversion of the rivers was heterogeneous; it brought together ecological concerns, revitalized after the Chernobyl disaster (the April tragedy clearly intensified the debate on the defense of the natural environment), and the pleas for a different approach to economic development by opponents of massive projects.

The decision to block the construction of the monument commemorating the Great Patriotic War was also an important sign. The work in progress had already leveled the entire Poklonnaya Hill, Bowers' Hill, at whose summit ambassadors to the tsar arriving from the West bowed down before the majesty of the Kremlin's golden domes.

This pharaonic project, described by the sculptor Koshkin as "a Byzantine-Vatican idea" in *Sovetskaya Kultura*, had raised waves of protests. In just a few days, more than twenty thousand people crowded the rooms of the Krimsky Most, where the blueprints and the scale models were on exhibition. The center of the monumental complex was supposed to be a dark-red granite column, seventy-two meters tall, as high as the Kremlin's Spasskaya Tower. For the entrance a kilometer-long stairway was planned, beginning at the Kutuzov triumphal arch and flanked by 1,418 fountains, to commemorate the number of days in the war against Hitler.

The project had had a troubled history ever since its beginnings in 1957. The partnership that received the commission included practically all of the most famous architects of the time. The final approval was granted by Brezhnev and Grishin in 1980. No one, or almost no one, objected to the idea of the monument per se. The Great Patriotic War was a memory that was communal, painful, and still very much alive. But the two basic concepts of what the monument should be represented two diametrically opposed groups: those who would commemorate the greatness of victory for centuries to come through gigantism, emphasis, and rhetoric, and those who objected to the idea that the "sacred" memory of those terrible days would be fixed in the "cold marble of bureaucratic ideas."[10] That this second concept was considered valid was a sign of new times. But above all, never before in this kind of debate had public opinion played such a large part in the deliberations of the highest state and party bodies.

In the meantime, heavier and heavier "moralizing" broadsides were being launched against the Brezhnev group. At the end of August as CPSU Central Committee resolution indicted the Kazakhstan party's Central Committee and its Council of Ministers. The agricultural situation was described as disastrous, and the party was accused of falsifying accounts and of being infested with corruption.[11] The attack was implicitly aimed at Kunayev. After nine months of work the famous Sokolov case was concluded in Moscow. This huge criminal investigation implicated hundreds of managers in the distribution sector. Sokolov had been the manager of Gastronom No. 1, the most famous food store in Moscow. In 1983 he was executed for economic crimes. His "circle" of friends included Kolevatov, the director of the Moscow Circus, and Boris Buryatsky, called "the gypsy," a friend of Galina Brezhneva. As a result of the new investigation, Nikolai Tregubov, the head of the Moscow Council on Trade, was sentenced to fifteen years' imprisonment; his assistant, A. Petrikov, received twelve years. The old political protections collapsed, even if the persistence of mafia networks became evident and reports circulated of continuous efforts to shelve all attempts to discover the truth. Boris Yeltsin, first secretary of the Moscow Party Committee, continued his moralizing offensive, incurring undying hatred.

While Gorbachev was returning from his vacation (between the eighteenth and the twentieth of September), he delivered an important policy speech at Krasnodar that would be broadcast in its entirety on national television. It announced the beginning of a new phase of the battle, in which the main enemy appeared to be the bureaucracy of the ministries, as well as the conservative resistance within the party that was tightly bound up with that bureaucracy. To overcome it Gorbachev once again played the card of public debate, glasnost: the card of "democratization" (this was the first time the term had been used) of Soviet society. The party itself was also directly accused in an unusually harsh tone. The television cameras transmitted to millions of homes the dark and disconcerted faces of the Krasnodar party cadres listening to the indictment. Gorbachev stated that it is true that the party directs society, "but comrades, the party is at the service of the people and its managing role does not represent a privilege. To those who have forgotten this, I am now reminding you from the podium." For Gorbachev, democratization meant information, first of all. The people must know how things are, "in order to form conscientious opinions."[12]

The Krasnodar speech caused a sensation. Gorbachev meant to establish the things he had said on that occasion as general policy. In fact, a formal resolution by the Central Committee summarized the results of his latest trip through the provinces:

> Although the society as a whole is favorable to changes, the process can be realized only with difficulty, in a contradictory and unequal way. It runs up against social, psychological, and organizational obstacles and into the op-position of those who, because of selfish interests, strive to maintain outmoded structures along with their privileges.[13]

At the end of September the Central Committee echoed these sentiments in two resolutions that seemed to indicate a new push toward more radical measures of reform. Starting on 1 January 1987, twenty ministries and seventy large industrial consortiums would be entitled to directly manage their own imports and exports, and would no longer have to go through the Ministry of Foreign Trade. At almost the same time *Izvestia* announced a salary reform for the beginning of the new year that would affect 75 million in-dustrial employees.[14] The raises would give priority to skilled workers; en-terprises could independently manage their own salary and staff levels; there would no longer be ceilings on salaries; and their level would depend directly on increases in productivity.

But the Krasnodar speech also provided new openings in the theoretical debate on the relationship between the party and democracy. *Pravda* carried a huge article signed by Viktor Vasilev, a doctor of law, who took a very critical look at the present conditions of socialist democracy.[15] Too many leaders, Vasilev wrote, "act as if the people existed for the apparats, and not the apparats for the people." The role of the soviets also had to be reexamined, together with a needed change in the electoral system: "We need to rid the elections of their formalism and their preorganized nature." Clearly, the process of democratization required a new body of laws embracing the entire realm of social, individual, and productive activities. The Presidium of the Supreme Soviet approved a legislative plan including the following: a law on referendums (provided for by the 1977 Constitution); a law that would grant labor collectives the right to elect their managing directors; a law on the citizen's right to appeal abuses of power by public officials; a law that would establish the subjects on which state institutions could not make decisions without first obtaining the approval of the social organizations. All of these measures were to be enacted by 1987. Other equally important steps were expected to be approved before the end of 1986, including a bill on information and the press that was rejected. One bill that was approved established new rights for "individual work activities." The reform laws scheduled to be discussed by the Supreme Soviet even included a bill on the activities of the KGB, the Committee for State Security. Chronologically, this bill was the last: the reform of the KGB was set for 1990.

By now perestroika was gaining momentum at an ever-increasing rate. The telluric jolts of "democratization" found an immediate and growing response among the intelligentsia. A chapter on de-Stalinization was re-opened; this was the fundamental matter left unresolved after the Twentieth and Twenty-Second congresses, the point that had thus far prevented perestroika from getting to the roots of the current problems of Soviet society. The debate on Stalin could no longer be postponed. And in one of the great ironies of history, the first stone against the dictator was thrown by his own homeland, Georgia, which still venerates him today, and not just in the snapshots stuck to the windows of taxis and trucks. The Moscow cinemas began to show "reserved" viewings of Tengiz Abuladze's film *Pokayaniye* (*Repentance*), the third startling episode of a trilogy that had begun with *Molba* (*The Plea*), and *Drevo Zhelani* (*The Tree of Desires*).

The film focused on the Terror of the 1930s, which was rendered even more upsetting by the surrealism of its images and by the density of references understandable only to Russians and, even more so, to Georgians. In the spotlight was Lavrenti Beria, with his unmistakable pince-nez, but dressed in a black shirt like Mussolini. Varlaam Aravidze, as the protagonist was called, wore a Hitler-type mustache that added another disturbing connotation to a figure who also recalled Stalin and who embodied the tragedy of coarse, plebeian, and destructive power. The film provoked great emotions in Georgia, where it had been shown on television and was already being shown regularly in the cinemas (thanks to the direct intervention of Eduard Shevardnadze, the minister of foreign affairs and a Georgian).

The film had been made in 1984, immediately after the death of Andropov and under the sponsorship of Shevardnadze. But the censors had not only condemned it to the archives, but to destruction. Only one copy had been saved. The Gorbachevs had liked the film. But it still took several weeks before the decision was reached to release the film to the wider public. Then the go-ahead was given, but not without objections. This was the sign of a directly political, not merely cultural, turning-point that could be compared to the Khrushchev-era publication of Aleksandr Solzhenitsyn's *Odin Den*

Ivana Denisovicha (*One Day in the Life of Ivan Denisovich*) in Tvardovsky's *Novy Mir*. From that moment the demolition of the myth of Stalin and the dismantling of Stalinism moved at an overwhelming pace.

When Yegor Ligachev spoke at the Kremlin's Congressional Building on the anniversary of the October Revolution, he also expressed strong support for perestroika. [16]

For October's traditional grand festivities the Moscovites discovered another change: the gigantic banners portraying Politburo members had not been hung. Moreover, *Moskovskiye Novosti* had taken the initiative of reporting a train wreck on 6 November in the Ukraine with a death toll of forty; the local and national papers had said nothing. Tass picked up the report from the weekly. This is the first time that information of this type and seriousness had been circulated by a source other than the official news agency. Furthermore, a new law was announced that would regulate the rights of citizens to leave the country on "personal business." In reporting this item, Tass acknowledged that the regulations enforced since 1970 were too arbitrary. Now a Soviet citizen would know precisely where his or her right to movement began and where it ended, which documents had to be presented, and the reasons why his or her request might eventually be denied (which the authorities were required to supply).

However, there was another notable change that would cause endless arguments and problems in the months to come. Gorbachev convened a large assembly of the industrial cadres for the fourteenth and fifteenth of November. The order of the day was the introduction of Gospriyomka (Gosudarstvenaya Priyomka Gotovykh Izdeli; State Inspection of Production). [17] Starting on 1 January, many enterprises would begin to use new systems of quality control for their products. In every factory a state commission would be instituted, "independent" from the company's management and from the ministry concerned, i.e., completely free from influence and pressure, at least in theory. All products that did not meet quality criteria, and international standards, would be rejected. Losses would be charged to the enterprise, whose employees would then receive cuts in their wages and premiums. Gorbachev did not hide the fact that the experiment could have a "painful" character. He presented his reasons frankly:

> I know if we were to say to many, "Okay, you are authorized to export your entire production abroad and everything that you earn will be yours, I repeat, everything, 100 percent," then they could go all around the world, but no one would buy their low-quality products.

His reasoning was impeccable, but this measure was not a reform. Rather it was another variation on old "disciplinary" methods that did not get to the roots of the problem. In effect, the introduction of Gospriyomka would lead to disastrous situations without reversing the state of things: in dozens of factories up to 40, 50, and 60 percent of the products would be rejected. In many cases considerable amounts were withheld from salaries. Discontent would grow rapidly, leading to episodes of violence that would even leak out in the press. While the figures on the economy in the early months of 1987 were more accurate than in the past, they revealed a slump in "real" production. The Supreme Soviet also heard a presentation by Aleksei Shkolnikov, chairman of the People's Control Commission, that drew an eloquent portrait of the moral, disciplinary, and productive climate of the country in the twenty months since Gorbachev's rise to power. In the last year alone thirteen thousand economic managers at various levels had been accused of "patent violations of productive discipline." About a hundred thousand managers had tampered with the books and financial statements or had been caught embezzling. The Kharkov tractor factory manufactured nine thousand machines (14 percent of the production) with such serious defects that they could not be marketed—and this was not the worst example.[18]

The Supreme Soviet finally approved the much-awaited law on "individual work activities," which would not take effect until 1 May 1987. "Individual" activities (the term "private" was carefully avoided) were permitted in twenty-nine basic sectors. But this was only a draft bill: it only set the main guidelines within which the various republics could "interpret" the rules based on "local conditions." Individual activities were recognized as "useful to the society"; "groundless restrictions" were removed; it specified that "income realized in this way should correspond to the expenditure of individual work and to the principal of social justice." Lastly, as proof of the law's net delimitation, adults "who work in social production" could engage in individual economic activities, i.e., as a "second job." To this category were added those who were not engaged in social production, such as housewives, invalids, retirees, and students. Precautions were taken to affirm that the new law "fully corresponds to the principals of socialist management," and "did not in fact mean a return to any form of private entrepreneurial activity, as they hope in some parts of the West." According to the first official estimates, reported by Ivan Gladki, chairman of the State Committee on Work and Social Problems, at least "2 or 3 million" Soviet citizens would engage in an individual or family economic activity. In reality, the law did not seem to facilitate even such limited development. Gladki himself hastened to explain that there were "substantial" differences between the law and the NEP, because in the earlier period salaried work was authorized, "while the new law categorically excludes it." The law thus represented a change of considerable proportions, more from a political and ideological standpoint than from an economic one. In any case, the implementation of the law dragged and is still in an experimental phase today.

But if the plan for economic reform was approached with great caution, the situation on other fronts seemed extremely lively and restless. For example, the weekly *Ogonyok* published a small collection of Khodasevich's poems—the same ones that the monthly *Znamya* had been forced to turn down—showing that the censors were no longer able to issue prohibitions in a uniform fashion. Indeed, 650 copies of Tengiz Abuladze's film *Pokayaniye* had already been printed, but permission still could not be obtained to show it in Soviet cinemas. The magazine *Znamya* announced the upcoming publication of Mikhail Bulgakov's *Heart of a Dog* (*Sobache Serdtse*), while *Novy Mir* announced its publication of Boris Pasternak's *Dr. Zhivago* starting in early 1987.

However, the most prominent cultural event in the capital was Mikhail Shatrov's play *Diktatura Sovesti* (*The Dictatorship of the Conscience*) at the Leninski Komsomol Theater, directed by Mark Zakharov. The subject was a "trial" of Lenin and of the October Revolution. It is in fact an invective against Stalinism and barracks communism. The main character is Pyotr Verkhovensky of Dostoevsky's *Devils*, and the play is a modern reading of that work with clear references to the past and the present.

The author, Mikhail Shatrov, spoke at the 6 December constitutional congress of theater workers. The entire Politburo was present, except for Gorbachev, and at the end of the speech Ligachev clapped vigorously. Extracts from Shatrov's speech were published the following week in *Moskovskiye Novosti* and caused a sensation. The speech consisted of a summary of alarming episodes of "resistance" to change, and concluded by lashing out at the culprits:

> Formalism and diffidence, intellectual inertia and perverted consciences. Absolute power corrupts absolutely. These words were said a long time ago. We realized this after having paid for distancing ourselves from the October ideals with the lives of millions of men, with spiritual impoverishment, with the spread of a slave mentality, and with social and political apathy.

The text published by *Moskovskiye Novosti* stops here. Shatrov, however, had said much more, confronting subjects that had still not found a public platform. Speaking to an audience immersed in a dramatic silence, he recalled 1929 ("the end of NEP, but also the end of socialist democracy") and the country's reawakening in the "spring of 1956, with the Twentieth Congress." Then, "step by step, the progress begun by the Twentieth Congress was gradually reabsorbed." His reference to Brezhnev was explicit: "Antidemocratic, basically antisocialist tendencies returned to halt our progress."

Remembering the March 1985 plenum at which Gorbachev had announced the political reform, Shatrov exclaimed, "We talk a lot about April, but I want to talk about March." Why? Because at that crucial moment "various alternatives" existed, including the alternative to choose:

We cannot forget the danger that weighed upon us in March 1985 and that, perhaps not immediately, could have led to a relapse to an uncontrolled power. When the problems that suffocated the country could have either been confronted with democratization or pushed back by an iron hand. *Tertium non datur.*[19]

Shatrov clearly stated that the danger stemmed from the former first secretary of Moscow, Viktor Grishin, who would be expelled from the Politburo just one year later, on 18 February 1986. This was the first confirmation that Gorbachev's election had been opposed up until the last minute and that Grishin was the candidate of the conservative opposition within the Politburo. Shatrov repeated, "I am absolutely convinced that the country arrived at perestroika suffering." This is why "we must not forget that before April there was March, nor must we forget who and what preceded March."

The writer's remarks hardly seemed casual. In the preceding weeks the rumor had circulated that a group of writers, clearly identifiable with the conservative wing (Chakovsky, the editor in chief of *Literaturnaya Gazeta*; Sofronov, the ex-editor of *Ogonyok*; the poet Nikolai Gribachev; and Feliks Kuznetsov, the ex-secretary of the Moscow Writers' Union), had written a letter to the Central Committee requesting an end to the spread of critical materials on the present and the past in order to prevent the celebration of the seventieth anniversary of the October Revolution from taking place in a climate that was not appropriately festive. This was not an isolated initiative. Since the beginning of December there had been persistent rumors of an upcoming Central Committee plenum on cadres, which would determine important rotations in the party's top leadership.

Suddenly, on Tuesday, 16 December, the plenum of the Kazakhstan Central Committee decided to "retire" Dinmukhamed Kunayev. He became the fourth member of Brezhnev's old guard that Gorbachev succeeded in removing from a leadership post, following Grigori Romanov, Nikolai Tikhonov, and Viktor Grishin.

Kunayev had formed a clan over the course of twenty-six years that proved to be much tougher than that of his neighbor Saraf Rashidov, who committed suicide after Yuri Andropov pulled out his dossier from the KGB archives in the struggle to succeed Brezhnev. His clan was so solid that even though Moscow had decided to end his rule, it could not find someone from Kazakhstan to take his place, forcing it to break the almost iron rule that demanded a local cadre in the top leadership post of a republic. A Russian, Gennadi Kolbin, took the reins of Alma-Ata.

But the protests began the very evening of the Kazakhstan plenum meeting at Alma-Ata, turning into mass protests the next day that led to serious disorders lasting until the following Thursday. On Thursday afternoon Tass took the dramatic initiative of carrying this news in a brief report that did not hide the political nature of the protest, though it did minimize the extent of the disorders and made no mention of the casualties (the official toll would not be made public, but direct mention in the local press and indirect mention in the national press would later confirm the existence of both dead and wounded). The nationalistic character of the protests was immediately obvious. But it was also implied that the demonstrations were not spontaneous, and that the protest had been the work of a specific, widespread organization.

The latter accusation portrays the events at Alma-Ata as an unequivocal political resistance to Gorbachev's "purifying" changes. The apparats, the syndicates of power and economics, had proven the extent of their aggressiveness. The Alma-Ata incidents thus posed a triple threat to Gorbachev. First, they proved that they would mobilize to protect their endangered interests. Second, they showed that the true goals of conservativism could be concealed behind the banner of nationalism. Third, it signaled that nationalistic claims that had been suppressed, distorted, or nurtured depending on circumstances, could now, after decades of fermentation, explode into uncontrollable forms in the new climate of openness.

Yet the spark was not strong enough to start a fire. Its promoters, the clan of Kunayev at Alma-Ata, had friends and protectors in Moscow and knew that discussions there were intense. But there was still no strategy or plan to fight the steamrollers driven by the center. The protest was quickly suppressed, while a drastic purge at every level of the local party organizations began.

The renewal moved forcefully in every direction. Gorbachev realized the need, vital to his strategy, to rid himself as quickly as possible of all the deadweight he had inherited. This included one boulder that loomed over the entire complex of relations with the West and that blurred every statement of goodwill toward the democratization of Soviet society. On Friday, 19 December, amid first the stupor and then the flurry of foreign correspondents rushing to the telephones, the deputy minister of foreign affairs read a declaration at a press conference that would prove no less "liberating" for Gorbachev and Soviet society than for Andrei Sakharov.

At the same time, Vladimir Petrovsky announced that the Presidium of the Supreme Soviet had decided to "pardon" Yelena Bonner. The text of the communiqué was labored, involuted, and legally obscure. But it was the last act in a series of events whose "legal" side had always been mysterious and incomprehensible.

The official reasons for Sakharov's Gorky exile, like the legal basis for the decision, had remained unknown. Only at the end of 1985, when the Soviet authorities allowed Bonner to travel abroad for medical reasons, was it learned that the Soviet physicist was named in a ukase of the Supreme Soviet, issued against him "individually" for having "damaged the economic and defensive potential as well as the political prestige of the country." Yelena Bonner's trip was interpreted as the Kremlin's first gesture of openness. Later there were other signals: the rumor, for example, of secret negotiations between *Literaturnaya Gazeta* and Sakharov for the publication of an article by the academician on the subject of the Strategic Defense Initiative (SDI; often referred to as Star Wars) and a commentary on the Reykjavik summit. Then, in the middle of December, after other confidential contacts, Sakharov's telephone in Gorky rang. On the other end of the line was Mikhail Gorbachev in person, to sanction not the leadership's defeat before the indomitable will of one man, but the rediscovered "wisdom" of repairing the damage caused by Brezhnev's "error."

The leadership had wanted to silence Sakharov, alienating him and isolating him. They had almost completely failed to accomplish their objective, and for that they had to pay dearly. As in many similar but less clamorous and emblematic cases, Soviet culture itself had suffered serious amputations and irreparable losses. On 28 December the death of the director Andrei Tarkovsky in Paris reminded everyone of the high cost of triumphant stupidity in power. Now Sakharov was unconditionally authorized to return. He came back with his earlier opinions and with the possibility of communicating them—and not just to foreign correspondents. This too was evidently taken into account by whoever made the decision to allow his return—to initiate a new phase that permitted the expression of a critical public debate on even the most controversial aspects of foreign policy and of civil rights. The importance of this signal went beyond that of a maneuver in foreign policy, or in protocol.

Perhaps the death of the dissident Anatoli Marchenko in prison helped speed up Gorbachev's decision. At the same time other dissidents were freed or received permission to emigrate. When on 23 December Andrei Sakharov—three times decorated with the Order of Lenin, a winner of the Stalin Prize, and of three gold medals as a Hero of Socialist Labor—stepped off train No. 37 onto the platform of the Yaroslavsky Station, there were no longer any doubts about the significance of the changes the new Soviet leadership was prepared to initiate. A few days later I would receive confirmation directly from Sakharov that he had no intention of emigrating and that he considered it possible and useful to continue his battle inside the country—a battle that was growing louder and more intense.

Around that time, the plenum of the Central Committee had been postponed twice. *Pravda* dedicated an editorial to the functioning of the party organizations, criticizing their growing resistance, their "tendency to supplant state and economic organisms" with party decisions that encroached upon every sphere of collective life, the selection of cadres made "by first secretaries of party committees without any collective evaluation of those decisions and without taking into account the workers' opinions."[20] In other words, what was forcing these postponements of the plenum meetings was "party reform," without which the perestroika of the economy and of the society could not take effect. Yet this was the very issue on which resistance focused. Gorbachev was about to face his most difficult obstacle: the democratization of Soviet society.

Second Conversation

Chernobyl and Its Impact on the Information System;
the Resolutions Against Unearned Income and the
Law Authorizing Individual Work Activities; the
Diversion of the Rivers; the Victory Memorial; Salary
Reform and the State Inspection of Production;
Kunayev and the Unrest in Alma-Ata

• • •

G.C. Chernobyl had made obvious the macroscopic inadequacies of the country's information system. I am speaking not so much about individual defects or politically mistaken decisions, but about out-and-out structural deficiencies deriving from the political system. I should emphasize that these structural problems have hardly been overcome at the time of this conversation. Centralized control of the mass media does not permit a quick response to current events. Those in charge of the media still do not have the necessary autonomy. In other words, centralization blocks an unbiased investigation into the truth and keeps the country from knowing itself and knowing its problems. This having been said, I should also add that there has been an enormous leap toward a more democratic dissemination of information. Do you agree with these assessments?

R.M. The greatest changes did occur after Chernobyl. There are, however, still structural defects. It is not hard to see them. In December 1986 Arkadi Raikin, a well-known Soviet artist, died. He was greatly loved by the public, and was one of the leading figures in our light theater. He died on a Saturday morning, but the announcement was not made until the following Tuesday. He was a friend of mine, but I was not able to find out if he was really dead, or where and when the wake and the funeral would be. It took three days to draft the obituary notice, which would be signed by all the members of the Politburo and by the best-known representatives of the cultural world— three days to establish who should sign the "state" obituary. But even then no news was given on where the funeral would be held. This may seem like

37

a minor example, but it is not. It raises many questions. For such an elementary piece of information, why was it necessary to wait for the official obituary? When the newspapers finally carried this late obituary, why was it undersigned by officials who had always refused to see Raikin, and not by his closest friends?

However, there is no denying that perestroika and the changes in the last three years have substantially improved our information system. Yet we still have not seen a broad improvement. The struggle has been two steps forward, one step back.

The leadership ran into many problems whose dimensions were unknown not only to ordinary citizens but to the leaders. This explains the many improvisations, the unexpected developments. It was as if the energy of perestroika found unexpected solutions whenever it faced a dead end. It is a mistake to represent the situation as if, starting in April 1985, the political leadership of the country was ready with precisely drawn plans and an outline of changes. There was a general dissatisfaction in almost all social sectors. A solid block of party and state leaders had reached the consensus that the situation and the country could no longer be managed in the same way. But no one could point out a clearly defined road to follow. In this respect our perestroika does sound like a revolution. For that matter, did the developments of the Russian Revolution follow a preestablished plan after February 1917? Even in the days of the October Revolution, the Bolsheviks knew they wanted to conquer state power, but they figured out the details as they went along. The events following the October Revolution often took shape quite differently from what the Bolsheviks had wanted. Some decrees could not be applied, others remained in the planning stages, and still others produced results that were the opposite of what had been expected.

Here and there you can see the same situation even today. Perestroika began in April 1985, but not under the watchwords of "democratization" and "glasnost," and not even with the intent of changing the information system. The new leadership's first idea was to accelerate and intensify economic development. Everyone was aware of the fact that the economy was limping, and that its growth had dangerously slowed down, if it had not ceased altogether. Everyone saw that the USSR could not keep step with the technical and scientific revolution that was taking place in developed countries. Yet in spite of the many meetings and appeals in 1985, there were very few changes in the economic situation. This led to a massive rotation of cadres at year's end, on the eve of the party's Twenty-Seventh Congress. But during the congress no one said the words "revolutionary changes" or even put forward the concept of "reform." In the spring and winter of 1986, though, almost nothing changed in the sectors of culture and information.

In this respect Chernobyl was both a serious tragedy and a crucial proof of the inadequacies of our information systems. This event spotlighted the grave insufficiencies of our nuclear power plants: in their planning, their construction, their security systems, and their technology in general.

But here we do not want to deal with all of the lessons of Chernobyl. Let's stick to the dissemination of information. At the beginning there was unmistakable and widespread confusion. The representatives of the mass media, the newspapers and television, could not reach the scene of the disaster. The only ones allowed into the area were special detachments of firemen, other special units, and members of government committees. The silence of the newspapers and Gorbachev's silence were a serious blow to the prestige of the Soviet leadership, and raised doubts about his statements on glasnost at the Twenty-Seventh Congress. The situation began to change after 10 May. First newspaper correspondents were allowed onto the scene, and then film and TV reporters. A policy decision was made, which was also extended to other domestic affairs, to restrict the censors' powers. This had a positive effect on cultural life as a whole, extending way beyond information in the strict sense.

Thus, by the end of 1986, the Central Committee had already found it necessary to change the editorial staffs of many publications. New editors in chief were appointed for *Sovetskaya Kultura, Moskovskiye Novosti, Ogonyok, Novy Mir, Znamya,* and a few others. The press started to become more active and more interesting. The first anti-Stalinist works were published. Criticisms of the insufficiencies of social life and of the party became more candid and more harsh. These developments were favored by readers, but they prompted protests in many sectors of the party's ruling cadres, especially at the intermediate levels. Here it helps to look forward to the later January plenum (1987), which was supposed to deal first of all with policy regarding cadres, but instead devoted most of its work to the problems of glasnost. Many of those who intervened denounced the "excesses" of glasnost and of freedom of the press; Gorbachev had no easy job in defending the policies of openness that had just begun.

Here I would like to underline an important change in the party's internal life introduced during the two-year period of our study. Western observers know very little about the more democratic way in which the Central Committee plenum has been run. Now at the plenary meetings of the party's ruling body, it is no longer decided in advance who is to speak, what can be said, and what subjects can be discussed. Sure, even today the party leadership closely controls media operations, but its control is no longer all-inclusive. This change was all it took to produce an information "boom" that has no precedent in all of Soviet political life. The press rushed to publish much of what had previously been prohibited. There was also a certain element of insecurity: this rush disclosed a fear that the party's new policies would not last long. In this rush not everything published was subject to adequate controls and verification, resulting in mistakes and inaccuracies that gave the conservatives and ideological watchdogs a chance to launch bitter attacks on the press.

G.C. The unleashing of a furious debate on the environment in 1986 is unique. But the question of the use of nuclear energy for peace, which is an integral and essential part of the ecology movement in the West, was virtually not discussed on a large scale. This was truly strange in the country that had experienced the greatest ecological tragedy in the nuclear age. Almost no one raised questions about the state program to accelerate the use of nuclear energy. It was as if there were an automatic or a self-imposed censorship.

R.M. The aftermath of Chernobyl demonstrated the persistence of clear restrictions and prohibitions on the dissemination of information. In the summer and fall we would learn many details about the catastrophe. Two novels and a play were published on the subject. The Mysl publishing house came out with a book containing observations of eyewitnesses and reflective essays. A long and apparently honest report on the causes of the disaster was published and delivered to the International Atomic Energy Agency. Representatives of the agency were allowed onto the site of the accident. These were all episodes of a highly unusual glasnost. Yet as you said, public discussion on either ecology or the economy was opened. Novels and plays were published, but scientific investigations and medical research on the effects of Chernobyl did not appear even in later months. As of this moment, the specialized press in the West has published over two hundred scientific articles on the effects of the catastrophe on the population, on the economy, and on the natural environment in various European countries. By contrast, in Soviet magazines, even in highly specialized ones with small readerships, these materials are presently almost nonexistent. This is even odder when you realize that in all probability similar studies were also conducted in the Soviet Union. Nor were the complete data on the economic damages suffered by the country made known. This is partially understandable, given the distressing questions they raise, to which perhaps no one can provide a reassuring answer. You would have to tell the people who live 40 to 50 kilometers from the site of the accident, and even those who are 100 to 120 kilometers or more away, that in the next ten to fifteen years there will be an increase in the incidence of cancer and of birth defects. All of this would raise the level of anxiety in the people who live near other nuclear reactors. It is much easier to keep the people in relative ignorance. The state monopoly over the media makes all of this possible. The public has many questions that for the time being no one is rushing to answer. This proves once again that glasnost and freedom of information are still in the preliminary stages.

G.C. Western "glasnost" has also been very reluctant to talk about nuclear accidents.

R.M. Exactly. Every accident at a nuclear power plant causes a drop in the value of the stocks of the companies managing the production of nuclear energy. Hence the attempts to withhold adequate information about the causes and effects of the accidents. Governments often support these attempts to cover up information. Unfortunately, there is no lack of examples. However, in Western countries the mass media is relatively independent, and consequently the public receives many facts despite the wishes of powerful industrialists and politicians. We still do not have such an independent information system. And we do not even have an opposition independent from the state, or independent criticism. Small ecology groups began to appear only after Chernobyl. This is why we still do not know many things. For example, there was another accident at a nuclear plant in Armenia, not as big as the one in the Ukraine, but even in this case there were very great dangers, considering the small size of this republic's territory. No information was provided about this, which is partly why such alarming rumors spread in Armenia. At the beginning of this conversation you recalled that Chernobyl brought to light various insufficiencies, including those of the political system. In effect, the abnormal centralization proved to be a powerful obstacle to an efficient response. Why, for example, did the local authorities not immediately warn the people in the endangered areas? The evacuation of people was very well organized, but came nearly thirty-six hours after the catastrophe; on the first day the children of Pripyat, a town with forty-five thousand inhabitants, continued to play soccer not far from the burning reactor. In Kiev on 1 May the traditional parade was held, as in Gomel and other towns. I have heard that Shcherbitsky wanted to declare a state of emergency in Kiev and in the northern areas of the Ukrainian Republic, but that Moscow would not give the authorization. Then in Moscow, in the first hours after the accident, extremely important questions were decided by incompetent people who were dealing with emergencies of this proportion for the first time. No one was able to react with sufficient decisiveness and authority. Many people had to pay the consequences for this. The alarm slowly rose from the bottom to the top, and everyone awaited Moscow's decisions and orders. Instead, crucial and rapid decisions should have been made right on the spot.

G.C. During the second half of 1986 there was a still uncertain debate and experimental, "halfway" measures. The two resolutions passed by the Central Committee on 28 May against unearned income showed a total blindness to and disdain for reality. Everyone knows the sizes (and the causes) of parallel markets in the Soviet Union. Yet the government chose exclusively repressive measures that were totally incapable of getting to the roots of the phenomenon.

R.M. The analysis of the economic situation in 1986 developed in different directions and on different levels. At that stage there was still no definite goal. Hence, as you observe, the contradictory nature of the political line followed. Let's not forget that this was the first year of the new *pyatiletka*, and that the five-year plan had been drawn up prior to the spring of 1985. In other words, we were prisoners of earlier tendencies. The orders were to "accelerate" and to "intensify," but thus far no one had raised the question in terms of radical economic reform. You may recall that the word "reform" was not even used at the June 1986 plenum. The plenum had been called to amend the economic development plan for 1986–90, while our economy was still based entirely on the methods of administrative command. In comparison with the growth projections of the previous five-year plan, the worst in the entire post–World War II period, the new plan had been formulated very cautiously. But there were still no criteria for calling it a reform.

In the summer of 1986 no major decisions were made on the economy, and it is also true that in the actual life of the country those months became a theater of unexpected and rapid changes—for the worse.

As the full seriousness of the economic situation manifested itself, huge sectors of the population began to express a growing impatience with the leadership. One of the causes of this discontent was the approval of the two resolutions against unearned income that you referred to earlier. They were not the only decisions in this area. Other minor, but similarly repressive, measures began to take effect on 1 July 1986 and they had an immediate negative impact on the daily lives of millions of Soviet citizens. Throughout the country, for example, the amount of farm produce shipped to the kolkhoz markets fell drastically, and at the same time the price of fruits and vegetables went up. In certain parts of Siberia and the Urals, the kolkhoz markets were deserted because the producers from the southern regions stopped sending food products there altogether; it was no longer convenient. In many regions the local powers began using their authority to curtail people's individual work activities; the greenhouses that farmers and city dwellers had built on family plots and in vegetable gardens were torn down. The fight against unearned income grew such that it took on a punitive character against all "private" forms by which families rounded out their incomes. The effect was very great in two ways: it struck the income of people who practiced these activities, and at the same time it left millions of people without services that the state was incapable of providing.

Additional factors should be noted. For decades the Soviet economy functioned alongside a complex and widespread network of underground business activities in numerous areas. This "second economy" is particularly active in the area of services, but it is also present in manufacturing, trade, education, health, farming, and transportation. It includes legal, semilegal, and illegal activities. In fact, most of the Soviet population is in daily contact with the underground economy in one way or another, which is why a careful and thoughtful approach was required. Certain forms of private activity were supposed to be legalized without any limitations. Others were supposed to be allowed only under specific conditions. Only some activities were to be prohibited.

For decades the authorities closed their eyes to some forms of "illegal" work activities rather than change the laws. Some economists spoke not only about the existence of a "second economy," but even about a third, fourth, fifth, and sixth. Others used colors to describe a variety of markets: black, gray, yellow, and red.

Let me give just a few examples. Millions of people who live at seaside resorts lease their apartments to tourists in the summer. As a rule, health regulations and the prices set by the local authorities are not followed because the demand is much greater than the supply. The harsh punitive measures adopted in 1986 deprived millions of citizens in the South of an extra summer income to which they had been accustomed for many years. At the same time, millions of people in the northern regions could not take their vacations in the South or in the Baltic Republics. Another example: Millions of people have small gardens. But not everyone can or wishes to go to the market to sell their produce. So a system of middlemen was created, both in the area of transportation and in the kolkhoz markets. The two 1986 resolutions classified both activities as "illegal." As a result, the markets were quickly emptied of sellers and of produce. A third example: Obviously, the principal of a school who accepts tips from the parents of future students should be punished. But how do you regulate the complex system of private lessons that prepares students for entrance examinations? How do you regulate the private tailors, the typists, and the home workshops for various types of repairs? Here there is no single response. In the springtime a tractor driver plows not only the fields of his kolkhoz, but also individual plots. He gets money for this, even if he works with a tractor that is not his. This activity could be prohibited because it is illegal. But who will do this work for the individual farmers who cannot do it themselves? Millions of empty buses from different organizations pass by bus stops packed with people waiting for the next bus. The ministries burned old office furniture because they were not allowed to sell it. All of this was "legitimate." But the elderly retiree from Kislovodsk who buys a bucket of cherries at the market and then sells them at nearby tourist hotels for a higher price could be stopped as a "speculator" and given a big fine. The underground economy is a huge iceberg. It has a considerable influence on the lives of millions of people, but it has not been adequately studied.

The impact of the two resolutions against unearned income was very serious. It was necessary to shift into reverse. By the end of August the local party organizations had already received a "confidential" circular on the "excesses of the fight against unearned income." Things had reached a point where in many regions the transportation of farm produce from one area to the surrounding areas had been prohibited. In other places the order had been given to tear down the greenhouses that farmers had built on their individual plots or in their vegetable gardens.

G.C. In the Volgograd region, for example . . .

R.M. In Volgograd, particularly harsh measures were taken against the holders of small individual plots. Since as a rule the law allowed only "summer" houses to be built on garden plots, the local authorities forced the chimneys in the little dachas to be torn down. And where there was an extra story, that too was torn down. So we are not just talking about greenhouses! These little houses were also places of rest and not just sources of additional income. These measures were explicitly punitive as well as damaging to both individuals and society. They resulted in great discontent—with Gorbachev. There is nothing strange in this: for simple people, especially in the provinces, perestroika is tied to Gorbachev's name, and he is its personification. This phenomenon also holds true for international public opinion.

G.C. Are the true dimensions of the underground economy obscured by ideology or by a political struggle in which certain sectors of the establishment try to make the situation even more difficult by continuing to act according to the old methods, ignoring all factual evidence in their refusal to engage in a realistic analysis of society?

R.M. I do not believe that the resolutions on illegal trading were deliberately conceived to exacerbate the crisis. First, they resulted from ignorance of the actual size of the underground economy. Unfortunately, as you said, there are many things which are known to literally all Soviet citizens, except for the party and state leaders. In the decisions we are talking about, I see the result, on the one hand, of a dogmatic concept of socialism, and on the other, of a dogmatic concept of the force of laws and resolutions. There are some leaders who think it is enough to pass this or that law to stop people from drinking, smoking, stealing, speculating, increasing their income, or selling their goods at prices different from those set by the government. From this perspective alone is it possible to speak of a political struggle "at the top" between the "pragmatists" and the "dogmatists," between those who understand that socialism does not exclude diversity in the forms of property and economic activity, who propose to provide incentives for all forms of reasonable work activity, in the interests of the individual and of the whole society, and those who do not understand all this in the least.

However, several points of view on the subject of the economy had already undergone their first corrections in the fall of 1986. In the press there were a number of articles criticizing the enforcement of the measures against unearned income. Various authors raised the issue of reexamining the concept of "speculation" to ensure that it did not include normal private commercial activity. In other words, if an inhabitant of the country transported potatoes and vegetables from his own plot to the city, and at the same time transported the vegetables and produce of his neighbors, this person should not be considered a speculator, but rather a normal businessman who substantially helped his neighbors, while also profiting himself, and provided a service to the city.

G.C. What do you think of the events surrounding the construction of the Memorial to Victory on the famous Bowers' Hill?

R.M. The decision to build large monuments commemorating the Soviet Union's victory over Nazi Germany was made over thirty years ago. One of the most majestic monuments was erected in Volgograd. It is a huge construction that took five years to build (1963–67) under the direction of the sculptor Yevgeni Vuchetich. There was no competition, nor was there any public discussion of the project. Brezhnev, Aleksei Kosygin, Mikhail Suslov, and Marshal Malinovsky liked the plans for the work. Earlier, Khrushchev had liked it, and that was enough. Even today that monument has its detractors and its supporters, but it has already been built and it cannot be eliminated. By contrast, the plans for the second colossus provoked much

45

more discussion. It took almost ten years to build it on the banks of the Dnieper River in Kiev. Once again it was under the direction of Vuchetich, who was a kind of dictator in the arts of sculpture and monument-building. The central part of the monument complex is a giant sculpture representing the Motherland, exactly as in Volgograd. The only difference is that the statue on the Volga was fifty-two meters tall, while the one on the Dnieper was sixty-two meters tall. Even though the majority of the people considered it just plain ugly, the complex was approved in the midst of protests.

But the most gigantic of the monuments was reserved for Moscow. The work began in 1983 on the famous Poklonnaya Hill. The funds for its construction had been put together through a popular subscription that raised 140 million rubles. Vuchetich died in 1974 and the project for the Moscow monument was entrusted to the sculptor Nikolai Tomsky, once again without any competition. The monument's structural deficiencies loudly proclaimed the decline in Soviet sculpture and monumental architecture over the last twenty to twenty-five years. Its primitive concepts were emphasized by its pharaonic dimensions; the complex was supposed to cover 135 hectares. But this time an active fight against the monument began with the first work on construction. This battle was headed by members of the Pamyat association, who are well known today, but the movement involved many people. Yet once again no one paid attention to public opinion. By the fall of 1986 almost the entire Poklonnaya Hill had been flattened and the pompous building for the Museum of the Great Patriotic War was being built. But the protests grew so loud that the authors of the project were forced to put their plans on display in a show open to the public. Not a single prestigious name came forth to defend the project. The Politburo had to interrupt the work. But the damage to the environment had already been done and almost 40 million rubles had been spent. After the Politburo's decision a public competition for a new project was announced, but a satisfactory new decision could not be reached. A second grand competition had to be announced whose results are not yet known. A show of all the projects presented was held at the Manezh in May and June of 1988.

G.C. And the story about diverting the rivers?

R.M. This is another old story. The first projects to redirect a part of the flow of the northern and Siberian rivers toward the southern regions were put forward fifty years ago, on the basis of rather elementary considerations. In the areas to the south of the RSFSR—in the Caspian region, the Stavropol region, in Central Asia, and in Kazakhstan—there are huge expanses of arable land; moreover, these areas are densely populated, with a high rate

46

of population growth. All of these regions suffer to some degree from a lack of water. Water for this purpose would have been drawn off the Volga, the Syr-Darya, the Amu-Darya, the Don, the Kuban, and the Terek. But present-day industrial development and urban expansion quickly proved that the water thus obtained was not enough. The level of the Aral Sea began to go down. At the same time 85 percent of the USSR's colossal water resources are located in the scarcely populated northern and eastern areas, which are almost unusable for farming. The grandiose plan to divert the rivers was born from this natural imbalance.

Before the war thousands of scientists and technicians began working on the project. In the 1970s, even before the final project had been approved, the Ministry of Reclaimed Lands began to move on it. Fifty or even twenty-five years ago, the need to defend the environment had not yet emerged with the urgency we feel today. The relationship between man and nature was seen in another way. But it was well known that various projects to improve agriculture that had been carried out in the past had not led to the expected results. Enormous man-made "seas," such as those at Zymlyansk, Kakhovka, Volzhky, and Kuibyshev, had flooded millions of acres of good land and upset the climates of the surrounding regions. In the Kuban, waterworks had often had the reverse effect of salinizing the irrigated lands. In Central Asia less than 50 percent of the irrigation waters were used efficiently. Moreover, the diversion of part of the flow of the northern and Siberian rivers could also have aggravated the situation in the northern farming regions, causing climatic changes that had not been adequately studied. In short, we had not yet learned how to use our water resources efficiently.

A decision such as the one to divert should have been preceded by a serious investigation of previous negative experiences. In general, the people's trust in projects like this had already been shaken by disastrous decisions such as the one to create a dam separating the Kara-Bogaz Gulf from the Caspian Sea. The Ladoga and Onega lakes were dying. The high-mountain Sevan Lake was in the same situation, and the waters of Baikal were polluted, as were the waters of hundreds of medium- and small-sized rivers. The ecosystem of the famous health springs in the northern Caucasus had been violated. Given this situation, to spend millions more for the construction of complex waterworks would have constituted an irrational economic alternative to the wiser decision to confront the problem of rational use of the existing land and water resources.

G.C. In the second half of 1986 there was a lot of talk about salary reform. A series of Politburo resolutions announced changes that were supposed to take place at the beginning of 1987. How would you evaluate those decisions?

R.M. At that point we were still very far from actual reform. The decisions made during that phase were partial and not at all radical. The existing imbalances in the price system for goods and services were at a level commensurate with those in the salary system. They were an integral part of the "restraining mechanism" that was now being denounced. It would be extremely difficult, if not impossible, to untie these knots in a short time. For example, in the last twenty to thirty years the average salary of factory workers has increased several times and today is two to three times higher than that of engineers and planners. But even among the factory workers there is a leveling system that makes little distinction between highly skilled and unskilled labor, and between a man who works well and one who doesn't work at all. Salary has ceased to be an incentive for quality work and efficiency.

Now everyone realizes that this is a vicious cycle that we must break, and not just in industry. For example, the salaries of doctors, lower-level health-care workers, many categories of office workers, and teaching personnel are absolutely inadequate. This inevitably leads to abuses, petty theft, corruption, the system of bribes, and so on. An engineer who earns from 120 to 140 rubles a month cannot be induced to work hard. A nurse who earns 100 rubles a month will not bend over backward to help patients. It is very rare to find male teachers, because a teacher's salary is not sufficient to support a family budget. This is an area that requires radical decisions. But the obstacles are both political and economic.

In 1987 the average salary of factory and office workers in the USSR was 201 rubles a month (it was 196 rubles in 1986). "Average" means that it includes those who earn high wages and salaries (by Soviet standards) of 250, 350, up to 500 and 600 rubles a month, such as metalworkers, miners, bus drivers, and workers at the enterprises in the North and the Far East. Yet not even the latter consider themselves well paid. We have about a hundred types of rather low-cost goods and services whose prices have not risen for thirty to forty years: rent, electricity, heating, bread, sugar, milk, meat, transportation, and so on. For these goods and services a salary of 200 or 300 rubles would suffice. But the problem becomes difficult for most workers as soon as a family procures goods or services that are not considered "prime needs," even if they can count on a decent or even higher-than-average salary. Even for a metalworker or miner it is not easy to find acceptable clothing for his wife or shoes for his children, buy a color television, go on vacation to Bulgaria, or buy a car. This is basically because the quantity of goods and services produced in the USSR does not correspond to the total amount of salaries paid: a "relative shortage." And this, *sic stantibus rebus*, would actually be aggravated by a simple increase in even the lowest salaries. Thus, savings accounts increase and money accumulates that cannot be spent because of a lack of goods. This being the case, a general increase in salaries, unaccompanied by a change in current economic structures, would aggravate the situation. The main problem is to increase the production of goods and services, without which no salary reform would be effective.

G.C. In the fall of 1986 a bill was passed that authorized "individual work activities." True, it would not go into effect until 1 May 1987, and it seemed extremely cautious, but it did constitute a step forward, don't you think?

R.M. This problem was raised in the early 1960s after decades of silence on the subject. Brezhnev brought it up again in a 1970 speech. The right of Soviet citizens to engage in an individual work activity is established by the Constitution. However, this question has never been resolved, at least from a legal standpoint, because in reality individual economic activity has always existed as part of what we earlier called the underground economy. Here I would emphasize that since these activities could only be performed illegally, they were and are accompanied by serious problems for both the state that would control and impede them and for the individual citizen. Let me give you just one more example. In the countryside there have always been the so-called "shabashniki," unlicensed construction companies. Without them the kolkhozes and sovkhozes could not handle all of their construction needs. But where do these shabashniki get their construction materials? On what basis are they paid? How many times have their interventions, which are indispensable to the normal operations of farm enterprises, ended in criminal trials with the foremen of these "unlicensed companies" and the accountants and chairmen of the kolkhozes as defendants? What should a kolkhoz do when it needs to build a new stable immediately? Wait for years until the state enterprises intervene? Many "illegal" private activities developed anyway, but not enough to make up for the deficiencies caused by state inefficiency. As a result, many services to the population are either inadequate or completely nonexistent. This holds true especially for the system of public food services and restaurants, one of the most backward in the world.

The law on individual activities also arrived very late. It has to be studied in the context of other important decisions, such as the introduction of contracts for work teams and for families, the development of cooperative trade, the increase in the number of private gardens, and so on—all decisions that indicated vast changes in concrete politics and in the economic ideas of the political leadership. However, the new law substantially altered the situation: the state ceased to be the only employer. A new social stratum was created—the artisans—whose existence had been ignored by official statistics and economics studies. Private and state enterprises could now compete in the area of services and the manufacture of consumer goods. The huge amount of compulsory savings (about 300 billion rubles) could partly be used to help finance these new private activities.

It is worthwhile recalling that on two occasions the extensive utilization of individual work had already helped save the Soviet economy from difficult situations. In the period from 1922 to 1928 Lenin's New Economic Policy helped prevent the economic and political collapse of the young Soviet republic. Thanks to the NEP, the country's economy was brought back up to its prerevolution level and even higher for a relatively brief period of time. The same thing happened during the tragic years of the Great Patriotic War, when production at all factories was geared to war needs and manufacturing for civilians was almost brought to a complete halt. In that time no NEP was declared, but millions of Soviets citizens, including women, old people, and adolescents, engaged in private economic activities, often working at night. At homes or in small workshops they made shoes, sewed garments and hats, produced knives, cigarettes, cigarette lighters, toys, furniture, and anything else that the state could no longer manufacture. During the war every big city had a flea market, the so-called *tolkuchka* early on Sunday mornings, where old and new goods were sold and traded. The government could not stick its nose into these spontaneous activities, but immediately after the war they were restricted and then altogether prohibited.

Today these conditions no longer prevail. Our industries provide thousands of different goods and services. Yet even today individual work activities, small industrial production, and private repairs and services still represent an essential component of people's everyday life. The law that has been approved should provide some order for this economic realm in different ways: first of all by finally authorizing activities that already existed *de facto*, but in semilegal or illegal forms; second, by lowering the exceedingly high taxes that had been set; third, by defining the responsibilities of local authorities and decreasing the amount of administrative vagueness. Thus, for example, it is now possible to privately renovate apartments and dachas, repair household appliances, and open hair-dressing salons or photography shops. A private car could be used as a taxi, and small handicrafts could be sold outside the area where they had been made, in other words, through the state stores. The proprietor of an "individual work activity" could employ his relatives and hire apprentices, either as salaried workers or as partners. Bank credit was allowed for these activities, and it was possible to lease space and to procure prime and semifinished materials from state enterprises. This should permit the immediate appearance of hundreds of small workshops, restaurants, repair shops, and private professional studios.

G.C. The law we are talking about was approved in the fall of 1986 and went into effect on 1 May 1987. Now it is the beginning of 1988. What has happened in these months?

R.M. It seems to me that however slow they were in coming, the first results were positive. According to official figures, the number of employees in private and cooperative enterprises had risen to 150,000 at the end of 1987 (at the beginning of 1986 the figure was only 15,000). The total production value of these individual enterprises amounts to 150 million rubles. But these rough figures do not include the vast majority of people already engaged in such activities, who are still not registered with the local soviets, where the permits are issued.

The local authorities did not always respond favorably to new legal guidelines. Even among the populace, reactions were not everywhere positive. No one denies that private activities play a useful role; most people use them every day. But many people do not like the exorbitant profits of the "privates" or the excessive prices of their services. For example, in Moscow in one year alone seventy cooperative cafés sprang up. Many people were happy, but many others were opposed and wanted them closed. However, a cooperative could not be closed by administrative decree—it could be forced out of business only by competition. There was no lack of bureaucratic obstacles of every sort when a cooperative's bylaws were approved, or later when its financial activities and income were audited.

Statistics show that in Moscow 25 percent of all roofs have holes in them; hundreds of cellars are flooded; thousands of meters of pipes need urgent repairs. A group of engineers and technicians decided to form a cooperative for emergency jobs like these. For many this would be manna from heaven, but authorization has still not been granted. Another example: in the Crimea the Temp cooperative was formed to make replacement pieces for textile machinery. The clothing factories immediately began to use their services, and the cooperative rapidly quadrupled its receipts—so the local authorities closed it on the grounds that it yielded too much income for its partners.

Craftsmen in every field made goods that no one had produced previously, despite strong demands for them. The earnings of these craftsmen were also very high, even when they duly paid their taxes. Once again, rather than letting free competition be the determining factor, restrictions and prohibitions were reintroduced. Let me cite another example. In a seaside town a cooperative was formed to manufacture footwear for the beach. Again a huge demand was discovered, since no one produced this type of article. The cooperative's earnings quickly reached incredible levels. But the local authorities and some of the populace counterattacked and the cooperative was closed. And always for the same reasons: these cooperatives earned "too much." For the sake of safeguarding a misunderstood principle of "equality" and "moderation," the populace was allowed to keep arguing in the midst of a shortage of goods and services.

G.C. Do you think that Gospriyomka is a solution to the production problem? Isn't it a disciplinary move rather than a reform?

R.M. I don't think we need to prove that the quality of production is one of the chief problems of the Soviet economy. The quality of the great majority of the goods we manufacture is significantly below international standards. We manufacture four times more tractors than the United States, but our farm yield is four to five times lower. This fact speaks clearly: our tractors break earlier and function worse. We manufacture 800 million pairs of shoes a year; this is too many, but our shoes don't last very long. To the list you could add televisions and hundreds of other products. But there is another side to the problem. Many goods in the stores cannot be sold, while large amounts of money in family savings accounts cannot be used. For these accounts alone the state has to pay from 5 to 6 billion rubles a year, despite the low interest rates. Soviet industry could increase its production of clothing, but buyers today want not just any clothes, but clothes that they like or that last.

Before Gospriyomka there was already a system of control: every enterprise had a technical control department (OTK) in charge of inspecting all outgoing manufactured goods. The OTK system, however, was subordinate to the enterprise's management. Ministerial commissions arrived from the outside to give a "seal of quality" to this or that product. Obtaining this seal meant a raise in salaries or wages. This was the only incentive provided for. Finally, another system of relative control was the right of the distributing companies to reject poor-quality merchandise. But this set of mechanisms did not work, and it could not work because there were not enough common points of reference accepted by everyone involved in the process. For example, what does poor quality mean? How could you measure it? This is the context in which Gospriyomka was born. Gospriyomka's bodies were independent of the management of a given enterprise. The Gospriyomka technicians and officials were employees of the USSR State Committee on Standards. They were very well paid, but their salaries were cut if a customer raised a complaint about goods received. Gospriyomka had great power: production that did not pass inspection could not leave the factory.

You are right when you say this was not a reform. Instead, it was an enormous new organization imposing a certain discipline on enterprises from the top. Gospriyomka began operations on 1 January 1987, but not every-where. Gorbachev himself, who had backed the proposal, did not hide the fact that this was a hard decision that could not be put into effect without conflicts.

About fifteen hundred enterprises were affected by the new measure on 1 January 1987. One year later there would be many more, including all the construction companies. At present, it is still not possible to give an overall assessment of the program, but already in early 1987 there were serious conflicts between Gospriyomka on the one hand and company management and workers on the other. There were more than a few enterprises in which more than half the production was rejected as it came off the assembly line. In some cases factories were shut down and workers were not paid because they did not meet the plan's quotas (rejected production could not be counted). But on the whole a certain compromise was found quickly.

In many cases the new controls led to an effective increase in the quality of production, even if there was no huge leap forward. In other cases the Gospriyomka technicians had to lower their demands to avoid completely shutting down a factory that was unable to produce anything that met the new standards. Compromises had to be made with other companies because they received defective parts from companies where Gospriyomka had not yet been introduced. In the early months of 1987 Gospriyomka rejected 15 to 20 percent of the production. By the end of the same year the rate had fallen to 10 percent. In one year these controls uncovered 6 billion rubles' worth of defective goods.

However, with the enforcement of the new law on state enterprises (approved in the summer of 1987), and the spread of self-managing, self-financing, and independent enterprises, Gospriyomka was destined to lose its significance. The control levers on production quality were pulled by economic interests rather than administrative supervision. I think that Gospriyomka will be kept and extended, especially to enterprises that manufacture valuable machinery, such as turbines for electric power plants, atomic energy plants, airplanes, and so on.

G.C. Was the Alma-Ata revolt a nationalist uprising, or the first response engineered by the local clans against the center's reforms? Do you see an All-Union significance in this event?

R.M. That is exactly the point: there were significant implications for the whole Soviet Union. But corruption and nationalism alone cannot explain the Alma-Ata revolt. Nor can you attribute the mafias, which were also built on a nationalist basis, entirely to Kunayev. In reality, the events at Alma-

Ata, like those in Uzbekistan, in Armenia, in the Baltic Republics, and those involving the Crimean Tatars, disclosed the existence of real, unresolved national problems. The USSR is a multinational country comprised of fifteen republics, each of which is inhabited by many different ethnic groups. According to statistics, there are in all over a hundred different ethnic groups, twenty-four of which consist of more than a million people each. Each of these groups has its own history and its own specific interests. Much attention was paid to these problems in the 1920s. There were special institutions at the state and party level to deal with these problems, such as the People's Commissariat for National Affairs as well as work groups in the Bolshevik Party's Central Committee. In the early 1930s Stalin proclaimed that the national question in the USSR had been resolved "completely and definitively."* All efforts to look into this area in greater depth were interrupted. From that moment most of the books and articles on the subject became praise for the "friendship among the peoples of the USSR"; they talked almost exclusively about the formation of a new social community, the "Soviet people." Thorny questions were simply erased and many real problems were ignored.

Kazakhstan is the republic with the second-largest territory, after the Russian Soviet Federated Socialist Republic (RSFSR): with its 2.7 million square kilometers it is four and a half times larger than the Ukraine. Originally, it had a small population; in the mid-1930s there were fewer than 7 million people, of whom about 60 percent were Kazakhs and 20 percent Russians. At the end of the 1930s the national structure of the republic began to change. Stalin deported many people to northern Kazakhstan and built many labor camps there. This policy continued into the war, when Chechens, Ingushi, Kalmyks, and a good number of Volga Germans were deported there. After the Twentieth Congress the people of the northern Caucasus returned to their lands, but the number of Germans increased. They were forcibly transferred there from various northern and eastern areas. When the era of land tillage began, almost 1 million Russians and Ukrainians arrived

---

* The "national question" refers to the complex network of relations among the various ethnic groups, nations, and peoples in the Soviet Union. The problem of mediating their interethnic relations and their linguistic, religious, cultural, and traditional differences has always been the source of grave difficulties for the central government. For decades, starting with Stalin, Soviet leaders have tried to "Russianize" the country, systematically violating the rights of ethnic minorities. This has led to a sharpening of preexisting historical conflicts. The explosion of the national question in the perestroika era is the result of this repression of the rights of peoples and nations. No sooner did glasnost open the gates to a genuine expression of national concerns than these conflicts erupted in all their uncontrolled virulence.

in northern Kazakhstan. The first experimental nuclear explosions were done in that area; a testing site for underground nuclear explosions was built in the area of Semipalatinsk. The Baikonur Cosmodrome and other centers for space research and control were built after the war. When leaders of the other republics expressed their reservations about the excessive pressures accumulating in Kazakhstan, they were not only harshly attacked by the center, but removed from office. Brezhnev, who was then the first secretary of the Kazakh Central Committee, laid the foundation for his political career here. He was the one who nominated Dinmukhamed Kunayev as his successor. Kunayev became first secretary of the Kazakh Central Committee in 1960 and became a member of the Politburo in 1971. Kunayev did not interfere in the activities of the central ministries involved in the northern part of the republic, and in exchange, he had a free hand in managing all the other internal questions.

The population of Kazakhstan grew to the current 16 million. About 5.3 million—33 percent—are Kazakhs. Russians now constitute 45 percent of the total; together with the Ukrainians they have become the majority. In addition to these two non-Asiatic populations, more than one million ethnic Germans live in Kazakhstan, to whom we should add the Byelorussians, the Tatars, the Uigurs, the Uzbeks, and other minorities. The Kazakhs live primarily in the South; the Russians, Ukrainians, and Germans instead have settled mostly in the North. There is such a sharp delineation that at a certain point the proposal was made to place all of northern Kazakhstan under the jurisdiction of the RSFSR. Moscow's noninterference in Kazakhstan's internal questions left the republic open to racketeering and patronage. Through Kunayev's personal connections, the corruption even spread to Moscow, even inside the Brezhnev clan. At the same time, the patronage structures were gradually tinged with nationalism.

If you go to the heart of the problem, you must recognize that the roots of corruption were as much in Moscow as they were in Alma-Ata. Together with Rashidov, his Uzbek neighbor, Kunayev would go to Moscow bearing expensive gifts for Brezhnev and his family, and for many other government leaders. These gifts frequently came in the form of hard cash. Obviously, Kunayev and Rashidov kept most of the plunder for themselves. This example was eventually followed by many local party leaders. I believe that presents for Brezhnev even arrived from Stavropol. But the most conspicuous flow was from the Krasnodar region, dominated by the mafia of Sergei Medunov, the first secretary of the local party.

G.C. Whatever happened to Medunov? Was he arrested after being expelled from the Central Committee?

R.M. Not at all. He is retired and lives in Moscow. He is still a Hero of Socialist Labor and in the Krasnodar park his name is still written in golden letters on the list of famous citizens. Vasili Mzavanadze, the former first secretary of Georgia, was not arrested, though he was fired from his position for corruption in 1973. Criminal investigations have not even been opened into the activities of Viktor Grishin and Grigori Romanov, ex-members of the Politburo who were no less involved in corrupt practices. This list could go on for as long as you like. Until recently, the party's top leaders could be kicked out of the Central Committee or the Supreme Soviet, and sometimes they could lose their party membership, but they were neither arrested nor sent to prison. This had been the practice since the times of Khrushchev, who did not begin legal proceedings against Molotov, Georgi Malenkov, or Lazar Kaganovich. Losing your position was considered punishment enough. Not even Kunayev has been arrested; he has been expelled from the Central Committee and he lives at his home in Alma-Ata. Instead, almost all of his assistants were arrested, along with many ministers and ex-secretaries of the local Central Committee.

G.C. Could you better illustrate the connection between corruption and nationalism?

R.M. Mafias are often built on a nationalist basis, making them close-knit. This is also the case in Kazakhstan, where even though the original inhabitants were in the minority, they held almost all the most important public offices. There were fewer and fewer Kazakhs in the factories; they came to occupy predominantly clerical jobs in the republic's ministries. Even places in institutions of higher learning reserved for Russians ended up going to Kazakhs. The republic's economy in the meantime grew significantly worse.

The fight against corruption began with Andropov, immediately after Brezhnev's death. Andropov refused gifts and appointed new ministers of the interior and of the KGB in the republic. Obviously, the Kunayev group was upset. The first arrests took place in 1985 and 1986. But the clan was close-knit, and Kunayev had no internal adversaries. Moscow realized that it would take a drastic "surgical" operation to turn the situation around, i.e., the appointment of a new first secretary for the republic, and, given the circumstances, a non-Kazakh. The choice was Gennadi Kolbin, a Russian who had never worked in Kazakhstan. In the party jargon that meant "breaking the *nomenklatura* chain."

Kolbin could be called an expert in the fight against corruption. He had worked with Shevardnadze in Georgia as the second secretary since 1975. He became first secretary of the Ulyanovsk Regional Committee in 1981.

The expulsion of Kunayev led to rioting. Tass quickly reported the news, but not in very much detail. For example, it was not reported that there were also disorders outside the capital in other towns. We do not know how many victims or arrests there were. The results of the inquest were never published. The disorders did not result from spontaneous combustion; you could make out clear elements of an organization. There were assaults on the Kazakh Central Committee building and the city prison. The disorders lasted for over two days, until special troops from the Ministry of the Interior intervened. Since then, in spite of Kolbin's exceptional steps toward cleaning things up, quite a few of Kunayev's men have remained in the republic's leadership. Some admitted their errors and were punished by a simple "reprimand" from the party. Informal associations have sprung up among the region's young people with names that tell you everything about their leanings: Golden Horde, and New Islam. To my knowledge there are two dozen other informal youth associations with different orientations.

CHAPTER 3

FOREIGN POLICY IN 1986

• • •

The Geneva summit at the end of 1985 had raised high hopes, but the new year began with an overcast sky and the distant sounds of a storm. The American refusal to halt underground nuclear experiments, the paralysis of negotiations, the Libyan crisis, and Reagan's steadfast insistence on Star Wars were all signs to Gorbachev of a reversal on the part of the U.S. administration. In Washington the president's most hard-line advisers were once again holding the reins. The administration's main strategy was to put continuous pressure on the Soviet Union, even though the country was at a difficult juncture and had little room to maneuver. The Kremlin replied by taking a harder line, and prospects for a Washington summit grew dimmer.

At this point Gorbachev went back on the diplomatic offensive, adopting a "reaction model" entirely different from the ones typical of former Soviet leaders. Gorbachev is a flexible and pragmatic man, who was well aware that the logic of opposing positions and toughness would not help his plans: it would aid the most aggressive circles in the United States, the same way it would the most conservative sectors in Soviet society. In the following months Western political circles would prove that they were not ready for this conceptual about-face, and as a result they would be slow to respond to the Kremlin's diplomatic initiatives.

The traditional "stone-faced" response was abandoned in a series of proposals that overturned all the consolidated doctrines of the cold war and of "traditional" détente. On 15 January the television newscaster read a thirty-eight-minute-long statement by Gorbachev on behalf of the Politburo and the Soviet government.[1] There were three proposals: to remove all American and Soviet medium-range missiles from Europe; to enact a program of total nuclear disarmament in stages over the next fifteen years; and to prolong the Soviet's unilateral moratorium on nuclear tests for another three months. The third proposal scored a victory in the propaganda battle. A negative reply by Reagan, who was "forced" to continue the detonations since most of them were designed for the SDI program, could only signify a weakening in the United States' political and diplomatic position.

The first proposal, in fact, was a striking exception to Reagan's "zero option," that had caused the failure of the Geneva negotiations in the fall of 1983, while Andropov was still alive. Gorbachev withdrew the request to count British and French missiles as part of the Western forces, and now he limited himself to asking France and Great Britain not to increase their current nuclear potential. The only difference between this and Reagan's zero option is that Gorbachev's proposal left out the medium-range missiles deployed in Asia. These concessions were as great as they were unexpected. Some Western commentators—and not without foundation—would see Washington's immediate perplexity as a sign that the zero option had been purposely devised so as to be unacceptable to the Kremlin. Now instead Gorbachev had appropriated it, and the tables were turned. The American administration could not argue against its own former proposal, while the European allies who had supported the original proposal now saw the olive branch being offered to them. It would not be easy for them to return it to the sender either.

But however ambitious the 15 January statement may have been, it covered a much broader agenda than a simple tactical, political, or propagandistic maneuver. The second of the three proposals contained the most important new concept. Global nuclear disarmament by the year 2000 meant a radical shift in theory: the end of "nuclear deterrence," of "mutually assured destruction," as an instrument on which to base future détente. This was one of the new ideas that Gorbachev would elaborate little more than a month later in his speech to the Twenty-Seventh Congress.[2] It was a strategic response to the Reagan-Teller "philosophy" of a strategic defense system. Gorbachev said essentially that if we can move toward an end to the mutual nuclear threat, then what sense is there in committing colossal resources to the creation of a system of defense from that threat? Especially when the SDI would not be ready before the end of the century—if it were even possible to create, a doubt shared by many even in the United States.

Gorbachev's plan certainly had its highly effective propagandistic elements, but its "theoretical" novelty and its "utopian" concreteness warrant careful consideration. Gorbachev realized that the strategy of nuclear deterrence was dying under the weight of the SDI, and he offered a diametrically opposed response: to renounce all strategic nuclear arms. Three stages were projected. In the first, which would last from five to eight years, the United States and the USSR would agree to a 50 percent reduction in their strategic arms, setting a maximum number of six thousand nuclear warheads per side (the zero option for Euromissiles would be enacted in this period). The second stage would begin no later than 1990 and would last from five to seven years. During this stage other powers would also join in nuclear disarmament, putting a freeze on their nuclear arsenals and agreeing not to deploy such weapons in Third World countries. The United States and the USSR would proceed by disposing of all of their tactical nuclear weapons. The third stage was to begin in 1995 and would provide for all the powers' disposing of their remaining nuclear weapons.

There was a further element to this turnaround. Gorbachev opened the way to every type of control mechanism, including on-site inspection. The Soviet leadership seemed to realize the proposal's actual implications. For NATO it meant giving up on the doctrine of a "flexible nuclear response," which had been conceived as a way of counterbalancing the Soviets' well-known "superiority" in conventional armaments. Moscow did not avoid the question and outlined the idea of a parallel, balanced reduction in conventional weapons and forces.

The Warsaw Pact's response to the latest Western proposals, made on 5 December 1985, came in February.[3] It had taken only two and a half months of study, as opposed to the ten months that NATO had needed to respond to the Soviet formulations of February 1985. The Warsaw Pact indicated seven points for a possible agreement: (1) The United States would withdraw 6,500 men from the central European area, and the USSR 11,500 men, along with their weapons; (2) the eleven countries of the Vienna Treaty would agree not to increase their armed forces on land and in the air in central Europe for a three-year period; (3) there would be a yearly exchange of information on troop rotations; (4) three or four fixed observation points would be installed on both sides with personnel from both sides: the troops that would enter and leave the areas targeted for reduction would have to pass through these checkpoints, and each side would have to inform the other of all troop movements involving more than 20,000 men; (5) on-site inspections would be allowed upon reasonable request; (6) a permanent consulting committee would be formed to study problems relating to the execution of the agreement.

The report to the Twenty-Seventh Congress represented the first attempt to systematize the new concepts. Some traditional views of the United States persisted: the accusation that United States defense policy was dominated by the military-industrial complex; the analysis of imperialism; and America's positive attitude toward the arms race. But Gorbachev introduced the new idea of "mutual interdependence." Neither of the two social systems could solve the huge problems of the contemporary era by itself. The question of security could no longer be dealt with in the traditional terms of every man for himself. Only a system of collective security is conceivable in the nuclear age, and this has to be jointly constructed. Autarchical solutions to matters like the ecology or a new international economic order are unthinkable because of the need for peaceful coexistence among nations. In other words, a new idea of "coexistence" was outlined that went beyond "peaceful competition" to hypothesize a vast system of worldwide interrelations. For the first time, a Soviet leader no longer looked at the world through the ideological prism of "strategic" opposition. Some form of cooperation between the two political and economic systems that dominate the planet had to be established, thereby creating the need for a radical revision of military doctrines.

In immediate terms, Gorbachev confirmed the possibility of rapid agreements on the reduction of medium-range missiles and the suspension of nuclear tests. A new summit with Reagan was possible, on the condition that it led to practical steps toward disarmament. Although Gorbachev's report criticized the American administration, especially on the difficult point of weapons in space, in general the report proposed a multilateral dialogue involving the United States, Europe, and China. The days of bipolarity were over. Now Moscow was looking for more partners in order to smooth the sharpest corners, partly because it was hard-pressed by the difficulty of improving relations with the United States.

But Washington did not respond to Gorbachev's invitations. The offer to suspend nuclear testing was turned down. The second summit seemed even farther away, and a series of irritations began when the United States asked the Soviet Union to cut its diplomatic corps at the United Nations by 40 percent. On 13 March the most disturbing episode took place, when two American ships, the cruiser *Yorktown* and the torpedo boat *Caron*, were detected cruising the territorial waters of the Crimean peninsula, six miles off the coast. The Soviets expelled Michael Sellers, the second secretary of the American embassy in Moscow; Premier Nikolai Ryzhkov met with Secretary of State George Shultz in Stockholm without any results; Washington accused Moscow of violating the Salt II Treaty and the ABM Treaty; Moscow newspapers polemicized Reagan's request to Congress for another $100 million in contra aid. These were all negative signs, compounded by the American fleet's continued incursions inside Libya's territorial waters. Tass stigmatized the "fourth demonstration of might in almost three months," and the "provocations" that "tended to make the situation in various parts of the world more tense."[4]

Soviet-American relations were once again heating up. When Gorbachev received the Algerian leader Bendjedid Chadli, he used uncharacteristically harsh language. The Soviet leader took advantage of the Moscow visit of Nilde Jotti, speaker of the Italian Parliament's Chamber of Deputies and one of the leaders of the Italian Communist Party, to deliver a message containing an appeal to the Western Europeans to act as moderators. Gorbachev wrote: "We are Europeans and we shall continue to give priority to the European direction of our foreign policy."[5]

Gorbachev apparently did not mean to let things go in the direction Washington wanted. A few days later he appeared on television to propose an "emergency" summit, since the one agreed on in Geneva already seemed out of reach. The sole objective was to reach an agreement suspending nuclear testing. This was his latest offer to extend the unilateral moratorium decided on by the Kremlin in August of the preceding year: Moscow would continue its moratorium until the first American nuclear explosion.[6] Washington replied by announcing the eighth nuclear test since 6 August 1985. Moscow reacted on 11 April by announcing the suspension of its unilateral moratorium.

The attack on Libya led to the moment of greatest tension between the two powers. Gorbachev called it "an illegal and arbitrary act" and decided to cancel the meeting planned in mid-May between Shultz and Shevardnadze. Yet at the same time a broad-ranging initiative on the part of Soviet diplomacy was extended to America's European allies, to Arab countries of different orientations, and even to Muammar Qaddafi. There was a strong fear of a chain reaction, and at the same time, of an even more serious rift. While the Kremlin promised "moral, political, and military" support to Libya, it also extended new offers. During a visit to Berlin, Gorbachev hinted that a summit with Reagan was still possible "if the appropriate international atmosphere can be created."[7]

Between May and June there were no improvements in the international political climate. Both sides were now unyielding, but the Kremlin was looking for a different way out of the dead end. When Gorbachev met with Felipe Gonzales, the Spanish prime minister, he stated that "if the rush to rearm spreads to new areas, and the ABM and SALT II treaties are violated, the level of distrust will increase geometrically."[8] At the same time, Gorbachev was working actively along the lines of the parallel diplomacy of "public opinion." It was the fourth side of a geometrical and diplomatic model that he was drawing to balance relations with Reagan's America. And it was another, untried variation on the behavior of the new Kremlin, to which the West paid scant attention. Moscow's initiative on "public opinion" was viewed with a certain smugness in the NATO capitals. They thought the USSR had no place in this territory: there were too many unresolved questions of human rights, and of civil and democratic freedoms weighing negatively on the image of Soviet power. Gorbachev was equally aware of this, and he was preparing a series of dramatic initiatives that would break with tradition. But first he had to break the internal opposition.

In the meantime, on 28 May in Moscow, Adrian de Wind, chairman of the Council for the Defense of Natural Resources, a private American organization, and Yevgeni Velikhov, vice president of the Academy of Sciences, signed a "private agreement" between the scientists of the two countries that provided for the installation of nongovernmental checkpoints, with personnel from both countries, near their respective nuclear ranges. The first was to be 145 kilometers east of Semipalatinsk in Kazakhstan, and the other a comparable distance from Yucca Flat, northwest of Las Vegas. The official American reaction was cautious but not negative.[9]

At the same time, other pawns were being moved around the chessboard. Ever since the previous fall, Gorbachev had been looking for a peaceful solution in Afghanistan. At the beginning of May, Babrak Karmal stepped down from the leadership of the Afghan party, but stayed on as chairman of the Revolutionary Committee. Mohammad Najibullah became the new leader. This was the beginning of Karmal's exit from the political scene and its meaning was obvious: he was not the man to lead the process of reconciliation.

The new Soviet leadership's initiative could not be completely unfurled without radically overhauling the previous foreign policy. At the end of May the entire Soviet diplomatic corps was called to Moscow for a meeting, chaired by Shevardnadze, at which Gorbachev delivered an "important" speech that would be published by the media. The official business was a discussion of ways to implement the decisions of the Twenty-Seventh Congress on foreign policy. The meeting not only sanctioned massive rotations of diplomatic personnel in the Foreign Ministry and in the departments of the Central Committee, but it set the premises for clear-cut alterations in the way the dialogue with the West was to be conducted.

Starting with the appointment of Shevardnadze to head the Ministry of Foreign Affairs, in less than one year Gorbachev had revolutionized the entire party and state leadership that deals with foreign policy. Anatoli Dobrynin had replaced the elderly Boris Ponomaryov in the Central Committee's Department of Foreign Affairs, and at the same time the department's functions were expanded. It would no longer just manage relations with Communist parties that were not ruling, with socialist parties, and with progressive and national liberation movements; instead, it would engage in an outright global "comanagement" of foreign policy. There were many changes in the staff of the Foreign Ministry. In a few short months thirty-four ambassadors had been replaced, including the ones in the most important posts: London, Paris, Bonn, Madrid, Washington, Tokyo, Beijing, Warsaw, Havana, and the United Nations. The Central Committee's Department of International Information was completely closed, and its head, Leonid Zamyatin, became the ambassador to London.

A considerable portion of Gorbachev's speech at the June plenum was dedicated to foreign policy. He gave clearer signs of a shift toward "greater flexibility" on some of the most controversial aspects of strategy toward the United States. Despite the harsh tones of the public dispute with the U.S. administration, Gorbachev proposed a global agreement containing interesting new cardinal points. The first point was a request to respect the ABM Treaty for the next fifteen years and to limit SDI experiments to the confines of the research laboratory. Then he proposed decreasing strategic nuclear arms to 1,600 carrier rockets per side, with a maximum of 8,000 nuclear warheads per side. Finally, there was a proposed separate agreement on medium-range and cruise missiles. The plenum voted for a special resolution on this issue, proof that Gorbachev had obtained collective endorsement of the new policy from the Soviet leadership.

Other clues showed that this policy implied a much more elastic relationship with the United States' own internal debate. During that same period, in fact, the House and Senate Foreign Affairs committees had turned down the administration's decision to abandon the SALT treaties, while the Senate cut funding for the Strategic Defence Initiative from $5.4 billion to $3.9 billion. There was intensive underground work toward a new summit, while Gorbachev kept his gaze steadily on Europe. On 7 July, French President Mitterrand arrived in Moscow. He was the first prominent Western spokesman to visit since the Chernobyl disaster, and his visit led to a broad convergence between France and the Soviet Union on some of the issues that divided the USSR and the United States. A clear consensus was reached to respect the SALT and ABM treaties, and combined efforts were made to prevent the militarization of space. "The road is open," Mitterrand said, in reference to the Warsaw Pact's Budapest proposal, which also called for the reduction of conventional arms and forces in Europe.[10]

The pressure of "the diplomacy of public opinion" was increasing. In mid-July Gorbachev met a large group of scientists from thirty-two countries, and in response to their urgings he announced that the extension of the Soviet's unilateral moratorium on nuclear testing would depend "to a significant extent" on the stance taken by the Americans.[11] There were still fierce arguments against the SDI. When Hans-Dietrich Genscher, West Germany's foreign minister, arrived in Moscow in mid-July, the SDI became the bitterest point of dissent in a most disappointing encounter. But Gorbachev held firmly to his new course, and in mid-August he made a surprise appearance on TV to announce another extension of the moratorium—until 1 January 1987.[12] At the same time, Nikolai Talyzin, the president of Gosplan and a candidate member of the Politburo, flew to Beijing. This was the highest-level contact that had taken place between the two countries since the time of the big break (1961). At the same time, there was no slackening in the strategy of attending to Europe. By now references to the European Community as a "political entity" with which the Soviet Union intended to establish economic and political relations had become more and more explicit.

However, the month of September was characterized by more heated arguments and below-the-belt punches. Nicholas Daniloff, a correspondent for *U.S. News and World Report*, was arrested in Moscow, following the New York arrest of Gennadi Zakharov, a Soviet official at the United Nations. The clouds of dust this raised, especially in the United States, seemed deliberately designed to burn away any residual hopes for a return to the relatively serene climate of the "Geneva spirit" between the two capitals. Gorbachev's interview with *Rude Pravo* made it clear that he was still looking for a minimal platform of "one or two subjects" that could help promote dialogue on international security.[13] The Soviet leader repeated his willingness to hold a second meeting with Reagan, "as long as it is useful."

Shevardnadze's meeting with Reagan and Shultz in Washington on 20 September took place under the cloud of a new, clear American provocation. Washington had just decided to expel twenty-five Soviet diplomats from the United Nations. It was an extremely difficult moment. Reagan's speech to the U.N. General Assembly, one of the toughest in recent months, met with violent opposition in the Soviet press. The only conciliatory sign was the positive conclusion of the Stockholm conference on 25 September— until the dramatic news of 30 September: the summit would be in Reykjavik on 11 October. This is not what had been agreed to in Geneva; it was a "presummit" that Gorbachev had proposed and that Reagan had accepted. But as *Pravda* wrote, the Reykjavik summit "was the result of a worsening in American-Soviet relations and not an improvement."[14] The decision signaled the American president's need to shake off the overly paralyzing pressure of the establishment's most extremist groups.

The political struggles inside the American administration kept the president from going to Reykjavik with any clear ideas. At the end of the summit Gorbachev would say that the United States "came empty-handed." This was the general impression. At the same time, the Kremlin was set on reversing tendencies. It proposed a package of concessions on strategic arms and it accepted the zero option on medium-range missiles, asking in exchange for a halt to SDI experiments "outside of the laboratory," and a ten-year observance of the ABM Treaty. This was the "Reykjavik package" that Gorbachev threw on the table of Hofdi House. The Americans did not expect such a development, but an agreement proved impossible because of an unbridgable gap in the two sides' views on Star Wars.

Was the summit a failure? Gorbachev did not hide the fact that he had hoped for success up until the final moments. But in spite of his disappointment, he formulated a conclusive judgment that would prove prophetic in many respects: "I think that the discussion with Reagan can be continued. . . . I don't think that we have to plunge into despair."[15]

The sense of shock all over the world was very strong. All at once, people everywhere became aware of both the encroaching dangers and the possibility of reversing the situation. But it would still take months to measure the traumatic effects—as well as the positive ones—of the Reykjavik "failure."

It was to a Reagan whose party had been defeated in the congressional elections that Shevardnadze renewed his offer: "Geneva and Reykjavik proved that Reagan can negotiate, and even in a profitable way."[16] Moscow realized that there were only two more years until the end of the president's term, and it offered Reagan an agreement before that time.

Only a few days later Ligachev announced a new gesture of goodwill during a visit to Helsinki, this time meant to encourage conciliatory changes in the European picture. Moscow had dismantled its launching pads for medium-range missiles on the Kola Peninsula and "most" of the SS-20s in the Leningrad and Baltic military regions. Even "some divisions of tactical-operative missiles" had been pulled out of those regions and moved further inland.[17]

Soviet Asian strategy also underwent consistent acceleration. At the end of November Gorbachev traveled to India on a highly significant visit. He reinforced the Moscow–New Delhi axis, but stated clearly to Indian spokespersons that his aim was much broader: to modify the other two sides of the Asian triangle that in the long term could influence the whole of international politics at the threshold of the new century: the Moscow–Beijing axis and the Beijing–New Delhi axis. His Vladivostok speech on 28 July announced the policy of a communal effort for Asian security. Naturally, the Soviet leader knew that Beijing and New Delhi were still divided by the debris from their 1962 war—in which Khrushchev had openly sided with Nehru—just as there were obstacles between Moscow and Beijing over the Soviet troops in Mongolia, Afghanistan, and Cambodia. Thus, the goal was not immediate, but research into it could not be deferred.

The "ten points" of the solemn joint statement at New Delhi spoke simultaneously of Asia and the Third World: a world free of arms and a new international economic order were conditions essential to worldwide collective security. The Soviet Union's friendship (and considerable economic interests) with India were further consolidated by this visit. But Gorbachev did not come to New Delhi just to play the card of India against Beijing. Instead, when Indian journalists assailed him with questions about the Chinese danger, Gorbachev answered: "China? I think that if relations between the USSR and China improve, than the atmosphere of the entire area will improve and have a positive influence on other relations. I have no doubt about this."

The New Delhi trip would also help him to announce the developments in Afghanistan: "No one thinks we will stay there forever."[18] In fact, the deciding match was underway in Kabul, in preparation for a radical internal political turnabout, the premise for a new international initiative. On 20 November Babrak Karmal was relieved of all duties and sent into retirement. In mid-December the new Afghan leader Mohammad Najibullah arrived in Moscow to discuss a strategy to "widen the social base" of the revolution. It was already clear that the Kremlin was beginning to recognize the internal problems of Afghanistan, aside from "foreign interference." More than one year later Gorbachev would disclose that since April 1985 he had brought up in the Politburo the need to reexamine the causes that had led to Soviet intervention. From that moment, then, Gorbachev had realized the need to identify "authentic national forces" that could steer the "process of reconciliation." The year would begin with a unilateral cease-fire proclaimed by the Kabul government and with Shevardnadze and Dobrynin's trip to the Afghan capital. Peace was still far off, but Gorbachev shortened the time it would take to create the conditions for Soviet withdrawal.

THIRD CONVERSATION

GORBACHEV'S FIRST STEPS IN FOREIGN POLICY

•　　　•　　　•

G.C. To grasp the dynamics of Gorbachev's foreign policy, one needs to go back to March 1985, when he first came to power. The unilateral moratorium on nuclear testing started on 6 August of that year and lasted 590 days (during which, incidentally, the Americans set off twenty-six nuclear explosions). It was written that the Soviet generals were pounding the tables in opposition to this approach. Yet it is interesting to note that high-ranking representatives of the military (Marshal Sergei Akhromeyev and General Nikolai Chervov) were actually the ones who effectively illustrated the significance of that move: the political advantages proved to be far greater than the losses of a strictly military type. Since this observation stemmed from Gorbachev's military entourage, it should have been analyzed promptly and carefully. It indicated one of the many "conceptual changes" that Gorbachev and his "team" were preparing. The "new way of thinking" in the international arena had systematically accompanied or even preceded every conspicuous domestic reform decision.

I would like to talk about the events surrounding Reykjavik. I have the impression that the Soviet perception of the Americans improved greatly before and after the summit. I think that men like Anatoli Dobrynin and Aleksandr Yakovlev played an important role in suggesting a more flexible, intricate, and differentiated approach. In other words, the new Kremlin had quickly learned that it could negotiate with Washington much better, especially by realizing that the American leadership is not a monolith. Many quick decisions by Gorbachev were undoubtedly made with an eye on debates underway among U.S. leaders.

Soviet policy toward the United States' European allies was equally flexible and varied, ready to take advantage of inclinations toward dialogue rather than adopting the brusque tones of rebuttal.

In short, Gorbachev had given more than one sign of his intentions of replacing Brezhnevite foreign policy with something completely different.

By the end of 1986 it was already clear that the policy on Afghanistan had shifted 180 degrees.

What are your thoughts on this?

R.M. Both the international situation and Soviet foreign policy changed significantly beween early 1985 and early 1988. The changes were in their own way much more comprehensive than anything affecting many internal questions. The *novoye myshleniye*, the "new thinking," had not yet won out, but now it constituted a factor that we and our partners had to reckon with. Let us say that the wheel shifted fifteen to twenty degrees, which is significant in itself. You must keep in mind that it is much easier to effect changes in foreign policy than in the economy. This country is like a big ship moving across an ocean buffeted by winds and by storms. To change course all you need is an expert captain who knows how to use the instruments to change speed and direction. These maneuvers require precision and skill because there are other ships in that same ocean moving in different directions. But the economy is another matter. It is as if you had to completely overhaul the ship, not in a port or a dry dock, but on the open sea while the ship is sailing— moreover replacing a good percentage of the officers and the machinery.

There is one more unresolved question. Too many prohibitions, secrets, and restrictions prevent public discussion of foreign policy. Despite a positive change in recent months, foreign policy is still discussed behind closed doors. This makes even our present conversation difficult. There must have been high-level discussions of medium-range missiles or of Afghanistan, but we know so little about this that we cannot compare different positions. The press limits itself to commenting (positively, of course) on decisions already made. We do not have even one scientific journal that deals with the problems of foreign policy. There are only mass-circulation magazines like *Za Rubezhom, Novoye Vremya,* or *Mezhdunarodnaya Zhizn.* But their job is to spread propaganda, not to analyze Soviet foreign policy. The military has a theoretical journal, *Voyennaya Mysl (Military Thought),* but diplomats do not. Diplomats and the military obviously have their professional secrets. Reagan and Gorbachev do not talk about their highly confidential colloquia with the thousands of journalists who cover the summits. That is their right. But we do not know a lot of things that the West knows about itself and about us. When our press prints military data, it generally uses information provided by the London Institute for Strategic Studies or the Stockholm International Peace Research Institute.

G.C. To the extent that the Soviet sources even had to use a Western name for its own medium-range missiles: the SS-20.

R.M. Exactly! When officers for the reserves underwent training, they used the designs for Western rockets. Our newspapers reprint Western designs for cruise missiles, neutron bombs, and so on. We learned from American sources that the USSR was building a huge radar station in the Krasnoyarsk area. All of this helped foster a climate of distrust that lasted for years. I should add that Gorbachev has now initiated a shift toward glasnost in this field. For that matter, it would not have been possible to reach agreements on arms reductions without concurring on broad measures of control. This struck a huge blow against the regime of complete secrecy. Regarding Afghanistan, I agree with you that Gorbachev understood the need for a policy of national reconciliation, and for a coalition government. Only now was it intimated—without ever explicitly being stated—that the "April Revolution" in 1978 was a coup d'état and not a "revolutionary situation" at all. Our tactics and policy changed several times after that. Finally, Gorbachev reached the decision to withdraw our troops, based on a much more realistic insight. Frankly, I must say that the speed of the developments in this area surprised even me. At the end of 1987 it was clear to me that Gorbachev wanted to change the Afghanistan situation, but I would not have been surprised if, in the face of complex internal and international problems, he had been forced to prolong the stay of Soviet troops in Afghanistan by another five to six years.

G.C. When you mentioned the serious restraints on the foreign-policy debate, I remember that Aleksandr Bovin of *Moskovskiye Novosti* became the standard-bearer of renewal, immediately after Gorbachev's statement that "untied" the famous "Reykjavik package." Criticism of the decision to "modernize" the Soviet arsenal of medium-range missiles was clear: if we accept the zero option today, then why did we decide to deploy those missiles in the first place? If we are no less secure today than we were before, Bovin essentially concluded, this means that those missiles were not necessary. Another standard-bearer for public criticism of Brezhnev's choices was Yevgeni Ambartsumov, in another article in *Moskovskiye Novosti* dated Spring 1987. The subject was Afghanistan, and Ambartsumov wrote that the prestige of a great power cannot be based on military might alone. These were the first examples of "breaking the ice."

R.M. There were others later on, it is true. But they were still exceptions. However, we must acknowledge that Gorbachev had to shoulder the heavy burden of the foreign policy he had inherited. In the last Brezhnev years it was no longer even clear how or by whom decisions were being made on crucial aspects of international relations. Brezhnev was no longer fit to guide anything. In his 1979 SALT II negotiations with President Carter, Brezhnev literally did not know what to say when the two met face to face. Andropov was even more inclined toward a politics of strength and not a search for compromises. It was a difficult moment, but it was Andropov who broke off negotiations with the United States when the Americans began to deploy missiles in Europe. The zero option was then derided as an American attempt to subvert strategic parity. Furthermore, both Andropov and Chernenko were gravely ill, and therefore in no condition to carry out an intensive foreign-policy initiative.

A reexamination of past decisions grew urgent, but it implied the elaboration of a new long-term strategy. Neither Andropov nor Chernenko had enough time ahead of them. Thus, it was a problem not just of mistakes made, but of time wasted. During that phase the United States succeeded not only in carrying out a huge deployment of Euromissiles, but it also declared that the preparations for the new SDI program were underway. This was an unexpected and unpleasant move for our military strategists, forcing them to take a new approach to every aspect of the political and military race with the United States.

When Gorbachev became general secretary I remember that his first comments indicated that Soviet foreign policy would be dominated by Gromyko. The new leader's experience was so slight that no one thought that he could take control in a short time. Gromyko's experience was unquestionable, but no one could expect new ideas from him. Gorbachev instead caught everyone off guard. Already in mid-July 1985 Gromyko had been given the honorary position of president of the Presidium of the Supreme Soviet. Eduard Shevardnadze, the party chief and interior minister in Georgia, became the new foreign minister. I am convinced that not even he imagined the possibility of such an appointment until a few days beforehand.

In this way Gorbachev let everybody know that he would be the person in charge of the crucial issues of foreign policy. A few days later came the decision for a unilateral Soviet moratorium on nuclear tests.

G.C. On 6 August 1985.

R.M. The appointment of Shevardnadze raised big questions and even prompted jokes. Instead, he proved to be a good choice. The new minister quickly took control of the ministry and its numerous branches, and became one of Gorbachev's closest associates.

G.C. Along with Dobrynin.

R.M. Exactly. Along with the man who, due to his diplomatic experience, many had seen as the most likely successor to Gromyko. Instead, Gorbachev wanted to use his twenty-year-long experience as ambassador to the United States—as well as his excellent personal relations with many American politicians—by making him head of the Central Committee's Department of International Affairs taking Boris Ponomaryov's place. In his new job Dobrynin entered the Secretariat of the Central Committee: another unusual event for a diplomat who had never worked within the party apparat.

These unexpected appointments immediately characterized Gorbachev's policy regarding cadres; in this way he broke solid ties and long-standing habits, creating situations that were easier to control and more innovative. Dobrynin's promotion also proved fruitful. In the Central Committee he became one of the key figures in the "brain trust" that designed the change, which also included men like Aleksandr Yakovlev, Georgi Arbatov, and others—a very strong group that for now has no counterpart in economics or ideology. Obviously, Gorbachev could not immediately make a clean sweep of all assistants and experts in foreign policy. For example, Andrei Aleksandrov-Agentov played a major role in the Soviet delegation that prepared for the first summit with Reagan. He had acted as an assistant to Brezhnev, Andropov, and Chernenko. Gorbachev took advantage of his extensive experience, but only until the beginning of 1986, when he replaced him with Anatoli Chernyayev, another important appointment. Chernyayev had been one of Ponomaryov's aides in the Department of International Affairs, but he was an honest and competent person, in no way tied to the Brezhnev group. He had entered politics through the Khrushchev apparat, and was a member of what we call "the generation of the Twentieth Congress." Another interesting personality with characteristics similar to Chernyayev recently appeared among Gorbachev's associates—I mean Georgi Shakhnazarov, who supervises relations with socialist countries.

G.C. To me the Soviet "team" at Reykjavik already seemed much better trained than the one for the Geneva summit.

R.M. Unquestionably. I even think that the observers' surprise—and especially that of the American negotiators—resulted from an insufficient analysis of what was happening in Moscow. The USSR arrived ready to make dramatic and unprecedented concessions. Gorbachev fully accepted all the preceding American proposals on various crucial issues, but tied them into a single "package" with our own proposals to limit the SDI program. The two sides seemed close to an important agreement, but it did not take place. However, Reykjavik represented a conspicuous diplomatic success for Gorbachev, even if no agreement was reached. It opened the road to negotiations on new bases, and as soon as the USSR had "untied" the package, the new meeting in Washington became possible, as did the signing of the agreement on medium- and short-range missiles.

G.C. We need to keep in mind that after the failure of Reykjavik, there were strong repercussions from America's European allies. Everyone had understood that the Soviet concessions were very big and many pushed Reagan not to let them slip by. Different West European countries, with France in the lead, made no mystery about their aversion to the SDI. I think that Gorbachev's statements on 28 February 1987, opening up the possibility of a separate agreement on Euromissiles, represented the final component in a prudent global realization of the effects that these events could jointly have on Soviet-American relations.

R.M. I agree with you that the untying of the Reykjavik package was a very clever political move, which succeeded in forcing the negotiations to develop. You can assume that in some predicaments Gorbachev had to overcome a certain resistance from the military. There are only a few indications of this and no definitive evidence. It was clear that Gorbachev wanted to reach an agreement with the Reagan administration, even if it meant making concessions that were technically disadvantageous to the USSR, but for the sake of achieving an exceptional success and a radical change in climate.

PART TWO
1987

CHAPTER 4

THE JANUARY 1987 PLENUM; THE SHIFT TOWARD DEMOCRATIZATION; PERESTROIKA'S FIRST POLITICAL CRISIS

•　　　•　　　•

"We have taken a road of profound transformations. This was a collective decision, yet there are still manifestations of repressive forces, of indifference, of the hope that one way or the other, everything will return to the old track."[1] Mikhail Gorbachev said these words on television in late 1986, in the midst of a decisive battle over the fate of perestroika. But the country and the world did not know of this. At that point the plenum of the Central Committee, which was supposed to have been held in December, had already been postponed twice, and it was still not clear when it could take place. The stakes were high: it was time to tally up the first returns on the political change in progress and decide what to do next. Gorbachev intimated that in the leadership there were those who asked "if" it should be continued. There was no doubt that there was a clash between powerful coalitions, which acted in the secret chambers of power and drew their strength from the country's existing uncertainties.

But Soviet society was now showing signs of a previously unknown or unexpressed vitality, responding differently than it had to equally bitter struggles in the past. This was one of the fruits of the first wave of glasnost, promoted by the leadership but sown on fertile ground. And it was becoming one of the factors in play that could influence political developments. The social formations still appeared fluid and uncertain: none of them probably knew the size of their troops or their degree of mobility. However, myriad signs indicated that the struggle in the Kremlin was not taking place in a vacuum. In some cases the hard blows each side inflicted on the other leaked out to the greater public. In other cases symptoms of a new climate made their way up through the chinks of glasnost. One little incident can prove this assumption. *Pravda* told the story of Viktor Berkhin, a reporter for *Sovetski Shakhtyor* who was arrested in Voroshilovgrad on the basis of fabricated accusations.[2] After a few days the party paper carried an article signed by Viktor Chebrikov, chairman of the KGB. In it he acknowledged the illegality of Berkhin's arrest, disclosed that the Ukrainian leadership had taken part in a conspiracy against an honest journalist, and announced that a series of high-ranking officials in the local political police had been fired.[3]

At a press conference Yelem Klimov, the first secretary of the Filmmakers' Union, announced that Abuladze's film *Pokayaniye* (*Repentance*) would be distributed at the beginning of February, and he described the reform of the Soviet cinema: Goskino (the State Agency for the Cinema) would no longer have the power to decide whether or not a film should be produced. Administrative censorship was over. Film studios had attained a broad independence of choice.[4] The latest edition of the *Soviet Encyclopedia* modified the entry under Khrushchev, now calling him "a Hero of Socialist Labor, a Hero of the USSR." The previous edition in 1979 had contained no biographical information, just the phrase "member of the party and of the Soviet State." Gennadi Gerasimov, the official spokesman for the Ministry of Foreign Affairs, announced that the jamming of the waves from the BBC and other Western broadcasts in the Russian language would be stopped; only the "most anti-Soviet and subversive" stations such as Radio Liberty and Radio Free Europe would continue to be blocked.[5] On the subject of exit visas for Soviet citizens, the editor in chief of *Pravda*, Viktor Afanasev, personally denounced the "bureaucratic delays and procedures" that "seriously damage the international image of the USSR."[6] The public also learned of a marginal but significant episode in the far-away Bashkir village of Oktyabrski where the local party leaders used every outrageous measure possible to prevent two thousand believers from exercising their right to build a church. The Committee on Religious Affairs intervened to right this wrong, but what matters most is that this episode became public knowledge, and therefore served as an example.[7]

This describes the situation at the end of January. The plenum was still a mystery, and its troubled preparation had become the subject of many rumors.[8] In early January Valentin Falin, the director of the *Novosti* press agency, confirmed that there were "new problems" during the preparatory phase that had made it necessary to "consult more people."[9] One of the issues to be confronted was the law on state enterprises, one of the cornerstones of the economic reform. But in his Krasnodar speech in the fall, Gorbachev had intimated that the issue of the cadres could no longer be postponed. The relationship between the party and society, and the party's guiding role, also needed radical changes, without which perestroika could not be achieved. It was no mystery that there were highly divergent points of view on both issues; in this period the newspapers were filled with heated debates on the subject. In those days I was informed of the existence of "thousands of letters" piled up in the offices of the Central Committee that expressed serious worries and protests over the "disastrous" effects perestroika was having on enterprises. The same source added that a selection of letters in the same tone had been presented to Gorbachev during an expanded meeting of the Politburo, along with a peremptory request to drastically review the tendencies thus far followed, or alternatively, to acknowledge the impossibility of the situation and resign for "health reasons" if need be. Gorbachev turned down the request; my health "is excellent," he replied sharply; there are "no alternatives" to the line taken; for every thousand letters against perestroika there are at least another thousand for it. The communiqué at the beginning of the plenum contained a revealing sentence:

> The participants have been given the opportunity to examine beforehand the theses and the report of comrade Gorbachev, with the USSR bill on state enterprises and with a selection of letters from workers on the issues of perestroika and the policy on the cadres. [10]

Thus, the clashes over these two subjects had caused the two earlier postponements of the plenum to December and at least a third postponement to January. The impact of these clashes would soon be felt. The Politburo would not succeed in finding a unifying line until 22 January, in a process that must have been anything but painless. The official communiqué of the meeting disclosed that it confronted "problems in the way the party is constructed."[11] This rarely used formula pointed to huge questions of domestic policy, including modifications in the composition of the ruling bodies and in the distribution of responsibilities in the leadership.

On the next day, while observers were awaiting the announcement from one minute to the next that the plenum was underway, Tass reported that there would be a All-Union meeting on agricultural policy, with the participation of hundreds of different directors, and with Gorbachev and Ligachev present (both of whom would speak), as well as Viktor Nikonov (the spokesman) and Vitali Vorotnikov.

Gorbachev himself announced that the plenum would take place the following Tuesday, 27 January; at the same time, he unleashed a violent attack on Brezhnevite farm policy. Thus, a compromise had been reached, but not on every problem. A broad spectrum of the Central Committee was faced with proposals and analyses that it did not share. Only later would we learn that conservatives had interrupted some speakers with rowdy protests, and that Gorbachev had to give them an ultimatum, saying in effect: either commit yourselves to reform or you will have to do without me.[12]

Gorbachev's report at the plenum constituted a broader and deeper change than what had been presented to the Twenty-Seventh Congress. To those who wanted to pull in the oars as soon as possible, the Soviet leader had a harsh reply: "We need a radical change because we have no other way. We cannot withdraw because we have no place to retreat to." Too many leaders had not yet understood that "the USSR is now forced into changes revolutionary in their substance." This indicated the need "to go back to the roots, to the reasons for what happened in the watershed period between the 1970s and 1980s." Thus, they could not stop at the denunciation of Brezhnevite "stagnation"; it was necessary to go further back in time, to the "concrete historical situation in which, while social theory and sciences were producing a lively discussion and creative ideas, authoritarian decisions and statements became irrefutable truths." This was an elliptical expression, but everyone understood it: Stalin's models of the state and the party are the distant cause of today's crisis—"a certain way of absolutizing the society's forms of organization," which fossilized the sciences, learning, and social [self-]consciousness.

Now it was necessary to drastically review what for decades had been considered "irrefutable truths," on whose basis the cooperative movement had been stopped, individual activity prevented, and "prejudices against the role of the relationship of goods to money and against the law of value (not infrequently presented as contrary and extraneous to socialism)" asserted. So the conservatives want to reinforce the idea of socialist property? But this is where "serious slowdowns occurred in control over who owned it and how they took care of it." The conservatives want to assert the plan's supremacy? But "the plan's authority as the main instrument of economic policy was impaired by subjective approaches." "Getting to the roots" meant telling the country "the whole truth" and naming the responsible party: "For primarily subjective reasons, the Central Committee, the country's political leadership, has not been capable of performing a timely and complete assessment of the need for the changes and the danger in the development of elements of crisis in the society." "Elements of social corrosion had a negative impact on the spiritual guidance of the whole society." A serious decline had struck the party itself and "violated the principle that all Communists are equal."

This criticism went far beyond any previous analysis. There was only one cure for the disease: "to reestablish the relationship between democracy and socialism." The idea of democratization was the most striking and substantive part of the entire report. It held true for both the sphere of productivity (and Gorbachev praised the democratic characteristics of the law on state enterprises) and for state institutions as a whole. The election procedures and the real powers of the soviets had to be changed and the principle of independent courts had to be achieved, because the party must not position itself above the laws of the state. And the party itself had to be democratized, introducing the principle of the secret ballot and open nominations in the elections for its ruling bodies. It had to democratize and to change its functions—to stop directly controlling the management of everyone and everything ("I repeat, proceeding with perestroika means reorganizing the work of the party"), and even leaving positions in public administration open to "non–party members."

Less than one year after the Twenty-Seventh Congress, Gorbachev could see that the consolidation of the resistance had to be blocked, and that the causes of the crisis, like its dimensions, were greater than they had appeared at the outset of perestroika. But the receptiveness of the party, the leadership, and the apparat was less than was needed at the moment. The plenum elected by the Twenty-Seventh Congress was still largely composed of forces that had everything to fear from the continuation of the new line and were in no hurry to restructure or move to the side.

Gorbachev decided to play a dangerous card at this point: he proposed that the Central Committee hold an All-Union conference on party organization by 1988, "at which we will take a broad overview of the progress being made on the decisions of the Twenty-Seventh Congress, and examine the results of the first half of the five-year plan." He posed the question in gentle terms: "I would like to consult you on an important matter." This was clearly a personal proposal, but even while he used the conditional, he insisted that "the very fact of such a conference, in harmony with the party's bylaws, would be a serious step forward toward the concrete democratization of our party life." His audience could not understand: the last conference of this kind, a sort of intermediate congress, had taken place in 1941, when Stalin was forced to pad out the Central Committee with new forces after having physically decimated the cadres.[13]

In a highly dramatic climate, only forty-three people signed up to speak, including numerous members of the Politburo. Only thirty-four actually spoke, and there were obvious conflicts on several points. The law on state enterprises was approved only as a draft bill.[14] In the final resolution there was no hint of the proposal to hold the conference. However, the document picked up almost all of the other innovative points in Gorbachev's report, including the blunt passage urging an "influx of new forces," a "change of the leaders for whom the new tasks have proved greater than their strengths, and of those who have been compromised by their dishonest behavior." Yet it also hinted at a difficult mediation that had forced Gorbachev to postpone the loosening of certain crucial knots. This same resolution clearly stated:

The changes proceed with great difficulty. The mechanism that has repressed economic and social growth for many years is still slowly being dismantled or giving up its positions; conservativism, inertia, and antiquated concepts have still not lost their force or influence.[15]

But there was another *coup de théâtre*. The plenum lasted two days, 27 and 28 January. One day later, on the evening of the twenty-ninth, after the newspapers had published the official communiqué and the final resolution, Soviet television made a surprise broadcast of Gorbachev's closing speech. It was an appeal to the Soviet people, reverberating with the echo of a tough and unending struggle.

On the same day, in obvious tune with Gorbachev's conclusions, *Novoye Vremya* published a violent article, written by Aleksandr Bovin in the heat of the battle, against the "Soviet conservative socialists," and extolling the "purifying downpour" of the Twentieth Congress. "We are faithfully expecting this plenum to confirm the irreversibility of the changes in our society."[16] Gorbachev had secured another round for himself. Once again his adversaries proved that they did not have a strategy, but the struggle would still be long and full of traps. In fact, just two weeks after the plenum Gorbachev had to go on the defensive. On 12 February he called a meeting at the Kremlin of about forty heads of the most important news organizations to explain what had happened, telling them "what used to be said to only a limited group of people in the past."[17] *Moskovskiye Novosti* would carry the news of the three postponements of the plenum. Its editor in chief, Yegor Yakovlev, was also authorized to report Gorbachev's key sentence: "If the plenum had reached the conclusion that perestroika has not stood the test and that we have to give up on it, I would have said, 'I cannot work any differently.' "

Gorbachev gave new proof of a tactic he had already used in the past and that he would systematically repeat in the following months: after every jolt, every sudden acceleration, he would put his foot on the brake in order to reassure the uncertain, minimize worries, and neutralize the most ardent conservative positions. He told the heads of the mass media and of the intelligentsia that criticism would not be blocked, but at the same time he urged them not to push beyond specific limits: "We cannot exhume in one day all the problems that have lain unresolved for decades." The blank pages in Soviet history had to be filled, but, he said, you cannot throw away "the years of collectivization and industrialization; this is the people's destiny, with all its contradictions, and with all its successes and errors."[18] Run with the hare and hunt with the hounds. At the plenum you could see that many people could still not digest glasnost. Gorbachev let them know that he would keep excesses in check, but he added sharply, "Criticism is a bitter medicine, but the disease makes it necessary. You can make a face, but you still have to take it!"

At the meeting, attended by Ligachev and Yakovlev, there were also representatives of the conservatives, who intervened to let everyone know their importance. Gorbachev's assurances were not enough—they wanted an "iron fist" against wrongdoers. Gorbachev responded almost ironically, "Why iron? It takes a knowing hand." At times, what was happening to the Kremlin and the whole country seemed like an eighteenth-century ballet. This is proven by the dramatic comparison that Gorbachev drew between perestroika and the Brest Litovsk peace, which Soviet Russia had been forced to accept. At the same time, Shatrov's new play, *The Brest Peace*, was the center of discussion in the press. It covered the sharp clash inside the Soviet leadership when Lenin was in the minority but still won by threatening to resign—how many references to the present! "Where does the analogy lie? The Brest peace was an example of how a historical change for the sake of strategic interests can be achieved by sacrificing the interests of the moment."

Then, German imperialism had dictated the "humiliating" peace, and Lenin's realism succeeded in prevailing over those like Trotsky and Bukharin who wanted to continue the war. Now Gorbachev made it clear that for the sake of realism, some steps backward had to be taken, but he implicitly compared the current internal enemies of Soviet renewal to the foreign enemies back then.

Many signals indicated that the January plenum had caused a violent jolt, and that those thrown off balance were struggling to regain their composure. The reform was progressing at a snail's pace rather than systematically; for now it was leading to more problems rather than to positive results. The Politburo disclosed that economic returns for the month of January were on the whole negative.[19] Since the beginning of the year all enterprises had been theoretically in a state of "independent management"; the salary reform for about 70 million industry employees had taken effect; Gospriyomka had been set up in patches here and there, having harsh repercussions on production and salaries. There were growing uncertainties and discontent both among the workers and in the management of the enterprises, which still had no unequivocal guidelines. In the months that followed, the debate on the economy came roaring back to life. The reformers sensed the precariousness of the situation and pushed for a more radical approach to the problems through the press. The magazine *Novy Mir* stood out in particular for its publication of a long essay by Vasili Selyunin and Grigori Khanin, "Lukavaya Tsifra" ("Arcane Number"), which essentially denounced the complete unreliability of official statistics on the economy for the past fifty years, and urged that they not be used to make projections for the reform. This caused a huge sensation.[20] Even if all the economists knew about the fabrications, not even all the experts—and the greater public even less so— had ever been able to read such a well-documented and impressive analysis. Thus, the state of the economy was much graver than had already leaked out. Four months later *Novy Mir* published an essay on the economy by Nikolai Shmelyov, entitled "Avansi i Dolgi" ("Credits and Debits"), which generally dealt with the inevitable social repercussions of an economic reform that means to actually break the repressive mechanism of the "system of administrative command."[21]

We know that Shmelyov's essay was read "at the top," and provoked various reactions. Nevertheless, the magazine was able to publish it, even those parts that demolished the myth of 100 percent employment in the USSR. The article stated not only that a fluctuating rate of unemployment already existed, but that it was useful, even indispensable, to invigorate the economy and put an end to a situation in which everyone is protected and no one works the way they should, knowing they will not lose their jobs or their salaries. Shmelyov instead proposed the study of concrete and timely measures of state protection for those who in the future would inevitably lose their jobs and have to be placed in new jobs because of the mobility the reform would create.

In a clearly calculated move, Gorbachev would enter the field to reply in person.[22] The Soviet leader met the voters at Polling Place 5 in the Krasnaya Presnya district and answered their pointed questions, thereby calming the general public. Shmelyov's operating proposals were incorrect, but his analysis "is close to the reality we will be talking about at the plenum." Thus, it was not a complete retraction.

In spite of these disputes, the political situation was affected by a series of extraordinary novelties. "Historical" and "literary" glasnost showed no signs of diminishing. The editor in chief of *Novy Mir*, Sergei Zalygin, announced the publication of *Dr. Zhivago* starting with the first issue of 1988, while a special committee of the Writers' Union "for the cultural heritage of Boris Pasternak" prepared to celebrate the centenary of his birth (1990) under the chairmanship of the poet Andrei Voznesensky.[23] Other participants included Dmitri Likhachyov, Bella Akhmadulina, Yevgeni Yevtushenko, Veniamin Kaverin, Vasili Bykov, Mikhail Ulyanov, Yevgeni Simonov, and others. The ostracism of Anna Akhmatova was finally over. Her poem *Rekviyem* (*Requiem*) appeared in the monthly *Oktyabr*, and was heralded by enthusiastic reviews in the press.[24]

Newspapers and television grew more lively and more candid, provoking waves of letters of protest from a significant segment of the public. Magazine and newspaper readership reached stunning levels, and TV programs such as "Twelfth Floor" were regularly watched by millions of viewers because of their frankness. Information about the "problems" of Soviet society—drugs, prostitution, social injustice, defects in the health-care system, and the restlessness of youth—was disseminated by the mass media, aiding the growth of a social awareness that many liked but that many others feared. It was made known that a mixed committee of experts and representatives of the security services had worked for months on the 1,109,086 documents that to date had been subject to a "regime of limited access." Just how many of the 340 million documents in the archives were still classified as top secret was not disclosed, but of those examined, 341,891 would remain secret. But a good 92,000 documents on the economy (out of the 154,000 examined) would be approved and published between 1988 and 1991 in ten volumes of economic statistics that were finally reliable.[25] An unprecedented episode occurred with the publication in toto of a letter from ten dissidents living abroad strongly protesting the Soviet interventions in Afghanistan, and in Czechoslovakia in 1968, and disdainfully calling Gorbachev's renewal an "ephemeral thaw."[26] The ten, including Aleksandr Zinovev, Yuri Lyubimov, Vladimir Bukovsky, Vladimir Maksimov, and Ernst Neizvestny, had issued a challenge: "The publication of this letter in the Soviet press would be the most convincing proof of the sincerity of the claims of glasnost." *Moskovskiye Novosti* accepted the challenge with a measured response from its editor in chief, Yegor Yakovlev.

Democratization also produced other changes that were substantial, but gradual and cautious, directed mainly at international public opinion. In Vienna the president of the Association of Soviet Jurists, Aleksandr Sukharev, stated that the liberation of the dissidents would continue and that the reform of the penal code "would affect two-thirds of the articles."[27] The next day Gennadi Gerasimov, spokesman for the Ministry of Foreign Affairs, announced that the Supreme Soviet had issued a decree (the text of which would not be made known) allowing the release of 140 people and the reexamination of 140 other cases. The freed dissidents revealed that as a condition for their release, they had to sign a sworn statement that they would not commit the same "crime" for which they had been sentenced. Not everyone signed the statement—including Iosif Begun—but they were released just the same.

Moreover in February, on the eve of the international forum on the problems of peace and disarmament, the Jewish refuseniks had begun their demonstration on Arbat Street. They would continue through April and May. The police and the KGB seemed to be getting contradictory signals. In some cases plainclothes agents pretending to be "indignant citizens" took forceful measures. In other cases there were brief detentions and turnstile trials that issued fines based on the existing penal code. Sometimes no repressive measures were taken and the demonstrators were left alone. In Leningrad, preservation groups had already called for demonstrations with hundreds of participants to protest the demolition of the old Angleterre Hotel and the renovation of the Astoria. Even here the local press and the police acted with uncertainty. In Moscow other kinds of demonstrations popped up. On 9 May a gathering of young hippies on Gogol Boulevard was immediately and violently suppressed by the police.

But on 6 May the capital's downtown became the scene for a genuine mass demonstration, followed by a protest march of about six hundred people from Pushkin Square to the Mossovet Palace ("Mossovet" is a shortening of "Moscow Soviet"). The demonstrators were received by Mayor Valeri Saikin and Boris Yeltsin, first secretary of the Moscow party, who listened to their claims and talked with them. The informal association called Pamyat had organized the protest in the name of perestroika. One of the requests written across their banners was the formal recognition of the association, which defined itself as "patriotic." In reality, highly ambiguous elements appeared alongside the clear slogans for the "preservation of urban culture" and the safeguarding of historical symbols, such as the three flags of the Russian, Ukrainian, and Byelorussian republics, i.e., the three Slavic and Christian Orthodox republics. But not just this. Many of the demonstrators wore the badge of the Order of St. George. In their meeting with Yeltsin, the newspapers reported, some shouted, "The Jews hold all the responsible positions." Viktor Vasilev, the head of Pamyat, asked Yeltsin to authorize the reconstruction of the Cathedral of Christ the Redeemer, torn down in the 1930s to make room for a Palace of Soviets that was never built.

Thus, Pamyat made its official entrance onto the political scene boasting strong support and a broad consensus even before it was legalized. Its political platform contained a strange mixture of words that were progressive, supported perestroika, and supported the fight against alcohol, in addition to obvious elements of Russian nationalism, and a more or less explicit anti-Semitism. Vasilev allowed himself to be guided by *The Protocols of the Elders of Zion* and made repeated public announcements that there was an organized conspiracy to destroy Russian culture—headed by "Zionist forces" that could exploit a bureaucracy "dominated by the international Masonry." The alleged aim of this conspiracy was to "Americanize Soviet society and sharpen its domestic, economic, and social conflicts." In a certain sense, Pamyat rehabilitated Stalin because he had saved Russia. The October Revolution, on the other hand, was one of the crucial moments in an international Jewish conspiracy (Vasilev alluded to this only in passing). The group's historical references were fairly explicit: to the "Union of the Russian People," the extreme right-wing party that had risen in 1905, and to the Black Hundreds, standard-bearers of the fascist ideology, who were also guided by the *Protocols*. The most recent precursor of Pamyat was the famous Rodina (Motherland) club in the mid-1960s, situated between a revival of nationalism and the Stalinist tendencies that permeated the then ultraorthodox magazine *Oktyabr*.[28] This was a potentially explosive mix, whose danger consisted not so much (or only!) in the truly mass base that Pamyat had at its disposal, but rather in its high-ranking supporters in the party, who allowed it to act in the light of day, though its platform included far more subversive words than the traditional language of dissidence.[29]

Pamyat was not the only group in a strong phase of expansion. In mid-1987 many Soviet cities witnessed the proliferation of dozens of "perestroika clubs," going by different names, that fostered and organized lively debates on the reform. All of this took place in forms that would have been considered illegal, and harshly suppressed, in earlier eras. These too were symptoms of a transitional phase in which the old rules were disappearing and the new did not yet exist; no one knew if, when, or how new rules would come about—or if indeed they could be established. This was the climate in which the first "unauthorized" magazine was born: *Glasnost*. Sergei Grigoryants promoted it in a gamble that would prove successful. Grigoryants was a literary critic who had just been released in February from a seven-year prison sentence, plus three years of internal exile, for crimes of conscience. Other sponsors of the magazine were Andrei Sakharov, Iosif Begun, Marchenko's widow Larisa Bogoraz, the Orthodox priest Gleb Yakunin, and the journalist Lev Timofeyev.

Despite obvious resistance to a reexamination of Soviet history, the January plenum opened the way to public stances of a more and more explicit anti-Stalinist leaning—and not just in the literary world, where the publication of novels by Aleksandr Bek (*Novoye Naznacheniye* [*The New Appointment*]) and Anatoli Rybakov (*Deti Arbata* [*Children of the Arbat*]) created a sensation. Yuri Afanasev, the director of the Institute of Historical Archives, was one of the first to light the fuse in an interview asking for a new probe into "what happened between 1917 and 1929, i.e., in the period of Lenin and immediately after his death, and from 1956 to 1965, i.e., after the death of Stalin and the Twentieth Congress, up to the attempts that were made at reform." It was time to reopen discussion on all of Soviet history, on the relationship between Lenin and Stalin, on Khrushchev, and on Brezhnev. In writing on Stalin in particular, Afansev commented polemically, "I personally fail to understand how the mass repressions perpetrated against honest people in the 1930s can be described as 'errors' or 'inadequacies' in the observance of socialist laws."[30] While the debate raged, Academician Aleksandr Samsonov echoed this view. For the first time ever in a widely read newspaper, he contested Stalin's role as a military strategist and as the "winner" of World War II, while praising Khrushchev for having courageously ended the cult of personality.[31]

These attacks were not in the least bit scholarly, historical, or literary. They were accompanied and highlighted by a steady stream of political blows that showed a bitter underground battle unraveling. In early February Gerasimov's spokesman made the official announcement of the arrest of Yuri Churbanov, former first deputy minister of the interior and Leonid Brezhnev's son-in-law. The accusations were very serious: corruption, embezzlement, and abuse of power. This was not only a blow to the already shaken prestige of Brezhnev, but a serious threat to the Rashidov, Kunayev, and Grishin clans. The offensive seems to have been particularly aimed at the Kunayev clan, to which *Pravda* had already dedicated a long article at the beginning of the year.[32] But the month of March saw a violent storm of official denouncements. The plenum of the Kazakhstan Central Committee mandated the bureau to "examine the issue of the party duties" of the former first secretary of the republic; in the meantime, two of Kunayev's direct collaborators were expelled from the party, and the Presidium of the Kazakh Supreme Soviet passed a resolution to confiscate buildings and apartments belonging to corrupt leaders.[33] At the same time, it was learned that two former members of the Central Committee, Kenes Aukhadev and Asanbai Askarov, respectively the first secretaries of Alma-Ata and of Chimkent, were under criminal investigation for serious crimes.[34] The party newspaper went back to the subject in a bitter personal invective against the former member of the Politburo. The accusations were so violent that some thought Kunayev might be removed from the Central Committee and himself be subjected to criminal investigation.[35] Clearly, someone in the offices of the Central Committee was moving pawns in a complex moralistic offensive with far greater political aims. In January the Voroshilovgrad scandal was followed by the retirement of Boris Goncharenko, the first secretary of the Ukraine region and a member of the Central Committee. In March another important first secretary of the Ukraine was ousted: Viktor Boiko, a member of the Central Committee, and Dnepropetrovsk's number-one man.

Differences in priorities grew more explicit within the Politburo, where Yegor Ligachev stressed both activism and clear-cut stands that tended to establish limits and draw solid boundaries. Between March and April there was a series of heavy broadsides and responses to them. The number-two man took the initiative in a trip to Saratov that was closely covered by television. His speech to local intellectuals confirmed the watchwords of "glasnost" and "democratization," but specified that "not everything can be denigrated," since even during the stagnation (i.e., the Brezhnev period), "works were produced that reflected the glorious pages of our history [i.e., the Stalin period] and consolidated socialist realism." His argument was directed against those who "try to limit the guiding role of state management in the realm of culture."[36] Such sharp emphases could not be ignored. The conservative elements in the *nomenklatura* immediately got the signal.

The plenum of the Secretariat of the RSFSR Writers' Union met without delay and tried to take advantage of the moment.[37] Sergei Mikhalkov thundered, "Behind the slogans of perestroika are hidden opportunists, speculators, and people with no talent." The main task of literature is "to resist imperialism's aggression toward culture and ideas with the maximum resoluteness." Many advocates of the most extreme cultural reaction joined the ranks after Mikhalkov—the same ones who had built their literary fortunes in the very midst of the Brezhnevite stagnation. The loudest cries of pain were from Yuri Bondarev, who performed a virtual parody of Gorbachev's references to the Brest Litovsk peace by launching another historical parallel: "If this retreat continues, if the time of Stalingrad does not arrive, the wealth of our national culture and everything that brings pride to the people will end up falling into an abyss." Bondarev was followed by Pyotr Proskurin, who openly attacked *Ogonyok*, and by Sergei Borzunov, who protested the publication of Pasternak, Nabokov, and others.

The opposite side replied to this explicit offensive with equal harshness, but with some signs of difficulty. After violent criticism of his intervention at the January plenum, Mikhail Ulyanov, a member of the Central Revision Committee and president of the RSFSR Theater Workers' Union, came back to speak as a guest of no less a publication than *Kommunist*. His emphasis was extremely alarming:

> They will oppose perestroika, it has become clear, in savage forms. Once certain vital interests have been questioned, it is clear that we cannot get away with exhortations and peaceful arrangements. Obviously no one is going to openly declare war on us, but a war is already underway using every means, even the basest, to the point of sabotage.[38]

What was at stake in the leadership was the control and the guidance of the mass media. Aleksandr Yakovlev called a meeting of the directors of the central news organizations and gave them quite a different speech, pushing the tiller in the opposite direction. Some opinions were final ("the repressive mechanisms, created over the course of years and years, must be broken without hesitation"); the defense of glasnost was unwavering. But there was also an invitation to be accurate in criticism, to avoid making accusations without proof, to consider various points of view, to "accurately represent the extremely complex structure of interests and points of view in the society's different strata and groups."[39] In short, it was an invitation to caution.

In that same period the signs that a big political debate was brewing grew explicit, but in coded forms. Gorbachev's trip to Prague was suddenly postponed for a few days, the official reason being that the Soviet leader had a cold. The Politburo meeting on the previous Thursday (30 March) had ended so late that the evening news on television, contrary to ordinary practice, had been unable to broadcast the text of the final communiqué. It was unexpectedly learned that a 31 March All-Union meeting of the Central Committee on the problems of the ideological and political training of government and party cadres had been presided over and opened by Lev Zaikov, with a long "Gorbachevian" speech. The report was delivered by Georgi Razumovsky, but both Ligachev and Yakovlev were absent: in other words, both the man formally in charge of controls over ideology and the man who—even if he was on the opposite side—seemed to preside over control of the mass media. The recent "exchange of blows" seemed to have led the Politburo to keep both men from the scene.[40]

On 16 April at the Twentieth Komsomol Congress, Gorbachev had already spoken about the new steps that would be taken. This speech focused entirely on the subject of "democratization": "It is time, it is truly time that everybody understand: socialism cannot exist without a consistent democracy." In anticipation of a concept that he would develop in his 20 May interview with *L'Unità*, Gorbachev firmly denied that perestroika had "political enemies" or "opposition." But at the same time, he stated that "the repressive mechanism was not created automatically," and that "concrete representatives of this mechanism exist both at the level of the Central Committee, of the government, of the ministries, of the republics, and of the regions," and further down, "in the work cooperatives, and even in Komsomol."[41]

But before the plenum, preparations for which were still far from completion, another event occurred like something straight out of the "Court of Miracles," halfway between the comic and the dramatic, and a symbol of the remarkable nature of what was happening. Mathias Rust landed near St. Basil's Cathedral after flying over the Kremlin in his Cessna and crossing more than a thousand kilometers of Soviet territory without being stopped, or perhaps even spotted and identified, by Soviet antiaircraft devices—on 28 May, the same day the USSR honors its border guards. The adventurous young German was the unwitting deus ex machina of one of the greatest spectacles of the Gorbachev era. The Soviet leader had just returned from East Berlin. He called a meeting of the Politburo and fired without consideration of extenuating circumstances both Marshal Sergei Sokolov, the minister of defense (who was also a candidate member of the Politburo), and Air Marshal Aleksandr Koldunov, the chief of air defense. It was later learned that forty-five other high officials were dismissed, many of whom were expelled from the party. Mathias Rust was arrested and tried under Soviet law, and given a mild sentence of four years in prison. But there were many both in and outside the USSR who thought that he was acting as an ally of the Gorbachev renewal. The solid blow he inflicted on the prestige of the military, and that Gorbachev proved quick to turn to his own advantage, restored a more attractive image to Gorbachev's USSR. The powerful Soviet military machine showed that it was neither infallible nor impenetrable, and therefore appeared less frightening. In logical terms, Rust almost deserved to be decorated with the Order of the Friends of the People. Politics rarely has anything to do with logic, and obviously no such thing occurred. Yet to no one's surprise he served only a small part of his sentence. He would be freed at the beginning of August 1988, little more than one year later. Whatever else, he can boast that he helped appoint a new Soviet minister of defense. The other surprise: the new minister was Dmitri Yazov, who in one leap jumped over the heads of four first deputy ministers: three marshals (Sergei Akhromeyev, Fyodor Kulikov, and Vasili Petrov) and one army general (Pyotr Lushchev).

FOURTH CONVERSATION

SAKHAROV'S RETURN FROM EXILE; ELECTION REFORM;
DISMANTLING THE MYTH OF STALIN; CHILDREN OF THE
ARBAT; PERIODICALS AND THEIR EDITORS IN CHIEF; THE
REHABILITATION OF BUKHARIN AND OTHERS CONDEMNED IN
THE TRIALS OF THE THIRTIES

•   •   •

G.C. Could you comment on the liberation of Andrei Sakharov from his Gorky exile?

R.M. Many people had been awaiting that decision, yet it still came as a surprise to most of us. As recently as the spring of 1986, after Yelena Bonner's return from the United States, a more rigid isolation was imposed on Andrei Dmitrievich. I think that Gorbachev had raised the problem of Sakharov's return to Moscow earlier than this. In fact, the new policy of glasnost had lessened the bitterness of Sakharov's conflict with the previous party leadership. The political price the Kremlin was paying for Sakharov's internal exile was clearly too high and no longer justifiable. The USSR's Academy of Sciences was boycotted by all the most important American and West European scientific associations. Sakharov had become a symbol, and no one could believe Gorbachev's democratic intentions as long as Sakharov remained in exile. However, as you can imagine, in the Politburo there were hesitations and even resistance. I believe that this development was hastened by the death of Anatoli Marchenko in the Chistopol prison. Sakharov and his wife were not in good health. If anything happened to them while they were still in exile, the reputation of the new Soviet leader would be irreparably tarnished. For the moment, I cannot dwell on Marchenko's plight. The Sakharovs were close to him and to his wife, Larisa Bogoraz. Marchenko's death was not due just to the deprivations he had suffered in the labor camp, but allegedly to the cruel violence of his interrogators in early 1986. This was immediately followed by a rapid series of events. On 14 December a team of technicians installed a telephone in Sakharov's apartment. On 15

92

December the guards were removed from around his house. On 16 December Gorbachev telephoned Sakharov personally to inform him that his exile was over and that his wife, Yelena, had been pardoned. Another day went by and Yuri Marchuk, the president of the Academy of Sciences, arrived in Gorky to discuss Sakharov's return to work in Moscow's scientific community. Sakharov came back on 23 December, and was received at the Yaroslavsky train station by more than two hundred foreign correspondents. His first interview with an American television correspondent was actually broadcast to the United States from the Ostankino studios.

But Sakharov's release also had a huge impact on domestic life. Over a period of two to three months, more than two hundred political prisoners were released, pardoned, and given amnesty, many of whom were well known abroad and among the intelligentsia. Since then each of the ex-prisoners has taken different stances. Sakharov immediately announced his support for glasnost and democratization. He criticized Reagan's policy on the Strategic Defense Initiative; he had opposed the SDI from the beginning, and made it known. At the same time, he called for the release of all political prisoners and the withdrawal of Soviet troops from Afghanistan. His position on these subjects had also long been well known. Sakharov took an active part in the international forum held in Moscow in February 1987; he spoke three times to criticize Star Wars. His participation in public life grew quickly, and not only through articles and interviews. He took part in a public discussion on nuclear reactors, proposing that they be built underground. I personally find this the most reasonable of the various proposals. Later on he became one of the founders of the International Fund for the Survival and Development of Humanity, and as such met with Gorbachev. But at the same time, he continued to work as a theoretical physicist and as an astrophysicist, holding seminars at the Academy of Sciences. The dissidents and émigrés reacted differently to his conduct. There were even those who called Sakharov a "traitor"—a shameful accusation. Even in the past Sakharov had never declared himself an organizer of the dissidents; he always spoke for himself. Yet this is precisely what allowed him to win an important moral and political victory for all of us. His victory helped to change the political atmosphere in the Soviet Union, as well as to score an important success for Mikhail Gorbachev's politics and prestige. Sakharov's release made a return to the past even less likely: this was the most important fact.

G.C. December 1986 was full of events. The eightieth anniversary of Brezhnev's birth was "celebrated" with an article in *Pravda* that was in truth not at all celebratory. In December too a new series of laws on emigration was approved. In the West discussions raged over the meaning of this new measure; many considered it a step backward, while others considered it a progressive move. Still others wrote that it favored only the emigration of Jews, which in fact grew noticeably during 1987. To me instead this period seems to mark the beginning of a considerable opening toward freedom of transit for Soviet citizens.

R.M. The article on the eightieth anniversary of Brezhnev's birth was definitely a further step in the criticism of the past. Attempts at forming a cult of Brezhnev failed to penetrate the mass consciousness. Even before his death people judged him harshly—only the officials continued to praise him, but their only motivation was career concerns. The new rules on entering and leaving the country that took effect on 1 January 1987 eliminated numerous previous limitations. For example, a Soviet citizen living abroad used to be permitted to come back to the USSR to visit his relatives only once a year—an absurd law. Moreover, the previous rules applied only to the "closest" relatives—parents and their children, brothers and sisters. But grandparents and cousins were not considered close relatives. The new change was significant. Not only could you return to the USSR more than once a year, without limitations, but you could also be invited by distant relatives. Finally, you could obtain a visa to go abroad, even for tourism, with the invitation of a simple acquaintance.

G.C. At the same time, however, a new restrictive clause was introduced that prevented a foreigner with a tourist visa from applying to marry a Soviet citizen.

R.M. I am not familiar with this rule. Often new instructions and legislative bills are published only in specialized periodicals, and few people know of their existence. I learned of the new rules on freedom of transit only by reading about them in *Golos Rodini,* a newspaper for former Soviet citizens that is distributed abroad.

G.C. What were Gorbachev's proposals for reforming the way that political and economic cadres were elected?

R.M. Gorbachev's proposals restored the system for electing party leaders that had existed in the 1920s but had been erased by Stalin. The facts would prove that this new situation would make life difficult for many officials in the intermediate and lower *nomenklatura,* who had already been upset by the waves of changes both before and after the Twenty-Seventh Congress. Gorbachev also proposed putting an end to the system of having only one candidate in the elections for the soviets, elections that had been discredited for having no "possibilities of choice." These were innovative and welcome proposals, but still did not constitute a revolution. The same could be said about the labor collectives' elections of managers at every level of their enterprises. This represented an important extension of democracy to the workplace. But the forms are one thing, the contents another. The electoral system could be good in theory but end up being terrible in practice. For example, it is known that kolkhoz chairmen have always been elected at the general meetings of members. Yet it is no secret that almost everywhere these elections were pure formalities, and everything had already been decided beforehand in the office of the local first secretary. Equally pro forma were the elections of department heads at institutes of higher learning, as well as the posts of president and vice president of the USSR's Academy of Sciences.

Another important proposal that the plenum finally approved was one to announce an All-Union Conference on Party Organization at the end of June 1988. Stalin had ended the tradition of holding these intermediate conferences with limited powers in the interval between two congresses with broad powers, and of renewing the membership of the ruling bodies. There had been numerous conferences and congresses in the 1920s, but in the twenty-three years after 1931, one can count only three party congresses and one conference, the Eighteenth, held in March 1941.

G.C. Could you talk about Abuladze's film *Pokayaniye?*

R.M. Initially, the director himself brought four copies of the film to Moscow. The film was shown only at the Dom Kino or at individual clubs. But many of the intelligentsia saw it. It's a very strong antidictatorial, anti-totalitarian, anti-Stalinist film. The audience watched it in shock, in tears. It seemed impossible that the film could be circulated to the greater public.

G.C. In Georgia they had already shown it on TV.

R.M. It had already been at the Georgia cinemas in the summer of 1986. In the fall it went on television at the express orders of the local party, with the support of Shevardnadze. The film caused a sensation in Georgia, where there was still a true Stalinist cult, especially in the villages. *Pokayaniye* had had a troubled history. It had been shot a few years earlier, but it was immediately blocked by the censors. Attempts were made to destroy the film. You have to remember that in the USSR we have individual spheres of local autonomy. So a film shown at the Moscow theaters could be blocked in the

95

Ukraine, as happened to the satiric film *Garazh* (*The Garage*) by Eldar Ryazanov. *Pokayaniye*, however, was authorized for general release in Moscow and Leningrad at the end of January, and had an exceptional public success. Equally huge was the success of the feature film *Legko Li Byt Molodym?* (*Is It Easy to Be Young?*) by the Latvian director Yuri Podnieks. Yet there had not been many good films made recently.

In literature, by contrast, there was a huge "reserve." The first 1987 issues of our "thick" literary magazines began to publish anti-Stalinist works such as Anna Akhmatova's *Requiem* and Aleksandr Tvardovsky's *Po Pravu Pamyati* (*By Right of Memory*). Neither poem had previously seen the light of day, even though they had been written in the 1960s. Yuri Trifonov's novel *Ischeznoveniye* [*The Disappearance*] on the repressions in the 1930s) and Anatoli Pristavkin's *Nochevala Tuchka Zolotaya* ([*And a Golden Cloud Spent the Night*] on the deportation of the Moslems from the Northern Caucasus) gained widespread attention. The magazines in Moscow, Leningrad, and Rostov almost competed to publish ferociously critical novels and short stories by Vladimir Dudintsev, Daniil Granin, Vladimir Tendryakov, Sergei Antonov, and Boris Mozhayev. There were poems by Anatoli Zhigulin, Boris Chichibabin, Olga Berggolts, Boris Slutsky, and Nikolai Gumilyov. Works began to be published by deceased or émigré writers, such as Andrei Platonov, Georgi Ivanov, and Vyacheslav Khodasevich. But the main literary event of 1987 was the publication of Anatoli Rybakov's novel *Children of the Arbat*. The action takes place in 1933 and 1934, and for the first time we can read a broad and truthful fresco of the life of the country and of the Kremlin during a period of dramatic changes. For the first time in our literature the figure of Stalin was placed in the center of a novel. Without stressing the horrors, the writer created a psychologically exact and historically reliable portrait of Stalin preparing what would later be called the Great Terror.

The plight of Rybakov's novel showed how deep the 1987 changes were. The first part of the novel had already been finished in the mid-1960s. Aleksandr Tvardovsky had announced its publication in *Novy Mir*. But it never happened. The "conservative turnabout" was already underway, and there were even some who wanted to rehabilitate Stalin. Rybakov did not give up. He kept working, and in the 1970s he finished the second and third parts of his great novel. Rybakov is a well-known writer in the USSR, the author of splendid books for young people, and honored by state prizes. A few years ago his novel *Tyazholy Pesok*, on the plight of the Jews in Nazi-occupied territories, was published both at home and abroad. It was very difficult to be silent about his work, and many of us read the manuscript for *Deti Arbata*. Yet the novel could not be published in 1985 or '86.

G.C. Even though more attempts were made in 1986.

R.M. Exactly. The magazine *Druzhba Narodov* refused to publish the novel for the second time in its history. The editor in chief explained that the novel was very good, but the figure of Stalin as portrayed was totally unacceptable. In the fall of that year a long list of writers sent a letter to the Central Committee firmly requesting that the previous decisions be reconsidered and that the novel be published. The undersigned included Yevgeni Yevtushenko, Fazil Iskander, Andrei Voznesensky, Veniamin Kaverin, Bulat Okudzhava, Sergei Antonov, and many others. The request was supported by Aleksandr Yakovlev, at that time secretary of the Central Committee, and by other officials of the partially renewed party and apparats. The novel was read by Gorbachev's personal assistants and the decision was finally made to publish it, but with a few small cuts. In April the first installment was published by none other than *Druzhba Naradov*, where in the meantime the editor in chief had been replaced.

G.C. How did the magazines and their editors change in these months?

R.M. *Druzhba Narodov* changed its policies, and as a result changed its reputation without substantially modifying its editorial staff. Many cultural figures considered cautious or even conservative lined up behind perestroika. Albert Belyayev is a clear example; for years he headed the literary sector of the Central Committee, where he was considered a very conservative functionary (and no less conservative a writer). When he left the apparat and was appointed editor in chief of *Sovetskaya Kultura*, he turned the newspaper into a leading publication for perestroika, for criticism of Stalin, and for support of cultural pluralism. Yet Belyayev was the same one who, obviously on Suslov's orders, arranged the 1970 firing of Tvardovsky from his position as editor in chief of *Novy Mir*.

Completely different was the behavior of Anatoli Sofronov, editor in chief of the weekly *Ogonyok* since 1953. He had always been one of the most assiduous conservatives, and was justly considered an outright Stalinist. Sofronov is a poet and playwright, even if no one has produced his plays for a long time and everyone has forgotten his poetry. Under his direction the readership of *Ogonyok* had plummeted, and 50 percent of its copies were sent to the pulping plant or sold at one-half or one-fourth the cover price. Sofronov had no intention of "restructuring," and therefore had to be replaced. He asked for an audience with Gorbachev, but was turned down. The new editor in chief, Vitali Korotich, and the new editorial staff turned *Ogonyok* into one of the most interesting magazines. Now it was almost impossible to buy it at the newsstands, even though more copies were printed. The editorial staff of *Znamya* was also changed. Vladimir Lakshin, who in my opinion is our best literary critic, was appointed first deputy editor. I remember because his appointment was provoked by a private battle. His candidacy was eliminated twice, and the case was only resolved when Baklanov threatened to quit unless he was joined by Lakshin.

From January on, the mass media had an enormous impact on public opinion. The proliferation of thousands of informal groups throughout the country was also the result of a new orientation in the central newspapers. The authority of some magazines grew so rapidly that it caught even the political leadership by surprise. This is how changing the head of a magazine like *Ogonyok* or *Moskovskiye Novesti* became more important than replacing the first secretary of the Kursk or Orel regions. But we should mention that after the January plenum the publication of important articles and essays, as well as the showing of bitterly critical films, came out of an extended and often dramatic struggle. Each of these events is a story in itself. We've already spoken about *Pokayaniye* and *Children of the Arbat*, but what about Tvardovsky's *Po Pravu Pamyati* or Akhmatova's *Requiem*, which appeared only after twenty years of struggle?

Western observers often fail to understand why major political leaders follow the destiny of a literary work so closely. One enlightening example: Aleksandr Bek's novel *Novoye Naznacheniye (The New Appointment)*. Bek was one of our best writers. His *Volokolamskoye Shosse (The Volokolamsky Highway)* is known all over the world, and is considered one of the best novels about World War II. *Novoye Naznacheniye* was written in the early 1960s. The protagonist was a people's commissar in the Stalin era. The prototype that inspired Bek was Ivan Tevosyan, the people's commissar for the steel industry. One of the main characters was Stalin, whose personality Bek describes with extraordinary accuracy. Tvardovsky enthusiastically accepted the novel. *Novy Mir* already had the printer's galleys ready. But Tevosyan's family rebelled against the publication. The chairman of the Council of Ministers, Aleksei Kosygin, who had himself been a people's commissar in Stalin's time, stepped in. Almost the entire Writers' Union then defended the novel and the author's right to choose his own models, especially considering that the protagonist was named Onisimov and not Tevosyan. The issue was confronted repeatedly by the leadership, but in the end the novel was not published in the USSR. Instead, it was published abroad in Russian. Aleksandr Bek saw the foreign edition only three days before his death in 1972. The novel was published in 1987 by *Znamya* and in the popular series "Roman Gazeta." Almost all the members of the Politburo supported its publication, including Yegor Ligachev, whom many had superficially considered one of the most conservative members of the party leadership.

G.C. Superficially?

R.M. At least in that phase. In his official speech on 6 November 1986 he had strongly defended perestroika, and I believe he was not just expressing the Politburo's point of view: he was speaking in his own name. Later on I believe Ligachev showed his limits: inability to understand the rapid changes that were taking place, and difficulty in learning from developments in the situation. Ligachev has slower reflexes than Gorbachev and his collaborators.

G.C. He had a more "traditional" training.

R.M. Yes, we could say that. Ligachev had been an energetic supporter of the fight against corruption, and defended perestroika and economic reform. He made a name for himself in the fight against alcoholism and against the so-called "unearned income." You could say that he was responsible for some of the most negative forays in this area. But in 1986 Ligachev supported all of the most important cultural events: Mikhail Shatrov's plays *Diktatura Sovesti* (*The Dictatorship of the Conscience*) and *Serebryanaya Svadba* (*The Silver Wedding*), and the film *Pokayaniye*. By contrast, in 1987 when cultural developments sped up, Ligachev clearly showed himself more inclined to support the cautious *Pravda* than *Ogonyok*.

G.C. Nineteen eighty-seven is also the year in which the question of "rehabilitations" was reopened. Why? And what forms did this process take in the courts and in the party?

R.M. The wave of rehabilitations began with a leap in the quality of the criticism of Stalin and Stalinism effected at the January plenum. It would grow to its highest point in the early months of 1988, with the reinvestigation of the trials of Nikolai Bukharin and of Lev Kamenev, Grigori Zinoviev, Grigori Pyatakov, Karl Radek, et al. This showed once again how incomplete and inadequate even the Twentieth and Twenty-Second congresses' denunciations of Stalin's crimes had been. Later we will get back to the problems of revising Soviet and party history. Here instead I would like to examine the question of rehabilitation from a historical perspective, and partly from a legal perspective. These problems have occupied a prominent position in the life of our society. Every wave of rehabilitations has been preceded by a bitter struggle, just as the preceding waves of illegal repressions were themselves expressions of violent cycles of party in-fighting. The issue closely concerns many Soviet citizens.

My father, a commissar in the Red Army, a political official, and a teacher of philosophy at the Military Academy, was arrested in 1938 and died on the golden sands of the Kolyma River in 1941. This was the tragedy that changed the course of my life and my ideas about society. In 1954 my father was rehabilitated by the Supreme Court of the USSR because of the "inexistence of a crime." In 1956 he was also rehabilitated by the party and posthumously readmitted into its ranks. Therefore, my brother Zhores and I were no longer sons of an "enemy of the people." However, the next twenty years were certainly not years of justice. Because of my manuscript on Stalinism (which still hasn't been published in the USSR), I was expelled from the party and lost the right to practice my profession in Soviet institutions. My brother was illegally tried and deprived of Soviet citizenship for having fought against Trofim Lysenko's abuses and for democracy in the sciences. Now he lives and works in London. Together we fight as hard as we can for his rehabilitation and together we are working to effect a change in the USSR's political and social situation.

Many examples affect me closely. Today there are millions of Soviets interested in rehabilitation for countless reasons, but I think that the crucial point is more political than legal. On my desk lies a copy of the *Legal Encyclopedia* recently published in the USSR. You can find entries for "amnesty," "pardons," "cassation," and "appeals," but there is nothing under "rehabilitation"—either here or in the huge volume of comments on the civil and penal codes of the Russian Federal Republic. In the *Great Soviet Encyclopedia* you can find "rehabilitation," but not as a legal term. Obviously, our legal handbooks don't even contain the terms "enemy of the people," "saboteur," or "cosmopolitan without a homeland"—all words that unfortunately weighed heavily on people's lives. In today's encyclopedias you will definitely not find the term "kulak," never mind "podkulachnik," although these labels were the reasons millions of peasants were deported or died.

G.C. Many people believe that the Twentieth Congress began the rehabilitations and de-Stalinization. In reality, it wasn't quite that way. The process began before the congress, almost immediately after Stalin's death.

R.M. It is true that de-Stalinization started immediately after Stalin's death. The first rehabilitations began in those same days. For example, Polina Zhemchuzhina, Molotov's wife, had been imprisoned in 1949; she was released the day of Stalin's funeral. Almost every member of the Politburo had relatives, friends, and collaborators in prison; they were the first to be rehabilitated, including Khrushchev's daughter-in-law, Lazar Kaganovich's brother, Otto Kuusinen's wife and son, and the wife of the army general Andrei Khrulyov. Marshal Georgi Zhukov, who hadn't been arrested but was "under investigation" at the headquarters of the Urals military recruitment center, was exonerated of all charges. The relatives of generals and marshals, ministers and members of the Central Committee, began to return from the camps. The Kremlin doctors' group was rehabilitated, after their January 1953 arrest on charges of being "spies for the United States and Israel."

This was a direct provocation against Beria, who rapidly succeeded in procuring the rehabilitation of Viktor Abakumov and Rukhadze, his collaborators at the Ministry for State Security (MGB). But this was short-lived: both were rearrested, this time along with Beria himself. The first year after the dictator's death saw the posthumous rehabilitation of Nikolai Voznesensky and Aleksei Kuznetsov, former members of the Politburo, along with a good many of the Leningrad party officials who had been suppressed in 1949–50 during the so-called "Leningrad affair." Famous actors, directors, heroes of the Second World War, and many others were also rehabilitated.

Gradually, the limits on rehabilitation were lifted. According to data I have available, up to the beginning of 1956, i.e., before the Twentieth Congress, from twelve to fifteen thousand people were rehabilitated. Approximately twenty thousand others were posthumously rehabilitated; their relatives received a certificate along with two months' wages as a form of compensation. However, I must specify that the rehabilitations did not begin after Stalin's death—there were also some while he was still alive. Every wave of repression that had taken place since the late 1920s had been accompanied by partial rehabilitations. For example, it is well known that between 1929 and 1933 millions of peasants were accused of being "kulaks" or "podkulachniks" and deported to the northern and far eastern regions. During the same years thousands of previously exiled peasant families were authorized to return to their native villages. There were various reasons, from the interest of relatives to the protests of the exiles themselves to later verifications by the authorities. But there was also a political calculation: the rehabilitation of a percentage of peasants who had been unjustly sentenced in a certain sense legitimized the actions of the leadership and justified the even more ferocious repression of the "kulaks."

Between 1928 and 1931 thousands of individuals were arrested on charges of "sabotage," "nationalism," and "counterrevolutionary activity." However, later on, a certain percentage of valuable specialists were released both as a result of the interventions of the organizations with which they worked and, in special cases, as a result of orders from Stalin himself. For example, the OGPU (Organization for State Political Leadership) had fabricated the case of a clandestine counterrevolutionary "government." The press had even printed a list of its membership, in which the "Ministry of Foreign Affairs" was entrusted to the well-known historian and academician Yevgeni Tarle. Obviously, all of the "members of this "government" were arrested. Who knows why, but Stalin was dissatisfied with the membership of this imaginary "counterrevolutionary government." The trial against the accused never took place, and Tarle, along with the other scholars, was able to return to work. Later on, Stalin sought consultation with Tarle on certain problems of history. Everyone knows how ferocious and large-scale the 1937 repressions were, but not everyone remembers that in January and February of 1938, after the Central Committee plenum, articles that harshly criticized the "slanderers" and "informers" appeared in the press. As a result, some party members who had already been arrested were released and even readmitted to the party. A few months later, starting in March 1938, a new wave of repressions began that sent 2 or 3 million new "enemies of the people" to the camps and prisons.

When Nikolai Yezhov was dismissed as head of the NKVD (People's Commissariat for the Interior) and arrested, once again thousands of people were freed. In one sense these partial rehabilitations served the purpose of emphasizing Yezhov's responsibilities and of strengthening the faith of millions of men hit by the repression under the "just" guidance of Stalin and the new people's commissar, Lavrenti Beria. After the 1939–40 war between the Soviet Union and Finland—a war that demonstrated the military leaders' weaknesses—Stalin authorized the rehabilitation of tens of thousands of Red Army officials, many of whom later distinguished themselves in World War II. During the war Andrei Tupolev was rehabilitated, along with a group of military planners. At the end of the war it was the turn of the scientist Sergei Korolyov, together with a group of researchers that later helped create the Soviet atomic bomb and atomic missiles.

Some events are not so well known, such as two examples of mass rehabilitation that took place during World War II. The Red Army suffered huge losses in the first months of the war. When the German troops approached Moscow, Stalin gave the order to transfer many divisions from the Far East, which were stationed there in expectation of a Japanese attack. This weakened defenses against Japan. But Stalin had no other choice. In order to fill in the gaps in his defensive lines in the Far East, General Iosif Apanasenko, commander of the Far Eastern Front, drafted not only the inhabitants of those regions, but also a number of the prisoners from the Kolyma and Siberian camps. This in fact represented their rehabilitation. General Apanasenko had been given a free hand directly by Stalin in 1941–42, and he ignored the NKVD's protests. In order to appreciate the significance of this rehabilitation, just compare the data. More than twenty divisions were transferred from the Far Eastern Front to the German Front in 1941–42. When Hitler invited the Japanese leaders to take advantage of the troop withdrawals on that front and unleash an attack from the East, the

Japanese replied that their intelligence sources indicated no weakening in the defenses: all of the Soviet divisions had kept and even reinforced their positions. Despite all this, General Apanasenko is almost unknown in the Soviet Union today.

There is another example of mass rehabilitation. In the summer of 1942 practically all of the men from Russia, the Caucasus, Central Asia, and Kazakhstan were in the army. However, in the Urals, in Siberia, in the Far East, and in northern Kazakhstan, there were many "special settlements," where the families of the so-called "kulaks" lived. Their children were not drafted, and they were not to be trusted—until 1942, when Stalin gave the order to conscript them too. This quickly came to mean that rehabilitation would be granted—after the invalids and wounded began to return from the front back to the "special settlements." Many had earned medals and honors, and were no longer willing to submit to the orders of the special-settlement commanders. Immediately after the end of the war almost all the inhabitants of these "special" villages were granted equal rights with residents of "normal" villages.

G.C. Was there a formal procedure for rehabilitation? What was it?

R.M. There is no legal procedure for rehabilitation. It has taken place in different ways during the various political phases—and not by accident. Stalin's repressions were arbitrary, but the rehabilitations were equally so. The prisoner was called before an official of the NKVD who informed him of his upcoming release and asked him to sign a declaration promising not to reveal what he had seen in the camps since it would be a "state secret." After which came a return to normal life. You can imagine the strangeness with which this all happened. This is the case of Sergei Kavtaradze, a noted Bolshevik from the Caucasus who had held important posts in the Supreme Court of the USSR and in the Attorney General's Office. He was arrested in 1936 and sentenced to a long prison term. In 1944 we suddenly read that he had been appointed deputy minister of foreign affairs. From 1945 to 1952 he served as Soviet ambassador to Rumania. I don't know on what basis Stalin decided to free Kavtaradze. In many cases it was simply the tyrant's whim. Another equally unique example: In 1942 there was a danger that epidemics would break out in the overcrowded cities of the Urals and Siberia. But the country's epidemiological services had also been dismantled by the repressions, so it was decided to free many specialists, the most famous of whom was Pavel Zdrodovsky. They brought him back to Moscow, but they neglected to rehabilitate him. He spent his nights in the Butirskaya prison and in the mornings he was taken to his job at the Ministry of Health.

Zdrodovsky took part in meetings with the minister while the NKVD guard waited for him outside the office door.

G.C. After the Twentieth Congress the situation changed substantially. How many people were rehabilitated then? How many came back home from the camps?

R.M. Let me take a short step back. When the first rehabilitations began under Khrushchev, there was immediate opposition inside the Politburo. Molotov, Kaganovich, and Kliment Voroshilov did not want millions of people to return from the concentration camps, nor did they appreciate the risk of a reexamination of the procedures that had led an even greater number of people to their deaths. This is why there was a fairly complex "procedure" from 1954 to 1956. Each "case" with all its related depositions and information had to be requested from the KGB prosecutor's offices; it was examined, checked and double-checked by special investigators; finally, it was sent to the Supreme Courts of either the republics or of the USSR. Even for a party rehabilitation every "case" took one or two years. At this rate rehabilitation would have taken hundreds of years, since in 1955 there were no fewer than 8-to-10 million political prisoners in the camps.

After the Twentieth Congress the situation changed rapidly, and unrest grew in the camps. There were numerous uprisings in 1955. Millions of statements started arriving in government offices from the prisoners' families. This pressure from below was augmented by the pressure from Khrushchev, Anastas Mikoyan, and other leaders at the top. In this way new decisions were made concerning rehabilitation procedures. A committee to investigate Stalin's crimes had already been formed before the Twentieth Congress, and was initially presided over by Molotov. Later Nikolai Shvernik became chairman, even when it split into two groups: a political commission at the Central Committee and a working group. The first was made up of high-ranking leaders; the second was mainly functionaries from the Party Control Commission and from the central apparats. The first dealt only with the most important party and state leaders. These cases were considered part of history, so the entire truth had to be known about them. Dozens of people took part in the working group because there were thousands—no, millions—of cases to review. There were not only the living, still in the camps: there were also the dead. There was a discussion in the Federal Prosecutor's Office, where Roman Rudenko was the chief. There were divergent points of view. To Mikoyan's credit, he proposed that the rehabilitation procedures for "ordinary" prisoners be simplified. His proposal raised objections in judiciary circles, but Khrushchev supported it. Thus, a hundred commissions were created, one for every main camp, with the power to grant pardons and rehabilitations, normally a prerogative of the Presidium of the Supreme Soviet. The commissions consisted of three members: a representative of the Prosecutor's Office, a party official, and an ex-convict reinstated in the party. From the end of 1956 to the spring of 1957, they examined the personal files of every prisoner without exception—an enormous task. An acquaintance of mine who was on one of these "troikas" told me that they spent an average of ten minutes on each file. First of all, prisoners who had been sentenced for criticizing Stalin were automatically released, as were those who had already served their sentences (there were thousands of these still in the camps).

Once these two categories had been taken care of, they dealt with the rehabilitation of former party members. In these cases the files were carefully examined and the decision to rehabilitate was made only after an interview with the prisoner. Most were rehabilitated without reservations, the only exceptions being members of opposition groups—the so-called Trotskyites, the Bukharinists, and so on. They were immediately released, but not rehabilitated. Finally, an examination of all the remaining prisoners followed, which was also simple and quick. Those who had collaborated with the Germans as prison guards were not released. With regard to former prisoners of war, simple soldiers were immediately released and rehabilitated, while officers were released without rehabilitation. During this phase I think that about 80 percent of all political prisoners left the camps. There were no statistics, but the figure of 3-to-4 million is considered reliable. Of the dead, about 90 percent had been arrested in the 1930s and were already dead at the time of rehabilitation. These rehabilitations continued past 1957, until Khrushchev made his exit in 1964, and even afterward. In 1957, for example, marshals and generals who had been killed in the 1930s were rehabilitated: Mikhail Tukhachevsky, Vasili Blyukher, Aleksandr Yegorov, Iona Yakir, Ieronim Uborevich, etcetera. The same happened for famous party representatives such as Fyodor Raskolnikov, Nikolai Krestinsky, and many others. It is impossible to list them all. I would, however, like to add something. Posthumous rehabilitation only began when the relatives of the deceased applied for it. This was one of its more loathsome features. When a prisoner died in the camps, his files were transferred to a central office in the NKVD, archived under the heading "Keep Forever." It would be pulled only on the request of a wife, a mother, or a child. A state with any self-respect would have gone through all the rehabilitations systematically, regardless of applications.

G.C. So how many people were rehabilitated during Khrushchev's time?

R.M. I think there were about 18 million people, about 10 million of whom were rehabilitated posthumously. But this figure includes other categories, and not just political prisoners. For example, it includes 3 million Moslems from the northern Caucasus: Chechens, Ingushi, and Kalmyks. Also 2 million Volga Germans. As I said, official statistics do not exist.

G.C. What happened after Khrushchev was ousted?

R.M. The mechanisms that had been activated continued to function, but more slowly. On Brezhnev's initiative, for example, the Uzbek party leaders who had been shot in 1937 were rehabilitated, like Kamil Ikramov and Faizulla Khodzhayev. The Crimean Tatars were legally rehabilitated only in 1967, even if they were not allowed to return to their native land. The rehabilitations were interrupted in the 1970s, thereby excluding many innocent people who had taken part in various opposition and "deviant" groups in the 1920s, thousands of specialists and engineers who had been denounced in the years 1928–32 for "sabotage," and "members" of nonexistent parties created by the imaginations of Stalin, Genrikh Yagoda, and Andrei Vyshinsky.

G.C. Gorbachev reopened the rehabilitation process with his speech in honor of the seventieth anniversary of the October Revolution, and the announcement that there was a special commission of the Politburo at work. Over the course of a few months, amid obvious difficulties, the trial proceedings of 1936, 1937, and 1938 were reviewed. The Supreme Court of the USSR publicly declared that the "right-wing Trotskyite block" had never existed, that the investigation and the trial had been fabricated and conducted with "inadmissable methods." In short, he acknowledged that the trials of Bukharin, Kamenev, Zinoviev, Pyatakov, Radek, and the others had been rigged.

R.M. The commission had to decide a huge number of cases. Bukharin, Pyatakov, Kamenev, Zinoviev, Radek, and Aleksei Rykov were fully rehabilitated in this new wave, but the problem of Trotsky remains open. Trotsky too was sentenced to death three times in absentia—and this sentence was carried out by a special group of the NKVD. I hope that we don't have to wait another twenty to thirty years for the decision.

Justice must be rendered to many innocent people—the list of whom grew longer during the Brezhnev years. Something in this direction was done in 1987, but it was only a first step. A huge chapter must be opened up on prisoners of war. After the war, prisoners who had survived Hitler's concentration camps (where about 5 million died) were subject to special investigations for "tendentiousness" in Stalin's camps. Another unsolved problem is tied to our relations with Poland: I am referring to the eight to ten thousand officers in the Polish Army shot to death in Katyn. Hopefully, the historical truth will be reestablished in all of these cases.

But I would like to linger for another moment on the rehabilitation of Bukharin. After Khrushchev's report at the Twentieth Congress it was already clear to every thinking person that the trials in the 1930s had all been rigged. The Soviet press in fact stopped describing Bukharin, Rykov, and the others as "spies for the Western secret services," "saboteurs," or "enemies of the people." In a 1962 All-Union meeting of historians, Boris Ponomaryov, secretary of the Central Committee at that time, answered a question by saying, "Comrades, if you read the materials of the Twentieth and Twenty-Second Congresses carefully, it will become clear to you that neither Bukharin, nor Zinoviev, nor Kamenev, nor Rykov were spies or enemies of the people." A few copies of the proceedings of that meeting exist, and I have one in my library. But that statement could not count as a formal rehabilitation. Bukharin and the others were not readmitted to the party, and their relatives did not receive either moral or material compensation. Although they were among the most famous representatives of the party and of the October Revolution, no one could write and publish works about them. When ten years ago Bukharin's son wrote his letter to Enrico Berlinguer (the late secretary of the Italian Communist Party) and the campaign for Bukharin's rehabilitation assumed an international character, the Soviet press maintained complete silence. In short, the fate of these men continued to be a "blank page" in Soviet history. It caused serious damage to our study of history.

G.C. Yet the latest wave of rehabilitations is the result of a heated political battle. Why?

R.M. You can see the conflicts with the naked eye. At first, Bukharin's rehabilitation had been scheduled for late December 1987, but for unexplained reasons it was postponed to May 1988. Gorbachev insisted that a special session of the Supreme Court of the USSR be held at the beginning of February. This dealt an especially strong blow to Stalinism. And this was not just a blow to ideology—the rehabilitation of Bukharin served the debate underway on economic reform. Many of the transformations planned by perestroika are in part a reproposal of the methods of the NEP for our own times. Resistance to the rehabilitation of Bukharin was also a sign of the resistance to perestroika.

G.C. In this respect, Gorbachev's speech for the seventieth anniversary of the October Revolution represented a compromise between two opposing goals: to reevaluate the NEP but also to justify the collectivization of the countryside. Yet the ensuing debate has already greatly exceeded the bounds of this compromise.

R.M. The revision is unquestionably moving far beyond that point. The Twentieth Congress had dated Stalin's main crimes after 1934. Today this periodization has been soundly criticized in the fields of literature, political journalism, and, to some extent, history. A reality emerges from the novels of Mozhayev, Belov, and Antonov—and from many articles describing the situation in the 1920s—of an effective and rapid growth of agriculture between 1926 and 1928. The NEP brought about this effect by providing incentives for family farms and for every type of cooperative. The campaign in those years was not without its contradictions, but they did not necessarily have to be overcome through violence and a "second revolution." The huge potential of the Russian farmlands was just beginning to reveal itself, giving the country an abundance of produce it had never before seen. Instead, between 1929 and 1932 we witness a violent break with the natural processes of the farmlands, the destruction of the productive forces, the liquidation of the most efficient farm enterprises, and the wholesale slaughter of livestock and horses. At the same time, millions of peasant families were ruthlessly deported, being absurdly equated with the category of "rich farmers." Millions of poor and middle peasants were persecuted or starved to death. Today most journalists contest the validity of the "dekulakization." Academician V. Tikhonov has proved that the increase in the number of rich farmers at the beginning of the century, and against which Lenin hurled himself so harshly (and not always justifiably), had already been halted in the years of the Civil War. Many of those rich farmers were frightened by the emergency confiscation of wheat, and had already abandoned the fields in 1927–28. In fact, many hardworking average farmers who had achieved relative comfort through their labors in the NEP years were defined as "kulaks" between 1929 and 1932. On the foundations of the NEP the country could have grown and developed much more efficiently not only in agriculture but in industry. The army would have had more cadres. I would like to add that in Germany the small farmer would not have been as terrorized as he was. It would have been very difficult for Hitler's party to triumph in 1933 if the fight between Germany's Communists and Social Democrats had not been set off by Stalin's orders. In short, a different line of conduct might have prevented World War II.

CHAPTER 5

THE JUNE AND OCTOBER 1987 PLENUMS; THE LAW ON STATE ENTERPRISES; THE SEVENTIETH ANNIVERSARY OF THE OCTOBER REVOLUTION; THE YELTSIN AFFAIR

•   •   •

The struggle to define the outlines of the economic reform had reached a crucial point, after a long incubation period marked by Gorbachev's sudden accelerations and by equally sudden attempts by powerful conservative groups inside the Central Committee to put on the brakes. In the midst of a "great debate at every level," which forced the Soviet leadership to postpone the plenum until the end of June, Gorbachev convened an unscheduled "consultation" on the eve of the Politburo meeting that would deliberate on the passage of twelve reform "resolutions."

The consultation lasted two days and was chaired by Nikolai Slyunkov, who was henceforth in charge of supervising the economic reform. Gorbachev asked the participants three specific questions: (1) how is perestroika going?; (2) what do you think of the bill we are bringing to the plenum?; and (3) what role should be assigned to the central bodies that manage the economy? The answers he received were not unanimous. Numerous ministers and representatives of the central bodies that manage the economy expressed vague inclinations that were at times opposed to the new measures. By contrast, many industry leaders clearly stated their support, and the economists who spoke took even clearer positions in favor of the reform. Gorbachev said, "Everyone is for perestroika," but there was obvious disagreement about the bill and about how much autonomy to give state enterprises. In essence, the consultation said "the bill must be approved," but with a series of revisions that led Gorbachev to say that the final text "cannot be called an ideal solution," though it was "a big step forward in the concrete phase of the reform through which we are now passing."

There was even sharper disagreement on the third question. Gorbachev emphasized that the "central bodies," i.e., Gosplan, Gossnab (State Committee on Supplies), the State Bank, the Ministry of Finance, and so on, should radically change their roles and structures, in order "not to contradict the law on enterprise." Instead, just the opposite was happening. Gorbachev turned to the chairman of the Council of Ministers and exclaimed, "Nikolai Ryzhkov told me a short time ago that every day he is forced to turn down a series of documents that go in the opposite direction of the new law." The ruling bodies were putting up a resistance that was insurmountable for the time being, and that was successfully imposing a "policy in stages" with the support of the party apparat. The way was open to autonomous enterprises— with some restrictions. But the reform of the central bodies would be diluted in the following trimester. The shift toward a "socialist market" (a term now used by many) would take place much more slowly and unevenly than necessary. Gorbachev made the best of the situation. He knew he could not push the situation any further, but for the record he warned: "One thing must be clear. The new law cannot begin to work unless we resolve the issue of central management."[1]

The June plenum thus opened under the sign of a new, difficult compromise that preferred a gradual approach over comprehensive solutions. But Gorbachev was intent on predetermining the stages and the path to follow, and he relaunched the offensive in every direction. His analysis of the "precrisis" situation was reiterated in even more dramatic terms, as if to remind those who asked for more time that there was not a minute to waste. The entire central structure of the economic leadership had to be "radically reorganized" and deprived of its prerogative to meddle with even the smallest details of a business's operation. It was time to shift from an "overly centralized" management system to another system, "based on democratic criteria and on the development of self-management." One goal was the "radical reform of the whole price structure," and the start of a "commercialization of the means of production." Horizontal contacts between enterprises and a structural reform of the finance system were essential components of the new responsibilities given to the enterprises to manage their production and their finances, and to utilize their profits. According to Abel Aganbegyan's explanations, initially the state work orders to the businesses would take up 60 percent of the productive potential, and later be gradually reduced to about 25 percent. In other words, market elements were being introduced into a socialist economy without touching the state plans' control over investments, natural resources, and the work force. Gorbachev specified that he was perfectly aware that as a whole these measures would produce "a discernible increase in the mobility of the work force," creating large-scale problems of unemployment and retraining. But "we have a duty to guarantee employment to workers, and the socialist system can accommodate this objective." This could not all be done with a single blow: we are "only in the first wave of perestroika." Instead, it would require a phase in which market elements would have to be reintegrated "with extraeconomic methods, with administrative pressure."

A timetable had now been definitely set. By 1987 the preparations for the enactment of the law (scheduled for 1 January 1988) were to be complete. In the two-year period 1988–89 every enterprise was to be ready to apply the law. By 1990 the reorganization of all the institutes for planning and centralized management was to have been carried out. The measures as a whole were to be gradually implemented over the five-year period 1991–95.

But Gorbachev did not miss this opportunity to note that the party was late. "The party cannot accept that perestroika sets the pace for the economic, social, and moral progress underway; that the changes in the lives and the moods of the people surpass the party's understanding of them." Here the leader's vehemence was unprecedented. "There are still voices that say that not everything is going badly, that maybe there's no reason to dramatize," so it was necessary to be even more explicit in denouncing the existing state of things. The crisis had, in fact, taken the shape of an outright "economic stagnation," whose components were an increasing delay in the country's technical and scientific growth (basically due to the rejection of innovation by an economic system that had become largely incapable of responding to external stimuli); a senseless policy of wasting resources and of making huge investments that proved less and less profitable; an obvious inflation (this was the first time the term appeared in an official speech); the shocking expansion in the production of alcoholic beverages (Gorbachev said that state income in this field had jumped from 67 billion rubles in the five-year period 1966–70, to 169 billion rubles from 1981 through 1985).[2]

In the midst of this downpour of dramatic allegations, the idea of holding an All-Union Conference on Organization, which had been blocked in January, was set for June. It would be held in June 1988 with powers and tasks similar to those of a special congress. Gorbachev had overcome the problems, but under heavy conditions. The plenum approved the entry of three new members to the Politburo: Nikolai Slyunkov, Aleksandr Yakovlev, and Viktor Nikonov. Yakovlev's positions were clear, but those of Slyunkov and Nikonov were much less so. But the fact that all three were also members of the Secretariat appreciably modified the balance within the party's two most important bodies, bringing the number of individuals in the leadership who belonged to both bodies up to six. The supervision of the economic reform was assigned to Slyunkov, the entire field of agriculture to Nikonov, and the upper hand in the direct management of glasnost to Yakovlev. The compromise did not allow the forces for restraint to make any gains, or even to present a credible alternative. Dinmukhamed Kunayev was expelled from the Central Committee. In homage to glasnost, a certain number of enemies of perestroika left the plenum "stamped" by Gorbachev's explicit personal criticism.

Gorbachev ended this round with a slight edge over his adversaries, but the match was not over. Many of the men surrounding the Soviet leader were hostile or unprepared to face his proposed changes. What the political and ideological resistance amounted to was often the less admissible fear of seeing one's consolidated privileges eroding away. Important segments of the party were implicated in illegal, if not criminal, activities. The panic that was spreading through the peripheral ruling groups was giving way to an angry desire for revenge. The difficulty of the political reform was proven by the conclusion of the summer session of the Supreme Soviet. In addition to the law on state enterprise, the Soviet parliament had on its agenda the approval of two emblematic laws: one on "the people's discussion of the most important problems," and the other on granting a Soviet citizen the right to file suit against public officials who had committed illegal acts in the performance of their duties. Both laws represented the first attempt to translate perestroika's innovative concepts into judicial terms, in the field of democratic rights and in the field of individual rights. But the debate in the political arena reduced the contents of both laws to little or nothing. The first should have concretized articles 5 and 48 of the 1977 Constitution. In reality, the final text did not even use the word "referendum." In entirely generic terms, it confirmed that important issues would be subject to public debate: an entirely formal and discredited practice that had been in effect for some time. The mountain was once more turned into a molehill; this judicial language was reminiscent of Brezhnev's time. There was great disappointment, at least in politicized circles. Nor did the other law approved introduce much of anything new. It confirmed the right to "bring suit" against a public official (that already existed, even if it was never applied), but its formulas were too convoluted and its clauses too complex for the law to truly defend the rights of the individual against the extreme power of the bureaucracies. In short, what came out of the offices of the Kremlin and of the Old Square continued to leave an aura of staleness in its wake.

However, the month of July saw more lively events, debates, and clashes in the country, and not just in Moscow. In the republics, and especially in the Baltic States, there were already marked symptoms of this great reawakening, deeply imbued with nationalistic claims. On 14 June there was a demonstration in Riga at the Monument to Freedom, a symbol, *Moskovskiye Novosti* wrote, "of the Latvian bourgeois state overturned by the people in the summer of 1940." A number of indignant readers (clearly non-Latvians), wrote letters complaining about the demonstrations to the Riga party organ.

The response came as a surprise: "It is time to stop seeing what are now unusual phenomena as subversion . . . the process of democratization is very complex, and perhaps that which is considered unacceptable today could become commonplace tomorrow."[3] These words anticipated the events of 1988. At any rate, there was an uninterrupted succession of breaks with tradition, and of unprecedented positions. Gennadi Lisichkin, a department head at the Institute for the Economy of the International Socialist System, made public at a press conference that he was studying a strategy to turn the ruble into a currency that could be exchanged in international markets.[4] The campaign against Stalin gained even greater force. *Ogonyok* published the letter that Fyodor Raskolnikov had written to the dictator in 1939, on the eve of the war: it contained stinging criticism that Soviet readers had never before been allowed to see, raising the question of Stalin's responsibility for the decimation of the Red Army leadership.[5]

There were more signals of a huge fermentation expressed in forms that were still uncertain and tentative. The first "unauthorized" magazine, *Glasnost*, came out; there were only fifty copies of the initial issue, reproduced on a photocopying machine. Promoted by the "political" ex-convict Sergei Grigoryants, this was an aboveground samizdat meant to test the reactions of the authorities. It was in clear violation of Soviet laws, but no one took the initiative to forcibly close it down.[6] This was on 3 July. Three days later a group of about thirty Crimean Tatars demonstrated in Red Square, demanding that they be allowed to return to their native land. Their head, Rishat Dzemelev, disclosed that their delegation had been received at the Kremlin on 25 June by Pyotr Demichev.[7] At Chernobyl a trial began against six defendants in the disaster. The public and foreign journalists were only allowed to follow the opening session. The common people lost out, but two days later, on 10 July, the TV news program "Vremya" announced that the chairman of the Ukraine Council of Ministers, Aleksandr Lyashko, had been dismissed. He was accused of "inefficiency" in the rescue operations in the days following the catastrophe.

Taken as a whole, these symptoms create the impression of a laborious search for legal certainty, a new system of relations between political forces, and standards to regulate social and democratic life. Glasnost had now made it possible to stare the country's problems in the face. Prostitution had always been considered nonexistent, but was now recognized as a social problem. The Supreme Soviet of the RSFSR introduced a new article in the Penal Code that defined prostitution as a crime punishable by administrative penalties, but not by incarceration. There was also news regarding freedom of movement. The head of the Visa Office at the Interior Ministry, Rudolf Kuznetsov, gave an interview with *Novoye Vremya* disclosing that the new law, which went into effect on 1 January 1987, would be even further expanded. Visas to travel abroad would be issued not only to those who had close relatives outside of the country, but also to those who were invited by acquaintances. Soviet citizens who lived abroad could now return to their homeland more than once a year. The limits on tourism were kept, but in practice the only obstacle remaining was currency. The newspapers published protest letters that asked for an end to the humiliating procedure known as *kharakteristika*; *kharakteristika* is the arbitrary power that party organizations have to make the irrevocable decision whether to issue or deny authorization to leave the country to anyone, including non–party members.[8]

Glasnost was also applied to the field of psychiatry. *Izvestia* was the first to denounce abuses and the lack of adequate regulations to safeguard citizens' rights.[9] There was also glasnost regarding the state of social and family morality. The sociologist Konstantin Kartsev published a disturbing article in the party's theoretical magazine that gave disastrous statistics on the condition of the family in the Soviet Union: a high number of divorces; a sharp increase in the number of illegitimate children and in child abandonment; an uncontrolled rise in congenital mental illness due to parental alcoholism; a third of all children were born out of wedlock. In short, the Soviets were getting to know themselves better and to search for remedies to the social ills that had been born—and neglected—in the long post-Stalin years.[10]

The only sign of opposition was Yegor Ligachev's visit to the offices of *Sovetskaya Kultura*, one of the newspapers most clearly on the side of renewal. His inspection lasted two days and ended with a report extremely critical of the editors. The writers, Ligachev said, must remain "profoundly faithful to party ideology."[11] It was time for some adjustments, which came just two days later. Gorbachev held a meeting of the representatives of the mass media, with Aleksandr Yakovlev present, and gave a cautious speech, clearly aimed at calming everyone down and preventing the dispute from getting worse. The main subject of a seven-hour discussion was the assessment of Stalin. The Soviet leader chose the road of mediation. On the one hand, he defended the supporters of glasnost (the debate, he said, "has been carried on till now within the limits of the struggle for socialism"). If someone wished to push "beyond the confines of socialism," then "the Central Committee would subject these positions to public criticism, and express in principle its own position within the limits of democracy and glasnost." Thus, the Soviet leader affirmed that he did not want to block debate through preventive measures. The party also had the right to criticize, since it was a participant in the debate. On the other extremely delicate point, "the party's guiding role," Gorbachev embraced the traditional formula. Radical reform of the party did not cast doubt on "its mission as society's guiding force." Finally, regarding Stalin, Gorbachev anticipated a formula he would use in November: "The Soviet people will never forgive or justify the repressions of the late 1930s."[12] His compromise restrained the debate, but did not end it.

At this point the conservatives decided to come out into the open. The celebrations for the seventieth anniversary of the October Revolution were approaching and the country's climate was not at all "festive." The conservatives' aim was not just to influence the speech that Mikhail Gorbachev would deliver in November. Various points of their argument focused exclusively on the general secretary of the party. The fuse was lit by the assistant editor of *Molodaya Gvardia*, Vyacheslav Gorbachev. His visible targets were the weekly *Ogonyok* and its editor in chief, Vitali Korotich; *Moskovskiye Novosti* and its editor in chief, Yegor Yakovlev; Aleksandr Bek's novel *The New Appointment*; the weekly *Nedelya*; *Sovetskaya Kultura*; *Oktyabr*; and the entire series of magazines that had embraced glasnost. Vyacheslav Gorbachev said that their editors in chief "direct readers toward shabby tastes, toward a petit-bourgeois morality that all too frequently coincides with the amorality and the consumerism of Western mass culture." Glasnost "is a double-edged sword, and in inexperienced hands it can hurt the person using it [who ventures to adopt] the rather suspect systems of glasnost and democracy in the Western press."

This seemed more like a mafia-style warning than criticism. Its almost obsessive leitmotif was in the classical Stalinist style: the reformers were the Trojan horse of Western penetration. While Mikhail Gorbachev had stated that he had no substantial criticism of the media's behavior, the deputy editor of *Molodaya Gvardia* lambasted *Moskovskiye Novosti* for the "grave and dangerous mistake" of exposing itself to "a provocation disguised as political ambition" in publishing the letter from ten dissident émigrés—with a response, moreover, "in a conciliatory style." Vyacheslav Gorbachev did not hide behind periphrasis. He quoted Vsevolod Kochetov in claiming that Stalin was "more of a victim of the bureaucratic apparatus than we realize." He attacked historians who, "instead of striving to explain history, prove that they do not want to forgive Stalin." (Here it is obvious that the argument was also directed against Gorbachev himself). Once again he raised the accusation of collusion with the West, where "there are certainly those who cannot forgive Stalin for winning the war against the Nazis."[13]

Rapid responses were heard simultaneously from *Ogonyok* and *Sovetskaya Kultura*. The latter carried a particularly harsh commentary, unsigned, but written by its editor in chief, Albert Belyayev: *Molodaya Gvardia* "does not want to let the changes through, and to that end, it defames those who are enacting them." Vyacheslav Gorbachev had peppered his article with heavy political allusions that needed clarification. For example, what was the meaning of the quote from Vasili Fyodorov: "Don't overturn the ancient tombs, they threaten new disasters"? To whom was it addressed? "Does *Molodaya Gvardia* really not know what the leaders of our party say about it?"[14] *Ogonyok* in its turn called Anatoli Ivanov's staff an outright Stalinist den that "is unequaled in this country for its adherence to old sympathies and ties, and for its factionalism."[15] At first glance, *Molodaya Gvardia* would seem to have taken a false step and to have left its sides exposed to a counterattack. But it would quickly become apparent that Vyacheslav Gorbachev's remarks had instead been a trap with an authoritative cover. Belyayev was, in fact, sternly reprimanded on the orders of men in Ligachev's entourage. As if that were not enough, *Pravda* would shortly thereafter publish a harsh criticism of *Sovetskaya Kultura*, accusing it of lacking "a tradition of debate."[16]

This was the most open clash since the beginning of perestroika, and it disclosed the existing level of tensions. It was based on unprecedented events: in the center of the capital, right in Red Square, the Crimean Tatars held repeated demonstrations. The police did not step in to suppress them. The evening news of 23 July correctly reported that the demonstrators "had addressed the party and Soviet bodies with the request to 'restore the autonomous republic of Crimea.' "[17] It was learned that on 9 July a special committee of the Supreme Soviet chaired by Gromyko had been formed to study the situation.[18] In the meantime, while similar protests were taking place in Tashkent, Samarkand, and Fergana, Gromyko himself (at the head of a weighty delegation from the Politburo that included Yakovlev, Vorotnikov, Shcherbitsky, and Chebrikov) received a delegation of the protesters and recognized the need to "do justice." The protest, however, did not stop, and only at this point did the police receive new orders: on 30 July a new demonstration in Pushkin Square was blocked, and many of the six hundred Tatars who had gathered in Moscow were sent back home with compulsory transit papers. On 3 August, in Dzhanzhul, in the vicinity of Tashkent, the police set up a blockade of armored cars to stop over five thousand demonstrators.

The duel between newspapers and magazines saw even more histrionics. At the beginning of August the party newspaper published a protest from a department head in the Ministry of Justice, Viktor Sukalo, over the "inexactness," the "distortion of the facts and the insulting tone," with which certain newspapers treated the magistrates. Sukalo wrote, "In the last two years in the Soviet press over two hundred articles have appeared criticizing the activities of the Prosecutor's Office, and about eighty of these have been about the magistrates."[19] The next week *Moskovskiye Novosti* "rehabilitated" Aleksandr Chayanov and a group of fifteen Soviet scientists suppressed by

Stalin. The paper stated that the "Peasant Party" had never existed, that all the accusations had been fabricated, and that all the confessions had been extorted.[20] In the meantime, the historian Yuri Afanasev disclosed to the Yugoslavian *Tanjung* that the Military Board of the Supreme Court was at work reexamining the trials in the 1930s, including Bukharin's. But these were only pinpricks compared to what was being prepared.

On 21 August *Pravda* published a full-page article entitled "The Fatherland Is Given to Us Only Once, and For All Our Lives." The article was signed by Vera Tkachenko, a relatively unknown editor on the paper's staff. But the presentation, the emphasis, and the content appeared to be "inspired" by an authority that was far greater than that of the "author." This was an outright attack on the "revisitation" of Soviet history. Tkachenko wrote, "We are proud of every day that we have lived." On the surface, her argument echoed formulations recently used by Mikhail Gorbachev. There are people "drunken with glasnost," who go too far with "denunciations and denials." It is alright to talk about "errors," but "we must not erase what we have accomplished through seventy years of Soviet power." The continued disclosures of the repressions raised the question "whether in this way we are not discrediting the history of the homeland itself." Tkachenko's prose gushed with pathos: "With sorrow we sometimes read statements that sound like apologies to the West. . . . It would seem that seventy years after the October Revolution, everything except the NEP was negative and weak, and now we want to correct ourselves." If Gorbachev described perestroika as a revolution, Tkachenko talked about it as a "continuation of our traditions, which does not mean giving up our historical patrimony." Gorbachev said more democracy, more socialism. Tkachenko inverted the factors and corrected them: "More socialism, more of our socialist democracy." Nor did her arsenal of topics neglect an allusion to the Jews: "There is only one fatherland: to say that the land of your ancestors is somewhere else and to want to go there is nothing more than a cover for treason."[21]

Mutatis mutandis, this was the same thesis presented by *Molodaya Gvardia*, but now with the more authoritative imprimatur of *Pravda*. Officially, Gorbachev was still in Moscow; Tass did not report his departure for the holidays. But the political climate was changing abruptly, and the capital was full of restlessness.

The first sign of a harder line was the central media's reaction to the waves of nationalist demonstrations in the Baltic Republics. Vilnius, Riga, and Tallinn were caught up in a controversial commemoration of the Molotov-Ribbentrop pact (also called the Nazi-Soviet pact) of 1939; ten thousand people demonstrated in Riga. Tass and *Pravda* wrote that the demonstrations had been instigated by Western radio stations. The official news agency claimed that the Vilnius demonstration had been a "fiasco" and that the Tallinn demonstrations had been witnessed by "many hundreds of bystanders."[22] In the same days the unauthorized magazine *Glasnost* disclosed that the Soviet judiciary archives for the 1930s, 1940s, and 1950s had been systematically destroyed at the rate of five thousand files a month because of a "lack of space." These were the archives of the Military Court and of the Supreme Court. The archives of the Justice Ministry had already been cleaned out in the 1960s and 1970s. No one knew where the KGB's archives were or what had become of them. *Glasnost* claimed that the beginning of the operation had happened when Justice Minister Vladimir Terebilov became head of the Supreme Court.[23] But cultural circles did not stop their criticism. The magazine *Teatr* published an interview with Andrei Sakharov, who was in the audience at a performance of Mikhail Bulgakov's *Heart of a Dog*, staged by the Teatr Yunogo Zritelya. This represented two firsts in one: Bulgakov's work had never been staged in the USSR, and Sakharov was being interviewed for the first time since the end of his Gorky exile. *Literaturnaya Gazeta* had tried in January, but Sakharov had refused to make any corrections to the text, so the interview was never published.

The tenor of the situation, however, was dominated by Ligachev's position. Three days after Vera Tkachenko's sortie, the party's number-two man gave a speech to the teachers of Elektroshtal, a small city, confirming his efforts to force a serious ideological shift, and to "theoretically" impose a restraining line on the "revision." Ligachev said, "Our country has committed errors, but they have always been accompanied by real successes." The events of the 1930s had been accompanied by excesses, but "in those years our country reached the number-two position in the world for industrial production; it collectivized agriculture and reached unprecedented levels in the development of culture, education, literature, and the arts." Criticism is necessary, but "there are some in the West, and even some in the USSR, who try to discredit the entire history of the construction of socialism in the Soviet Union; through their talk of unjustified repressions, they end up overshadowing the achievements of the people who consolidated socialist power in the USSR."[24] The object of his reprimand was the surge of revelations regarding Stalin's crimes. But the tone and content of Ligachev's speech appeared quite different from what Gorbachev's words had been in mid-July. The secretary-general had limited himself to denouncing the repressions of 1937 and 1938, but he had used scorching words: "There were heavy losses. We know what the years 1937 and 1938 led to, and how they struck the party cadres, the intellectuals, and the military commanders." And there was his crucial sentence: "The people will never be able to forgive this."[25] There was an obvious split in emphasis, revealing, among other things, that there had been a sharp evolution in both Gorbachev's position and in the public debate. In fact, in February 1986, the Soviet leader had been high-handed and disdainful about Stalinism in an interview he gave to *L'Humanité*: "Stalinism is a concept invented by the enemies of communism and is widely used to portray both the Soviet Union and socialism in dark colors." Thus, the term "Stalinism" had no validity and was radically rejected by the party's top leader. But one year later Gorbachev's words already expressed a different approach, and in the midst of the festive climate of the summer of 1987, the denunciation of Stalin's crimes was giving way to a more comprehensive criticism of the political and economic system constructed in those years. Use of the term "Stalinism" become widespread in a few short months. But there was a not so subtle component in Ligachev's approach: the relationship he posited between foreign "plots" and criticism on the home front. This was a constant that could easily be traced back to positions expressed both by *Molodaya Gvardia* and by Vera Tkachenko's article. Reading between the lines, the entire conservative front was expressing a vision of an ideological struggle on a worldwide scale, and of a division of the world into two opposing systems—an approach that differed substantially from that of Gorbachev, Yakovlev, Shevardnadze, and Dobrynin.

The other subject Ligachev touched on forcefully was economic reform. In the mind of the number-two Soviet citizen, perestroika was quite different from what Mikhail Gorbachev thought and said. At Elektroshtal, Ligachev repeated more clearly than before that the "class enemies" would gladly see "the Soviet Union move away from socialism and move toward a market economy, pluralism, and Western-style democracy." Undoubtedly, positions of this type were widespread among the Soviet intelligentsia, and Gorbachev himself had argued with them. But none of the top economists on Gorbachev's team had ever talked about installing a "market economy" in the USSR. The real debate centered on the question of "how much market" was needed to revitalize the economic mechanism and in what new terms to cast the relationship between the plan and the market. Here Ligachev left no doubts: "moving toward" the market meant "moving away from socialism." The whole debate about Lenin's NEP and the "rehabilitation" of Bukharin's ideas was thus canceled in one fell swoop. Here his differences with positions expressed by Gorbachev were clear, not only because in June the Soviet leader had indicated the need for a "radical reform of prices," which hypothesized a broad intervention into the way the market determined them; not just because Gorbachev had spoken about enterprises that "must start to compete with each other to better meet the demand"; but especially because in January Gorbachev had bared the roots of the "once indisputable truths" of the administrative command economy, which had been transformed into "prejudices against the roles of the relationship of money to goods and the law of value, which are not infrequently presented as contrary or alien to socialism." There were no doubts: Ligachev's arguments were not so much aimed at the most extreme reformist wing as they were at the political line of the general secretary of the Communist Party.

Gorbachev had departed for his summer holiday, and his absence from Moscow was felt immediately. But the hints of a struggle underway remained contradictory. Gennadi Gerasimov, the spokesman for the foreign minister, was invited to Warsaw, partly to follow up on the decision made by Gorbachev and Wojciech Jaruzelski in April to create a bilateral commission of historians with the task of "filling in the blank pages" on relations between the Soviet Union and Poland.[26] The Polish people could read long excerpts from an essay by Jaruzelski published in *Kommunist* that contained an open condemnation of the "political and military plots by the Soviet government" in 1939, which he called "anti-Leninist and opposed to Poland's right to independence." This was the first explicit condemnation of the Molotov-Ribbentrop pact, of the deportation of Polish citizens in 1940–41, and of the 1939 purges of the Polish party on the grounds, wrote General Jaruzelski, of "inflammatory and baseless accusations."[27] Thus, the anti-Stalinist offensive continued, and also spread to the leadership of "brother" countries.

The only member of the Politburo who publicly and systematically supported a "different" interpretation of perestroika was Yegor Ligachev. The others kept their mouths shut. But the evolution of the situation left an opening for other opinions. Now it was Viktor Chebrikov's turn. His attack was harsh and unequivocal. At the celebration of the 110th anniversary of the birth of Feliks Dzherzhinski, the chairman of the KGB said: "Among us there are carriers of ideas and viewpoints alien and even openly hostile to socialism"; people who "due to political naivité or some other reason have ended up perceiving the process of spreading democracy as a chance to do whatever passes through their minds." These include people "who are under the influence of the Western secret service." There is no shortage of "representatives of the artistic intelligentsia . . . enthralled by stances of hypercriticism, demagogy, and nihilism, and the denigration of certain stages in the historical development of our society."[28]

His "arguments" are typical of Stalinism. He wanted to close the debate, and label anyone who offered alternative ideas as "enemies of the people," guilty of "collusion with the enemy." A plot to silence the most exposed wing of perestroika had become evident, but it took place in a hidden, evolutionary way, carefully avoiding any emphasis on clashes with the ruling group. One of the "spokesmen" of the conservative line, Viktor Afanasev, the editor in chief of *Pravda*, brilliantly applied this tactic during a press conference in Paris. According to his version, the history of disagreements between Gorbachev and Ligachev was nothing more than "an invention of the West." Afanasev used his own personal experience to support his statements. He disclosed that he had a permanent invitation to meetings of the Politburo, and that he had been to every one; never had he heard "Comrade Ligachev say anything in disagreement with Mikhail Gorbachev's ideas." Obviously, they expressed "different points of view," but in a "common language."[29] This triumph was fitting for a man who for all his importance was still the supporting actor.

The true protagonists instead spoke a less cryptic language. Once again Ligachev called a meeting of the leaders of the mass media, the directors of the "creative unions" and of propaganda, where he heavily criticized "some publications" that "haven't known how to find the right orientation." The official text gave no names of persons or publications, but shortly afterward it was learned that there had been well-targeted denunciations at the meeting. The party's number-two man supported his criticisms with "the sentiments of public opinion," as evidenced in a flurry of letters published by *Pravda*. Ligachev said that the people do not like "certain episodes of history to be represented at times in a unilateral way." Like many of *Pravda*'s readers, Ligachev maintained that to deal thoroughly with the reexamination of party history was equivalent to "showing a disrespectful attitude toward the generations who constructed socialism." To that end the editorial boards were peremptorily told to "refer to the materials of the Twenty-Seventh Congress, to the plenum of the Central Committee, and to Mikhail Gorbachev's speeches." But not just these: now they also had to take into account speeches "by other party and state leaders." It was quite true, Ligachev continued, that starting with the April 1985 plenum various materials had appeared in the press that reflected different points of view:

> This constitutes a manifestation of democracy . . . [but] certain editors gladly publish only what corresponds to their own points of view, while what doesn't correspond is either not published, or it is accompanied by critical editorials. In this way a one-way democracy will emerge, which we must put a stop to.[30]

This had unquestionably been the most energetic reprimand yet effected during the age of glasnost. The journalistic and intellectual world was in an uproar. The report given by Tass was fairly reliable, but there were immediate leaks to the press about the "true" contents of the discussion.[31] Ligachev had explicitly criticized *Moskovskiye Novosti* and its editor in chief, Yegor Yakovlev; *Ogonyok* and its editor in chief, Vitali Korotich; *Sovetskaya Kultura*; and the authors of various articles that had appeared in other magazines. *Moskovskiye Novosti* was targeted in particular for providing a voice for

121

"enemies from abroad" who "are reorganizing their ranks," and who are uniting all the reactionary forces into "a single front," rekindling "suggestions of nationalism." This was the tone and the logic of the cold war. The ideological bridge with Chebrikov's speech was clear. But Ligachev also pointed to the example of Vera Tkachenko's article, which had stimulated a flood of letters of agreement. By contrast, he said, there are some journalists who "have exceeded the limits of the trust given to them." He was asking for resignations, a fact made even clearer by Ligachev's stating that the policy "is still firmly in the hands of the Central Committee"—in other words, in his own hands. He ended with a warning not to criticize *Pravda*, because it was the publication of the Central Committee and therefore to be considered above reproach. At this point the unpredictable happened. Yegor Yakovlev, who had been put on the defendant's bench for having published Viktor Nekrasov's obituary, asked for permission to speak and stated his disagreement with these opinions. "If you ask me to leave, I will," he said in essence, "but I would argue that I have been consistent with the directives of the party's Twenty-Seventh Congress." The only other person who asked to speak was Sergei Mikhalkov, who expressed his support for Ligachev's line. Everyone else was silent. Gorbachev was still officially on vacation. In Moscow many thought that Yegor Yakovlev would be fired from the staff of *Moskovskiye Novosti*, and there was great unrest.

But not everyone was overcome by fear. One of those who signed Nekrasov's obituary, Grigori Baklanov, editor in chief of *Znamya*, decided to publish an essay in response to "Incognito," by Yuri Karyakin. It was the most violent indictment of the Stalinists that had yet been published by a Soviet newspaper. It was known that "Incognito" was a specific person: the rector of the University of Rostov on the Don, Yuri Zhdanov, son of the man after whom the University of Leningrad is named. Karyakin offered a behind-the-scenes look at a letter against Boris Mozhayev.[32] Yuri Zhdanov had initially sent the letter to the magazine *Don* and then withheld it "until a more favorable time." Was everyone waiting for a return of the flames of prohibition and censorship? If this was the objective, then the reactionary conspiracy must be denounced immediately. *Znamya*'s move was a challenge. Ligachev could not silence Baklanov, and Yegor Yakovlev's position was unchanged.

But Gorbachev still did not return to Moscow after what had seemed like an unusually long vacation. Rumors were flying. *Bild Zeitung* wrote that Gorbachev had been the victim of food poisoning, hinting that he may have been deliberately poisoned. The Swedish daily *Expressen* reported instead that Raisa Maksimovna had been operated on for appendicitis, and that there had been serious complications; Gorbachev had stayed by her side to help her through the two-week recovery period in the hospital. Semiofficial sources leaked that the Soviet leader's vacation was not as long as it seemed, since he had not left until 22 August. The fact remained that Gorbachev's last public appearance had been on 22 August, at a reception in the Kremlin for a group of American teachers of Russian. The spokesman on duty for the Foreign Ministry, Boris Pyadyshev, had to respond to the foreign correspondents' entreaties by saying, "Gorbachev is still on vacation and he is in perfect health."[33] The uncertainty lasted for a few more days.

On 29 September Mikhail Gorbachev reappeared in public, visiting and conversing with 370 French guests, including Pierre Mauroy, the former prime minister. Soviet TV broadcast the entire event. He had been absent from the political scene for fifty-two long days, during which many revealing things had happened. He said: "I think that some people think that I took too long a vacation. But I can tell you that I've earned it." He wrote a book, *Perestroika*, that would quickly become an international best-seller. But in the meantime his line had been hard hit. "There is no political opposition in the Soviet Union," he said to French guests. But he added a sentence with multiple meanings, raising even more questions. The hopes of those who would use glasnost and democratization to "instigate social upheaval . . . are in vain." Where was this warning addressed? Home or abroad? Gorbachev certainly didn't give the impression that he was in any difficulty. The day before, *Pravda* had "taken note" of his return to Moscow by publishing as an editorial a collection of six letters from workers, all in favor of perestroika and glasnost.[34] This abrupt change in direction looked like blatant revenge after the repeated "discourtesies" that the party paper had allowed itself in August. Gorbachev, however, did not stop in the capital for long. On 1 October he was in Murmansk, where he delivered a solid speech: The political climate of the country has changed, but the people are waiting for concrete things. The new economic mechanism has one protagonist: the people. Two tools by which it can be accomplished are democracy and adequate incentives. The month of October began with obvious signs of glasnost's progress. *Ogonyok* told the story of Vasili Grossman and his novel *Life and Fate*.[35] *Sovetskaya Rossia* commemorated the figure of Nikolai Vavilov.[36] A few days later Boris Yeltsin shocked the diplomatic corps with an entirely unusual initiative. He held a meeting of the ambassadors and told them about the problems of perestroika in the capital. This was a kind of rough report, as a result of which a good twenty-three *raikom* (district committee) secretaries were replaced. *Literaturnaya Gazeta* threw new light on the Stalinist repressions. In a debate between Feliks Kuznetsov and the historian Yuri Polyakov, it leaked out that the 20 million who died in World War II were not the only victims of that period; another 6-to-7 million died "of other causes" between 1940 and 1946 alone.[37]

There was no lack of counterattacks from the opposite side. Tass attacked the unauthorized magazine *Glasnost* (which had continued to come out regularly since its creation) and the police detained two activists and sequestered seventy copies of the latest issue. The detainees were accused of using the materials and press equipment belonging to a state organization.[38] On 13 October Gorbachev departed for Leningrad. In his speech to the party rank and file he announced the preparation of the Nineteenth Party Conference, the Conference on Organization, and emphasized the need for perestroika in the party. On the same day the first joint venture was born in Moscow. It was to be called "Sovetprodmash," formed by an Italian multinational corporation, FATA of Turin, and the Ministry for the Construction of Food Industry Machines.

Meanwhile, the celebrations of the seventieth anniversary of the October Revolution were approaching, leaving many questions unanswered. Would Bukharin be rehabilitated? What new theoretical outline did Gorbachev and the ruling Soviet group have for the numerous problems opened up by democratization? On 18 October, the eve of the opening of the Supreme Soviet, Gorbachev spoke before hundreds of managers of the agroindustrial complex. "If the people notice serious changes in the supply of foodstuffs, that will be the best propaganda for perestroika."[39] This was a grave problem, but in this area there has still been virtually no progress. Then, all of a sudden, it was officially announced that a plenum of the Communist Party's Central Committee would be held. The business of the day was Gorbachev's speech at the Kremlin Palace of Congresses to celebrate seventy years of Soviet power.

The meeting was held on 21 October. At the end of the preparations it was learned that there was one more item on the agenda: the "organizational issues." Geidar Aliyev was forced into retirement, making him the fifth member of the Politburo to be removed from the political stage since April 1985. But a surprise awaited Gorbachev. The first to speak was Boris Yeltsin, but not to discuss the business of the day. He gave a short, explosive speech. The Moscow party chief announced that he was resigning because it had become impossible to continue work because of the meddling and the outright sabotage that Yegor Ligachev had been practicing against him. It was a virulent attack: perestroika is not moving forward, Yeltsin said, because there are too many uncertainties and because too many opponents of change are given a free hand. He started by saying that Gorbachev had asked him to be patient and to "defer the question until after the celebrations." But he could not wait any longer. He personally attacked Yegor Ligachev, accusing him of having a "work style" that did not correspond to perestroika. Secondly, he accused "certain members of the Politburo" of deliberately lapsing into an exaltation of the general secretary of the party, thereby imitating "past errors." Finally, he stated that it was necessary to put an end to the practice of proclaiming objectives that were either unachievable or that could not be achieved in the space of "two to three years." All of this, along with his ascertainment of the "lack of help especially from Comrade Ligachev" led to his request to be excused "from the functions and duties of a candidate member of the Politburo."[40]

Yeltsin's speech upset the programmed course of the plenum. Many of those present reacted angrily. He had upset sensitive balances and had shattered the illusion of unanimity. This set him against all the apparats. But he also said that perestroika was not moving forward. By so doing, he alienated himself from the reformers, who were well aware of the current difficulties, but could not acknowledge the strength of the pressures on them without further weakening their position. Twenty-five people signed up to speak, including ten members of the Politburo. Almost all of them declared their opposition to Yeltsin and rejected his pessimistic judgment on the progress of perestroika. Ligachev led the demolishing offensive himself, accusing Yeltsin of worsening the situation in Moscow by his replacement of cadres "without criteria," and by his populistic moralism. At this point Gorbachev tried to salvage what he could.[41] Yeltsin's "rash act" had provided the occasion for a conservative onslaught. Thus, he proposed suspending discussion of the subjects raised by Yeltsin until after the celebrations. But Yeltsin, who by now had decided to push for an accounting—perhaps convinced that he could garner support, and possibly convinced that he could no longer sustain his position in Moscow, where the apparat considered him public enemy number one—asked to speak once more and restated his wish to resign. After his second intervention, ninety-four members signed up to speak. Gorbachev could do nothing to save Yeltsin, even if he had wished to, and at this point there was no knowing if he did. The resignation of Moscow's first secretary would be studied by the Party Committee. The issue of whether some other candidate members of the Politburo would stay or go would be decided by the Politburo and brought to the attention of the Central Committee at its next meeting. But the overwhelming majority of Central Committee members had already expressed their opinion—Yeltsin had to go.

The game, however, was not over. Abroad, people would learn what had happened only nine days later. On 30 October, the *New York Times* and *El País* revealed the outlines of the political clash inside the plenum. The news traveled around the world. The next morning Vadim Zagladin answered reporters' questions by categorically denying these disclosures, but he was in turn rebutted that evening by Anatoli Lukyanov, a member of the Secretariat of the Central Committee and head of the General Affairs Department. Lukyanov held a press conference at the Foreign Ministry and verified that at the plenum "different points of view were disputed," and Boris Yeltsin "issued his request to resign" after conflicts with other members of the Central Committee who had rejected his interpretations. Finally, Yeltsin himself acknowledged that his intervention had been "mistaken." As a result of this occurrence, "the Politburo and the Moscow Party Committee found it opportune to examine the issues stemming from such a statement." For decades there had been no such public disclosures about what had gone on behind the scenes at a Central Committee meeting. But Lukyanov indirectly denied the leaks regarding attacks on Gorbachev. Yeltsin had indeed personally criticized "members of the Politburo," he said, but on the issue of policy lines added: "All the participants of the plenum, I underline 'all,' shared the formulations of the Politburo of the Communist Party of the Soviet Union and of Comrade Gorbachev." In other words, what Gorbachev would say to open the celebrations of the seventieth anniversary of the October Revolution had been unanimously approved.

When Tass reported Lukyanov's speech, however, it added a note nineteen minutes later (only on an internal cable meant for Soviet newspapers) "categorically" ordering journalists not to use "Lukyanov's response to questions concerning the first secretary of the Moscow party."[42] The "internal" blackout probably signaled uncertainties over what line to follow, as was seen in Zagladin's denials immediately followed by Lukyanov's confirmations. Yeltsin's ouster would clearly be interpreted as a victory for Gorbachev's opponents, and as proof that the general secretary's allies were within firing range. The fear that this dispute could have significant repercussions was entirely justified: Yeltsin was extremely popular among the people in Moscow (and in Sverdlovsk). The people eagerly read his heated condemnations of misdeeds by the apparats. Everyone remembered that his speech at the Twenty-Seventh Congress had been the most courageous. The intelligentsia were not the only ones to interpret his appointment as party chief in the capital as a concrete sign of renewal. Young people especially saw in him an honest man ready for openness. This is why in this period people were under the strong impression that efforts were being made to save Yeltsin. It could not be ruled out that the disclosures to the *New York Times* and *El País* had been planted by others in order to explode the case in public and prevent a "restitching." A few days later came confirmation that the situation was still open. During the course of a press conference on Gorbachev's speech, Aleksandr Yakovlev said that "no one is raising the issue of his [Yeltsin's] dismissal." Yakovlev specified that there had been an argument, since "we argue things out in the Politburo, and the opposite would be strange." Yakovlev stated his agreement with the things said by Yeltsin, on the merit of "certain points."[43] The climate of public opinion was still white-

126

hot. Yeltsin himself spoke at the Bolshoi Theater (with Ligachev and She-vardnadze sitting next to him) and did not deny his own combative intentions:

> Are we ready to promote the cause of perestroika with perseverance? Is our revolutionary spirit high enough? Are we doing everything possible to live and work according to Lenin's commandments? These are the positions on the basis of which each one of us must evaluate his or her own place in the general formation.[44]

These words were a challenge to those sitting next to him on the stage, and certainly not the farewell speech of someone who had resigned. There were fiery debates at the Writers' House with Aleksandr Bovin requesting the publication of Khrushchev's "Secret Report." The Vakhtangov Theater gave the first performance of Shatrov's new play *The Brest Peace* to a highly select audience. The first fliers in support of Yeltsin began to appear on Gorky Street. There was a restless atmosphere all around. Nobody knew exactly what was happening, or what the terms of the dispute with the Central Committee were. Many people feared that the conservatives, who had issued warning signs in August, had begun their offensive. Some thought that the battle was already lost.

Gorbachev's speech at the Palace of the Congresses would dispel many, but not all, of the reformers' apprehensions. It was a compromise that allowed one to read between the lines the conditions binding the Soviet leader. He did not give up on the general line. In his three-hour speech Gorbachev presented a great historical fresco of this phase of the battle, with restorations and finishing touches that were so cautious in places as to seem uncertain. He made an energetic defense of perestroika against those "who try to intim-idate us by arguing that the costs are too high. Our answer is that the cost of stagnation is much higher." But there was also a broadside—and here the reference to Yeltsin is obvious—against "impatience." In the area of historical reflection Gorbachev succeeded in going much further than the things he had already said at the January and June plenums. It is true that he repeated that the forced collectivization of the countryside and accelerated industrial-ization had been "necessary" choices. But now he said that they had been accompanied by "huge losses," and he denounced the mistakes that had been made, the lawlessness, the indiscriminate repression of average farmers, the spread of central administrative methods, the scorn for economic laws, to the point that "the brutal violations of the principles of collectivization took on a general character." His condemnation of Stalin was unprecedented. He was the one who "mechanically applied" the same methods of battle against the revolutionaries as had been adopted against the enemies of so-cialism. The theory of the intensification of the class struggle in the process of building socialism was constructed in an atmosphere of "intolerance, hostility, and distrust." "Outright crimes and abuses of power" were perpetrated. "The repression of the masses struck thousands of militants and nonparty members. This, comrades, is the bitter truth." It is "indispensable" to say so openly. Did Stalin have any virtues? Gorbachev said that he did, but the idea that he did not know about the repressions was no longer acceptable. The crimes of Stalin and his entourage "are unforgivable." The Twentieth and Twenty-Second congresses told us that "the repressions and political incriminations . . . were the result of a premeditated falsification." Yet the reestablishment of justice had not been completed. Gorbachev disclosed that at the October plenum he had formed a special committee to examine "new or already known facts and documents referring to these problems," thereby announcing that the process of de-Stalinization would continue. "Not to do so would hurt our reflections on democracy today." The historical reconstruction was still completely traditional in many respects; the much-awaited rehabilitation of Bukharin did not take place. But Lenin's opinion of Bukharin was cited, rehabilitating him as a revolutionary and as a Leninist. Trotsky was still an enemy of socialism, but the veil of silence enshrouding him, Aleksandr Zinoviev, and Lev Kamenev was rent.

One figure who did emerge almost completely relegitimized was Nikita Khrushchev. He too had made mistakes, but one had to recognize the "great courage" he had to have to unleash the attack against the cult of personality. If his efforts at reform had failed, Gorbachev said, it was because he had not known how to combine them with a proposal for the development of democracy in the country.[45] This is probably not all that Gorbachev wanted to say. The caution with which he confronted the historical revision of the seventy years that had gone by was the sign of a tense political struggle within the leadership. It would still be a mistake to consider this speech a mediation of the different tendencies inside the leadership. The Soviet leader knew well that these pressures reflected deep moods in the country, and not just in the apparats. The shocks he was causing were already strong enough. A celebration conducted under the banner of critical reflection was already such an innovation that it would be rejected by the most conservative sectors of society. To many the step taken seemed excessive, while to others it seemed to represent little more than an intention. But in reality it was a big step onto a new road.

Just how big would be shown a few days later, on 12 November, by the meeting of the Moscow Party Committee that ousted Boris Yeltsin. He was thrown out roughly, accused of "showing grave insufficiencies as a political leader"; by not simply accepting his request to resign, the Moscow plenum disclosed the depth of the fierce resistances in the capital's apparat. In an unprecedented move, the stenographer's report of this dramatic meeting would be published in its entirety by a few central newspapers.[46] Gorbachev opened the meeting with heavy charges against the former Moscow chief. He said that his intervention at the October plenum had been "politically immature . . . extremely confusing and contradictory . . . demagogical in form and content." The unquestionable popularity he had won in a short period of time had gone to his head, and he "ended up placing his own personal ambitions above the interests of the party." He demonstrated "complete theoretical and political inconsistency in his analysis of the progress of perestroika," and "he was incapable of understanding that there are short-term and long-term tasks."

But the accusations hurled at Yeltsin from the floor were far more violent and angry, an attempt to lynch him both morally and politically. The tone and language of this trial was very reminiscent of the trials in the 1930s. Gorbachev himself seemed surprised. The only thing he could do was to leave Yeltsin to his fate, though he nevertheless was forced to acknowledge the offensive launched by the most reactionary and intransigent sectors. This was not just a defeat for Yeltsin; his misjudgment reflected on Gorbachev too. This was one more reason to criticize him. But in his conclusions the Soviet leader sought to somehow soften the outcome of a disastrous meeting— if for no other reason than for fear of the image of the Moscow party that would emerge—by issuing a challenge to the floor:

> Our enemies call us Utopians and predict that we shall fail. They say this out of fear of our perestroika. . . . After the January and June plenums they were gripped by fear. . . . Sometimes you hear mountains of words about perestroika . . . but when you listen carefully you begin to perceive such a stale odor of mothballs that it makes you nauseous.

He did not wish to hide this bitter note, both political and human: "I suffer personally over what has happened." Then he suddenly shifted from the second-person plural to the singular: "I have to say, Boris Nikolayevich, they have really gotten in the way of your personal ambitions." At that moment Gorbachev realized that the apparat's offensive was really aimed against himself. Yeltsin's mangled, confusing, and contradictory speech dramatized his own fall and the political crisis it disclosed. He criticized himself, and acknowledged that he had lost, but he defended his right to dissent, and the validity of at least some of his criticisms. This was a speech by a man on the edge of psychological and physical collapse. The publication of the stenographer's report turned the public against the Moscow party and in favor of Yeltsin (perhaps the decision to disclose the contents of the discussions was really meant to provoke this response). The people wanted to know the truth, and they asked to hear exactly what Yeltsin had said on 21 October, along with the names of the leaders he had criticized. The official silence on this point showed the winners' weak spot, but it cast a shadow over Gorbachev, who could not comment. Seven months later, during the Nineteenth Party Conference, he would acknowledge that it would have been better to publish Yeltsin's speech to the October plenum immediately. But publishing this speech would have meant opening a case even more difficult to manage—the "Ligachev affair."

Unlike the first political crisis of perestroika, which took place inside the rooms of the Kremlin, the second took place under the sign of a public opinion excited by the first sparks of glasnost. This context could not tolerate the old methods of managing information about events that took place in the "palace of power." There were demonstrations in support of Yeltsin in different parts of the city, especially at the university. Although these episodes involved only a minority, they expressed a widespread unrest. The whole city was openly discussing and criticizing the decision to oust Yeltsin. It still was not clear if he would also leave the Politburo, nor what physical condition he was in. There were mounting rumors that Yeltsin was dying. The truth was, as official spokesmen gradually confirmed, that the former first secretary of Moscow had been taken to the hospital after the October plenum, and he had been brought to the Moscow plenum in precarious physical condition, heavily medicated and almost incoherent. Moscow intellectual circles, the groups that had bet everything on perestroika, took the blame. But the first signs of a counterattack began to appear. For days everyone in the stores and on the buses was talking about the Yeltsin case. Perhaps never before had the common people shown such an interest in politics.

Moskovskiye Novosti publicly stated its opinion in an article by the economist Gavriil Popov. Yeltsin had made a mistake, but attempts to lynch him for it were inadmissable. Many of those who attacked him had no right to pose as defenders of perestroika: "People who through their behavior have restrained the renewal of society are making themselves out to be authentic heros of perestroika, while a leader who truly supported it is fired for having made some mistakes."[47]

There were signs of discontent, demands for clarification, and outright protests among the party rank and file, and emergency meetings to explain what had happened to them. The official explanation, which made Yeltsin a scapegoat, did not convince even party members. It was at this point that the surprise announcement came that Yeltsin had been appointed deputy chairman of Gosstroi (State Committee for Construction) with ministerial rank. Yeltsin had been stripped of his rank and dismissed from the Politburo (his official expulsion would not be announced until the next plenum), but he had not completely left the scene. At the end of November the voice of the Moscow apparat would let itself be heard in a column in *Sovetskaya Rossia*, with an embarrassing query by the worker Vladimir Zatvornitsky, a Central Committee member and one of Yeltsin's most intransigent critics.[48]

But those who sensed the danger of an irreparable step backward had gone back into battle in an almost enraged state. *Ogonyok* published a letter to Gorbachev from Anna Mikhailovna Larina, Nikolai Bukharin's widow, requesting the full rehabilitation of her husband.[49] It seemed almost like a personal request from the Moscow intelligentsia to the general secretary of the party. The Moscow apparat had to face waves of criticism from the people. The appointment of Lev Zaikov to take Yeltsin's place proved that the conservatives' success had not been complete. Zaikov, who did not lose his place in the Secretariat of the Central Committee, carried a lot of weight in the Politburo and had the reputation for being an independent. Therefore, the Politburo maintained that the party in the capital city had to be kept under strong surveillance, demonstrating that the state of the organization was hardly satisfactory or sound. This was not a prize. The control of Moscow did not pass directly into the hands of the antiperestroika forces.

At the end of November, Gorbachev tried to give another sharp tug to the reins and called a meeting of the party's central apparat. He clearly realized the risk that the "Yeltsin affair" might spread to the provinces as a signal that perestroika was over. He repeated his criticisms of Yeltsin, but he also launched heavy broadsides against the Moscow party. It acted the same way it did before, he said, "doing nothing except making the society feverish, irritating the people, and agitating the social consciousness." Boris Yeltsin had virtually been put on trial. But, Gorbachev exclaimed, deliberately quoting one of the few balanced opinions heard at the Moscow plenum: "Where were we, the members of the Secretariat, the members of the Party Committee? For all of this was taking place in front of our eyes." In the next few months the preparation for the party conference would take place amid a fiery debate on the party itself. Party members were invited to participate, using "all the rights they are guaranteed in the bylaws," and to fight against efforts to organize rigged debates and against efforts (of which Gorbachev was well aware) to avoid, restrain, or repress criticism. Yeltsin's mistake was not knowing that "we do not make perestroika with ideal cadres, but with the cadres that we have." This was no compliment to the cadres. But "when you realize that a given person does not accept the new and refuses democratization, than he or she has to be put to the side with the greatest determination."[50]

The year ended with uncertainties. The unrest had not been quelled. The seesaw of news on rehabilitations saw successes and failures; but the names

Bukharin, Zinovev, and Kamenev still did not see the light. There was still formidable resistance to the reopening of those trials, but Soviet public opinion was already showing an unprecedented vitality. It was already known that two years of glasnost and of greater freedom of information had produced a sudden increase in the readership of newspapers and magazines. Now facts emerged proving that the people, reaching the millions, preferred the most unbiased and outspoken magazines. The subscription campaigns for 1988 saw a huge increase in orders for *Druzhba Narodov* (which had published Rybakov's *Children of the Arbat*), *Znamya*, *Novy Mir* (which would start publishing *Dr. Zhivago* in the next year's first issue), and *Ogonyok*. *Pravda*, which had stood out for its conservativism and its antiglasnost tactics, lost a million subscribers. At the same time, *Izvestia*, which had become one of the most interesting and critical newspapers, saw an increase of more than 2 million subscribers. At year's end Soviet TV broadcast an outstanding documentary by Igor Izkov and Mikhail Babak entitled "More Light," which carried images that Soviet viewers were seeing for the first time: pictures of Trotsky, Bukharin, and other Bolshevik leaders. These were accompanied by commentary that restored them to their rightful place in the history of the revolution. There had still been no official rehabilitations, but Soviet television had not expected any. It was a giant fresco reserving the harshest words for Stalin, and giving Khrushchev full credit for the Twentieth Congress; the only thing it left to Brezhnev was a list of his medals. The Dom Kino showed *Komissar*, Aleksandr Askoldov's first and only film, which had been buried for twenty years and miraculously saved from the destruction it was condemned to. Many members of the audience cried openly out of sadness for a time gone by; because many who worked in that troupe had not lived to see that day's triumph; because each individual remembered how many talented minds were forced not to produce, or to produce only for themselves. Many still feared that the transition to a new age was still being opposed by powerful and indomitable forces. The events of 1988 would prove that these fears were justified.

FIFTH CONVERSATION

THE YELTSIN AFFAIR AND OTHER UNIQUE DEVELOPMENTS

·   ·   ·

G.C. The "Yeltsin affair" marked a sharp political about-face. It was the first crisis inside the leadership that had come out of the Twenty-Seventh Congress.

R.M. The Yeltsin affair was the result of serious political problems. However, I don't think it can be called either a crisis or a political crisis. It was simply a political and personal conflict with what we'll call the "renewal coalition" for the sake of convenience. Officially, there are no factions or groups inside the Communist Party of the Soviet Union. According to the party bylaws, "The indestructible law of the life of the Communist Party of the Soviet Union is the unity of ideas and organization, the monolithism of its members . . . any manifestation of factionalism and of the creation of groups is incompatible with the Marxist-Leninist concept of the party, and is incompatible with membership in the party."[51]

However, the party, like any living organism, cannot exist, much less enact profound reforms and perestroika, without a struggle over ideas, without clashes over specific policies among its members and its leadership. The party had always had "informal" groups, gathered around specific ideas or programs, or specific leaders, or specific regional bases. From this perspective we can safely ascertain the existence of a conservative "Brezhnevite" group inside the party and its leadership. Its existence is well known to both party members and to common people, and it was derisively given labels such as the "Dnepropetrovsk mafia." After the exits of Tikhonov, Kunayev, Aliyev, Romanov, and Grishin—all members of the Brezhnev group—the group had only secondary importance. Yet it would be hasty to say that the conservative groups have no influence on the party leadership.

There are already differences among the leaders of the "renewal coalition" over the programs and the depth and extent of the changes they propose, as well as over the methods they would adopt to realize them. The only way to understand the conflict centered on Boris Yeltsin is by taking these differences into account. Yeltsin had replaced Grishin as chief of the Moscow party; he worked very energetically, and changed many things in the capital, replacing numerous bosses and modifying the leadership's style and methods. When he initiated a particularly bitter fight against corruption, apparat officials lost many of their unearned privileges. As a result, Yeltsin became one of the most popular leaders among young people and workers, to the extent that he was often named with Gorbachev as one of the men who best personified perestroika. This is why there was so much unrest and so many questions about Yeltsin's exit, while Geidar Aliyev's retirement went unnoticed, even though just three or four years earlier he had been considered a "new star in the Kremlin firmament."

The January and June plenums were events of great political momentum and acceleration. During this same phase there were signs of disagreement inside the party leadership. It was no accident that the January plenum had been postponed twice, and that the June plenum had been postponed once: first an agreement had to be reached on decisions inside the Politburo. The *Pravda* articles that you mentioned show that many people did not want to go too far with democratization and glasnost, or with the critique of Stalin's crimes and of the Stalinist system—at least not as far as Gorbachev, Yakovlev, and newspapers and periodicals such as *Izvestia, Moskovskiye Novosti, Znamya, Novy Mir, Ogonyok,* and others seemed to want. Judging from the articles in *Pravda,* its editorial board must have thought the only changes required were a few cosmetic improvements in the party line, in ideology, and in the representation of party history. The same held true for the economy. There were influential groups of economists who were afraid of supporting profound reforms. I still think, however, that the "Yeltsin case" ran parallel to these forms of dissent. This issue did not deal so much with the direction in which perestroika was moving as with the methods that should be used to administer it; it concerned the personal qualities and the work style of a major leader.

G.C. Is that all?

R.M. To my knowledge Yeltsin has never said anything against glasnost, against democratization, or against radical economic reforms. Nor did he say anything against the decisions of the January and June plenums. The problem is that he was unable to administer the exceptionally difficult situation in Moscow. Anyone might have run into problems or made mistakes: any member of the Politburo, the Central Committee, or the Council of Ministers. But Yeltsin had to face more problems than anyone else, since

Moscow was the headquarters of so many organizations, institutes, and ministries that acted independently of the city Party Committee. This was the source of continuous conflicts. Yeltsin couldn't handle the tension, and didn't demonstrate the leadership qualities needed to deal with the problems in the capital. He often tried to use his power to iron out problems, only to see higher authorities rescind decisions made by the Moscow Party Committee. I would add that in the past two years most of the leaders of the Moscow organizations were changed, while life in the city, especially in the areas of food supply, transportation, and social life, had not changed for the better. Prices at the kolkhoz markets in Moscow had actually gone up. Yeltsin was psychologically unequipped to deal with this situation. I don't have enough information to judge, but I don't think that anyone was paving the way for Yeltsin's dismissal; he was the one who said he wanted to resign. It was as if he were either delivering an ultimatum or suffering from a psychological breakdown. My closest friends and I were saddened by this conflict, and almost all of us felt sorry for Yeltsin. But after calmer and more cautious reflection, I realized that Yeltsin himself had caused the most unbearable and controversial situations. In many cases he expected instant changes where it was practically impossible. Let me give you a few concrete examples.

It is well known how energetically Yeltsin fought from the start against privileges for party leaders. On the first day of his arrival at the Party Committee, he decided not to eat in the small dining room reserved for Moscow Gorkom (City Committee) secretaries and officials, but in the cafeteria open to all Gorkom functionaries. The next day the executive dining room was closed. Soon after, several "special stores" were closed, places where functionaries could procure foodstuffs and consumer goods unavailable to the general public. Immediately after this he decided to lower the number of personal cars in administrative service. Not far from where I live is a complex of beautiful brick houses built for Gorkom functionaries. Every morning a large number of chauffeur-driven black Volgas arrived. These cars drove downtown, passing by bus stops crowded with people waiting in line, leaving behind the hustle and bustle of the subway stops. I never once saw a driver in one of these cars stop to offer a ride to a woman, or to a mother with a child, except maybe to the nearest subway stop. Yeltsin put an end to this situation, and now every black Volga carries not one but four passengers. Obviously, the man on the street approves of changes like this.

There are even more stories about Yeltsin's energetic attacks on abuses in the commercial sector. He would personally go into stores posing as a normal buyer, and when he discovered abuses he would call the police. When he knew ahead of time that a certain store had received a shipment of imported food, he went there the next day to ask for a kilo of German beef. The meat was neither on the counter nor in the store; it had been sent to the Cheremushki kolkhoz market, where it was sold at prices two or three times higher. Each of Yeltsin's incursions into Moscow stores ended with arrests and criminal investigations. The existence of a mafia network was discovered in the capital's distribution and commercial system, headed by the functionaries of the Moscow soviet commercial management. Hundreds of people were arrested. When Yeltsin spoke to the Moscow salesmen in April 1986, he said: "In the last few months eight hundred managers of the commercial sector have been arrested in Moscow. We keep digging, but we still haven't found the bottom of this black hole. But we must get rid of this filth. We are trying to sever these criminal connections, to identify the leaders, and to replace them with honest people who can get to the bottom of things. The work ahead of us is difficult and long, but we have decided to get to the bottom of this."

What was there to say? Most Moscovites were happy about this. However, the affair turned out to be more difficult than expected. Dozens, or rather hundreds of employees in the commercial sector, who had to work within a complicated distribution network that suffered from shortages, were unable to substantially change a situation that had built up over the decades. Many were immediately implicated in the abuses. New arrests followed. Many state stores underwent two or three changes in management over a two-year period. Many salespeople, cashiers, and other employees were caught committing minor crimes. As a result, the service in Moscow stores has gotten worse. Wages in the commercial sector are very low, while the work is hard and tiring. Many stores, especially the ones on the outskirts, had a permanent staff shortage. You can often read advertisements saying, "Help Wanted: Salespeople, Cashiers, Men to Do Heavy Lifting." The salaries for the last category in particular are extremely low, and so at the end of the day a bottle of vodka or a bag of food was often thrown in. This practice was so widespread that no one considered it illegal, but rather a form of payment in kind. With the new, tougher controls, many people ended up losing this form of compensation. This is why today you often see trucks loaded with vegetables parked behind stores while the men who are supposed to unload it puff on their cigarettes, as if to say, "Let someone else worry about it!" The store workers were not the only ones waiting—the customers had to wait too, and the lines that were formed were not only due to a shortage of goods, but also to the slowness of distribution, or to a shortage of salespeople and cashiers. By this I don't mean that you shouldn't fight against abuses, theft, and corruption, but you cannot limit yourself to the symptoms. You have to get to the causes and distinguish between the organizers and bosses of the thousands of commercial mafias and simple working people who often get involved in these things against their will.

Yeltsin had criticized the high prices at the kolkhoz markets since 1986. But in 1987 prices increased. His theory was that the food supply to the capital was calculated according to the resident population, without figuring that every day Moscow is visited by 2 to 3 million occasional visitors or commuters. Therefore he asked the appropriate ministries to increase the food supply by 25 to 30 percent. This was the wrong approach. Everyone knows that Moscow is supplied much better than the other cities in the Russian Federal Republic. As a matter of fact, most of the visitors come from the provinces every day to purchase things that they cannot find in their towns and cities. The situation could improve only if there was a significant increase in the food supply to all the towns within a two-to-three-hundred-kilometer radius of Moscow.

The slump in fruit and vegetable crops lasted through 1986 and 1987, and made the shortages worse. Asking for an increase in the supply to the capital meant doing so at the expense of smaller towns. If goods in the capital increased, so would the number of commuters who came to do their shopping. I remember a joke from the Brezhnev days. Nixon and Brezhnev met, and the first said, "We do things in America so that in every small rural town you can buy exactly what you can buy in the big cities." Brezhnev replied: "We do even better. We bring all the goods to Moscow, and the people themselves take care of the distribution to the rest of the country." In essence, what Yeltsin was proposing would have completed the vicious circle that had turned the capital into a city for the elite, where one can buy anything, while the rest of the country suffers from a dearth of even the most basic goods. At any rate, Yeltsin's request was rejected, and commercial distribution got no better than it had been under the previous leader—and may have actually gotten worse.

G.C. Yeltsin also suffered similar defeats. This might explain the conjecture that he had a psychological breakdown.

R.M. His battle against the *limitchiki* system didn't go too well either. This phenomenon began in the 1930s, when huge public works were being done in the capital. Even back then the Moscow work force was not large enough, so workers were recruited in the provinces. These workers were willing to work under difficult conditions, and live in dormitories (*obshchezhitia*) and barracks. But they gradually become Moscovites, received their certificates of residency, and improved the conditions of their lives. The first *limitchiki* abandoned the heaviest and most unpleasant jobs, and found easier and better-paying jobs. Thus, it became necessary to find new *limitchiki* for heavy and low-prestige jobs. It's common knowledge that individual Soviet citizens have very limited possibilities of moving from one place to another in the

USSR, and that Moscow has many advantages over other cities. Thus, it's no surprise that almost no one wants to move away from the capital. Young people in particular don't want to move to the provinces, so the certificate of Moscow residence is much sought after. At the same time, young Moscovites don't seem too enthusiastic about heavier jobs. In the last thirty to forty years there has been an acute shortage of workers in the construction industry, in sanitation, on the assembly lines, and so on. I too moved to Moscow as a *limitchik*. There were very few people during those years who were willing to become school principals in Moscow, and in the 1950s the city office for public education was authorized to recruit principals and mathematics teachers, who were also in demand, in the provinces.

Lately, the average annual flow of *limitchiki* into Moscow has numbered between seventy and eighty thousand. This situation was clearly abnormal. The *limitchiki* would obtain a *propiska*, a certificate of temporary residency that was good for five to ten years. They could not bring their family members with them, nor could they change jobs; they were at the mercy of the business managers who hired them. The growth of the Moscow population was essentially due to an influx of *limitchiki* that surpassed all the security barriers set by the city authorities. Thirty years ago it was decided to contain the capital's population at six million people. Then the figure was raised to seven million. Today there are more than nine million people. This is one of the reasons why there is no solution to Moscow's housing problem.

Yeltsin immediately stated that over a two-year period he would put an end to this problem. He issued a warning to business managers who hired *limitchiki* when they could solve their labor problems differently, by mechanizing and automating procedures and thereby reducing the number of employees. The police were given rigorous instructions: go after the idlers, the citizens who don't work but make their living through a variety of illegal activities: illegally leasing state apartments, exploiting prostitution, and so on. As a result of these measures only twenty thousand *limitchiki* were registered in Moscow in 1986, and the inflow was completely stopped at the beginning of 1987. But it proved to be impossible to solve the problem this way. The gaps in the assembly lines at many factories had to be filled by engineers, technicians, and office workers. The most serious problem was with the companies that build the subways, where all the underground work was done by *limitchiki*. At this point the Secretariat of the Central Committee made the decision to revoke Yeltsin's orders, and to allow the Metrostroi company to hire another five thousand *limitchiki*. It was learned that Ligachev had backed this decision while Gorbachev was on vacation.

There had been other quarrels between Yeltsin and the Secretariat in the preceding months, but this last one proved to be the proverbial straw that broke the camel's back, provoking first Yeltsin's protests to Gorbachev and then his dramatic resignation at the October plenum.

G.C. But Yeltsin had appealed to Gorbachev for help and mediation a number of times in the preceding months. I wonder what concrete circumstances led to his taking the floor at the plenum.

R.M. My data also indicates that Yeltsin had turned to Gorbachev and hinted at the idea of resigning well before the October plenum. Gorbachev asked him to wait awhile. Yeltsin evidently couldn't hold out anymore. I should add that he quarreled with certain Politburo members after his meeting with Gorbachev. I don't feel like justifying Yeltsin's behavior. He was not up to the task of confronting the difficulties that the Moscow party chief inevitably has to wrestle with. As first secretary of the Sverdlovsk Regional Committee (for about ten years), he had been the absolute number one in a crucially important area—a region with forty cities and towns and hundreds of factories of national importance. During the Brezhnev years the first secretaries of the regions and republics had practically a free hand, and the territories assigned to them were at their complete disposition. Today the secretary of a regional committee still has more authority than anyone else in a given region.

But the situation in Moscow is completely different. There are hundreds of institutions in Moscow whose instructions and decisions are completely independent of the party committee. It takes special political talents and "diplomatic" abilities to steer such a situation. In his fight against privileges, Yeltsin shouldn't have neglected the strength and the origins of his opponents. For example, let's take the special middle schools where certain subjects are taught in French, English, or Spanish, or where the teaching staff is highly qualified. These schools had for some time been transformed from centers for the education of intellectually gifted children into schools for the "gifted" children of famous people. It was certainly fair to take a moral stance on the situation, but since it was a delicate and difficult situation, it would have been better to seek the support of the Ministry of Education first. Yeltsin instead thought he could solve the problem by himself through sudden decisions.

G.C. I've heard that the city apparat reacted furiously to Yeltsin's decision to close certain "special" stores reserved for the cadres.

R.M. The decision certainly wasn't greeted with enthusiasm. You could say that Yeltsin concentrated special efforts in that direction, and this made him extremely popular. When he visited a factory, the first thing he did was to find out about the supply system for simple workers and for "bosses." In one large factory he discovered to his indignation that there were not two but four cafeterias, with different levels of service. Moreover, it turned out that the particularly luxurious executive dining room was only open to a selected few. After this visit the party organizations received harsh reprimands for their lack of control over the managers' work styles. There was another episode regarding the party secretary of a neighborhood who had had an individual fireplace built for his apartment, with his own personal chimney. Another secretary had the walls of his home covered with animal hides rather than with ordinary wallpaper. Yeltsin fired both of them after reminding them that they were "only" party leaders and not princes. He closed both the special food store and the consumer goods store of the Party Committee. On that occasion he said, "The party functionaries must become more acutely aware of the insufficient supplies in the capital that so trouble ordinary citizens." This clearly upset the functionaries, who under Yeltsin had already seen their work days grow longer, up to ten to twelve hours. He himself disclosed that for two years in a row he hadn't slept more than four hours a night: he began work at six in the morning and left the office at midnight. To me it stands to reason that this affected his nervous system.

G.C. Do you think that his speech at the October plenum came as a surprise to Gorbachev?

R.M. It wasn't a complete surprise, nor is it fair to describe Yeltsin as Gorbachev's best friend. They had had disagreements and quarrels before then. When Yeltsin complained that he wasn't receiving enough support, he was obviously referring to Gorbachev. When the Soviet leader was about to go on vacation, Yeltsin sent him a letter that included a request to consider his resignation. At the Moscow committee plenum Gorbachev himself disclosed that he had met with Yeltsin right before the October plenum. They spoke about various issues, and Gorbachev proposed that he not raise the issue in Moscow, because the meeting was supposed to examine other issues. There was really no rush. They were on the eve of the celebrations of the seventieth anniversary of the Revolution, with an important speech by Gorbachev; a meeting of the leaders of left-wing parties; and the imminent summit with Reagan. Yeltsin's request could have been held off until January or February, but he did not want to wait. His intervention was badly timed: in certain respects it was fair, but in others it was an unfair criticism of the Politburo and the Secretariat of the Central Committee. Thus, Gorbachev was well aware of Yeltsin's requests and his mood. What he didn't know ahead of time is that Yeltsin would speak at the plenum and what he would say. I only want to add, in these regards, that today the plenums are more democratic. The only limits concern the length of the speeches: the speakers have to hold to a fifteen-minute limit. The plenum itself must decide if a speech can be longer. Furthermore, the assembly decided ahead of time whether or not the speeches would be published (an "open plenum"). Obviously, the participants act differently if they know that their speech is going to be published. Unfortunately, there have only been a few "open" plenums in recent years. This is why today there are many calls from the party press to publish the minutes of the discussions as a matter of course.

G.C. What do you think about the meeting between Boris Yeltsin and the Pamyat group?

R.M. The Pamyat (Memory) association can be clearly characterized as nationalistic, anti-Semitic, and "anti-Masonic." We could say simply that it was a neofascist organization. The demonstration took place not far from Red Square, and as far as I can tell, the size of it took the authorities by surprise. Demonstrators carried signs and banners that read: "Down with the Jewish Masons!"; "Down with Vitali Korotich, Editor in Chief of *Ogonyok!*"; "Down with Yegor Yakovlev, Editor in Chief of *Moskovskiye Novosti!*" There were more than eight hundred people. There were other demagogic slogans, such as: "We Defend Perestroika!"; "We Ask for the Recognition of the Historical-Patriotic Association Pamyat!"; "We Want to Be Received by Gorbachev and Yeltsin!"

I don't know the intentions of the Committee for National Security, the KGB. In previous years demonstrations by civil rights activists or by Jewish people who wished to emigrate, usually numbering fewer than fifty participants, were rather quickly and unceremoniously broken up. However, while the KGB was perhaps still making up its mind what to do, Yeltsin invited the demonstrators to a meeting in a Moscow soviet hall. He answered their questions for almost two hours and talked with the Russian neofascists, in his own words, "as an equal." It was later learned by reading the materials of the Moscow Party Committee plenum that Yeltsin had personally made that decision and that he had conducted the discussion in a manner inappropriate for a leader of the Moscow Communists. In fact, through this he legalized the Pamyat association in Moscow and helped its rapid growth in Sverdlovsk, Leningrad, and other cities.

G.C. That's a very strong criticism. Yeltsin made a democratic and unusual gesture. Moreover, I get the impression that the true nature of Pamyat still requires study.

that repressive and prohibitive methods should be applied
on't understand why, for what purposes, the decision was
iese Russian Nazis and talk with them "as equals." I can
ng the summer of that year there were disagreements be-
l the KGB when the Crimean Tatars were demonstrating
ably as a result of that Chebrikov intervened at the October
iate Yeltsin's accusations that he had meddled in affairs of
the Moscow Party Committee. He said on the contrary that Yeltsin was the
one who tried repeatedly to dictate the law to the central government institutes, including the KGB. Let me repeat that I don't think that the KGB is
better qualified than others to manage relations with Pamyat, with the Crimean Tatars, or with the activities of numerous informal groups that are
rising up. I only want to point out that there were quarrels between Yeltsin
and Chebrikov.

Let me tell you an interesting story. A little while after these events I had
an interview with the Italian daily *La Stampa* in which I harshly criticized
Yeltsin's approach to the *limitchiki* and the reorganization of commerce.
This interview was published in Yugoslavia by the newspaper *Borba*, after
which I received a phone call from an acquaintance, an intellectual whose
Russian nationalist tendencies I am familiar with. He had translated the
interview and forwarded the text to the Pamyat activists, who reacted furiously. He also told me that Pamyat had protested Yeltsin's dismissal and
considered it the result of a "Masonic plot." One of their fliers says that
Academician Andrei Sakharov and the historian Roy Medvedev are among
the ringleaders of the "Moscow Masons." The use of these base tactics can
be attributed to the fact that both Sakharov's wife and I have Jewish relatives.
My answer to this person was that I didn't understand why the Russian
nationalists were so interested in calculating percentages of Jewish blood. In
a multiethnic country like Russia everyone is mixed, and Yeltsin himself is
from one of the ethnic minorities in the Urals. As it turns out my observation
was very interesting to Pamyat, and another intellectual close to the group
contacted me to learn more about Yeltsin's national origins. At that point I
stopped talking with them. Let them do their racial investigations by
themselves.

However, there was a huge reaction from the populace, especially from
the young people, and it took the authorities by surprise. Besides demonstrations in the cities of Togliatti and Naberezhnye Chelny, there were also
numerous protests in Moscow. In many factories the workers wanted to hold
assemblies to obtain a thorough explanation of Yeltsin's resignation. There
were expressions of protest at some institutions of higher learning. People
talked about it openly on the subways and buses, and there were small

demonstrations here and there organized by the informal groups. There were outright demonstrations to defend Yeltsin in Sverdlovsk, where he had long been first secretary of the party's regional committee, and where he was held in high esteem. I was told that in Sverdlovsk thousands of people marched, and it was the first time in thirty years that the removal of a Politburo member (and Yeltsin was only a candidate member) had raised such emotions, protests, and debates among ordinary people. This clearly required a serious analysis. No one tried to publicize Yeltsin's personality or his actions. The press didn't say too much about it.

Yeltsin had become one of the most popular leaders of the new ruling group. It was not just a question of the ideas of perestroika, which many people still found not particularly congenial and often incomprehensible. I think that the main reason for his popularity was his fight against the privileges of power, his personal honesty, his frugal life-style, and his clear condemnation of industrial and political leaders who didn't care about the people's everyday problems. When he visited factories and companies, he enjoyed spending time with the workers rather than with the managers. Earlier I mentioned his mistakes and his excessive haste. But the people believed in his sincerity. In the Brezhnev years the people's intolerance was not aimed at the top leaders, but at the bosses with whom they were in closest contact: bullying managers, arrogant *raikom* secretaries, police officers who accepted bribes, store managers who stole, and so on. Under Yeltsin these characters were fired or arrested. They grew afraid. Thus was built the well-founded legend of Moscow's new chief. Except that he threw himself into the fray to the point of hysteria, to the point of creating conflicts everywhere, to the point that he had to leave by slamming the door as loud as he could. It was no coincidence that immediately after the October plenum he ended up in the hospital on the verge of a heart attack. Now he's the minister of the State Committee for Construction. Perhaps he will return to the political leadership, maybe after some new development. As the Russian proverb goes, "One who's seen a beating is worth two who haven't."

G.C. Do you think a return to the past is still possible?

R.M. Unfortunately, the possibility of a move backward is still possible. No one in the Soviet leadership is opposed to more rapid scientific and technical progress, to the development of agriculture, and to the improvement of transportation and communications. But many do not like the spread of glasnost and democratization. They would enact the reforms through authoritarian means, and maintain all their privileges of power and information, as well as their material privileges. This way is feasible, although it would lead to state capitalism rather than to socialism. At this time the situation is very complex. There were tumultuous protests over the dismissals of Yeltsin and Kunayev. The corrupt reactionary bureaucracy was still very strong and it was beginning to pose a solid resistance to perestroika. Moreover, in the provinces very little has changed in the past two to three years. I read various provincial newspapers. From their content it's often impossible to guess that restructuring is going on in the country. Some papers are interesting, but they're in the minority. Even an important newspaper like *Leningradskaya Pravda* is practically unchanged in content and quality. The mechanism of glasnost still hasn't been elaborated, and glasnost is still in its early stages.

A number of rumors and interpretations surrounded the Yeltsin case. Some people said that he was dead, or that he had committed suicide. Phony transcripts of his speech at the October plenum appeared, and one of these was actually published in the British newspaper the *Observer*, and then broadcast in Russian over the BBC radio station. This dealt another blow to Gorbachev's reputation, and in particular to that of his wife, Raisa. This was possible because of a lack of glasnost. To complete the picture, informal youth organizations, in Leningrad for example, publicly approved of Yeltsin's dismissal and identified him as an enemy of perestroika. I spoke to the leader of one of these groups, and asked him why they thought that way. He responded that Yeltsin had acted like a dictator and that he had supported Pamyat in Sverdlovsk and Moscow. But this opinion is based on hearsay rather than on reliable information.

G.C. I would like to go back to the question of Gorbachev's long vacation in August and September 1987. According to the official version, he was working on his address for the seventieth anniversary of the October Revolution and on his book *Perestroika*. However, without casting any doubt on the veracity of the official version, I get the impression that there was a vacuum in the leadership during that period. A vacuum that others immediately filled by expressing their own points of view—which were very different from Gorbachev's.

R.M. Gorbachev's prolonged absence during that period did indeed prompt doubts and fluctuations, but I wouldn't exaggerate their importance. I heard that Gorbachev continued to follow the press closely and phoned Moscow when necessary. The general secretary's vacation always creates certain difficulties. When Stalin went on vacation, Molotov usually took his place, and later on Malenkov did; in some cases another Politburo member would replace him. However, they could only decide on secondary issues, and postponed everything else until Stalin's return. When problems arose that couldn't be postponed, Stalin was still the one to decide, either by telephone or by holding a meeting of his associates at his dacha. It was not uncommon for all the members of the Politburo, except for the one or two whose "shift" it was, to go on vacation at the same time as Stalin. More or less the same thing happened with Khrushchev and Brezhnev. In August and September of this year, Ligachev took Gorbachev's place. Ligachev has a different work style, and the two men seem to have different points of view on a number of issues. It is likely that this facilitated the appearance of a series of articles and speeches that worried the intelligentsia. But the importance of the phenomenon was overestimated. Not even the most progressive circles of the intelligentsia could have anticipated the changes in the area of culture, and the harsh criticism of Stalin and Stalinism that had taken effect after January. Not even the most progressive groups were certain of the solidity and the irreversibility of the changes. Thus, there was a certain apprehensiveness.

Many asked openly how long glasnost would continue. The resistance of the conservative forces increased and uncertainties appeared. Rumors circulated that put everyone on their guard. Are we going too far with criticizing the mistakes of the past? Are we talking too loud? Are we exaggerating by raising too many different issues? Are we tarnishing the love for the fatherland and for its history? Glasnost and freedom of speech were spread, but it seemed evident that in the uproar you could hear the loud voices of demagogues of every sort. It was inevitable that conflicts would arise. Thus, for example, the newspaper *Moskovskiye Novosti* published an obituary in September "In memory of Viktor Nekrasov." Nekrasov had died an émigré. He was a wonderful and honest man who had fought honorably on the front in the Great Patriotic War and had joined the party. He began to write after the war. His V *Okopakh Stalingrada* (*In the Trenches of Stalingrad*) was one of the best books on the war, and was read by every Soviet schoolchild. We owe many other beautiful books to him. He was a beloved friend of Aleksandr Tvardovsky. But Nekrasov, who lived and worked in Kiev, had various quarrels with the political leadership of the Ukrainian party. He spoke against many repressions, signed letters in defense of Ukrainian dissidents, and requested that heavy sentences be reduced, maintaining that you couldn't send someone to prison for freely expressing what he or she believed in. At first he was warned. Then he was expelled from the party, and later from the Writers' Union. In the end, Nekrasov emigrated. He lived in Paris, nostalgic for his land, the Ukraine, and for Kiev. But he did not get mixed up with other émigré spokespersons, even if he did severely criticize the Soviet situation under Brezhnev, and the Ukraine under Shcherbitsky.

Nekrasov died at the age of seventy-nine, and many of his friends publicly expressed their condolences. The obituary in *Moskovskiye Novosti* was taken by the intelligentsia of Moscow (and of the Ukraine, I hope) as an example of understanding and conciliation. You must keep in mind that the death of the great film director Andrei Tarkovsky (who had also refused to return to the USSR, but without losing his Soviet citizenship) had been commemorated with obituaries in almost all the newspapers and cultural magazines. Nekrasov's obituary instead raised a storm of protests from the world of cultural functionaries and among the conservative intelligentsia. The editor in chief of *Moskovskiye Novosti*, Yegor Yakovlev, was so harshly criticized by his superiors (and probably by one of the party leaders) that he decided to resign. The situation was only turned around by direct intervention of Gorbachev, who phoned Yakovlev in Moscow from his vacation spot to ask him to remain. Thus, *Moskovskiye Novosti* is still a bastion of glasnost, targeted by the conservatives, but enthusiastically supported by the majority of the intelligentsia and the young people. This example shows how a relatively minor publication can provoke significant activity in the leadership, even if the greater public can't see it. This shows the difficulty of making even slight progress in glasnost and democratization. Under these conditions Gorbachev's long absence from the Kremlin didn't go unnoticed by careful observers, who remarked the changes in emphasis in the press during this period.

G.C. At the same time, it was during this phase that the debate on rehabilitation accelerated. *Ogonyok* even published excerpts from a letter to Gorbachev by Anna Mikhailovna Larina, Bukharin's widow. If this initiative hadn't been "agreed on," then it must have been a form of pressure. *Ogonyok* and *Moskovskiye Novosti* published memoirs by Anna Mikhailovna and other materials that "rehabilitated" not only Bukharin and Rykov, but also Fyodor Raskolnikov, and that exhumed the "Leningrad affair." In general the debate on history was still tense, but it showed no signs of weakening and didn't seem hard hit by the political standstill. It was as if the group of reformers wanted in some way to prove that the blows struck in the Yeltsin case had not touched the balance of forces.

R.M. I don't think that these tactical considerations had any weight. The question of the rehabilitations, which we will return to in more detail, is important to the intelligentsia, to the elderly, and to foreign observers, but it doesn't affect a large part of the population as a whole. Young people barely know who Bukharin and Rykov were. I think that the push toward the rehabilitations, and the reinvestigation of the so-called deviation of the right, of the whole history of the party, and of Stalin's crimes, was simply

146

the "logical" result of the economic policies of the past two years, and of the beginning of glasnost. The ruling group was already preparing the terrain for the formal rehabilitation of Bukharin, Rykov, and other major leaders from the 1920s, which was scheduled for late 1987. The letter that Gorbachev sent to Bukharin's widow, and her memoirs, have to be seen as preparing public opinion for an important event. I am convinced that the publication of the materials you cited had been agreed to by Gorbachev and by the entire Politburo.

CHAPTER 6

FOREIGN POLICY IN 1987

•　　　•　　　•

After the Geneva summit, 1985 ended with an exchange of greetings from the television screens. After Reykjavik, 1986 ended with Gorbachev letting President Reagan know that the current climate did not permit such cordiality. The American president sent a radio message on the Voice of America to the Soviet people anyway, and Soviet radio broadcast it for seven to eight minutes. Gorbachev replied by granting an interview to the prominent U.S. journalist Joseph Kingsbury-Smith. Rather than dialogue, there was an exchange of barbs that reflected the worsening of relations. But the tone on both sides was still moderate. Gorbachev said to Kingsbury-Smith:

> Nothing should be done that would modify or break the ABM agreement. . . . We are for its being preserved without time limits. . . . Without it, an agreement on the reduction of strategic nuclear weapons cannot be reached.

In his end-of-the-year television message, Gorbachev evoked the dramatic moments of Reykjavik and repeated that on that occasion the Soviets had demonstrated "the best goodwill":

> This was a moment in which humankind could have, so to speak, taken a look at the horizon and made out the outlines of a world without nuclear weapons. Unfortunately, the reaction of many political spokesmen in the West proved how strong the stereotypes of old and conservative positions still are. [1]

However, the year began with a series of stunning developments regarding Afghanistan. Gorbachev did not sit around with his hands in his pockets to contemplate the difficulties of dialogue with the West. There were many signs that he was convinced of the need to get rid of the deadweight of a war being fought at the USSR's doorstep, directly involving Soviet troops, that had tarnished the Soviet Union's international image for seven years. On close inspection, the year that had just ended had already seen complex developments in Kabul that clearly originated in the Kremlin's reflections. A month and a half after the Geneva summit, Afghan President Babrak Karmal issued the first proposal for national reconciliation, and appointed to his government a group of ministers who belonged to no political party. At the end of January 1986 the Kabul government sent a plan through their U.N. representative to Pakistan for the withdrawal of Soviet troops in exchange for a guarantee to "end foreign interference."

Washington responded coldly. Moscow still had to make a crucial step, and recognize that there was not only a problem "around" but also "inside" Afghanistan. This was difficult, especially considering that the Soviet public had been told exactly the opposite for years. Gorbachev could not put a stop to this deception in one bold move, even if later it would be discovered that he had been raising the problem of Afghanistan in the Politburo since April 1985, immediately after his election as general secretary. But on 4 May 1986, Karmal was fired from his position as head of the People's Democratic Party of Afghanistan (PDPA) and replaced by Najibullah. In Vladivostok during the month of August, Gorbachev announced an upcoming trial withdrawal of six Soviet regiments by the end of the year. On 20 November Karmal left the political scene for good and was relieved of all his duties. Clearly, he could not effect a policy of "controlled disengagement." Instead, he was trying to lay the basis for a political solution, independently of the American willingness to assist the process.

Moscow understood that no help would be forthcoming from Washington in the very moment that the Soviets were trying to correct the improvident decision made in December 1979. Gorbachev knew that he had to proceed by himself, and he set about doing so without wasting any time. On 1 January a resolution by the PDPA announced a unilateral six-month cease-fire, to start on 15 January. It proclaimed the beginning of a program of national reconciliation, dialogue with the opposition groups, including the armed groups based on foreign soil (this was the first time the proposal had been extended to guerrillas following foreign orders). It was announced that the Afghan leadership wanted to make contact with "the most highly visible representatives of the past regime," with the objective of creating a coalition government. Najibullah said the withdrawal of Soviet troops could take place "after" the creation of a national unity government.[2] After a few days, Shevardnadze and Dobrynin suddenly left for Kabul. At the end of his meeting with the Afghan leader, Shevardnadze said that "a political solution is not a long-term objective but a reality of today." He specified first of all that "foreign interference" had to stop, but he assigned the policy of national reconciliation the "task of creating the real internal presuppositions for a political settlement." This recognition was not enough to assure the end of foreign interference, and a base of social support for the Kabul regime had to be constructed.

In the meantime, Moscow launched another signal that it wanted to ease tensions with Asian countries, hinting at a slow but constant development of attention toward China. The Defense Ministry announced that one motorized division and other military units would be withdrawn from Mongolia between April and June of the next year.[3] But the barometer continued to indicate bad weather in relations with America. The Soviet press reacted bitterly to America's setting off its twenty-fifth nuclear explosion since the beginning of the Soviet moratorium. The Novosti agency wrote that the moratorium was "over," even if the USSR did not immediately resume experiments.[4] However, the Soviet leader did not take the pressure off his initiatives. In mid-February he created one of the most original forms of unconventional diplomacy by inaugurating the Moscow Forum. The topics of debate covered practically the entire gamut of foreign-policy controversies: disarmament, human rights, economic cooperation, culture, and ecology. A heterogeneous group of scientists, clerics, artists, men of culture, actors, and businessmen came to Moscow for the forum, committed to free and unbiased confrontation without formulas and propaganda. Many of them probably came to see up close the phenomenon of the changing USSR. The effect was astonishing, and it was widely amplified by Soviet television, which broadcast unprecedented images and speeches to the public. The forum thus turned into a show of international support not so much for Gorbachev's foreign-policy proposals as for his policy of domestic renewal. The Soviet experts each had their say, including Andrei Sakharov, who had been released from his Gorky exile only three months before. Gorbachev ended the forum with a speech dedicated entirely to the philosophy of the *novoye myshleniye*, the "new thinking." "What happened in Reykjavik irreversibly changed the nature and the essence of the debate on the future world." He did not make the sensational proposals that many people expected. This may have been because he did not want to "exploit" that frontier, or maybe because the *novoye myshleniye* still had to convince a part of its own managing group.

Gorbachev made no mention of the Reykjavik package. This was a relevant "lapse" on the part of Gorbachev, who spelled out his ideas on a new approach to world security from the podium ordinarily used for the Supreme Soviet. Nuclear deterrence was no longer an adequate response, for "considered in its historical context it does not reduce the risk of nuclear conflict—on the contrary, it increases it." Therefore, it was necessary to get rid of the psychological conditioning of the past and take note of the risks humankind was running. In the nuclear age, human beings "had lost their immortality as a species." The only way out was to destroy the nuclear arsenals and the drive to create new weapons. The idea of the Strategic Defense Initiative embodies the old concepts of peace and war as a whole, Gorbachev said. Its substance was old, even if it appeared to be based on the most modern developments in military technology.

Gorbachev did not avoid the many questions about "his" Soviet Union:

You have come here in a moment of essentially revolutionary changes, which have an immense meaning for our society, for socialism as a whole, and for the whole world. Only by understanding their contents, meaning, and goals can you form a correct idea of our foreign policy.

He reiterated the idea of transformations "along a socialist line," that can be judged by a "socialist unit of measurement," but that implied "more democracy." He added, "Our new approach to humanitarian problems, to Helsinki's third canister, is before everyone's eyes, and it too is the result of a new way of thinking."[5] Many experts who attended the forum asked Gorbachev to further extend the unilateral moratorium on nuclear experiments, in spite of the Americans' refusal to respect it, but the Soviet leader could not grant this request. After 569 days and 26 atomic experiments in America, the moratorium that had previously been extended four times came to an end. A device with twenty kilotons of power was set off on 26 February at the Semipalatinsk range. General Geli Batenin commented: "Washington's irresponsible policies have confronted us with the need to end the unilateral moratorium. The historical opportunity to end nuclear experiments once and for all has, for the moment, been lost."

But he added that "we will immediately interrupt [our experiments]" as soon as the United States decides to do the same.[6] This meant that Gorbachev had been forced to take a blow. But only forty-eight hours later the Kremlin was back on the offensive with a dramatic and unexpected move. The "Vremya" newscaster read a statement by the general secretary "on behalf of the Soviet leadership of the Defense Council" that announced the USSR's willingness to reach a "separate and immediate" agreement on medium-range missiles. The Reykjavik package had been untied. The questions of the SDI and the reduction of strategic missiles were still tied together, but the road was open for a separate agreement on Euromissiles. The outlines of the proposal indicated substantial and significant Soviet concessions: the zero option for theater missiles; a hundred missiles per side in Asia; the withdrawal of tactical-operative missiles from East Germany and Czechoslovakia in the event of an agreement; and the willingness to immediately enter into separate negotiations to eliminate short-range missiles.[7] Moscow had quickly grasped signs of movement in Western countries regarding the ABM Treaty. The Italian foreign minister, Giulio Andreotti, had arrived in the Soviet capital

a few days earlier to communicate Europe's support for a restrictive interpretation of the ABM agreement. A world that had been paralyzed by the
shock of Reykjavik was set back into motion. A few days later the deputy
minister of foreign affairs, Aleksandr Bessmertnykh, disclosed that George
Shultz had received an invitation to come to Moscow as soon as possible.[8]
Now the plot thickened on both sides. Someone in Washington was trying
to put an immediate end to any possible openings. *Pravda* bluntly rejected
statements by anonymous "officials" who accused the Soviet Union of having
violated the SALT I and SALT II agreements.[9] In the meantime, Gerasimov
described a meeting between Shevardnadze and Assistant Secretary of State
Michael Armacost as "satisfactory."[10] The meeting between Shevardnadze
and Shultz was set for 13 April, and Armacost stated that "the Kremlin has
unequivocally made a commitment to withdraw its troops from Afghanistan."[11]

Under the new Soviet leader, efforts to reestablish a dialogue between the
two superpowers took a form quite different from the old "bipolarity" typical
of the long years of Brezhnev's (and Khrushchev's) policies. The *novoye
mishleniye* presupposed an active multipolarity. The Kremlin needed to find
new partners at a time when their main partner was reluctant to engage in
dialogue. The time was ripe for a vigorous European initiative. U.S. allies
warned apprehensively that Washington was pulling the reins too tight; they
could feel a shift in the public, which had become very receptive to the new
image of Soviet leadership.

On 24 March the second round of talks between the EEC and Comecon
opened in Geneva. During the same period the first delegation of Christian
Democrats from the European Parliament arrived in Moscow. These new
developments were the first results of a consistent policy of rapprochement
that Gorbachev had advocated ever since his first remarks on "his" foreign
policy. The situation had been frozen since 1980. The first formal move
toward a thaw came from the East in July 1985, with a letter sent to the
European Community by the secretary of Comecon, Vyacheslav Sychev.
This was the immediate result of the opening toward Europe as a "political
entity" that Gorbachev had proposed in April. He had described it to Be-
nedetto Craxi when the latter came to Moscow in May of the same year,
and he had shown it to Mitterrand during a visit to Paris; he had also repeated
it in Moscow to a delegation from the Italian Communist Party in January
1986. The first round of talks between the two economic communities had
taken place in Geneva in 1986.

George Shultz arrived in Moscow after the violent accusations on both
sides regarding espionage at the embassies. According to Tass, the story of
irresistible Mata Haris who had surrounded the Marines on guard was thrown

on the negotiating table like a "dead mouse." Yet in spite of domestic pressures, Shultz had brought two hundred advisers with him, and the discussions were profitable. Reagan sent a conciliatory letter to Gorbachev, and the Soviet leader replied with an offer of a more substantial agreement than any previous ones: Moscow was willing to insert "into the agreement on cruise missiles the commitment to completely eliminate its operative tactical missiles in a relatively brief and precisely determined period of time."[12] This was another step toward a double zero option. When Shultz left, he stated, "We have made good progress on missiles," but Washington still kept its hand covered. The dialogue was clouded by the muffled noise of arguments in the background. Gorbachev visited the Baikonur Cosmodrome with Chebrikov and Zaikov in mid-May, where he delivered another bitter indictment of the SDI.

In an interview with L'Unità a few days later, the Soviet leader complained energetically about the hesitations of the West, and of Europe in particular, to respond to the Soviets' repeated offers.[13] The statement of 15 January 1986, and the proposals for nuclear and conventional disarmament were still on the table, but no one had made any moves. The responsibility for the stalemate, for the lack of reaction, and for the paralysis of the Geneva negotiations could certainly not be blamed on the Kremlin's bad will. But during the course of a conversation with the Italian Communist journalists, Gorbachev made an allusion to Afghanistan that international observers would immediately grasp:

> The USSR does not interfere and in the future will not interfere in the question of where our Afghan comrades will search for interlocutors in order to achieve their program of national reconciliation: in their country, among Afghan refugees or émigrés, or even in your country, Italy.

Only one Afghan émigré famous enough to deserve mention lived in Italy: the former king, Muhammad Zahir Shah. Thus, Moscow was intimating that it had no prejudices against the expansion of national reconciliation, and this may have been meant as an explicit invitation to Kabul to make more substantial openings. Gorbachev added that "it was profoundly mistaken" to believe that the USSR would accept a political settlement only on the condition that "it kept Afghanistan in its sphere of influence." In spite of the obvious difficulties, Gorbachev continued to work on eliminating the obstacle Afghanistan posed to dialogue with the West (and with China). Two months later Najibullah would make a new, unexpected appearance in Moscow. On 14 July Kabul announced it would extend the unilateral truce for another six months, even though in point of fact there hadn't been much of a truce during attempts to achieve national reconciliation. Najibullah met with Gorbachev to study new initiatives that could shift the situation. Najibullah's last move was to approve the new Afghan constitution, which provided for a bicameral parliament elected by universal suffrage.

In the meantime, a new law went into effect that authorized the existence of different political parties. In Moscow, Najibullah disclosed that opposition groups could occupy important positions in the government, such as vice president of the new Afghan Republic, the deputy chair of the Council of Ministers, or the president of the Supreme Court. He even told reporters, "I am ready to step aside if the supreme interest of the people requires it."[14] But the "Peshawar seven" (the leaders of seven guerrilla groups based in Peshawar, Pakistan) did not reply. On the other hand, Gorbachev, who reiterated Soviet support for the policy of reconciliation and continued to denounce the increasing aid to the guerrillas by Pakistan and the United States, was pressed by unavoidable demands. America's European allies insisted on considering Afghanistan a litmus test of Soviet intentions. Even Soviet dialogue with China, which was still cut off by the Cambodian problem, could be restored through Afghanistan. But for the moment there was no alternative. There were no new developments until September. The Geneva negotiations, under the aegis of the United Nations, proceeded slowly. When talks between Pakistan and Afghanistan resumed, with Diego Cordovez acting as mediator, Kabul presented a new schedule for the withdrawal of Soviet troops. The previous session had ended with Pakistan asking for the withdrawal in seven months, and Afghanistan instead proposing eighteen months. Now Kabul proposed a withdrawal in twelve months. The comings and goings between Moscow and Kabul hinted at other developments. The new proposal was made official by Najibullah in November, when he was elected head of state.

The seesaw of relations with Washington, however, was quickening its rhythm. Gorbachev used his interviews with foreign newspapers to issue signals and proposals in public, while his confidential contacts thickened. In a talk with the editor in chief of the Indonesian newspaper *Merdeka*, the Soviet leader outlined the entire double zero option: the elimination of all medium-range missiles, including the hundred per side in Asia. There were some low blows. The proposal had been anticipated by General Nikolai Chervov (who was the General Staff's chief of controls on armaments) in early July in a confidential talk with U.S. negotiator Maynard Glitman. It was meant as a way to take the pulse of the White House. There were those in Washington, however, who decided to "burn" the operation by divulging its contents ahead of time. Moscow was clearly irritated, and sharply denied the reports.

In Geneva the negotiation mechanism ran into engine trouble on the last curve: the Pershing IA. This was an unexpected and clearly artificial obstacle, raised by Chancellor Kohl, dealing with short-range missiles, with conventional warheads commanded by the Bonn government, and with nuclear warheads under American command. By playing on the ambiguities of the interchangeable warheads, the West German government refused to dismantle its seventy-two missiles. Marshal Akhromeyev replied that Moscow was not asking for the elimination of the Pershing IA's but that it did expect the Germans to dismantle their nuclear warheads, which belonged under the double zero option since they were "American." For almost two months discussions had focused on splitting hairs, which obviously helped extremist groups in Washington to block further progress. Finally, at the end of August, Chancellor Kohl submitted to pressure from other European governments and heated debates at home and decided to unload the Washington hawks and announced that the Pershing IA would be retired in 1991. Moscow's positive reaction was instantaneous. Gerasimov received the evolution in the German position "with interest" and he invited Washington to follow suit. The spokesman said that Moscow had not liked Reagan's recent speech in Los Angeles, but intimated that there were several issues, in particular the section on control, on which "an agreement can be reached in Geneva."[15] Once more a summit seemed to be within reach, even if Washington intermittently fired disturbing shots, such as the controversy over the Abalakovo radar station, near Krasnoyarsk. The American administration, which did not lose sight of its wish to get rid of the ABM Treaty, claimed that the radar station violated the 1972 treaty. At this point the Kremlin allowed an American delegation to visit the construction site and its plant. This was the first time ever that the Soviet Union had permitted an inspection on its own territory without a reciprocal gesture. At the beginning of September the American experts, headed by Democratic Congressman Thomas Downey, concluded their on-site inspection. Their findings are still confidential, but the Krasnoyarsk visit dealt another blow to mutual distrust.[16]

However, the rhythms were quickening. It was now clear that Gorbachev's and Reagan's designs coincided: both needed results urgently, before Reagan's term was over. Gorbachev, who was officially on vacation, published an article in *Pravda* and *Sovetskaya Rossia*. The occasion was the eve of the forty-second session of the U.N. General Assembly. The Soviet leader needed to illustrate the key concepts of his détente strategy and expand it. Essentially, the secretary-general said that all traditional military doctrines had to be revised for the nuclear age. Neither nuclear deterrence nor a flexible nuclear response could be considered. At the U.N. Security Council, Gorbachev ascribed a new, important, and unprecedented role to the control mechanism established for the two sides, which would have the authority to restore order

155

where it had been disturbed, and to prevent conflicts. The tactical alternative that the Americans took in the Persian Gulf was well received. But the issues were broader, and not just tactical. A safer world would be the result of joint efforts toward a new economic order, "ecological safety," and nuclear and conventional disarmament. In a completely unprecedented Soviet formulation, the concept of "mutual interdependence" was stretched to the point of recognizing that "the world cannot be safe if individual rights are violated."[17] This was the first hint of a new concept that would be confirmed in more and more explicit terms. At international gatherings Gorbachev's Kremlin had decided to face up to the thorny question of human rights, both social and individual; in fact, individual human rights would be given full recognition in the institutional reform bills approved at the party's Nineteenth Conference in June of the following year.

The actual turning point, which had been carefully prepared by the two sides, came on the occasion of Shevardnadze's trip to Washington. The agreement "in principle" to eliminate short- and medium-range missiles was the first positive reversal in the tendencies of Soviet-American relations in the last decade, and it resulted from the groundwork done at Reykjavik. But the effect exceeded by far the important area of Euromissiles. In fact, the decision was made to start new international negotiations on nuclear testing by December 1987. This too was a compromise because Moscow wanted a speedy end to the tests, while Washington intended to continue them in its development of the SDI. But the two sides agreed to move toward reductions in stages, along with joint verification of the control systems and ratification of the restrictive treaties of 1974 and 1976 (which the United States signed but did not ratify). The joint communiqué also mentioned future agreements in the field of strategic weapons ("active measures to draw up an agreement on a 50 percent reduction in strategic nuclear weapons"). There was no mention of the Soviet request for "strict observance of the ABM Treaty." However, the Soviet foreign minister's visit had been preceded by an American Senate vote that required the president to obtain the authorization of Congress before conducting tests on elements of the SDI that might exceed the bounds of a "traditional" interpretation of the ABM Treaty. The discussion of human rights was also "constructive." The two foreign ministers decided to meet in Moscow in the latter half of October, after which a summit would be held, as both Reagan and Gorbachev seemed to want, as did the Democratic majority in the House and Senate.

Worldwide reaction was enthusiastic, proving that this reversal had been awaited and hoped for. This was a success for both men, but especially for Gorbachev. He had had the more difficult task of fighting the current, and he had brought two fundamental arguments to the peace table that could break the vicious circle of mutual distrust: he affirmed that the task of internal reform in a country facing difficulties was irreversible, and that a radically new foreign policy was an unavoidable necessity. Gorbachev also won, however, against ideas and concepts that were anything but dead inside his own country. The sincerity of his proposal to the rest of the world ("our reform-revolution is the other side of the coin of our proposal for détente") was part of a difficult and unresolved struggle on the home front to make the reform prevail over its adversaries. Decades of isolation and suspicion that had been tolerated and often proudly kept alive could not be swept away all at once. Among the opponents of perestroika, it is not hard to make out the ranks of those who often and gladly resort to talk about the "foreign enemy," or the omnipresent "subversion," that can only be overcome by ending critical reflection on Soviet experience, going back to withdrawal, and eyeing with suspicion the interest that Gorbachev's reversals had excited all over the world. Thus, in one of history's fortunate paradoxes, Gorbachev helped Reagan to conclude, on a happy note, his second and last term. And Reagan, who may have continued to think that he was facing the "evil empire," or the new Faust, helped Gorbachev.

Optimism was spreading. But before the final stretch there were some tricky curves to negotiate. When George Shultz came to Moscow in early October, there was a sudden slowdown after a good beginning. The Soviet side went back to asking questions about Star Wars. Was Washington willing to provide a list of devices whose deployment in space could be forbidden by common agreement? Shevardnadze hinted that an agreement to respect the ABM Treaty for a ten-year period required some guarantees from the American side. Essentially, this would constitute a new Soviet concession, given that the possibility of "something" being deployed in space was now admissible. But it looked like a stiffening of attitude. George Shultz had not come to talk about the Strategic Defense Initiative; for President Reagan this was a nonnegotiable question. After an animated meeting between Gorbachev and Shultz, the Soviet foreign minister told reporters that "the conditions do not exist to set the date for Mikhail Gorbachev's trip to Washington." This was a cold shower. Perhaps Gorbachev had wanted to drive another wedge between Reagan and the Congress, which was now aiming to observe the ABM Treaty, and which Reagan accused of "often being on the other side" of the negotiation table. Perhaps members of the Politburo or of the military leadership had objected to Gorbachev's excessive compliancy.

The world reacted to the Soviet move with disappointment and surprise. Gorbachev quickly realized the risk of a sudden blurring of the line thus far followed. So on 27 October, Shevardnadze met with Ambassador Jack Matlock and proposed new talks with Reagan and Shultz while the drums were still beating. At the same time, various Soviet sources disclosed that any pessimism was "unjustified," and that the USSR "had not raised the price."[18] Washington accepted in a split second. Three days later, on 30 October, Shevardnadze was already in Washington with a letter from Gorbachev to Reagan. On the same day, the Soviet spokesman, Pyadyshev, explained that Moscow was favorable to a summit that would achieve "a serious exchange of ideas on offensive strategic arms and on measures to reinforce the conditions of the ABM Treaty." There was an obvious, even dramatic mellowing. Gorbachev's letter actually proposed two summits with specific agendas— one to be held in Washington immediately, and one to be held in Moscow in mid-1988. The first of the two encounters would "complete definition of the agreement to eliminate short- and medium-range missiles," and elaborate a "basis of understanding" on the reduction of strategic nuclear weapons, "on the condition not to use the right to abandon the ABM Treaty for a period of time to be agreed upon." The second summit would "draw conclusions from these premises"; in other words, it would allow for the signing of a treaty for the reduction of strategic arms.

In Moscow, Gorbachev intended to untie the link between the ABM Treaty and START (Strategic Arms Reduction Talks). A clear choice had been made. After some hesitation, the Kremlin realized that it was more convenient to follow the policy of untying the Reykjavik package. The distance between the two sides on other matters of strategic importance was still so wide that to bind oneself to a preliminary clarification of these topics would have meant freezing everything again, even the possibility of a separate accord on short- and medium-range missiles. The positions had not shifted very much. The USSR wanted the 1972 treaty to remain in force for another ten years just as it was. The United States proposed a shorter period of time (seven years) and a more "extensive" interpretation. The head of the Soviet agency for disarmament, Viktor Karpov, would only explain that "there is already a mutual understanding between the sides in principle," that "the ABM Treaty constitutes the basis for achieving strategic stability during the time period agreed upon." But as far as the SDI was concerned, Karpov specified that Moscow was not inclined to consider it a separate subject of negotiations."[19] The formula was not an ultimatum, and it had been deliberately studied to indicate a shift of attention to the ABM Treaty, but it also showed that Moscow had not given up on the link, that for now it would limit itself to postponing this round until the middle of the following year. This was exactly what Reagan had been waiting for: the summit would be held in Washington on 7 December.

Once the last tactical hesitations had been overcome, the way was clear.

In the later half of November the last meeting between the heads of the two diplomatic corps took place, while consultations grew more intense. John Whitehead had just left Moscow, after speaking with Shevardnadze about the general topics, with Aleksandr Bessmertnykh about bilateral relations, and with Anatoli Adamishin about humanitarian problems. Yuli Vorontsov flew to Geneva to talk about regional conflicts with Michael Armacost. The final difficulties—and there would be no lack of them in the final hours—were being ironed out.

On the eve of his departure for America, Gorbachev gave an interview to an American television correspondent and stated clearly that "the SDI is not the subject of the Washington negotiations." In fact, the Soviet leader had agreed to meet the American president for the third time with a platform that was virtually identical to what Andrei Sakharov had suggested one year earlier. When the academician returned from his Gorky exile, he had criticized Reagan's plan for a space shield: he claimed that it was "technically impossible," and unusable for strategic purposes because one of the two sides would always be able to find sufficient, though not necessarily identical, countermeasures. At the same time Sakharov had criticized the Soviet position that at the time was rigidly linking any progress on the reduction of strategic arms to a preliminary agreement on the Americans' giving up the SDI. The famous physicist had said the following:

> For us the most important thing is to respect the ABM agreement. The United States can go forward with their SDI, as long as it does not violate the treaty. Why do we say this? Lately, there has been a continuous change in the importance that the Americans attribute to the Strategic Defense Initiative. It seems to be a bottle with variable contents: the SDI is at the bottom, but the liquid inside keeps changing. At the beginning it seemed something like cognac, now it seems like wine, and perhaps in a little while it will turn into Coca-Cola. Since we don't know what the SDI is, we cannot tell the Americans whether or not we agree with it. For that matter, the Americans even refuse to begin discussions with us on the SDI. So we should tell them something else: let's agree that what they are doing will not violate the ABM Treaty for a given period of time. That is all.[20]

This was an effective and spirited way of spreading a layer of continuity to a substantial evolution. But Vorontsov was correct in emphasizing that Washington's positions on the subject had also undergone deep changes. Reagan was now almost alone in his stubborn defense of his "creature." On the other hand, it was clear that Moscow was no less rigid in its attempts to bind the United States with its current requests (in fact, the ABM Treaty "as it stands" excluded the possibility of installing any space shield), but it eliminated an insurmountable obstacle from the negotiating table and also offered—on close examination—a possible way out for Reagan. Gorbachev knew that Reagan would not abandon a flag he had waved for four years, and on which he had spent millions of dollars in public money. The American public, which did not understand the technical fine points, would think that its president had beaten the Russians on the subject of Star Wars, while in essence the SDI could be indefinitely postponed.

The Washington summit thus took place with a well-reshuffled deck of cards. All of the details of the agreement on medium- and short-range missiles had already been prepared. The only thing missing was the solemn signature that would mark the historical event and admit a gust of fresh air into relations between the two superpowers. The rest of the talks were aimed at the future and at entering new stages. Now the discussions were taking place between two "teams," both of which wanted to reach an understanding. Gorbachev was surrounded by the same team that had accompanied him to Geneva and Reykjavik. Reagan had reorganized his own team, replacing Caspar Weinberger with Frank Carlucci.

In one of history's frequent ironies, the Washington summit would witness the creation of an "improper" alliance between the two leaders, each of whom, for different reasons, wanted to strike a blow against the opponents of arms control. Once the agreement on Euromissiles had been signed, each man needed further results, and needed to broaden its implications. Each needed to pave the way to the next summit. Each needed to come to terms with clear and unavoidable obligations. Gorbachev could not agree to a 50 percent reduction in strategic arms without receiving in exchange a guarantee that the ABM Treaty would not be rescinded. Reagan could not make a guarantee that would leave him vulnerable to attacks from the right wing on the eve of an election campaign. Therefore, both men knew that they had to take advantage of the moment and foster progress and a better mutual understanding, and both knew that there would be no other practical results.

However, the summit concluded with a dramatic political success for both, and it became a milestone in Soviet-American relations and in international détente. Reagan had won. The opinion polls indicated an 80 percent approval rating from the American people. Gorbachev went back to Moscow even stronger than before. The Soviet polls still have little value, but to those who viewed the agreement suspiciously he proved that even America could be led to fruitful negotiations—even the America of the "hawkish" Ronald Reagan. More than anything else, he proved that the road to further developments was open. The summit had two other results. Gorbachev won the hearts of the American people. The era of the "evil empire" was over. But the agreement also opened a breach in the Soviet world's historical impenetrability before foreign eyes. The treaty provided for mutual inspections and controls that would throw open a window of trust that had never before existed. Its impact would also play a favorable role in the internal struggle for perestroika.

The next meeting was scheduled for mid-May 1988 in Moscow. The exact date could not be set, but everything was in motion. Arthur Schlesinger, Jr., wrote the epigraph for the third Gorbachev-Reagan summit in the *Wall Street Journal*, saying that "Reagan himself seems to have forgotten Reaganism." At the final press conference, Gorbachev gave the following summary:

> Today we can talk about a new stage in relations between the United States and the USSR and in the international situation . . . at the highest level the two sides recognize that they are exiting from the phase of opposing positions. . . . Geneva and Reykjavik were not in vain. [21]

There was great euphoria, but behind the scenes, beneath the sparkling veneer of smiles, the problems were still there. The summit had just ended and Reagan repeated his unshakable determination not to abandon the SDI. In a televised allocution on 14 December, Gorbachev also returned to the problem to remind everyone that substantial problems persisted. The "new atmosphere" had to be safeguarded. But "I have to tell you that it is still too early to talk about a drastic reversal."

The year that was ending had witnessed significant successes in Gorbachev's new foreign policy. New developments had affected the entire system of relations inside the "socialist camp," by introducing objective elements of "destabilization." Gorbachev had moved in this very delicate area with particular caution. The Soviet leader was at the center of a dilemma in both practice and principle. On the one hand, his position would be strengthened by the development of "perestroikas" among allied countries. But situations in the socialist countries varied, and did not allow for uniform solutions. On the other hand, some of the ruling powers in Prague, Bucharest, Sofia, and Berlin, were openly hostile in varying degrees to the innovations elaborated by the Soviet leadership. Pressures and impositions from the Kremlin in some situations could provoke uncontrollable crises. The last four months of the year had witnessed a rapid succession of political uprisings, of various types and intensity, in Rumania, Hungary, Czechoslovakia, Poland, and Bulgaria. The most recent had been the changing of the guard in the leadership of the Czechoslovakian party, with the appointment of Miloš Jakeš as general secretary and Gustav Husak as president. This did not represent a clear shift toward reform, but at least on the surface it signaled the Prague leadership's difficult need to adapt. In November the Rumanian dictator had

161

to face a workers' movement in Brasov. The referendum announced by General Jaruszelski did not solve the problems of political relations in Poland, and had no effect on the size of the economic and social crisis. In Hungary, János Kádár's position had been weakened under the pressure of ultrain-novators like Károlyi Grosz. Todor Zhivkov, who had quickly converted to perestroika, was forced to postpone the party conference that was supposed to launch the Bulgarian economic reform. The situation remained fluid and uncertain. Not all of the changes were in tune with each other or with what was going on in Moscow.

In April, during a trip to Prague, Gorbachev had rejected the idea of proposing a new Muscovite model to the allies. He had reassured the skeptical by saying that each country had to find its own solution: the important thing was not to be immobilized. The inevitable differences could even be useful. But clearly the implications of perestroika were so broad that they upset fifty years' worth of ideas consolidated inside the "camp." Even if for the time being the allies had not yet been fully included in the "brain trust" of the Kremlin's foreign policy, they speculated over possible repercussions with increasing restlessness.

Gorbachev organized his "dress rehearsal" on the occasion of the festivities for the seventieth anniversary of the October Revolution by holding one of the largest assemblies of "left-wing and progressive" forces ever in Moscow. One hundred forty parties and movements participated: Communists, Socialists, Social Democrats, and liberation movements. The preparations had been painstaking, and not without fluctuations and initial uncertainties regarding the form and composition of the gathering. The largest Communist party in the West, the Italians, had let the Soviets know beforehand that they were willing to participate as long as the encounter remained informal and no documents were approved. Completely opposite voices were raised by other Communist parties that were not in power and by "brother" countries.

Gorbachev took the approach of opening up as much dialogue as possible with all the forces of the left. This was already new. In his short opening speech he once again brought up the issue of interdependence. "No one has Ariadne's thread in hand to escape from the labyrinth of the contemporary world." This is why "it is no longer possible to watch international devel-opment solely from the point of view of a struggle between two opposing systems." This did not mean the "unification or convergence" of the two social systems. Socialism still represented "an alternative" to capitalism. But today one had to realize above all that an explosive "critical mass" had been created that could threaten the very existence of human civilization. This expression was deliberately borrowed from nuclear terminology, and his speech was addressed to the West as a whole. Yet Gorbachev also wanted to use that platform to deliver a speech to the international left, urging the forces for progress, each with its own identity, not to limit themselves to copying Moscow. According to Gorbachev, it was time for "a correlated action, obviously in modern forms." "If it can be put this way, what is needed is a more modern culture of relations among progressive forces." The reactions varied from the general applause of the Socialist, Social Democratic, and some of the Communist parties, particularly the Italians, to the complete coldness of Ceauşescu, Husak, and numerous Communist representatives who had come to Moscow to express their perturbation and even their open dissatisfaction.

Gorbachev brought to everyone's attention one of the most devastating deconstructions of dogmatic myth that had ever been expressed in the Soviet capital. "The usual formula of a growing general crisis in capitalism" had lost all worth. Gorbachev insisted that it was partly negated by the realization that "the forces of the Old World have the possibility, with every twist of history, of eliminating the most dangerous contradictions." It was also useless to conceal the fact that "for the moment, real socialism is behind capitalism in terms of technological growth." Therefore, it was necessary to come up with new ideas and concepts. If at the beginning of the century not all of Marx and Engels' formulations were still applicable to the age of imperialism, "it's even less possible to do the same thing today, and evaluate the contemporary world according to postulates formulated in the 1950s and 1960s, or even in the 1930s." As far as the Communist movement was concerned, Gorbachev confirmed its "prominent position among the forces of the avant-garde." But it too "needs to renew itself, to change qualitatively." This is where the Soviet leader inserted a sentence that seemed to echo closely what Enrico Berlinguer had said after the events of the Polish crisis regarding the "exhaustion of the propelling force of the October Revolution." The general secretary of the Communist Party of the Soviet Union acknowledged that "during the times of stagnation, we too were strongly aware of how much the international impulse of socialism had decreased."[22] There is a considerable difference between "exhaustion" and "decrease," but both shared a common realization. This was an invitation to a difficult discussion that no longer involved just the Communists, but all the forces of the left.

Sixth Conversation

The Gorbachev Team; the Military; Disarmament

•   •   •

G.C. The Washington summit was an indisputable personal success for Gorbachev, partly from the perspective of the image he succeeded in conveying to the American public. No one can doubt that the general secretary is fully in command of his public image, but there are legitimate questions regarding which of his associates at the Politburo or in the Secretariat of the Central Committee has the ability to help him so shrewdly plan his public appearances and define his style. The impact of Gorbachev's behavior is surely enhanced by the fact that he represents an enormous change from his predecessors. But Gorbachev's character is also radically different from Ligachev's, and it meets the Western public's expectations with astonishing accuracy. It's as if Gorbachev had lived in the West for a long time and knew how a leader produced by a representative democracy should behave, move, and speak. On the contrary, we know that in this regard, Gorbachev's prior experience was very limited. If you exclude his trips to Canada and to Great Britain before his election as general secretary, Gorbachev had never been abroad in an official capacity. He had been to Italy on vacation many years earlier, and he had attended Enrico Berlinguer's funeral in Rome. This is why I ask how Gorbachev utilized his associates' experiences. But even before that, how did he chose these associates? How did he know they would be useful? What kind of background did these men have?

R.M. There is no doubt in my mind that the Washington trip was very carefully planned, not only regarding the political content of the talks, but also regarding his image. All the meetings that took place in Washington—with Sovietologists, congressmen, businessmen, journalists, and so on—had been prepared even before his plane took off from Moscow. Even in the preparatory phases, Gorbachev played the main role. But no one could predict ahead of time what issues would be raised. Gorbachev was certainly helped by his direct associates, especially in writing his personal speeches. He received specific advice. Even Gorbachev's unexpected stop on the way to the White House, when he got out of his limousine to shake hands with the citizens of Washington—taking the American Secret Service by surprise—had undoubtedly been planned beforehand. I think that you can't underestimate the experience he gained on previous trips abroad. It's true that as a member of the Politburo he traveled only to Canada and England, but he was part of various delegations when he was the first secretary of Stavropol. Earlier, in 1969 I believe, he had been to Czechoslovakia. In 1972 he went to Belgium. In 1975 he visited West Germany. As you mentioned, he attended Berlinguer's funeral, and in 1985, when he was already general secretary, he went to Paris. However, I agree with you that his last trip to the United States highlighted a milestone in his development as an international leader.

A highly qualified team on foreign policy had formed around him. I believe that Anatoli Dobrynin played an important role; today he is secretary of the Central Committee, but he had worked in the United States since 1957, first as the deputy to the secretary-general of the United Nations, and then, starting in 1962, as ambassador to Washington. In my opinion he is our greatest expert on the United States today, having represented the Soviet Union to seven different American presidents. A very important role is also played by Aleksandr Yakovlev, who takes an active part in planning Gorbachev's foreign trips. A historian and an economist—and now a full member of the Politburo; he studied at an American university for one year. For ten years he was ambassador to Canada, and he visited the United States frequently.

One of Gorbachev's closest advisers has been Georgi Arbatov, a member of the Central Committee, a scholar, and an expert in American studies who had directed the Institute for the United States and Canada since 1967. Dobrynin, Yakovlev, and Arbatov were the "brain trust" for Gorbachev's first trip to America. But let's not leave out Eduard Shevardnadze. I think that until 1985 not even he had imagined he would ever have a diplomatic career, yet he demonstrated exceptional diplomatic skills, and in a short time mastered the new area that had been assigned to him.

Obviously, the staff of associates is huge. It includes people from the Foreign Ministry, from the Central Committee, from the KGB, and from the intelligentsia, including editors in chief of newspapers and magazines. Fashion designers and cosmetologists also took part. The doctors, who had played a crucial role in Leonid Brezhnev's trips abroad, had little to do this time.

G.C. And the military? Their attitude toward Gorbachev's policies remains largely uninvestigated. In a 1987 speech at Murmansk, Gorbachev said that "even" the generals agreed to the line he had adopted (but this expression was later cut from the published text). This expression was reassuring, but it also indicated that there had been arguments before the Reykjavik package could be "untied." I think that it's at least probable that they thought Gorbachev was making too many military concessions to America. I was very struck by a press conference in Moscow in the fall of 1987, attended by Georgi Arbatov, Valentin Falin (then the director of *Novosti*), and a representative of the military. The correspondent for *Krasnaya Zvezda* stood up in uniform and asked a question from a written text. "Don't you think that Reagan's consent to sign the agreement to eliminate medium- and short-range missiles was dictated by primarily tactical reasons and by considerations of domestic policy?" Arbatov, Falin, and the military expert acted surprised, and all three gave a response to *Krasnaya Zvezda*. But to me that question sent a definite signal. I remember that at a previous press conference, Marshal Akhromeyev had answered an American reporter's question regarding the relationship between politicians and the military by saying, "I am a military man, but I am also a party member. And as such, I believe that concessions can be made on a strictly military level that are worth making because of their overall political and diplomatic advantages."

Shevardnadze spoke in Geneva after his final meeting with Shultz before the Washington summit, and he also addressed the question of whether the Soviet Union's concessions were more significant than those of the United States. He answered, "No, we have respected the interests of the USSR and the United States." In the USSR, this sentence means: we have given America what it was reasonable to give without jeopardizing our own security. Finally, another topic has to be explored. What is the relationship—and I believe that one exists—between resistance to perestroika, to democratization, and to the opening of the country to dialogue and to foreign influence, and conservative attitudes in the area of military doctrine?

R.M. In his Murmansk speech on 1 October, Gorbachev appeared completely convinced that he had the full agreement of the military leadership. I don't mean to say that there were no arguments or disagreements between politicians and the military, and among different groups of military leaders. There had been a repeated debate on various questions of military policy in the USSR in the past. This was during Stalin's time, before, during, and after the war. I have no doubt that a discussion is underway today as well. Modern Soviet military doctrine is the result of the work of many specialists who can and do have different and valuable points of view on the prospects of military relations. When Brezhnev was still alive, his negotiations with Reagan produced no results. The confrontation with the Americans had gotten so bad that Andropov interrupted all talks on restricting nuclear arms.

When Gorbachev came to power in 1985, an agreement like the one he would later sign in Washington was almost unimaginable. It is certain that in the Supreme Council on Defense, chaired by Gorbachev, and whose members included army and navy leaders, there was an argument. But no one knew its contents, its various hypotheses, or its alternatives. However, I think that the military leaders exercised no discernible opposition to the process of democratization and glasnost.

I am convinced that the crux of the debate in military circles concerned verifications and on-site inspections. On this point, at the very end, the USSR accepted the basis of the American proposals. Today you can even read in the Soviet press the acknowledgment that the USSR faced the new round of negotiations by making broader concessions than the Americans. But the first step had to be taken in order to lead the talks out of the quagmire into which they'd sunken. I think that the military understands better than anyone else that there are too many weapons in the world today, and that more of them can no longer increase the country's security, but they would instead increase the unpredictability and risk of an "accidental war." The military experts aren't blind. They have not failed to notice the weakness of the Soviet economy, which keeps them from keeping up with the competition in the frenetic arms race. Military engineers are well aware that even in the area of missiles we are now forced to use certain elements of Western devices, acquired, copied, and obtained through technical and scientific espionage. It is true that we could build them too, but certain sophisticated components produced in the West are far better than their Soviet prototypes. In the long term, this situation would become intolerable. We need to revive our economy, both in military and nonmilitary sectors. The army leaders realize this, which makes them allies rather than adversaries of Gorbachev.

G.C. François Feitö's thesis is that the military is the only sector of the Soviet population that for years has lived in active and total competition with the West.

R.M. Exactly. We claim to have reached military parity with the West, and the Western experts agree on this point. But this is a temporary parity. At the next turn in the arms race the USSR could once again find itself dropping behind. The military does not want a repeat of the powerlessness they faced in the years that American spy planes could fly over Moscow and Leningrad at an altitude of twenty kilometers, and we weren't able to do anything because our missiles and aircraft couldn't go higher than sixteen to seventeen kilometers. In 1962, during the Caribbean crisis, the USSR had one-tenth the atomic potential that NATO had. To preserve our parity it is thus indispensable to stop the arms race. You could write that the SDI program is irrational, wasteful, and inefficient: these are fair considerations. But it is also true that the USSR is incapable of developing its own SDI.

G.C. So you don't see disagreements between the political and military leadership, at least on the subject of defense strategy. But the army is a colossal presence in the Soviet Union. How is it possible for it not to have a strong influence on the country's political and social relations?

R.M. The military has repeatedly taken positions different from the party's decisions, for example, when Stalin was denounced at the party's Twentieth and Twenty-First congresses. This was one of the reasons why the military leaders supported Khrushchev's dismissal, and later on put pressure on Brezhnev to rehabilitate Stalin. Here they were aligned with the party's most conservative sectors. But the new generation of generals had a much less nostalgic attitude. They had begun their careers during the war, but as lower-ranked officers. Their ascent to the leadership took place during the Khrushchev and Brezhnev years. The defense minister, Dmitri Yazov, had been a company commander at the end of the war. His first deputy, Marshal Akhromeyev, had been the commander of a battalion. These cadres clearly saw things differently than the "Stalinist" marshals and generals. But it is equally true that they are not men without character, completely subservient to the politicians. Within their capacities they took part in the definition of all the most important decisions.

G.C. It's very interesting to examine the developments in Gorbachev's position toward dissidents. At the end of 1985, for example, he said that the Jewish problem was "imaginary." In February 1986, in an interview with *L'Humanité*, he returned to the subject, mentioning that in the USSR anti-Semitism was forbidden by law, as were all other forms of racial discrimination. He added that the accusations of anti-Semitism made against the USSR were part of a psychological war. He admitted the existence of censorship, but he limited the areas in which it was applied. He claimed that in the Soviet Union there were no political prisoners. However, he admitted that there were about two hundred people currently incarcerated for crimes against the state. His first policy decision in this regard was the exchange between Anatoli Shcharansky and a group of Soviet agents. Later a new series of more permissive procedures for obtaining an exit visa from the USSR were approved. Yelena Bonner was allowed to come to the United States for hospitalization at the end of 1985. In November 1986 new regulations for entering and leaving the country were passed that were decidedly more liberal than previous ones. Finally, there was Sakharov's liberation from his Gorky exile. We will return to the subject, but up to this point you can see clear developments.

R.M. The change was visible even if it was slow. Ms. Bonner had already been abroad three or four times, once in order to receive her husband's Nobel Prize. Even exchanges of secret agents for dissidents was nothing new; there had been an exchange between the secretary of the Chilean Communist Party, Luis Corvalan, and Vladimir Bukovsky. The reversal took place with the release of Sakharov. After that moment, in a three-month period, about three hundred people were released. Fifty to sixty of them asked permission to emigrate and their requests were immediately granted. Some of those who remained completely stopped all political activity. The majority, on the contrary, began to do once more what they had done before, except at this point the state machine had adopted a different attitude. Many demonstrations took place without obstacles. The Crimean Tatars were sent back home only after several demonstrations in downtown Moscow. To my knowledge there were no later arrests. The publication of samizdats increased considerably without too many repressive interventions. Pamphlets that in the past would have constituted proof of a crime, since they were "anti-Soviet," were repeatedly distributed in Moscow. In some cases there were detentions, and some fines were issued for "unloading trash in public places." In other cases the courts handed down sentences of five or ten days' confinement for "minor delinquency." But I think it would be a mistake to focus only on the dissidents—some hundred of them—from the 1960s and 1970s. The political picture had changed a great deal. Glasnost, the first forms of democratization, the end of fear, and the invitations from the top to a "revolutionary perestroika" changed the terms of the problem.

In 1987 the so-called informal groups began to proliferate. At the beginning there were about one hundred of them. By September 1987 there were already a few thousand. In mid-1988 they were counted at no fewer than thirty thousand. Millions of people were directly involved. All of this had nothing in common with the dissident movements of the past. New leaders, other forms of organization, and other themes emerged. I only wish to add that all of this shocked the bureaucracy a great deal, and it would have been impossible if Andropov had not stayed in the party leadership. He too projected great changes, but not in the area of democracy. The harsh battle that he had begun against the Brezhnev gang was in fact accompanied by even more repressive steps against all types of dissidents. Gorbachev also shared some responsibility for the policy against the dissidents during the Brezhnev years. He became secretary of the Central Committee in 1978 and entered the Politburo in 1980. Some of the decisions on dissidents, such as Sakharov's exile, were made at the level of the Politburo. I think that Gorbachev probably didn't agree back then, but probably didn't want to expose himself. Nor could he do so immediately after April 1985, and as we have seen, he proceeded very gradually at the beginning.

G.C. But it's also true that the shift toward democratization didn't take place until January 1987. Only at that point did Gorbachev fully realize the problems of reforming the political system. In the first two years he focused his attention on economic reform. The first signals of a new approach to "human rights" seem to have been based on strategic concerns rather than on a philosophical position.

R.M. Maybe. Through his international contacts, he must have realized what a high price the country was paying for the war it was conducting against a relatively small group of dissidents. But his reflections on domestic affairs were also maturing. The first two years of drawing up the reform proved the need for a deep political change.

G.C. This is why we are going back to the debates that flared in the party leadership on the eve of the January plenum.

R.M. That was the phase in which the debate on glasnost and on freedom of information sharpened. It was only logical that the subject of dissent would enter into the debate. The official press leaked the news that many of the dissidents' criticisms were right. Freedom of discussion had to include the freedom to criticize mistaken positions.

G.C. In an interview with the *Financial Times* in December 1987, you said that there were almost twenty-five hundred political prisoners in the USSR. On the basis of what data?

R.M. Obviously, we have no official data. When our police talk about "political" prisoners, they mean individuals convicted on the basis of articles 70 and 190 of the RSFSR Penal Code (or the corresponding articles in the penal codes of the other republics). But many others should be added to the list: people convicted for "nationalism," the "religious," and so on. The truth is that all you had to do was criticize official policy on religion or the nationalities to run up against numerous articles in the penal code. Many "dissidents" were jailed for breaking the rules of residence, for disturbing the peace, or for "attempted rape" (this is what happened to the Ukrainian dissident Vyacheslav Chernovol). Others were confined to psychiatric hospitals for "misdemeanors." The well-known dissident Aleksandr Podrabinek was incarcerated for "illegal possession of a firearm."

G.C. I myself have witnessed this. In the past five years I've been approached by fourteen people who were sentenced to different periods of detention for "crimes of conscience." Most of them had stayed in psychiatric clinics. I've kept the documentation of their stories. All of them were unknown to the international press, and they had trouble finding my address. I imagine there were others who didn't succeed, even if they tried. And there are still more who didn't try.

R.M. I know dozens of similar cases of victims of official abuse. In all honesty, I have to admit that some of them didn't seem mentally fit. Yet these people were not at all dangerous, and in some cases their forced detention in a psychiatric clinic worsened their condition. Almost all of them asked me to make their unhappy cases known. However, I didn't have the means to verify what they said, and the Western correspondents only write about the most famous cases. I met with other ex-convicts who had no desire to meet with foreign journalists. Not all of the dissidents wanted to be "publicized" in the West, for different reasons. Based on these considerations, I came up with the figure of twenty-five hundred "prisoners of conscience." The figure of two hundred is an obvious understatement.

G.C. I would define the situation in late 1987 as "transitional." In that period at least three unauthorized magazines were being published in Moscow in different ways. The authorities didn't seem sure about what they wanted to do.

R.M. The situation was truly unprecedented. The magazines you mentioned are *Glasnost* (editor: Sergei Grigoryants), *Press Khronika* (editor: Aleksandr Podrabinek), and *Referendum* (editor: Lev Timofeyev). But these are only the best-known. In reality, hundreds of them are being published: typewritten, photocopied, etcetera. Their circulations vary widely: from twenty to thirty copies to as many as a thousand. Very few end up in the hands of foreign journalists. Many groups have published their "manifestos," "platforms," or "declarations" in this way. Many declared themselves "political parties," such as the "Democratic Union." The activities of all these groups clearly exceed the limits of "socialist pluralism" proclaimed by Gorbachev. Moreover, some of them openly express their hostility to socialism, yet up to now there has been no wave of repressions against them. Every now and then, articles appear in the press criticizing these formations. Many people targeted the Pamyat group of Russian nationalists. There were repeated attacks on *Glasnost*. There was particular hostility toward magazines that had contacts with Western correspondents or who received economic aid from abroad. The official press ignored the other small "illegal" magazines. In my archives I've gathered more than fifty different samples published in many Soviet cities. Most of the writers are students, young people who want to communicate. I think this phenomenon is natural and necessary. Besides the political magazines, there are other magazines on specific subjects: the economy, ecology, literature and poetry, religious or national themes. There are also extremist groups and magazines that publish advice on organizing underground work.

G.C. At the same time, existing laws still haven't been changed, and they could squash this swarm of initiatives in an instant.

R.M. The debate on the subject is also open in the official press. Different sides have asked for the repeal of article 190 of the penal code. It was introduced in 1966 and constitutes the legal basis for most of the repressions. The famous article 70 on "anti-Soviet activities" was also the target of criticism. It was a legal monstrosity, both for the harshness of the penalties inflicted and for the indeterminacy of a statute that under the label of "anti-Soviet activity" could be applied to artistic works, the expression of convictions, and completely peaceful creative activities. Today the official press publishes material and articles that would have been punishable five to ten years ago based on articles 70 and 190. In recent months the courts haven't used them, and I know that a vast amount of work is being done to prepare the new penal code.

G.C. Ever since 1985 it has been clearly stated that there was a need for a huge legislative reform. Later on, the formulation "rule-of-law socialist state" would be introduced.

R.M. A work plan prepared by the Supreme Soviet was approved providing for an entire system of new laws. However, it has proven extremely difficult to make progress in this direction. The deadlines set were not respected. For example, at the beginning of 1988 the new law on the press had still not been drawn up (it was supposed to be studied by the end of 1986). And there is still no law on social organizations, even if thousands of informal groups have been pressing for official recognition.

G.C. On 20 November 1987, Gorbachev held a meeting of the Central Committee apparat. Ligachev also spoke, but the texts of their speeches were not published. We know that a tough fight was going on in the leadership over economic reform, glasnost, rehabilitation, and the history of the party and the country. On each of these points, from what I can tell, Ligachev's position was more and more openly opposed to Gorbachev's. The Soviet leader himself disclosed this in a 8 January 1988 speech to the heads of the mass media: "The process of perestroika cannot develop without a struggle; if we are conducting a truly revolutionary policy, then the fight is inevitable." The risk you can discern is that in the absence of rules the discussion could degenerate into open conflict. Gorbachev seemed to foresee what was being prepared against him.

R.M. In reality, a meeting of the central apparat was nothing new. These meetings have always been held, and the contents of the debates which take place have never been made public. Among other issues that came up, there may have been a discussion of the idea of reducing the apparat. We have more information about the Central Committee meeting on 1 December, to which the heads of the media in Moscow and in the republics were invited. This was the first time that Aleksandr Yakovlev spoke as a member of the Politburo, and his speech made a big impression by its decisive tone and its support for the transformations underway. He stated that conservativism had been weakened, but not yet defeated. It was still possible it could make a comeback. At the same time—the "Yeltsin case" was still closed—one had to guard against a "pseudorevolutionary avant-garde." Monopolies had to be eliminated in every field, getting rid of the "tens of thousands of 'Bonapartists' " and the "haughty tribes of lackeys who block our way more than all of the shortages taken together."

G.C. In mid-December, however, Ligachev held another meeting of newspaper editors and gave a speech of a completely different tenor.

R.M. Indeed. The discrepancy was so great that Gorbachev held a third meeting on 8 January to restate his position.

G.C. What are the main differences?

R.M. First of all, the development of glasnost. Starting in December 1987, political journalism became the most "effective" literary genre. Dozens of essays and articles unleashed a frontal attack on Stalinism. The problems of Soviet history and the Soviet economy were dissected with increasing frankness. Materials began to be published that in the last twenty years had been limited to confidential memoranda. The facts about prostitution and drugs, crime, and accidents at the workplace were discovered. Facts previously unpublishable were disclosed regarding the police and the judiciary. Disclosures were made about the field of psychiatry and the fact that healthy individuals were confined to mental hospitals. There were countless articles against corruption and the abuse of power by high-ranking party functionaries and ministers. There was still a ban on discussing the activities of the KGB and the members of the Politburo (including the ones who had been forced into retirement, such as Romanov, Grishin, Aliyev, and Kunayev). Writings about the situation in Rumania and North Korea were also very cautious.

But glasnost had reached such a level that it provoked an angry reaction from the apparats, which were incapable of adapting to democracy. Ligachev's mid-December meeting confronted these very problems. Even if the press provided scant information about the discussions, it was heard that Ligachev argued with Yakovlev at different points, that he had expressed his own personal points of view and not those of the Politburo. Many of those who attended felt disoriented. In effect, the situation was very strange, with two members of the Politburo working on the same problems. In part, there was a certain "division of labor" between them. Yakovlev was in charge of propaganda and the press. Ligachev presided over public education, the cinema, and cultural institutes. But there was no clear division of the areas in which they could intervene. Thus, for example, it's not difficult to notice the different emphases of *Pravda* and *Izvestia*. The former is very cautious, when it is not being outright hostile to criticism. It is no accident that Ligachev went to visit the editorial office in mid-December and expressed his positive opinion of the work done by the party organ.

This took place at the same time it was learned that *Pravda* had lost almost half a million subscribers (even though party members were required to subscribe). On the other hand, everyone knew that *Izvestia* always sold out at the newsstands. The most popular weekly was *Moskovskiye Novosti*, followed by *Ogonyok*. An examination of the circulation differences among various publications could act as a referendum in favor of glasnost. *Izvestia* gained 2 million new subscribers. Its readership increased by 30.4 percent, practically overtaking *Pravda* (10.4 million copies versus 10.7 million for the party organ). The readership of *Selskaya Zhizn* went down by 14.6 percent, while that of the more courageous *Sovetskaya Rossia* went up by 15.4 percent. *Literaturnaya Gazeta's* readership went up by even more— by 22.6 percent, with 700,000 new subscribers. The readership of *Sovetskaya Kultura*, which had stood out recently for its clear anti-Stalinist positions, rose 12.8 percent. Both *Ekonomicheskaya Gazeta* and *Za Rubezhom* saw their influence decrease.

The situation with magazines was even more interesting. *Druzhba Narodov*, which had been virtually unknown until recently, jumped from 35,000 to 150,000 copies in 1986. Today the number of subscribers has reached the 800,000 mark. There is an explanation for this amazing 433 percent increase. *Druzhba Narodov* published Rybakov's novel *Children of the Arbat* and announced the publication of a sequel, *Tridtsat Pyaty i Drugiye Gody (1935 and the Years That Followed)*. In 1986 *Novy Mir* printed 500,000 copies, a good number. This was high for a "thick" magazine. But the 1988 subscription campaign reached the figure of 1,100,000—an absolute record for a Soviet literary magazine. *Znamya* increased from 300,000 to 500,000 copies. *Ogonyok* is a special case. It increased the number of subscribers several times over, but was forced to reduce the number sold at the newsstands. As a result, it went from 1,500,000 copies to 1,700,000.

The conservative *Molodaya Gvardia* also increased circulation, but to a lesser degree (9.4 percent), going from 640,000 to 700,000 copies. The other conservative magazine, *Nash Sovremennik*, increased by 9 percent (from 220,000 to 240,000 copies). There was a net decrease in the readership of the party's political magazines, like *Kommunist, Molodoi Kommunist, Partiinaya Zhizn*, and *Politicheskoye Samoobrazovaniye*.

But let's get back to the subject. After the clash between Yakovlev and Ligachev, Gorbachev had to step in to restore order. In his 8 January speech, he substantially supported Yakovlev, and even went beyond his formulations. The firmness with which he argued against critics of perestroika seemed to prove that the "November crisis" had not affected the determination of the renewal group. Gorbachev did not express his opinion of the arguments. He urged a continuation of the debate that would respect the different points of view and not turn it into a riot. The party was in favor of freedom of criticism, even if it confirmed its right to control the press—which is not a "private shop." Nevertheless, everyone noticed that he praised *Izvestia* twice, and did not even mention *Pravda*.

A bitter debate followed Gorbachev's speech. For example, the head of *Novosti*, Valentin Falin, said that the party and its press "have depleted their credit of trust or are close to depleting it . . . this is why we do not have the right to make more mistakes, only to correct them again in ten to fifteen years." In his conclusion, Gorbachev added another important pointer on method: the decision of the October plenum on the interpretation of USSR and party history were not "the last word," but rather the starting point for a more thorough analysis of the past.

G.C. An invitation to continue.

R.M. Exactly. I should add that the situation now is much different than it was in the 1960s, when *Novy Mir* was the only periodical to openly fight against Stalinism and for a truthful examination of history. Now there are more than ten magazines committed to this cause. Then, speaking figuratively, *Novy Mir* fought "in defense" of the policies of the Twentieth and Twenty-Second congresses. Now magazines like *Oktyabr, Znamya, Neva, Argumenty i Fakty, Druzhba Narodov, Sobesednik*, not to mention *Moskovskiye Novosti, Ogonyok*, and *Nedelya* are clearly on the attack.

G.C. Nevertheless, there is also relentless opposition.

R.M. Many magazines and newspapers, such as *Moskva, Zvezda, Rabotnitsa, Krestyanka*, and all the historical magazines are virtually unchanged, and have maintained their previous characteristics and positions. *Nash Sovremennik*, that counts among its contributors writers like Valentin Rasputin, Vasili Belov, and Viktor Astafev, expresses a "pro-Russia" nationalistic line. It often propagates ideas that in their extremist form are expressed by the "patriotic" association Pamyat. These same ideas are present in the official press of the other republics as well.

G.C. At the 8 January meeting, when Gorbachev said that it was necessary to study the history of the Bolshevik period, the editor in chief of *Moskva*, Mikhail Alekseyev, replied that the history of the Soviet period was after all well known, and that it would be better to study the preceding one thousand years of Russian history. There are those who say that *Moskva* is the organ of Pamyat.

R.M. Alekseyev has never been a progressive. In 1969 his signature was at the top of the collective letter denouncing Tvardovsky and *Novy Mir*. However, I think that the magazine closest to Pamyat is *Nash Sovremennik*. *Moskva* takes a more complex and contradictory position. For example, it recently published an article by the late film director M. Romm in clear anti-Stalinist tones and denouncing anti-Semitism. And their publication of Nikolai Karamzin's fundamental work, *History of the Russian State*, was a praiseworthy initiative.

G.C. Where exactly does *Molodaya Gvardia* stand?

R.M. It is the most conservative magazine. It is openly hostile to all anti-Stalinist criticism, opposed to the publication of works that were forbidden by the censorship of the 1950s and 1960s, opposed to rock music, and to everything that was emerging in our cultural and political life. Their slogan is, "Don't uncover the ancient tombs, because they will lead to new tragedies." In their opinion, everything was fine in Brezhnev's day, while now a demolition is underway that threatens the prestige of the fathers of the literature of the 1970s.

Part Three
1988

CHAPTER 7

1988: A YEAR OF LESSONS; THE CONSERVATIVE
OFFENSIVE; SUMGAIT AND THE ARMENIAN CRISIS; THE
FEBRUARY PLENUM; NINA ANDREYEVA

• • •

Nineteen eighty-eight was the year of the dragon, the year that in its very first days a restless press predicted would be full of battles. "What will the Soviet Socialist conservatives do?" "I don't think they'll attack again this year," predicted the economist Gavriil Popov, "I think they'll only move into action when they can blame perestroika for the failures due to previous restraints." Moreover, "the conservatives are only now, I wouldn't say becoming afraid, but seriously reflecting on the development of events." He closed with a cold gibe: "The conservatives don't have leaders."[1] These were the prevailing ideas in the forefront of perestroika, and perhaps even in the leadership of the reform group. This prediction couldn't have been more wrong. The conservatives were already at the peak of their restlessness. The country was at the threshold of the Nineteenth Conference on Party Organization. The election of the delegates was about to take place. The campaign to renew party cadres was in full swing. This was a crucial moment for anyone who wanted to set up the chessboard to their own advantage. The political atmosphere was changing rapidly. The process of democratization was gaining strength, and Gorbachev's popularity was on the rise. The conservatives still had not attacked, but they had succeeded in landing some important blows without moving. True, they had no leader who could be compared to Gorbachev, but in the face of imminent danger, they had men and forces they could count on.

Mikhail Gorbachev knew that the most difficult moment was approaching. On 8 January he called in representatives of the mass media and heads of the "creative unions" and outlined the steps that needed to be taken in the new year. This was the third meeting of this type in one month. At the beginning of December, Aleksandr Yakovlev had presented the policy. Fifteen days later a similar meeting was chaired by Yegor Ligachev. This was striking proof that there was conflict at the head of the sensitive Ideology Department. Their two speeches so stridently contradicted each other that Gorbachev had to step in with an authoritative clarification: "The preparation of perestroika is over. Now comes the most difficult moment [because] now things have become acute in many respects . . . [the process] cannot develop without a fight." Anyone who was surprised did not understand that what was going on was "the continuation of a revolution." Therefore, the fight was "inevitable." The problem was to understand "what forms the fight would take and who the participants were." The "forms," the rules of the game for this revolution, still had to be defined. Gorbachev limited himself to a quick description of his adversaries: there were no antagonistic interests, but "instead you could speak of the temporary interests of groups, and sometimes even of personal ambitions."

Gorbachev had no interest in explaining the extent of the current conflict. He seemed determined to prevent any steps backward, even if he appeared cautious regarding steps forward that had to be made in any event. This is why he made his attack on two fronts. He told the conservatives: "You cannot agree with those who propose to forget history or to use only some parts of it. Now we understand that this approach is unacceptable." Without a thorough examination of the past, "we will not know the roots of many tendencies that have afflicted us." There are also those who "demand more decisive measures," the "ultraperestroikists," the "representatives of the revolutionary phase." Thus, Boris Yeltsin made his entrance without his name even being said. Gorbachev did not hide the fact that "a certain percentage of the intelligentsia, especially young people," interpreted the October events "as a blow to perestroika." He reassured them that this idea "is the biggest mistake." There would be no turning back.

Gorbachev saved his next blow for the conservatives, who warned of the dangers of cracking the foundations of socialism. "Will socialism be overturned when the people raise their heads, when they extend their efforts to confront the country's problems?" The resistances were the natural effect of the fact that "we are striking a blow to the administrative-command methods, and to their actual bearers, to their interests." But be careful, Gorbachev warned, the restraint mechanism had not yet been broken. There may be "inevitable steps backward" that should be faced "without panic." "They will literally say, 'Where is perestroika going in the next two or three years?' Two or three years!"[2] The debate that followed, which *Pravda* covered extensively, was lively and polarized. "Revanchists"—such as Yuri Alekseyev, editor in chief of the magazine *Moskva*—came out into the open. Others—such as Valentin Falin, the head of *Novosti*; Pyotr Fedoseyev, vice president of the Academy of Sciences; and Valentin Chikin, editor in chief of *Sovetskaya*

Rossia—expressed the air of uncertainty in the party, and tended toward conservative positions. Viktor Afanasev, editor in chief of *Pravda*, launched a harsh attack on Shatrov's latest play, *Dalshe! Dalshe! Dalshe!* . . . (*Further, Even Further.* . . .) Chikin and others followed suit. The playwright's latest work had just appeared in Grigori Baklanov's magazine, *Znamya*. During the debates Baklanov had said, "This is the last chance we have." Gorbachev interrupted him, but to agree. "If we stop, it will be fatal." And Baklanov replied, "This is exactly what many people are hoping for."

Instead, the march continued, even if storm clouds began to form. One month later the Supreme Court of the USSR legally rehabilitated Nikolai Bukharin and nine of the other twenty-one people convicted at the 1938 trial. A crucial page of Soviet history had been reopened after fifty years of silence, thirty-two years after the Twentieth Party Congress, and three months after the celebration of the seventieth anniversary of the Revolution. It was not only one of the "blank spots" being filled with thick and tragic lines of truth. It was a decision that reopened the debate on what socialism could have been had the hot and pliable material of the revolution not been struck by Stalin's mallet. It is easy to explain why the decision was so controversial: without this step perestroika could not have gone to the heart of problems. Rehabilitating Bukharin did not just mean affirming the full legitimacy of historical research into the revolutionary past, but above all it set the foundation for understanding the deep, structural origins of the "restraint mechanism" that had to be destroyed.

In the exhausting tug-of-war between various conflicting tendencies in the party leadership, Gorbachev thus scored another important point, recovering at least in part from the repercussions of the Yeltsin case. The Soviet leader made an even more explicit readjustment at the February plenum. It's true, he said, that there are various interpretations of perestroika. The situation "is not easy, either politically or ideologically." There were reactionaries who could not be ignored. The "defenders of Marxism and Leninism" who rend their clothes and ask "Where will we end up?" Those who would simply like "to give the façade a fresh coat of paint." Those who would like to "dismantle the system from the foundations up." And finally those who "urge us to skip the stages of socialist growth." The political struggle is "acute," but it does not just contain danger: "For the first time in many decades we have actually achieved a pluralism of points of view." Gorbachev showed further evolution in the lively debate on history. One must recognize with all frankness that "convincing research into our history was not carried out thoroughly after the Twentieth Congress." The roots of the restraint mechanism must be sought much earlier than the years of stagnation, in the "systems of administrative command created in the 1930s."

Gorbachev's reasoning was clear: be careful about forcing a showdown between the different tendencies, for it was time to bring them together. This invitation was especially addressed to the most relentless supporters of renewal. We cannot ignore the "logic of perestroika"; in other words, we need to come to terms with a complex network of political, cultural, and economic forces. The plenum's "organizational conclusion" represented a synthesis of difficult compromises. Where there was voting, i.e., in the Politburo, there would be no change in membership. The power balances among the top leadership remained unchanged. Boris Yeltsin left, as was inevitable. Georgi Razumovsky and Yuri Maslyukov became candidate members. Oleg Baklanov was promoted to the Secretariat. These were important touches, but clearly secondary.

The main episodes of this battle took place outside the Kremlin, and its rules were unwritten. Gorbachev seemed to be restlessly predicting attempts to split the compromise by the opponents of perestroika. Again he proposed the necessity of democratization, and for the first time he explicitly associated it with a problem that had become acute: nationality. On 18 February, the Soviet leader proposed to dedicate one of the next Central Committee plenums to this subject, "of primary, vital importance."[3] This was not just a premonition. At the October plenum Geidar Aliyev, first deputy chairman of the Council of Ministers, a member of the Politburo, and for many years first secretary of the Azerbaijani party, had been forced into retirement. The official excuse, "for health reasons," fooled no one. Karen Demirchyan, the first secretary of the Armenian party, had been harshly criticized in public at the June plenum. After this, the rank-and-file members of the Armenian party replaced their first secretaries, 450 deputies, and leaders in more than two hundred party organizations. At the beginning of January there was a violent political clash at the republic's plenum. The party apparat drew into a compact formation to defend Demirchyan against an offensive that was clearly inspired by Moscow.[4] After Alma-Ata there was unrest in Moldavia, Georgia, and in the three Baltic Republics. This was enough to foster unrest in the center. In the same period, protests began in Nagorno-Karabakh, an autonomous region with an Armenian majority that Stalin had artificially sectioned off inside Azerbaijani territory in 1923.

This was unquestionably one of the effects of the new climate of democratization that was filling the country. The Nagorno-Karabakh problem did not arise in February 1988. It had existed for decades, suppressed and unmentioned. Like other, analogous problems, it began to manifest itself as soon as the fear of harsh repression by the authorities abated. But it was equally clear that someone had been blowing on the smoldering ashes. The Nagorno-Karabakh Regional Committee unexpectedly voted in favor of the annexation by Armenia, the Armenians voting yes and the Azerbaijani minority abstaining. In a few days all of Armenia would march in support of this request. The first "official" death toll was given: two in Nagorno-Karabakh and dozens of wounded. The huge demonstrations in Armenia took place peacefully, but economic activity was blocked for days. The Central Committee of the USSR reacted with an alarming communiqué: "Actions and claims that tend to revise the nation's territorial structure are contrary to the interests of the workers of the Azerbaijani and Armenian republics, and prejudicial to relations between nations."[5]

Three candidate members of the Politburo—Demichev, Dolgikh, and the newly promoted Razumovsky, in addition to a secretary of the Central Committee, Lukyanov, were sent to Yerevan and Stepanakert (the capital of Nagorno-Karabakh) to oversee the crisis. The first step Moscow managed to impose was the immediate dismissal of the first secretary of the Nagorno-Karabakh party, Boris Kevorkov (an Azerbaijani), replacing him with an Armenian, Genrikh Pogosyan. But Tass criticized the "passive position of the Soviet and party organizations" and spoke about "irresponsible elements" who had set off the tensions.[6] A shroud of silence regarding the true extent of the events descended on all the central mass media. Glasnost was disappearing day by day. The Soviet people knew almost nothing about what was happening. Central television did not broadcast a single image of the events. Workers for Armenian TV threatened to go on strike unless at least a few images of the demonstrations were broadcast. There was fear of "contagion." But the silence and the reticence of the mass media made the Armenian people indignant, and it nurtured the spread of uncontrolled rumors that increased unrest and panic in both communities.

At this point Gorbachev asserted his own personal authority. Vladimir Dolgikh read an appeal from the general secretary into the microphones of Armenian and Azerbaijani radio. The message was an invitation to peace containing no clear refusal of the Armenians' claims. Gorbachev confirmed that the sense of Leninist national politics was to "give every population the freedom to fulfill its own needs in every sphere of social and political life, in its own language and culture, with its own customs, and its own religious beliefs."[7] This was a vague promise. After decades during which the Azerbaijani political leadership violated the rights of the Armenian majority while Moscow remained silent, faith in the central government could hardly be restored with a few words. Yet Gorbachev's prestige and the belief that he could meet and wanted to meet the Armenians' demands led to a turnaround in events. On the same Friday that Dolgikh read the radio appeal, Gorbachev received two well-known Armenian intellectuals at the Kremlin: the poet Silvia Kaputikyan and the writer Zori Balayan. On Saturday, 27 February,

185

these two representatives of the Armenian intelligentsia told thousands of people who had gathered in Opera Square about their talk with the Soviet leader. Gorbachev had told them: "You are for perestroika, but the way you are applying it is too uncompromising. You have to give us enough time to change things."[8] This was not the answer that the demonstrators were expecting, nor was it a rejection. However, it was enough to restore the peace— a conditional peace. The campaign committee decided not to meet until 26 March, until Moscow took concrete steps.

It was in this delicate situation that the "provocation" was unleashed. On Sunday, 28 February, a crowd of enraged Azerbaijanis launched an outright pogrom in the small industrial city of Sumgait. The "witches' Sabbath" lasted for a day and a half. The official toll of casualties, which was not released until several days later, was thirty-one dead and hundreds wounded.[9] The local police stood by and watched the massacre. Some local party leaders were later implicated in the cover-up of the massacre. The official version spoke of "thugs," but the fact that political orders were being carried out in the Azerbaijani "vendetta" was all too clear. Moscow sent the army to quell the riots, which in the meantime had spread to many Azerbaijani towns. A curfew was declared in Sumgait, while thousands of Armenians (there were over four hundred thousand in Azerbaijan) began a mass exodus, abandoning their homes. At the same time, thousands of Azerbaijanis fled from Armenia.

A few weeks later Gorbachev would confide in a prominent European Communist who was visiting Moscow that the Central Committee had heard about the events in Sumgait only after a serious delay.[10] This was the reason for the late arrival of the troops from the Interior Ministry at the scene of the massacre. But, as the Soviet press would later reveal, the preparations for the aggression against the Armenians had taken place in broad daylight during the preceding days. It was impossible to accept the hypothesis that the Secret Service, the Azerbaijani KGB, and the Sumgait and Baku party organizations knew nothing about the atmosphere that was building up and the mobilization of criminal and violent elements. The delay in the reaction of the local authorities and in relaying information to the central government hinted broadly at the existence of a conscious political maneuver designed to aggravate the situation. But the central political leadership, in its turn, proved uncertain in its decisions and its behavior. This was partly due to its ignorance of the actual extent of the threat, and partly to conflicting positions inside the Politburo. This uncertainty was reflected in the contradictory behavior of the mass media. Some things leaked, but the truth was surrounded by reticence, by rhetoric about "the friendship among the peoples of the USSR," and by the hypocritical equidistance between Armenians and Azerbaijanis that served to increase tensions in the region rather than to alleviate them. Gorbachev either could not or did not know how to reveal the outlines of the political maneuver then underway. Whoever was managing information inside the Politburo either did not understand the dimensions of the events, or most likely did not intend to encourage the public to think about who or what was responsible for what had happened. The only clear voice to be heard—but not until ten days after the tragedy—was Yegor Yakovlev, editor in chief of *Moskovskiye Novosti*:

> Whatever the forces that want to take advantage of this critical situation, that are upset, one thing is clear: there was an error in estimating the mood of the masses, and in the prediction of what it was capable of producing. . . . The road to democratization has two lanes. It is not just taken by the perestroika patriots, but also by their opponents. [11]

The succession of events was uncontrollable. When the horrible dimensions of the Sumgait massacre became clear, the feud between the two ethnic groups became even worse. Strikes and demonstrations spread all over Armenia. In Stepanakert the party's regional committee approved a resolution requesting that "the issue of uniting Nagorno-Karabakh with Armenia be resolved in a positive manner." This initiative dramatically proved that, as the resolution stated, "the overwhelming majority of Communists in the region share the people's hopes." [12] The force of the Armenian movement had become so great that the local party was forced to negotiate, unless it was willing to risk total political isolation. But the Yerevan party was also the sorcerer's apprentice, which at the very least had helped ignite the blaze, and was now moving to save itself and to find a solution to the problem that it had initially raised to cause trouble for the Gorbachev leadership. In effect, the Kremlin was now faced with unavoidable problems. Objectively speaking, there were tight boundaries on mediation. The local party organizations, both Armenian and Azerbaijani, were either inactive or completely unreliable. The tools of government power were also completely unusable, such as the police, the courts, the investigative bodies, and the soviets. The steps that were taken—with delays—were partial, insufficient, and inadequate. The first secretary of the Sumgait party, Mamedov, the mayor, Muslim-Sade, and the police chief, Dzhafarov, were all fired from their jobs. The latter two were ousted from the party. But the search for the responsible parties proceeded slowly, even though the Prosecutor's Office of the USSR had sent a team of investigators from Moscow and other republics to the site. The instigators of the pogrom remained in the shadows. The decision to transfer the trial to another place, made because of legitimate suspicion, was unexplainably delayed.

The Armenian national movement, by contrast, proved to be extraordinarily mature. Portraits of Gorbachev and properestroika slogans continued to appear at the ceaseless demonstrations of the following weeks, which in spite of everything maintained a peaceful and orderly character. The Nagorno-Karabakh committee chose a political line "within" perestroika, and aimed to use the legal tools provided by the Constitution. Signatures from the 340 deputies in the Supreme Soviet were now gathered to request the convocation of the Supreme Soviet of the USSR. This would be the first time in post-Revolutionary history that article 112 of the Constitution had been applied.[13] Moscow's response was awkward, to say the very least. *Pravda* broke the silence on the events—which had been almost total for more than a month—with an article impartial in form, but substantially directed against the Armenian movement. It dismissed the Sumgait tragedy with a few lines of cautious criticism. The article's coarse and insulting distortions of the events in the party newspaper were signed by three authors: Yuri Arakelyan, Z. Kadymbekov and Gennadi Ovcharenko.[14] The reaction from Yerevan was scorching. Less than twenty-four hours later, there was a dramatic denial: Arakelyan said that he had never taken part in the writing of that article, and for this he was fired.[15]

At the same time, there was an "institutional" counterattack from the center. An emergency meeting of the Presidium of the RSFSR Supreme Soviet was held to ask the USSR Supreme Soviet to restore order in the two republics. The "older brother's" stance served as a cue for the other republics to follow. Gorbachev tried to anticipate the events before the demonstration announced for 26 March. In the space of forty hours every republic's presidium had expressed itself similarly, while Armenia and Azerbaijan remained silent. On 23 March it was the turn of the Presidium of the USSR: the Armenian request is "inadmissible"; the Interior Ministry of the USSR must "take the necessary steps to restore order"; the Council of Ministers of the USSR was assigned the task of drawing up a plan for economic, social, and cultural development in Nagorno-Karabakh.[16]

The army garrisoned its forces in Yerevan. Paruir Airikyan, leader of the Union for National Self-Determination, was arrested along with three activists. The Nagorno-Karabakh Committee was stripped of its authority. On television the deputy chairman of the State Committee for Social Development, Vladimir Lakhtin, illustrated the resolution adopted by the Central Committee and the Council of Ministers. This resolution made the following provisions for Nagorno-Karabakh: an accelerated program of construction; the opportunity to pick up "the television programs of Yerevan and Baku"; an increase in editions of Armenian-language books; and the opportunity for Armenian students in the region to attend secondary school in Yerevan. But it was not hard to figure out that this line of conduct would not solve the problem. In fact, the truce lasted very briefly and dramatic new developments arose.

In mid-March, there occurred an episode that would prove crucial to later events. At the January 1987 plenum there had been a change inside the ruling group. The coalition that had won at the March and April 1975 plenums was splintered, but not broken. The shift toward democratization was not fully accepted by the whole leadership. There were conflicting views inside the Politburo. Hostility toward a reform of the political system was even more explicit in the Central Committee. The membership of the party's leading body was mostly characterized by balances created before Gorbachev's assumption of power. The many rotations of leaders in the party's regional committees did not change the power relations among full members of the Central Committee—the ones who had the right to vote. And the membership of the Central Committee could be changed only by a party congress, or by a conference on organization.

When Gorbachev decided to do battle and push for political reform, he knew he was running a high risk, considering the current balance of power. But he had no choice: economic reform could not be achieved without a system of social alliances, which could not, in its turn, be formed if the debate stayed behind closed doors. This was the paradox already examined here: the party promoted the reform revolution, but it was also one of its main obstacles. Therefore, the reform group was facing the unknown, but along with the risks, it could figure on some advantages that were not to be overlooked. The most conservative members, who were still strongly represented in the Politburo, had tolerated the general secretary's political initiative without losing their composure. They were aware of their clout in the party and in society—although they lacked a comprehensive alternative— and they waited by waging an unflagging underground resistance. Now democratization was, to a certain extent, forcing them to enter the field, to actively organize themselves, and to "show their cards"—in other words, to speak out. In 1987 heterogeneous groups were formed who, despite their differences, were united in their support of perestroika. The tensions within this loose coalition already seemed intolerable in October, when the first breakdown took place—the "expulsion" of Boris Yeltsin from the "left." But simultaneously, they also appeared intolerable at the opposite extreme, more and more clearly embodied by Yegor Ligachev. The protagonist of the crisis on the "right" would, in fact, be the party's number-two man. The tip of the iceberg was an article signed by Nina Andreyeva published in *Sovetskaya Rossia* on 13 March 1988.

The title itself demanded attention: "I Cannot Deny My Principles." It took up a full inside page under the heading "Polemics." The front page featured a picture of the author, surrounded by her students at the Technological Institute of Leningrad. It was an explicit all-out attack on perestroika. It was an attack on the "liberal socialism of the left" (meaning against the progressive intelligentsia), and against "cosmopolitanism" (meaning against the opening of the country to the rest of the world). But it also made a general criticism of the broader ideological implications of Gorbachev's new foreign policy. Peaceful coexistence, the chemistry teacher wrote, is "no more than a class struggle in the international arena." The West is only a threat, whose pressures are manifested in many insidious forms (one must defend oneself in every way, beginning with a rejection of bourgeois and capitalistic "mass culture").

However, the article was mainly a complete defense of the Stalinistic cultural, economic, and political "model," against every "revision," and it repeatedly gave off clear chauvinistic and anti-Semitic signals.[17] Regarding Stalin, whose myth the reformist intelligentsia was demolishing through a systematic campaign, Andreyeva peremptorily stated that "there is no doubt about the fact that the judgment of Stalin's actions and scholarly approach to the subject must even today conform to the Central Committee's 1956 resolution." She used the same style of invective that had characterized the Stalinist and Brezhnevite "cultural pogroms." The playwright Shatrov (who was Jewish) was accused of borrowing from Suvarin's works. The writer Rybakov (who was Jewish) was accused of having taken many of his ideas "from émigré publications." The "insinuations" they and many others made regarding Stalin's responsibility for the assassinations of Trotsky and Kirov were "tendentious." Andreyeva's axioms were elementary: Stalin continued the work of Lenin; to hold Stalin up to questioning meant casting doubt on socialism. These were the "principles" that Nina Nikolayevna Andreyeva could not renounce.

But why did a letter from an unknown Leningrad teacher become the object of so much attention, upset the highly politicized public opinion of the entire USSR, and galvanize broad sectors of the party? And who was Nina Andreyeva? Why did she become so important all of a sudden? Why did Nina Andreyeva create more alarm in *Sovetskaya Rossia* in March 1988 than even Vera Tkachenko had in *Pravda* on 21 August 1987, and remind so many people of the notorious Lidia Timashuk?[18] Why, as Yuri Karyakin would ask publicly in a debate at the Writers' House, did the article in *Sovetskaya Rossia* take on the characteristics of a "micromodel for a coup d'état"?

The reconstruction of events (that would come out after a few weeks) revealed a disturbing panorama. The "letter" had a complex history. A first draft condensed two articles that the Leningrad teacher had mailed to *Len-*

ingradski Rabochi in the summer of 1987, after the paper had published two articles by the writer Aleksandr Prokhanov.[19] In September Andreyeva decided instead to send her letter to *Pravda, Sovetskaya Rossia, Sovetskaya Kultura, Nash Sovremennik,* and *Literaturnaya Gazeta.* No one published it. *Pravda* and *Nash Sovremennik* thanked her, and the latter even praised her letter. Someone on the editorial staff of *Sovetskaya Rossia* encouraged Nina Andreyeva to continue.[20] Her second letter, which she sent only to *Sovetskaya Rossia,* was twenty-six typewritten pages long. The newspaper replied by proposing that Andreyeva quickly prepare a shorter version; in the end, the letter was eighteen typewritten pages long.[21] But the text was left in the drawer until February. At that point someone decided that the moment had arrived to use it. A group of editors, under direct orders from the editor in chief, Valentin Chikin, set to work rewriting the material.[22] An editor was sent to Leningrad in great secrecy to contact Andreyeva and her husband Aleksandr Klushin.[23]

The operation was both risky and clumsy at the same time. It would not be easy to hide its genesis. The people chosen as protagonists were not model citizens.[24] On the other hand, it's hard to find "clean" individuals willing to lend themselves to an undertaking of this kind. But whoever masterminded the idea did not have much time to act. The conservative offensive couldn't wait any longer. On the one hand, Mikhail Gorbachev put his foot on the gas pedal once again at the February plenum; glasnost was becoming a growing threat for all the apparats, especially those at the periphery; signals of an increasing activism in the intellectual strata were circulating in various parts of the country. On the other hand, these obstructions were no longer enough to halt the tumultuous course of events. In the Communist Party leadership, Gorbachev was repeatedly placed in difficulty, and a few times tensions boiled over. There were rumors, for example, that the rehabilitation of Bukharin had already been decided on in December, and that the Supreme Court was supposed to deliver its opinion before the year's end.[25] But Ligachev and other members of the Politburo succeeded in blocking it, taking advantage of the fact that Gorbachev and Yakovlev were busy with preparations for the Washington summit. There was another danger signal for Gorbachev at a Politburo meeting that was supposed to approve a bill on cooperatives. The general secretary suddenly found himself in the minority.[26] The explosion of the Armenian crisis and the Sumgait tragedy lent credence to the idea that Gorbachev was "destabilizing" the country.

However, the objective was much greater. The party conference was entering its most delicate phase: the preparation of the platform and the election of delegates. The problem of its "powers" was still unsolved. Would it be the equivalent of a party congress? Could it change the membership of part of the Central Committee? A difficult tug-of-war was going on over these two points in particular. The conservatives had to make a show of strength to all the apparats, gather their forces, and come up with a political platform before Gorbachev succeeded in tilting the balance in his favor. The opportunity arose with Gorbachev's departure for Yugoslavia. *Sovetskaya Rossia* published Nina Andreyeva's letter on 13 March. On the fourteenth Gorbachev was in Belgrade, and Yakovlev was in Ulan Bator for a meeting of the heads of ideology in the brother parties.

The entire press was silent, for specific reasons, as would later be learned; orders had been given to that effect. On Friday, 18 March, a few hours before Gorbachev's return to Moscow, Ligachev held a meeting of the heads of mass media and praised Nina Andreyeva's letter as an "example to follow" for every editorial staff.[27] He added that "The Barricades of Perestroika," a roundtable discussion in the latest issue of *XX Vek i Mir*, was a "glaring example of counterrevolution." The press did not carry any reports of this meeting. Some of those who attended leaked the contents of Ligachev's speech. Now the cards were "almost" on the table. The editor in chief of *Izvestia*, Ivan Laptev, went back to his office visibly shaken and held a meeting of a group of close associates. "The time to choose has arrived," he stated. "Personally, I am for Gorbachev, but I am getting ready to retire. The youngest of you here must make your decisions, knowing what the risks and the stakes are."[28] In an instant the news spread that at some papers photocopies of the page from *Sovetskaya Rossia* were distributed to all the editors. This happened, for example, at *Trud*, the unions' publication. Outside Moscow, many party organizations picked up the signal enthusiastically. In Leningrad copies of the article were passed out at all the neighborhood committees, with instructions to use it as a "preparation manual for the Nineteenth Conference."[29] At the same time, probably in compliance with instructions from the center, numerous provincial newspapers reprinted Ms. Andreyeva's article.[30]

Gorbachev returned to Moscow on 18 March. Aleksandr Yakovlev arrived on the nineteenth. Both had already been informed of the article's contents, but they still did not know all the background details. Gorbachev's assistants were sent to investigate Andreyeva, to analyze the article, and to uncover its genesis. Academician Yevgeni Primakov, for example, had some of his colleagues check the Churchill quote about Stalin used in the article. They combed through the complete works of the British statesman, but the quotation could not be found. In fact, Isaac Deutscher, and not Churchill, was the author of the "panegyric." This "technical" oversight would help discredit the editors of *Sovetskaya Rossia*. Gorbachev was given a detailed report of Ligachev's speech to the newspaper editors. Almost nothing was leaked to the foreign press, but numerous newspaper editors and members of the intelligentsia asked Aleksandr Yakovlev to authorize a public response. He urged everyone to calm down: "It is up to *Pravda* to respond." In the meantime, Gorbachev held a meeting of the leaders of the mass media and harshly criticized the behavior of *Sovetskaya Rossia*. Immediately afterward, sometime between 21 and 27 March, the Politburo met to address the issue. The debate was stormy. Ligachev, Chebrikov, Shcherbitsky, and Solomentsev formed a coalition. Other members of the leadership were reluctant to take sides. But the first showdown ended in a victory on points for Gorbachev: Yakovlev was given the mandate to write a reply to *Sovetskaya Rossia*.

In the meantime, the first signs began to appear of an outside counterattack by the supporters of perestroika. On 25 March, while conferences praising Andreyeva's article were being held at Moscow University, there was a meeting of the party organization of the Filmmakers' Union. The playwright Aleksandr Gelman delivered a harsh criticism of Andreyeva's article, and the "open" assembly unanimously approved his proposal, to be sent to the Nineteenth Conference as a "formal mandate."[31] On Sunday, 27 March, Ligachev left for a three-day trip to the provinces, in the Vologda region. On one of these days, probably 30 March, Gorbachev held a special meeting of the Politburo that was not announced by the press. All the candidate and full members were there, with the exception of Ligachev. Gorbachev explained the facts he knew, and noted the total discrepancy between the contents of Andreyeva's article and the policy that had been decided on collectively. He spoke about an "antiperestroika manifesto." In fact, he raised the issue of confidence. "Perestroika cannot stop at the halfway mark. We have to go all the way. I am not willing to continue performing the duties of the general secretary of the party unless a clear choice is made in this direction. Therefore, I ask all of you to declare yourselves."[32] Everyone criticized the article's contents and the method followed by *Sovetskaya Rossia*, but with varying gradations and nuances. A resolution was approved containing harsh criticism of Valentin Chikin (member of the Central Committee) and a "warning" to Yegor Ligachev.[33] The resolution, which would stay in the minutes, but secretly, mandated *Pravda* to publish an "editorial" response to *Sovetskaya Rossia*, which in its turn would have to publish *Pravda*'s response in its entirety. Aleksandr Yakovlev was chosen to write the response. At the same time, the first public response to Andreyeva appeared in *Moskovskiye Novosti*, an article by Aleksandr Levikov in the 30 March issue. This broke a wall of silence that had lasted for seventeen days.

A third secret meeting of the Politburo took place on 4 April. This time Ligachev was present. The response written by Yakovlev was approved with some amendments. Ligachev was isolated within the ruling group, even if the die he had cast was producing effects throughout the party organization. The conflict ended to his disadvantage, but the decision—tacit or explicit— was not to make the fracture public. Ligachev appeared in public on 4 April (the day before the *Pravda* response) at an All-Union meeting of only secondary importance, where he gave a speech that would not be published until 7 April. The speech contained these two lines of contrition: "The party says there will be no return to the past. This is guaranteed by the irreversible process of democratizing our society." The rest followed the line of his well-known cultural conservativism, allowing room to attack rock music and to defend "popular and classical art, as the solid ramparts holding off the penetration of bourgeois mass culture."[34] But very few people knew what was happening. Not even Nina Andreyeva knew. On Friday, 1 April, she held another conference at the KGB's Leningrad training institute.[35]

The full brunt of Gorbachev's counterattack appeared in *Pravda* on Tuesday, 5 April. He called the *Sovetskaya Rossia* article a "manifesto of the forces opposed to perestroika." "For the first time the readers have been able to read in a highly concentrated form, in this 'letter to the editor' . . . the intolerance of the elementary idea of renewal, the brutal exposition of fixed positions that are in essence conservative and dogmatic."[36] In various places *Pravda* emphasized that its reply was not meant to put a stop to the debate. It did not want to ban expressions of dissent from the official line. The objection was to specific positions that had been taken. The criticism of the article's treatment of the past was scathing:

> In the article a substantially fatalistic concept of history prevails that has nothing in common with a scientific opinion, justifying everything that happened in the name of historical necessity. The thesis that when you cut down the forest, flying splinters are dangerous, is incompatible both with a scientific view and with socialist morals.

Regarding Stalin:

> Not only did he know about [the illegal acts], but he organized them, he directed them. This is an established fact. The responsibility of Stalin and his entourage for the repressions of the masses and for the violations committed cannot be forgiven by the party and by the people.

But there was still the question of why it was still necessary to return to these problems, *Pravda* asked, going to the heart of the political issue. The answer lay in the fact that the dispute was not about the past, but about the present. This was the only way to explain the virulence of certain positions, their turbid ambiguity, and the attempt to confuse the merits of the Soviet people with the merits of Stalin:

By defending Stalin they fight to maintain in our life the practices and the methods he created for a "solution" to problems . . . above all they defend the right to use power arbitrarily.

The next day *Sovetskaya Rossia* was forced to carry the *Pravda* article in its entirety. But it did so with no comment. It seemed as if the reformers had achieved victory, but the conflict still had not reached its peak. Gorbachev and Shevardnadze were busy on the international front. On 6 April, they flew to Tashkent to see Najibullah. Between 6 and 8 April, Ligachev had another go at it, and held a meeting of the Politburo, in the general secretary's absence, at which he requested a special meeting of the Central Committee. The situation had reached a peak of uncertainty, almost a "diarchy of power," as a noted intellectual would comment.

As Gorbachev was boarding the plane for his return flight from Tashkent, he replied with an outright battle cry: "Don't wait for instructions from the top. The success of perestroika is in the hands of the people."[37] Some people did not want to take notice of the seriousness of the problems, and of the fact that "the destiny of our country and of socialism are in question." There were those who were scared, or puzzled, and "there is only a short step from here to sounding the retreat." His reference to Ligachev was transparent, at least for those who knew what was going on. Gorbachev said that ideology has "a crucial significance," but "without definite, revolutionary breaks in our way of thinking, we cannot achieve radical transformations." The signal was unequivocal. Control over ideology had to be placed in new hands. Resolute though this speech was, it could not dissipate the real, incumbent danger. Ligachev thought, and rightly so, that the majority of the plenum would take his part and reverse the situation of risky disadvantage that had been created in the Politburo and in the Secretariat. Gorbachev was perfectly aware of this, and he made recourse to an unusual maneuver. He did not hold a plenary meeting, where he might have been in the minority. Instead, he met separately with three distinct groups of plenum members, for the sake of "consultation." In this way he did not reject the request for clarification, but none of the three groups could vote. The meetings were held on 11, 14, and 18 April.[38] At the same time, according to some sources, all the commanders of military districts were called to Moscow, where each was received privately by Gorbachev.[39]

The uncertainty persisted. On 13 April another member of the Politburo broke the silence. Chebrikov gave a speech in Cheboksari in sharp reaction to glasnost and democratization, but without once mentioning Gorbachev. He bitterly attacked the Armenian movement, and insisted that foreign secret services were creating diversions. On that date one can gather that the match was not yet over. The crucial moment took place at a new, dramatic meeting of the Politburo held on Friday and Saturday, 15 and 16 April. Gorbachev opened the discussions by showing all his cards. He informed the Politburo that he had ordered his personal assistant, Ivan Frolov, to conduct a thorough investigation of Nina Andreyeva's letter, which proved beyond a shadow of a doubt that it "started inside here." Obviously, very few people know what happened at that moment. Sources report that an extremely bitter debate followed. Ligachev defended himself and launched a counterattack. Chebrikov took his side, as did others. The normally taciturn Ryzhkov blew his top and pounded his fist on the table. He said it was time to put an end to this state of affairs: "Comrade Ligachev has continuously stepped into areas that lie outside his competence. There are at least ten ministers who spend hours in his office taking instructions different from those that I give." His complaints literally echoed Yeltsin's outburst in the previous October.

Ligachev ended up in the minority; even Slyunkov and Zaikov criticized him. This was a final defeat, and inevitably he was stripped of some of his duties.[40] The preparation of the Nineteenth Conference was assigned to Razumovsky, who was also assigned the task of delivering the public speech for the celebration of the 118th anniversary of Lenin's birth. But the three meetings with the first secretaries had provided a "real" picture of the forces in the party leadership. Ligachev's positions had a profound echo in the apparats. Making dramatic changes and redistributing Politburo positions was an impractical and possibly dangerous solution. Thus, by common consent, it was agreed to keep the outcome of this clash closed behind the Kremlin doors. During this period Aleksandr Yakovlev would tell a close friend, a famous writer, "We have crossed the Rubicon."

From abroad everything would look the way it did before. Those who needed to know were informed of the new geography of power relations. In a private colloquium, Shevardnadze told Shultz plainly: "It was a tough battle and there will still be great difficulties, but the outcome is unquestionable. I share Gorbachev's positions." It was indispensable to inform the antagonist, in order to avoid possible misunderstandings or manipulations of internal dissent. Gorbachev in his turn put the American secretary of state on guard: "Don't think you can play on our divisions." The same had to be done with allies. On a visit to Budapest, Ryzhkov confided to an old Hungarian diplomat: "I am with Gorbachev. The confrontation ended in our favor." But the American journalists who were allowed to attend the first meeting between Gorbachev and Shultz on 22 April were discreetly forewarned: anyone who asks questions about the conflict between Gorbachev and Ligachev will no longer be invited to the Kremlin.

On 15 April, *Sovetskaya Rossia* finally published an editorial retraction in which it made amends for what had happened. Replies to Nina Andreyeva, and the analyses and the denunciations that had been locked in the editors' drawers, now flooded the press. *Komsomolskaya Pravda* published an article titled "The Reversal That Wasn't" which epitomizes this response:

> This situation is not the last and maybe not even the most dangerous of the ones that require resolution, courage, and steadfast principles . . . [because clearly] the antiperestroika forces will not step aside . . . we still have not duly appreciated how difficult and tough the fight before us really is.[41]

Ligachev had not appeared in public since 4 April. On 21 April, a spokesperson for the Foreign Ministry announced that Ligachev had taken "a brief period of rest," and that "recently no reorganization of duties inside the Politburo had taken place."[42] The next day, at the Kremlin's Palace of Congresses, millions of Soviet citizens witnessed a stupefying scene, almost a pantomime before the well-focused lenses of the television cameras. Ligachev reappeared at Gorbachev's side, in his unofficial "number-two" position. Both men were smiling and relaxed, and continued to converse in an conspicuously relaxed fashion, while Georgi Razumovsky spoke at the podium and confirmed the perestroika line point by point. The "micromodel" of a coup d'état had failed; Ligachev had been demoted. But it had been decided to keep the issue inside the Politburo.

The month lost in this harsh internal confrontation, however, caused a serious setback in the preparations for the conference. Now Gorbachev was forced to correct the course again and to cut corners. Once again he held a meeting of the leaders of ideology, the mass media, and the creative unions, where he delivered a speech making it clear that "the confusion, to be frank, is not only at the lower levels but also at the top," and that "the Politburo thought it was necessary for the general secretary to talk about the ideological content of the second stage of perestroika."[43] To avoid misunderstandings of any kind, Gorbachev added bluntly that the decisions made at the February plenum "have even today retained the full weight of their value." The delegates to be elected had to be "resolute supporters of perestroika." But Gorbachev urged listeners not to generalize: the conservatives had to be fought, but not everyone who was uncertain or restless could be labeled an enemy of perestroika. Many people are "marked by the climate of stagnation," and changing 66 percent of the ministers and 61 percent of the first secretaries of the regions still did not mean having the human resources needed for perestroika.

The conference could be compared to a special party congress, and it required a reexamination of critical issues: the party's guiding role, the structure of the apparats, and judicial and legal reform. The objective was to make a resolute shift toward the "rule-of-law socialist state," and to "define the criteria: what is socialism really, and what is the opposite of the idea of socialism." However, the idea of giving the Nineteenth Conference the power to change the membership of the Central Committee, at least in part, did not go over. In the second half of May, a new plenum approved the conference's "Theses," accepting the approach of a "radical reform of socialism." "A task that cannot be postponed," it was said, "[is] the creation of political mechanisms and guarantees that exclude future violation of the Leninist principles regarding the party's leadership of the society." The party's guiding role was thereby confirmed, but "within the limits of a sharp separation of duties" with respect to the state, and with the recognition that the party's monopoly of politics had ended. A rule-of-law socialist state implied that the party agreed to act "within the limits of the Constitution of the USSR and of the Soviet laws," while the activity of the social organizations, the voluntary associations, and the autonomous unions finally had to be supported by distinct rights. With a single criterion: "Every social activity that is realized within the limits of the Constitution and that does not contradict the Soviet socialist state's interests in development must be recognized as valid." This was a cautious formula that was still open to various interpretations and applications, but it fit into a general picture of profound conceptual changes. For the first time in Soviet history an institutional system of succession inside the party and inside the state was provided for: the limitation to two elective terms.[44] Actual power had to return to the soviets through a reform of the Constitution and of the system of elections, and with a new law on local autonomy.

The April conflict did, however, make it possible to iron out the problems of the law on cooperatives. The new law was one of the cornerstones of the plan for economic reform, and one of the most important measures in the past three years. In principle, it confirmed a citizen's right not to work in state enterprises, but to form autonomous cooperatives. In actual fact, things went differently, and the development of a powerful sector of cooperatives was consistently blocked by a series of conservative restraints at the end of 1988 and the beginning of 1989.

In the meantime, the unprecedented and relentless battle for the election of about five thousand delegates to the conference took place without holding back on the punches. The supporters of perestroika were still in shock over the Andreyeva affair, and were vexed with uncertainty and pessimism. They proved to be relatively unprepared to grasp all the possibilities that the new situation offered. A large percentage of the public was involved in the process of choosing delegates. There were several episodes of apparat candidates being successfully challenged. In the final tally, however, most of the delegates were still noticeably conservative. But unlike the situation at the Twenty-Seventh Congress, this time a tough properestroika group would be present in the convention hall, armed with the "Theses" document. Gorbachev would help this minority to have a decisive influence on the debates by pitting the two sides against each other. The most significant episode to reveal the high level of political tension on the eve of the historical assembly took place during the Moscow Party Conference, where Gorbachev tried to break down the conservative resistance, and succeeded only in part. Left out of the delegation was a group of perestroika's leading intellectuals, including the playwrights Aleksandr Gelman and Mikhail Shatrov, the sociologist Tatyana Zaslavskaya, the economist Nikolai Shmelyov, the writer Yuri Karyakin, and the theater director Oleg Yefremov. The apparat reacted furiously, but at the last minute it was forced to include the economists Leonid Abalkin and Oleg Bogomolov, the director Yelem Klimov, and the historian Yuri Afanasev, the most disliked of the bunch.

The month preceding the conference saw a succession of dramatic developments that both reflected and heightened the conflicting sides' restlessness, tensions, and covert and overt offensives. The Nagorno-Karabakh crisis exploded again. Starting on 23 May powerful strikes and demonstrations paralyzed the autonomous region and all of Armenia, while increasingly serious fights broke out between the two ethnic groups in Azerbaijan. *Pravda* acknowledged that the authorities were not in control of the situation, especially in the disputed region.[45] But the leadership of the Armenian movement still stood substantially on legal ground. The "Theses" for the Nineteenth Conference actually provided a legal platform on which the Armenians tried to legitimize their demands. They argued that if all the power had to return to the soviets, then it was up to the republics' soviets to say where they stood. On 15 June, under massive and organized public pressure, the Armenian Supreme Soviet declared itself in favor of the request by the Nagorno-Karabakh regional soviet to enter Armenian jurisdiction. This was a perfectly legal action guaranteed by the Constitution, but entirely unprecedented in Soviet experience. Two days later the Azerbaijani Supreme Soviet rejected the request as "unacceptable."

There was a total stalemate, while the risk of a popular uprising increased by the minute. The dismissal in May of the first secretaries of the Armenian and the Azerbaijani parties, Karen Demirchyan and Kyamran Bagirov, was not enough,[46] just as a policy of impartiality was no longer sufficient. Therefore, precious time was wasted, while disappointment and anger gradually built up in Armenia; in Azerbaijan subversive forces began to win a consensus, which at times verged on appeals to a sort of "holy war" of Muslims against Christians. If Moscow continued to hesitate, in a few months people might be carrying portraits of Khomeini through the streets of Baku. Clearly, a much broader underground political game was exploiting these forces and setting them in motion. Gorbachev and his group did not seem to either understand the danger of the situation, or to have identified ways to avert it. There was fear that any radical solution, such as accepting the Armenians' request, would immediately touch off an Azerbaijani backlash, and possibly set off a chain reaction in the entire Muslim world of Soviet Central Asia, where various territorial and national problems in the Caucasus had been left unsolved for decades.

This was heightened by the wave of mass-based independence and separatist movements raging in Tallinn, Vilnius, and Riga, forcing the party to ride the tiger of nationalistic claims. In June the first secretary of Estonia, Karl Vaino, was replaced by Vaino Vyalyas. Demonstrations in the three republics multiplied. They demanded economic autonomy, the recognition of the national language as the official language, and the restoration of the flag and the national anthem from the "bourgeois" period. The police did not intervene.[47] The same happened in Moscow, where the huge panorama of informal groups was generally set into motion. One of the most influential, Memorial, sent a petition to the Nineteenth Conference with about thirty thousand signatures (including noted intellectuals like Sakharov, Korotich, Zalygin, Yevtushenko, and Boris Raushenbakh), asking that a memorial to the victims of Stalinism be built in the capital.

In the same period, the Supreme Court rehabilitated Zinoviev, Kamenev, Pyatakov, Radek, and the entire group from the 1936 trial. The wave of perestroika seemed to be advancing, overcoming every obstacle in its path, but carrying with it the rubble from the past and an uncontrollable undertow. The apparats grew even more restless. But the conservatives knew that they were guaranteed a majority of the delegates, and they hoped to dictate law. On the eve of the great assembly, the editor of *Pravda*, Viktor Afanasev, reminded everyone that the Politburo meetings were chaired by Gorbachev, and "in his absence, by Yegor Ligachev."[48]

SEVENTH CONVERSATION

GORBACHEV'S TACTICS; THE DEBATE OVER THE POWERS OF
THE NINETEENTH CONFERENCE AND THE FIGHT FOR
DELEGATES; EDUCATIONAL REFORM; NINA ANDREYEVA'S
LETTER; NAGORNO-KARABAKH; THE REHABILITATIONS; THE
CULTURAL REBIRTH

•   •   •

G.C. At the February plenum Gorbachev invited the "left-wing" critics not to ignore the "logic of perestroika." What is your opinion of the general secretary's position?

R.M. It's not easy to analyze. His critical remarks about the different tendencies coming out in the party seemed cautious. For the first time, the term "pluralism" was used in a positive context, but with the connotation of "socialist." In my opinion this was the most important concept expressed at the plenum. If you read Gorbachev's speech carefully, you can see that he did not have ready answers to many questions. Much ground had been covered in three years, but even more remained. The general objectives had been defined: more socialism, more democracy, a higher standard of living for the masses, more social justice, and more culture. But these ends could not be achieved by just any means. Gorbachev did not seem in any hurry to condemn certain opponents and support others. He encouraged discussion without getting into bitter clashes. For example, regarding the debate on history, Gorbachev stated that every element had to be kept in mind—contradictions, transitional phases, dark pages and bright pages. Not everything should be painted black, nor should the crimes that were committed be forgiven. In other words, all of the contenders could quote Gorbachev to maintain that they were in the right. He was the same with economic reform. Yes, we have to make radical changes, but we cannot skip stages. We cannot forget that we are creating a new management and operational system for the economy, but within the limits of the existing plan, conceived according to the old criteria. Therefore, every step has to be made on solid ground, and at the same time, be radically new.

G.C. To me Gorbachev didn't seem at all uncertain. For tactical reasons he simply didn't say everything that he was thinking. Concerning reflection on the past, in fact, he said that "it takes time, ability, and responsibility." His thoughts were clear: there was still much to be said, but not right away. He stated that the Revolution's potentials had not been achieved because of the cult of personality, because of the administrative and bureaucratic system of command, because of dogmatism and arbitrary power, because of voluntarism, and because of the consequent stagnation in the 1970s. In this way his criticism associated Stalin and Brezhnev, indicating that the roots of the crisis went much further back than the immobility of the Brezhnev administration.

R.M. That sentence is indeed interesting, but in our political vocabulary, "voluntarism" is associated with the Khrushchev period. In this way Gorbachev revised the entire historical period following Lenin's NEP. In my opinion it is a clear sign that he thought it was necessary to reexamine all previous concepts of socialism. His words recall almost to the letter what Lenin had said in 1922 about the transition period between barracks communism and the NEP. This demarcation line was not even clear to Lenin. Gorbachev seemed to be preparing his audience for what he would say later at the party conference. Every sentence at the February plenum had been accurately weighed so as not to close debate, excluding categorical formulas and overly precise instructions. Gorbachev did not specify in depth the dimensions and the limits of the process of "socialist democratization." On the other hand, it is true that the economic situation was very serious, and more so than had been thought in 1985. Now it could be grasped that economic growth reported, which was clearly unexceptional, was for the most part artificial.

The growth of industrial production as a whole was almost imperceptible if from the gross national product you were to subtract oil production—which had quadrupled in fifty years and increased even more in terms of specific weight if you counted price increases on the international market. Add to that the fact that we squandered our earnings from oil exports to purchase grain that we ourselves could have produced. We have at our disposal the largest area of farmland in the world; colossal technical resources; the largest rural population; and the world record for the production of chemical fertilizers. In short, this was no economy, but rather an elaborate fiction. For the first time, Gorbachev disclosed that in 1987 many of the plan's objectives had not been achieved.

We lowered the production of alcohol, but did not replace it with other goods. Thus, state revenues lost billions, compounded by the 10-billion-ruble loss of foreign currency due to the fall in the price of oil. This, in its turn, kept us from purchasing consumer goods on the foreign market. The situation of the state budget had become highly critical. Moreover, for the first time it was disclosed that in the last twenty years the USSR had achieved absolutely no growth in national income. Up to this point it had been said that the growth rate for national income was shrinking. The figures showed instead that in many cases, this was a fabricated growth, often resulting from falsified data. For example, the actual cotton crop was 5 million tons, but the figures reported 6 million (and salaries were based on this imaginary figure).

Gorbachev's analysis showed other unpleasant things that weren't new either. Juggling the books was common practice in many industrial sectors, especially in construction. The growth was also fictitious when examined from other angles. We produce more fertilizer than all the other countries in the world, but we use it irrationally. We manufacture obsolete equipment, but we calculate it in our growth statistics. However, the most serious problem was human resources. Gorbachev insisted on the need for a compromise because he realized that he couldn't impose decisions that, right though they might be, could not be effected due to the unpreparedness of the cadres. This was the basic logic behind perestroika. "Perestroika" means "restructuring"—not "replacing," but if you don't have the human and material resources to accomplish the restructuring, then all you can do is wait.

It was clear that Gorbachev still did not have suitable cadres or enough cadres to bring about his political and economic reform. By force of circumstances, he had to give it time and create the right conditions for new cadres to grow, and the process of training these cadres was much more difficult from a political standpoint than from an economic one. When Gorbachev spoke about the need to change the political system, many people believed that this meant more than a broadening of the soviets' powers. In fact, this had been spoken about many times in the past, even during the Khrushchev and Brezhnev years, but nothing substantial was done. Now instead it seemed as if the attempt was serious and relations between the party organizations and the soviets were to be radically altered, with an expansion in the powers of the latter. It has already been stated many times that the party had to maintain its duties of control and policy, and abandon the rest. Our political system is not only characterized by a "single party," but by the circumstance that the party performs a countless number of functions that normally lie within the purview of government bodies.

G.C. The February plenum opened with a report by Ligachev on educational reform, but almost nobody paid any attention to it.

R.M. Ligachev's report actually deserved to be forgotten, since he said almost nothing new. In reality, educational reform, which had begun in 1983 on Andropov's instructions, was a half-step. For example, it was decided to begin elementary school a year earlier, with six-year-olds rather than seven-year-olds. They should have predicted that millions of new schoolchildren would crowd the existing educational structures, which were already highly inadequate. The use of double and triple shifts was common. Where would the new students be put? Instead, very little was done to meet the material needs created by this decision. Moreover, Soviet schools did not even provide an adequate education for the cadres. Ligachev justifiably criticized educational standards and teacher training. But it was impossible to enact a reform of this type without providing for a huge increase in investments in this area. Teachers worked more than eight hours a day, but received a salary that was lower than the national average. This is why most teachers were women—almost 85 percent! The male teacher had almost disappeared from the Soviet schools.

Ligachev justifiably pointed out that schoolchildren in Central Asia work two months a year on cotton plantations. This meant that for them basic schooling lasted 8.5 years, not 10. And in the republics they had to study the national language in addition to Russian. He added that in the Asian republics there were currently two or three million people who were unemployed because of their lack of professional skills. A survey conducted at local institutes of higher learning showed that 70 percent of the students were unable to solve elementary arithmetic problems. But this was not just a problem in the "provinces." In Moscow up until a short while ago students at the technical institutes spent more than half their classroom time on various "social" subjects, on military education, and on other occupations—like the harvest—that had nothing to do with their own specialization. Ligachev's report urged a more serious reflection on the state of public education, but it did not respond to the central issue of how to overcome the actual current situation.

G.C. Is there any truth to what the press writes about the "conservativism" of the Soviet schools, faithfully reflecting the conservativism of the society during and before the period of "stagnation"?

R.M. The Soviet educational structure is undoubtedly very conservative. Decades of authoritarian pedagogy left a deep mark which is hard to erase today. When I read Ligachev's report, I tried to put myself in the shoes of a school principal—actually, I used to be one—and to establish new goals in light of his instructions. I would have to check the teaching practices, get rid of the bad teachers, or at least get rid of the ones whom it was no longer possible to change, and create an advisory board, enlisting the best teachers, many parents, representatives of the community, and some students. There are some elements of democratization, but nothing more. For example, there's no answer to the problem of how to get better-trained teachers and administrators.

G.C. Now I would like us to address the "Nina Andreyeva case." You are already familiar with the reconstruction of events I have presented in chapter 7. But maybe you have other information.

R.M. In some ways Andreyeva's letter is similar to one written by Pitirim Sorokin, a leader of the Socialist Revolutionary Party. When Lenin examined Sorokin's letter and his gesture, he came to important conclusions regarding changing attitudes toward the revolution by specific intermediary social groups in Russia, especially the average farmer. Sorokin was a professor of sociology, not a farmer, but he expressed deep-seated moods that Lenin took note of when he wrote that the Bolsheviks had to substantially alter their policies.

Today the situation of the country is obviously completely different. But Nina Andreyeva's letter reflected the shifting moods of a broad stratum of the party and of the apparats that was not crazy about perestroika and that was beginning to mount a growing resistance, especially as far as changes in ideology were concerned. Once again a letter or an article became the occasion for important political developments and constituting the premise for strategic reversals. But there was an obvious plot behind this case. For example, Ligachev was clearly involved in some phases of the operation. I think that the rumor that Ligachev had been informed of the letter before its publication is well founded. The fact that he praised the letter and that the editor in chief of *Sovetskaya Rossia* published it was beyond doubt. Ligachev had been in favor of perestroika during the two-year period 1985–86. In the current phase he still supported some of its features, but he was a "traditional" leader who was used to being in command, not a "modern." Glasnost, democratization, and the reexamination of ideology and history went beyond the boundaries of perestroika as he pictured it. Ligachev had many supporters in the party, though they weren't organized. In the case in question, he clearly tried to direct the action. However, one should realize that Ligachev also started to become a point of reference for many enemies of any type of perestroika, who saw him as the "lesser evil."

Nina Andreyeva's educational background was typical of certain circles. Thousands of high-school teachers in the so-called social disciplines, most middle-school history teachers, and the majority of cadres in the ideological apparat share the same orientation. These people are used to working with the manuals and the methods of the past, to praising the "unique and heroic" history of the party and the country. And here were waves of denouncements of the past, textbooks being taken out of circulation, and history exams no longer being given. Students asked questions that the teachers couldn't answer. They had to think a lot, but they weren't used to doing this. The teachers had to read a lot, but without the help of dogmas or stereotypes. This was not easy for most of the cadres, and hence their intolerance of perestroika. This is just one example. Similar situations confronted many social groups.

G.C. Why did the initiators of the offensive choose a teacher as their instrument—in other words, why a representative of the "widespread" intelligentsia* rather than a worker?

R.M. Their choice indicates a search for social alliances. The teachers are a large, influential, and very stable group whose membership hasn't changed substantially since the time of Stalin. In Khrushchev's time too the social studies teachers were the ones who mounted one of the most relentless resistances to the attacks on the "cult." In the 1960s the social science department at Moscow University was considered a reactionary hotbed. Add to this the huge mass of "political lecturers" of the Znaniye association, and the party propagandists and agitators at every level, an army of a few million people, for the most part hardly enthusiastic about perestroika, even if they were not all as hostile as the department heads at the high schools. The lower levels of the propaganda apparat were more subject to the public's moods, and many of them realized the need for change. In this specific case, however, Ligachev tried to use the most conservative and most dissatisfied groups in the intelligentsia. I think that the creative intelligentsia that supports Gorbachev is still a minority of the "humanitarian" intelligentsia as a whole. However, Gorbachev's supporters, even if they are a minority, held positions

* This term refers to the producers and disseminators of culture at the intermediate and lower levels, i.e., production technicians, strictly speaking, but also schoolteachers, engineers, and others.

of power in this phase and built up the offensive. The reaction by the conservative forces was partly a result of this situation. They felt that they had a numerical advantage and they meant to exploit that as long as they could. Their attack would be thwarted for two main reasons: in the first place, because Gorbachev had a solid position inside the leadership; in the second place, because Gorbachev's reasoning was more solid than that of his adversaries.

G.C. The editor in chief of *Sovetskaya Rossia*, Valentin Chikin, was considered "progressive" by many people. Under his leadership the newspaper had courageously supported perestroika, but at the beginning of the year there was an abrupt change. In the debates over Mikhail Shatrov's play *Dalshe! Dalshe! Dalshe!* . . . , Chikin suddenly became one of its sharpest critics. Why?

R.M. Chikin never stood out very much for the clarity of his positions. In the 1970s he was the deputy editor of the same newspaper, when it was conformist like all the other dailies. Chikin limited himself to obeying orders both before and after. In this case he made the wrong choice. During this phase many newspaper editors found themselves in a difficult and uncertain position. For example, in the last two years *Pravda* actively declared itself in favor of rehabilitating party life, against corruption, and against the mafia groups in the republics. But it sided with conservative positions every time that it touched on the subjects of history and ideology. Its editor in chief, Viktor Afanasev, is not only a journalist. He is first and foremost a politician and a philosopher, who has often shown that he tended toward the conservative side. His scholarly work was on the "scientific leadership" of the society, analyzing the role of information, especially information on the society. Now it emerged that there was no "scientific leadership of the society" in the USSR, and that the party leaders ignored the information about the society that they had available. One would have to deduce that Viktor Afanasev's work did not correspond to reality, and therefore guess that the new direction was not to his liking.

The events of April and March can be considered a victory for perestroika, but they were not accompanied by any changes in the cadres. Chikin kept his job, even though he deserved to be fired for playing a key role in the conspiracy (not for having different viewpoints from Gorbachev). As far as the editor of *Pravda* was concerned, there had been talk about replacing him for some time, but for now nothing changed. Now Chikin and Afanasev could continue their policies. One can only suppose that they would do so with greater caution.

207

G.C. One more question on the "Andreyeva case." The reconstruction of events in the *Washington Post*, which matches my own in many details, also says that Gorbachev had changed the composition of his bodyguard in 1987, and that now it was formed by the army, not by the KGB. Do you know about this? There's also another version that introduces a variant from my own. The current assistant editor of *Kommunist*, Otto Lazis, referred to it during a lunch with Italian journalists. According to Lazis, the Politburo met for three days without interruption after Gorbachev returned from Yugoslavia.

R.M. I too have heard some of these rumors, although I am not yet able to confirm them. They said that for six hours the country had no general secretary. It is perfectly possible that in those six hours, according to another rumor, Gorbachev held a meeting of the Defense Council, over which he presides and whose members include all the heads of the different armies and the main military districts. A complete reconstruction of those events can only be made in the future. It was definitely a true crisis, even though I don't think it verged on a coup d'état. It is also clear that Gorbachev had enemies in the Politburo, but no one who could replace him. I do think that what you said about Gorbachev's bodyguard is true. He does not want to entrust himself completely to the KGB. In this he follows Stalin and Brezhnev, not Khrushchev. However, on the surface the KGB did not play a visible role in the events of March and April.

G.C. After the Twenty-Seventh Congress, at least fifty members of the Central Committee had to abandon the posts that were the basis of their membership in the party's most important ruling body. Another ten died. But Gorbachev's attempt to perform a "'remixing" of the Central Committee midway between the two congresses fell through, for the resistance was too strong. Thus, the preparation of the conference focused on ideological issues, on the "rule-of-law state." Organizational issues were postponed.

R.M. In the months preceding the conference a bitter but invisible struggle took place over the powers that it could and could not be granted, including the power to change the face of the Central Committee. The bylaws of the Communist Party say very little about party conferences, but there is no prohibition on changing the membership of the leading bodies. The last party conference had been in 1941. On that occasion Stalin changed the Central Committee in part. But he was not fond of holding large party forums. There were no conferences during the "stagnation." They were of no use, since even the congresses had been turned into sheer formalities whose main task was simply to approve the new five-year plan.

G.C. The crisis of March and the following months was coupled with the uprising in Nagorno-Karabakh. Up to now no one has been able to uncover whether or not there was a direct link between the two issues. I also think there were at least some elements of "political maneuvering" intertwined with the "nationalistic" spark.

R.M. There are some clues. After the retirement of the first secretaries of the Armenian and Azerbaijani parties, four Politburo members were sent into the region. Yakovlev went to Armenia and Ligachev went to Azerbaijan. Dolgikh was sent with Yakovlev, while Ligachev was accompanied by Razumovsky. Knowing the factions in the Politburo, it's not difficult to see that Moscow wanted to maintain a system of checks and balances. Ligachev wanted to take a hard line toward the Armenians. During the crisis *Pravda* maintained a not entirely impartial line, opposed to the Armenians. On the other hand, I think the men close to Gorbachev suggested to the new Armenian first secretary, Arutyunyan, that he allow the Armenian Supreme Soviet to vote on supporting Nagorno-Karabakh's demands. However, the balances in Moscow did not allow this policy to take effect.

G.C. Even the way the investigations were conducted, and the subsequent trial for the Sumgait massacre, proved that in Moscow there were forces that were more or less consciously "blowing on the fire." The very fact that an obvious pogrom was classified as a simple crime could only make the Armenians indignant.

R.M. Who knows why, but the court examined the Sumgait events by subdividing them into single episodes and not as a programmatic act of genocide. At the same time, it was decided that the trial would take place in an Azerbaijani court, even though for the obvious reasons of its gravity and importance, the trial should have been under the jurisdiction of the Supreme Court of the USSR, and not in Sumgait but somewhere else. Although the Armenians were obviously being provoked, their reactions remained under control. The attempt to take the issue to the Supreme Soviet, which was absolutely unprecedented in Soviet history, aimed to open up an "institutional crisis," whose end point would have been a modification in the Constitution of the USSR.

G.C. But Ligachev's behavior at Baku threw oil on the fire.

R.M. The situation in Baku was already hard to control between May and June. Later it would become even harder because of indecision in Moscow. In Baku, Ligachev did not find even one Azerbaijani leader who could take Bagirov's place. A partially "foreign" solution had to be invented, leading to the appointment of Abdul Vezirov, the former ambassador to Pakistan, who was Azerbaijani by nationality, but in actuality Muscovite. This choice led to public demonstrations. Ligachev wanted to appease the demonstrators, and he promised that Nagorno-Karabakh would always remain under Azerbaijani jurisdiction. The truth is that in that moment Nagorno-Karabakh was being run by Moscow. Ligachev's careless public statement upset the delicate balance that had been temporarily established.

G.C. In the meantime Kamenev, Zinoviev, Pyatakov, Radek, and others were also rehabilitated.

R.M. These were strictly legal rehabilitations, but that is no reason to consider them secondary. They filled in another "blank spot" in our history. The case of Bukharin was also a question of rehabilitating his political ideas during the period of the NEP. Here we were dealing with the so-called opposition "from the left," whose politics in substance was wrong.

G.C. The sentencing of Zinoviev and company included a sentencing of Trotsky in absentia. But there was no mention of this in the actual rehabilitation documents.

R.M. When Bukharin was rehabilitated, Yagoda's name was obviously stricken out. Now Trotsky's name was also left out. Clearly, the trial against Zinoviev and the others was more difficult to deal with in light of current events. The "left-wing" opposition was arguing with the NEP in the mid-1920s. Trotskyism still exists today as an ultraleft-wing organization in many Western and Latin American countries. However, it's indispensable, for the sake of historical truth, to officially erase all the false accusations made against him at the Moscow trials and that provided a justification for his murder and the assassination of thousands of his followers. These lies include the well-known accusation that he performed "intelligence" services for fascism. It should also be noted that the party press did not report the rehabilitation of Zinoviev and his comrades. Only *Izvestia* mentioned it. This confirms that the question of their rehabilitation in the party had been postponed. But Pyatakov, for example, was Ordzhonikidze's deputy and a member of the Central Committee and of the party. All of these strictly political problems will probably be settled later, and on an individual basis.

G.C. How would you judge the election campaign for delegates on the whole?

R.M. The last days before the conference were actually tumultuous. Never before had the party rank and file taken such a large part in the debates on the candidates. Thus, it was possible for many worthy individuals, including many important intellectuals, to enter into the group of delegates. At the same time, the apparat abuses began, with widespread attempts to get rid of candidates whom the local party bosses didn't like, meetings held at the last minute in order to prevent other candidates from being nominated, and unlawful acts. Scandals were registered in Moscow too. This is how many delegates got elected who were open adversaries of perestroika, or supporters of a perestroika without glasnost. The bigger picture was highly complex. In many cases there were open and free political debates. In very many other cases, on the contrary, the antidemocratic arbitrary power of the apparats prevailed. However, the new feature of the situation was a growing involvement of the party rank and file. I myself was able to participate in a discussion of the "Theses" at a meeting at the Institute for Social Sciences Information at the USSR Academy of Sciences. It was my first public appearance before a Soviet audience in many years.

G.C. Political tensions grew sharper, accompanied by accelerated cultural production. Even if for the moment, in literature, the works published were predominately those that had been forbidden by censorship in the past decades.

R.M. I would like to review the most significant events in this field. *Novy Mir* published Boris Pasternak's *Dr. Zhivago* for the first time in the USSR in 1988 [nos. 1–4]. We all read it with great interest, even if the novel didn't provoke any particular emotion in the greater public. However, there was a great deal of discussion among critics. The novel, which won the Nobel Prize for Pasternak in 1958, received general critical approval, but there were some venomous reviews, such as D. Durnov's in *Pravda*.

In my opinion the main event in the first months of 1988 was the publication of *Zhizn i Subda* (*Life and Fate*) by Vasili Grossman. This is an epic novel about the war, about Soviet society, and about the Soviet people's lives and struggles during the crucial months of the battle for Stalingrad, on the front and in the rear, in the POW labor camps in the West, and in Stalin's gulag in the East. Grossman wrote his novel between 1956 and 1960, in the climate produced by the Twentieth Congress. The novel was "arrested" in 1961, when every copy of the manuscript, even his rough draft and his notes, were sequestered from the author and from his friends. When Mikhail Suslov received the already famous writer in his Kremlin office, he told him that the novel could not be published for another two hundred years. The novel was a huge critical and public success.

To the same group of valuable works written in the 1950s and 1960s, but never before published, we must add Varlaam Shalamov's *Kolymskiye Rasskazy* (*Kolyma Tales*). Once again *Novy Mir* began an initiative that would upset the general public [no. 6]. In my opinion this was one of the finest literary investigations of life in the camps; it was written before the famous *Gulag Archipelago*, and was in many respects superior to and more profound than Solzhenitsyn's work. In the 1960s Shalamov's work circulated in samizdats, and many knew of it in this form. In the 1970s it was published in the West, first in Russian and then in various translations.

An equally great event was the publication of two classics, which were also unknown to the general public: the novels *My* (*We*) by Yevgeni Zamyatin [*Znamya*, nos. 4–5, 1988], and *Chevengur* by Andrei Platonov [*Druzhba Narodov*, nos. 4–5, 1988]. *My* was written in 1920, and is known to the Western reader as the forerunner of a new literary genre: the antiutopian novel. George Orwell wrote his *1984* in 1949, under the obvious influence of Zamyatin's work. While we're on the subject, *1984*, which had long been considered "slanderous" and "anti-Soviet" in the USSR, was published by the Progress publishing house and by *Novy Mir* at the beginning of 1989. In the meantime *Literaturnaya Gazeta* published a few selections on the Ministry of Truth.

Less famous was Platonov's novel *Chevengur*, one of the bitterest representations of Soviet reality in the late 1920s. Its linguistic, stylistic, and formal particularities as well as its complex symbolism made it a work difficult to translate and not easy for the general public to read. However, it is unquestionably a fundamental work. I have to say that the quality and the quantity of publications in these months made it difficult to choose. For example, you cannot ignore Vladimir Tendryakov's short stories [*Novy Mir*, no. 3, 1988], and Konstantin Simonov's diary, *Glazami Cheloveka Moyevo Pokolenia* [*With the Eyes of a Man of My Generation*; *Znamya*, nos. 3–5, 1988], which describe the reflections of a writer. No less important were the publication of books and verses by many poets and writers who had already died, such as Aleksandr Yashin, Boris Yampolsky, Yuri German, and Boris Slutsky.

G.C. Many works of Western literature were published that had previously been inaccessible to Soviet readers.

R.M. Kafka's *The Castle* was published for the first time in 1988, simultaneously by *Inostrannaya Literatura* and by Neva in Leningrad. *Znamya* published Mario Puzo's *The Godfather*. Vladimir Nabokov was also repeatedly published. His autobiographical novel *Drugiye Berega* (*Other Shores*) came out in *Druzhba Narodov* [no. 5, 1988]. But I would like to continue by also remembering the Soviet writers whom I would define as "average," like Vladimir Orlov, whose novel *Aptekar* was published, or David Gai, whose *Bodyguard* was published, with General Nikolai Vlasik, the head of Stalin's bodyguard, as its protagonist. The highly original poet from Kharkov, Boris Chichibabin, whose poetry has long been published in the West, was finally introduced to Soviet readers.

G.C. There was a true renaissance of social and political essays.

R.M. Yes, we witnessed a real explosion. In this field the weeklies competed with the huge political and literary monthlies. Some articles and essays were epoch-making. Yuri Karyakin's article in *Ogonyok* [no. 19], entitled "Zhdanovskaya Zhidkost, ili Protiv Ochernitelstva" ("The Liquid of Zhdanov, That Is, Against Slander"), raised a torrent of arguments because it accused Zhdanov not only of persecuting writers in the 1940s, but also of coauthoring the 1937 trials and being a protagonist of the closing of many party organizations in the 1930s. Equally explosive was Vasili Selyunin's essay "Istoki" ["Origins"; *Novy Mir*, no. 5, 1988], in which the author analyzed not only the events of the 1930s, but also the mistakes of Soviet power in the first years of its existence. Arkadi Vakhsberg distinguished himself in *Literaturnaya Gazeta* with vehement articles against former Minister of the Interior Nikolai Sholokov that reconstructed the event of the shooting of Soviet generals on the eve of the Second World War.

G.C. Up to this point you have only mentioned the offensive of the forces for renewal, yet we know that the conservatives were not standing around with their hands in their pockets.

R.M. Hardly. I have already mentioned that *Molodaya Gvardia* and *Nash Sovremennik* headed the cultural reaction. For example, M. Malakhov openly came to Stalin's defense, calling him "an illustrious personality, to whom many of his contemporaries paid homage: Roosevelt, Churchill, Maurice Thorez, and so on" (*Molodaya Gvardiya*, no. 4, 1988). Igor Shafarevich and Vadim Kozhinov also took reactionary stances, but for them an explicit defense of Stalinism is unacceptable. They saw Stalinism as a kind of international phenomenon, that was not due to the intrigues of Stalin and his entourage, but to the plotting of the liberal Western intelligentsia (especially those of Jewish and French origin: Albert Einstein, Lion Feucht-wanger, Henri Barbusse, and so on) [*Nash Sovremennik*, no. 4, 1988]. It was the same idea, but better camouflaged, of the secret power of the "Jewish Masons" directed against the Russian people and against the "Russian spirit."

But the quality of the conservative and reactionary positions in the Soviet press is much inferior to that of the reformers. Mikhail Ulyanov's vehement articles in *Sovetskaya Kultura* caused a sensation. They appeared more and more frequently, denouncing corruption and the organized mafia. *Izvestia* and other periodicals denounced the use of psychiatry for political repression. Even the KGB was openly criticized for the abuses of the 1960s and 1970s, but with a certain caution. At almost the same time, different newspapers and magazines published articles on Beria's crimes and on his arrest at the Kremlin. New material appeared on the 1953 "doctors' plot," and on the repressions of the Komsomol leaders from 1937 to 1939. More than anyone else, Stalin was attacked from every side for his crimes and mistakes, both in the prewar period and in the first months of the war, when he proved that he didn't know how to confront the situation.

The rehabilitation of Bukharin and the other Bolshevik leaders put down in the 1936–38 trials gave vent to a wave of publications that opened the eyes of millions of readers to our history in the 1920s and 1930s. A totally unprecedented debate grew on collectivization, industrialization, and the so-called "revolution from above." The name of Nikita Khrushchev and the events of the Twentieth and Twenty-Second congresses appeared more and more frequently and positively. This was especially important when you consider that the latest generation of Soviet youths knew nothing or almost nothing about either one or the other.

G.C. Even Roy Medvedev was published now.

R.M. For the first time in twenty years my articles, interviews, and essays appeared in the Soviet press—in the weeklies *Sobesednik, Moskovskiye Novosti*, and *Argumenty i Fakty*, and in the dailies, *Komsomolskaya Pravda, Moskovski Komsomolets*, and so on. However, I would like to point out other significant facts, such as the evolution of the monthly *Inostrannaya Literatura*. Under the direction of the ultracautious sinologist and diplomat manqué Nikolai Fedorenko, the monthly had been losing readers month after month. His place was taken with great acclaim by a member of the editorial board, Chingiz Aitmatov. *Inostrannaya Literatura* began to publish truly important Western writers. Aitmatov explained his platform in a long article published in *Izvestia* that may have been the best essay in 1988 for its vigor and depth (4 May 1988). There was significant growth in the readership of the most progressive newspapers, and a sharp increase in the number of letters to the editor.

G.C. Television did not fall behind in this panorama. Of all the mass media, it is the one that underwent the most sensational change.

R.M. Millions of people can watch programs of unprecedented frankness every night. Materials were pulled out of the Gosfilm archives that had been collecting dust for decades. The cinema also began to produce interesting things. For example, the film *The Cold Summer of 1953* was a big hit with the public; it was a kind of adventurous Western with anti-Stalinist content and unusual psychological depth. Other films that had been blocked in the 1960s were finally released. Among these I wish to note Aleksandr Askoldov's *Komissar* and Andrei Mikhalkov-Konchalovsky's *Asiya-khromonozhka* (*The Story of Asiya Klyachiana Who Loved Without Getting Married*). The theater also began to reawaken after a long lethargy, and the audiences started to fill the theaters again. Among the best works in the new year you have to include Bulgakov's *Heart of a Dog*, staged by the Teatr Yunogo Zritelya. The Little Theater of Moscow University was crowded every day for *The Black Man, or Poor Soso Dzhugashvili*. Some of the provincial theaters had already staged Shatrov's controversial play, *Dalshe! Dalshe! Dalshe!* . . . But in Moscow no theater was able to surmount the bureaucratic obstacles and opposition. The Taganka Theater returned to the center of attention with Vladimir Vysotsky's show, staged by the new artistic director A. Gubenko along the model of Lyubimov's script. This was a major event since this work was one of the *casus belli* that made Lyubimov decide to leave. Taganka also staged another play that had been forbidden in its time: Pushkin's *Boris Godunov*, according to Lyubimov's original directions. The director obtained a visa to reenter the USSR and see the opening night. I also wish to mention a show at the Dramatic Theater of Baku, *Zolotaya Chasha* (*The Golden Cup*), a pitiless satire of the times of stagnation, which were still alive in Azerbaijan, as the events were proving.

Perestroika in the theater took place very slowly and through hard work, in the midst of clashes, slander, panic, and in some cases open demagoguery. Clearly, the long phase of immobility had created a void of ideas and of leaders in almost all the most important theaters. But conversely, there was a widespread growth of small theater groups and theater studios that were often housed in makeshift structures, and in many cases attracted great interest.

By contrast, there were still very few signs of renewal in music, sculpture, and the figurative arts. A major event was the first show in the USSR of Salvador Dali's works. Ilya Glazunov could finally exhibit in the USSR his work *The Mysteries of the Twentieth Century* as part of a one-man show at the Manezh that was extremely successful with the viewers. I have to admit that I'm no fan of Glazunov, but I am ready to fight any attempt to block him or others from exhibiting their works. The magazines began to reproduce paintings by Chagall, Kandinsky, and Malevich. Soviet rock music grew refined and it spread among young people, causing protests from those who praised the "official" music. As you can see, 1988 began with a very crowded picture, full of problems and contradictions, but also of great novelties and openings.

CHAPTER 8

THE NINETEENTH PARTY CONFERENCE; THE
SEPTEMBER PLENUM AND THE REFORM OF THE
POLITICAL SYSTEM

•   •   •

Even before Gorbachev stepped up to the podium, it was already clear that
the Nineteenth Conference was the equivalent of a special party congress;
however it ended, it would become a watershed in the history of the Soviet
state and of the Communist Party of the Soviet Union. Nothing had been
predetermined except for the temporary and fragile balances of power inside
the leadership and the party body. The agenda of ten "Theses" approved by
the Central Committee included the creation of the "rule-of-law socialist
state"—an outright revolution. But the majority of delegates in the convention hall physically embodied the very past that was slated for change: the
establishment, power, and privilege. Many of them did not understand where
they were being led; they did not know what role they would have under
the new conditions appearing on the horizon, or even if they would have a
role.

Gorbachev was not guaranteed success. This may be why media proposals
to broadcast the proceedings of the conference live were turned down. This
was the wish of the conservatives, who wanted an accounting sheltered from
indiscreet eyes. But so did the reformers, who were not interested in showing
the whole country that they were in the minority. Gorbachev said that
"perestroika is in the hands of the people," but the people were not inside
the convention hall. However, their presence was felt as never before, through
the 150,000 from Tallinn, the 10,000 from Vilnius, the 500,000 from Yerevan, and the thousands of citizens in Sakhalin and Omsk, Sverdlovsk, and
Tyumen, who had challenged their corrupt party leaders, imposed their own
delegates, and created "popular fronts" and informal committees and perestroika groups.

Most of the thirty-four authors of a book that summarized the ideas of
perestroika were also left outside of the hall. Their ideas went well beyond

what Gorbachev would and could say in his report. The volume was entitled *Inovo ne Dano* (*There Are No Other Possibilities*). It was printed in record time, boycotted until the last minute, but distributed to all the delegates. These ideas were the launching pad for the "inevitable" changes that awaited the country. They had been written in the midst of the turmoil of the last few months by a handful of intellectuals, but in reality they were the distillation of long silent years when it was not possible to tell the whole truth in public. Gorbachev had already drawn extensively from that well-known but "unutterable" truth. Without knowing or sharing that truth, the group of reformers in the party could not have effected the shift at the April 1985 plenum. But it went over the heads of most of the delegates assembled. It was as "unpolitic" as it was "true." But the more "unpolitic" it was, the more "necessary" it was for the great, decisive political match being played before the country and before the world.

The Nineteenth Conference would represent Gorbachev's masterpiece partly from this perspective. Gorbachev's staunchest supporters—Ulyanov, Abalkin, and Baklanov—were paradoxically his harshest critics. When Ulyanov spoke, he exclaimed:

> I thought about it all night, you must believe me. Now I am telling you that I am not only against three consecutive terms, but also against two terms. In our country every exception becomes a rule. . . . Therefore, I propose that as an exception we decide on only one, for Gorbachev. We are making a revolution that will take time. I trust Gorbachev.

This passage from his speech caused an ovation, but when Ulyanov raised the topic of glasnost, asking that the local first secretaries not be allowed to strangle it, the way they were doing almost everywhere, threatening murmurs rose from the hall. "We know that it is a weapon," Ulyanov said, turning toward the panel onstage, "we have to realize that it can hurt someone." Gorbachev stopped him: "We must avoid falling from one monopoly into another. We cannot even settle things through the press. But I think we agree." Ulyanov replied, "Mikhail Sergeyevich, the example of Nina Andreyeva's letter is a lesson that must not be forgotten . . . it put everyone on his guard."

Dialogues like this between Gorbachev and the delegates were repeated several times. Today you can say from the podium, "I don't agree with Gorbachev." And it is his most ardent supporters who do this most often. It's an obvious paradox. They knew that not everything that Gorbachev put in his report to the conference was entirely "by Gorbachev." The others, who accepted a difficult compromise, stated their agreement, but rushed to limit its significance. In this way, with the passing hours Gorbachev came to find himself in the most favorable position, the one who smoothed out conflicts, the only key figure who could unify, lower tensions, and reduce the distance between extremes. The more this scenario took shape, the more television and radio came into the conference halls, spreading and amplifying the debate. Millions of onlookers watched a show never before seen, at times of a crude frankness. On the second and third days of debate, the decision made on the eve of the conference was effectively subverted; the Soviet reporters received the go-ahead and interviewed the delegates, recording and broadcasting even the bitterest phases of the discussion.

On the third day Gorbachev spoke again to draw the line down the middle that had been so badly trampled that it was almost unrecognizable. Too deep a split could compromise the conclusions of the entire conference. He was shrewd in delivering blows, arguing on the left with Leonid Abalkin, who had questioned the idea of a single party. He urged those who were pushing too far ahead "not to force," because "there are no shortcuts." You had to look for a "possible" compromise. "Some people say that we should pound our fists. If we agree on this, we can do it." He spoke with bodily gestures, carried away by the heat of his speech. But the thunderous applause that followed his pounding his fist on the table surprised him: the different factions in the convention hall found themselves united for a second in the hope that a strong hand could solve the many uncertainties of the moment. Gorbachev waited for a minute in silence, while the television cameras scanned his expressionless face. Then he doused the enthusiasms in both camps with a devastating and sarcastic remark:

> Comrades, as far as pounding hard goes, we truly have accumulated quite an experience. I think instead that we should restrain ourselves, because otherwise we will find ourselves once again adopting old methods—at the very time that we are on the verge of renewal. . . .

Now everybody understood—before they had not. And the applause was even more thunderous. Only Gorbachev could allow himself the luxury of getting two ovations for opposite reasons in the space of one minute. Perhaps in that very moment he realized that he had won the battle. He chased it abruptly, dramatically, with "I am telling you loud and clear that I will never give in to this temptation." Then he made a jab in the opposite direction:

> If the people are not involved in the reform process, then we will not succeed. We have an apparat of 18 million people that costs us 40 billion rubles a year. Has it worked? No, it hasn't worked! The system doesn't work, the management of the economy doesn't work, and not even the society works.

The magic trick followed, in a breathtaking succession of surprises and broadsides that rocked the floor like a wheat field in the wind. He gave a second of comfort to the apparatchiks, who had just been branded as incapable before the eyes of millions of Soviet people: the role of the party could not be held up for questioning. "I see no other force . . . the smallest doubt about the function of the party would be a big gift to the enemies of perestroika!" But the party in its turn knew that it had to "understand, undergo the criticism of a courageous analysis." You cannot be avant-garde by decree. You have to earn this role in every moment.

This task was quite strenuous for the many cadres who were only used to commanding. An exchange of blows followed, live on television, moment by moment. The session turned into an exceptional moment of glasnost, in which the conservative and reactionary spirits of the party showed both their arrogance and their inability to organize an alternative. The writer Yuri Bondarev made inflammatory accusations against *Ogonyok* and its editor in chief, Vitali Korotich. The first secretary of Altai, Filipp Popov, upped the ante: on the eve of the conference, he said, the "slanderer" Korotich had published the "revelation" that some of the delegates were implicated in criminal proceedings. If that was true, then let him publicly expose them! The spirit of revenge once again blew heavily through the hall.

Razumovsky reported that the general prosecutor of the USSR and the Party Control Commission knew nothing about any of this. They knew of no delegates under investigation. But *Ogonyok*'s move was anything but reckless, and Popov's attack boomeranged. The article had been signed by two "special investigators" from the Federal Prosecutor's Office, Telman Gdlyan and Nikolai Ivanov, who had headed an investigation into the Uzbek mafia for more than five years. Korotich explained to the podium what could already be read in *Ogonyok*: the corrupt could not be prosecuted because "there are unwritten laws, on the basis of which it is not easy to file suit against a member of the Central Committee." Gdlyan and Ivanov could not write the names of the alleged criminals who were seated in the hall with the delegates for the obvious reason that secrecy had to be maintained during the preliminary investigation. However, Korotich could give their names to the president in a sealed envelope. The Central Control Commission had to choose either to strike the accused or to punish the investigators and the journalists who had uncovered the scandal. The assembly watched in icy silence: along with the four "who knew," many others felt the same threat weighing down on them. Less than five months later a series of arrests would prove Korotich to have been completely right.[1]

But the culminating moment was yet to arrive. The delegate Boris Yeltsin asked to speak. His request was granted, and he would be the last speaker at the second session on the last day of fiery debate. His speech was contradictory, yet he made almost no retractions, and he reiterated his criticism of Ligachev, even more explicitly this time. Now Yeltsin repeated in public much more than he had said in the closing moments of the October 1987 plenum, and he expressed his opinion of the progress of perestroika, partly critical of Gorbachev's position and partly supporting it.[2] When he asked for "political rehabilitation," he was interrupted by noises and shouts. Gorbachev stepped in with a broad smile: "Boris Nikolayevich, go ahead and speak," using the familiar form; "they are asking you to." Then he turned to the floor, which was having a hard time calming down: "Think, comrades, that we must remove every shadow of secrecy from the Yeltsin affair. Let comrade Yeltsin say whatever he needs to say. And if it seems necessary to us or to you, we will say what we need to say."

This gesture was both proper and magnanimous. In making it, Gorbachev gained even more prestige and strength. But he also subtly hinted at the need for a response from the accused party—Ligachev. Yeltsin's speech had been tentative until the last minute.[3] Allowing him to speak meant forcing Ligachev to respond.[4] And Ligachev would be the only member of the Politburo to step up to the podium—to defend himself.

This was a speech that would not help his image: harsh, dense with allusions and messages, he did not succeed in rising above his "antagonist." In places he was weakened by invectives against Yeltsin, and by his attempts to legitimize himself as a supporter of perestroika. Ligachev defended himself, Chebrikov, Solomentsev, and Gromyko, claiming that they had solved the crisis of succession to Chernenko. It was as if he were saying: Watch out, without us you would have had Viktor Grishin in Gorbachev's place. Thus, we also deserve some credit for perestroika. And this gives us the right to ask for our "interpretation" to be taken into account. Especially since—and here Ligachev showed his teeth—I am the one who chairs the meetings of the Secretariat. Everyone understood the meaning of his message: don't tilt the balance. The floor applauded, but the repercussions were huge, and certainly did not favor maintaining the balances that Ligachev wanted to preserve.[5]

The conference, which was supposed to decide whether to approve the "rule-of-law socialist state," was itself an affirmation of the right to criticize. *Pravda* published the complete texts of the speeches, even the heavy accusations against Mikhail Solomentsev for having protected corrupt high-ranking leaders of some of the republics; even the vehement denunciations of social inequalities and of the privileges of party cadres; even Yeltsin's sarcastic remarks about the "hungry *nomenklatura*" that continued to receive its "food packages" at reduced prices, or for free. This had never been said in public. Yet such sincerity was not only attributable to Yeltsin. The assembly was for the most part conservative, but it showed surprising variety. Whoever expected that a platoon of avant-garde intellectuals would play a primary role was not mistaken. But the intellectuals also showed a very different face, with explicit invitations to moderate glasnost (Vladimir Karpov, for example), or even with snarling appeals for new forms of censorship (Yuri Bondarev, for example).

The struggle was intensified in every group. The first man who had the courage to name the Politburo members who had to go was not Yeltsin, but Vladimir Melnikov, the first secretary of the Komi Republic and a member of the Central Committee. And the worker Veniamin Yarin, from the Nizhni Tagil rolling mill, was the one who asked to finally know the way duties were divided up in the Politburo, in order, he said, to determine individual responsibilities. The simplified diagram of an "all-conservative" party was no longer adequate. Those who really were conservatives also found themselves almost unexpectedly having to contribute to glasnost. Even Gorbachev himself was subject to jabs—sometimes provoked—which had never been allowed in a congress hall.

He was the sorcerer's apprentice who knew he was invoking powerful forces that could get out of control, but also knew that he had to take this risk to ensure his project's success. Thus, the conference was a kind of experimental laboratory for a "controlled" chain reaction. Whoever wanted a closed meeting realized too late that they were swimming inside a transparent aquarium in which, unlike the mute fish who usually swam there, there was a noisy battle. We do not know if the decision to let Yeltsin speak was made collectively, or by Gorbachev, or by someone else. Ligachev only hinted at it, enough to intimate that he had no part in it: "I knew that he would speak; I expected that he would speak."

Thus, the ship of the Nineteenth Party Conference arrived in port under full sail. It was a triumph for Gorbachev, who came out of it even stronger than when he went in. Perestroika still could not be considered irreversible, but with Gorbachev as its champion it was now unassailable. Gorbachev would be the future president of the Supreme Soviet of the new "rule-of-law socialist state" that was being formed. Even Boris Yeltsin helped; he showed that a pluralism of ideas is not only permissible, but useful. In his closing speech, Gorbachev was even able to "forgive him"—something he wouldn't have been able to do in the dramatic month of November 1987 in which he had to be cruel and pitiless in order to defend himself. He would do so by acknowledging the "mistake" (which was not his alone) of not having immediately told the whole truth at that time.[6]

The conference had just closed its doors when the Politburo announced a new plenum for the end of the month. The resolutions approved by the conference clarified the outlines of institutional reform. Part of the new

Congress of People's Deputies would be elected by universal suffrage (1,500 delegates), and another part would be made up of representatives elected directly by the "social organizations" (750 deputies).[7] The Congress would meet once a year, and elect from among its members two houses totaling 542 deputies who would constitute the new Supreme Soviet. The Supreme Soviet would meet for prolonged sessions three times a year (rather than the previous system, where meetings of this body were pure formalities that lasted only a few days every year). The Congress would elect the president of the Supreme Soviet by secret ballot.

The separation of the functions of the party and the state, and the preeminence of the elected bodies over the executive bodies of state power were established as principles, though in highly contradictory terms. The local soviets would elect "presidiums" as permanent working bodies. In fact, these were "councils" that were quite distinct from the "executive committees." The membership of the latter consisted of functionaries, who were not allowed to serve as deputies in the soviets. Anyone who held the position of judge, prosecutor, member of the government, or member of the central or republican ministries was also ineligible. At the same time, the highly controversial issue of the overlap between the offices of president of a soviet and first secretary for the corresponding party committee, was settled with a "recommendation, as a rule, to increase the role of the representative bodies." Finally, the document on democratization sanctioned an extremely important principle, establishing for the first time an institutional mechanism for the succession of powers. The duration of an elective term was established as only two consecutive terms.[8]

There would soon be a signal indicating shifts of balance in the leadership. Aleksandr Yakovlev held a meeting of the mass media to provide an "authentic" interpretation of the Nineteenth Conference, in which he said:

> The shift toward glasnost is not only a policy line corresponding to the interests of perestroika. It is a stage in the development of the revolution. Blaming glasnost for something amounts to blaming a doctor for formulating an accurate, even serious, diagnosis of a disease. In this respect, the conclusions of the Nineteenth Conference are not at all compromising.[9]

But there was not a single day of truce in Nagorno-Karabakh. The events in Moscow changed nothing in the Caucasus crisis. On 12 July the deputies attending that day's session of the region's soviet, 104 out of a total of 144, voted unanimously for formal separation from the Azerbaijani Republic. Baku's reaction was immediate. On 13 July the presidium of the Azerbaijani Supreme Soviet called the decision "illegal." Once again Armenia was paralyzed by strikes. Gorbachev tried to step in. The clash had reached the institutional level, and required a formal response. At an emergency meeting of the Supreme Soviet of the USSR there was an extremely bitter discussion that would be widely broadcast on central television. The interventions disclosed the seriousness of the conflict between the Armenian and Azerbaijani leaders. "Intermediate" proposals proved worthless, such as Academician Yevgeni Primakov's formulation to raise the status of the autonomous region to that of an autonomous republic, while keeping it inside the borders of Azerbaijan. The first secretary of Armenia, Arutyunyan, also ventured a reasonable proposal: leave the region in the temporary administrative care of the central bodies. This was the same suggestion made by the poet Razul Gamzatov, who invited everyone not to forget the irreparable harm caused by Sumgait, which he called a "Chernobyl of the spirit."

However, completely uncompromising positions were taken inside the Presidium. In no uncertain terms Lev Zaikov asked that public order be restored by using "every means available." Gorbachev appeared to be incapable of getting out of the dilemma. He spoke about the need to look for a "compromise," but then he allowed himself to be led into a dispute that was at times disrespectful toward the chairman of the Presidium of the Armenian Supreme Soviet, Grant Voskanyan. The "logical" arguments against the Armenian request were highly unconvincing. The concrete fact that the rights of the Armenian majority in Nagorno-Karabakh had been violated was not mentioned.

Gorbachev tried to remain "impartial," which was no longer possible after the Sumgait massacre. This was perhaps the moment when Gorbachev displayed the greatest uncertainty and confusion since taking power. The final "unanimous" decision was to "confirm that Nagorno-Karabakh belongs to Azerbaijan." There was little compromise. "The Presidium of the Supreme Soviet of the USSR is sending its representatives to Nagorno-Karabakh," who would act "in close cooperation with the representatives of the Azerbaijani and Armenian republics." Legally, it was an innovative decision, since it gave Armenia the right to intervene in decisions regarding Nagorno-Karabakh, even though Armenia had no sovereignty over the territory in that region. Later events would prove that the line adopted to confront the situation was completely inadequate. Gorbachev did not seem to have understood that continuing in this direction would dangerously reinforce the extremist elements. The absence of a "real" mediation pulled the rug out from under the moderates leading the Armenian movement, while it convinced the rebelling Azerbaijanis of their own impunity. Undoubtedly, there were already those who were blowing on the fire. The arrests struck only the leaders of the Nagorno-Karabakh Committee, which in that phase represented the only possible and still relatively responsible leadership for a huge mass movement.

The July plenum held a surprise. Many observers expected it to sanction the new political balances within the Politburo. But everyone kept their positions. However, two resolutions were approved on "party reform," and Gorbachev himself headed a special commission of the Central Committee assigned to prepare concrete proposals to carry out the decisions of the Nineteenth Conference. The Soviet leader was on a tight schedule, and he did not intend to delegate control to anyone. The stages for the political reform were scheduled in extremely close succession. In the fall the new constitutional reform and the new law on elections had to be approved. The elections for the Congress would take place in March 1989. Immediately afterward the new government had to be approved. The moment Gorbachev became president would thus be the time to establish the new political balances in the leadership. The reform of the party and of the apparat had to take place before that date, for the party's duplication of governmental functions could not continue under the new directives.

The course of events would upset this "work calendar" and force Gorbachev to do many things that had been scheduled for later. But Gorbachev was also worried about what was happening in the country. It was no accident that almost all of his report at the plenum was on the economy. He insisted on the need to "draw up the next five-year plan and strengthen its social aims." As far as the food situation was concerned, he insisted on the need to achieve a change by 1990. The figures given at the plenum were self-explanatory: in the last seventeen years the state had invested in agriculture the astronomical sum of 680 billion rubles. The increase in gross production in the corresponding period was 25 percent, equal to an average of 1.4 percent per year. This was a huge waste of resources for such a meager yield. Gorbachev said it was useless to throw good money after bad "unless the economic relations in the countryside change." He proposed a variegated solution to the problem: family and team contracts; independent management for existing farm enterprises; but especially "the leasing of lands to families and to cooperatives." This was another "radical" proposal: to give the land to single farmers and to groups of farmers for periods of "twenty-five to thirty years, up to fifty years." This represented, in short, a change in property relations in the countryside. Gorbachev said, "I hope that no one will be disturbed if the means of production are made available to the farmers, and for a long time." Instead, some people were disturbed; in fact, many of them. But Gorbachev cut it short: "Come on, comrades, let's reach an agreement at this plenum. We will not put up with any more small talk on this issue." Actually, he *would* have to put up with it.

Once again the resistance of the "leadership cadres, at different levels, who don't know how to do anything, but stubbornly keep others from showing their initiative," tried to ambush him.[10] Added to this was the fact that the farmers were not used to considering the land as their own. Another six months would go by—until 15 March 1989—before the "agricultural" plenum could be held that would implement these recommendations. Up to the last minute there was opposition from those—Ligachev would make no attempt to hide it—who wanted production relations in the countryside to be left unchanged.

This was already happening to the law on cooperatives, approved by the Supreme Soviet at the end of May. Along with the law on state enterprises it constituted, in its intentions, a cornerstone of the economic reform. In fact—for in theory cooperative property had always existed, although in reality it was "as if it didn't exist"—the fifty articles of the law sanctioned the end of the complete nationalization of the means of production. However, applying the law would be highly controversial, and by the end of the year and in early 1989, bureaucratic hostilities (greatly favored by popular hostility to the "nouveau riche") would succeed in imposing substantial limits on the development of cooperatives.

During his summer vacation, however, Gorbachev clearly realized the need to move faster. There were troublesome signs of social and political tensions in different parts of the country. The apparats' inertia threatened to produce a wave of public discontent. Therefore, Gorbachev decided to dramatize the situation and he had "crowd scenes" organized, which the television would amplify throughout the country, in one of the most depressed and difficult areas. In mid-September, before returning to work, Gorbachev visited the Krasnoyarsk region. From his encounters with the people the Soviet leader found out what he already knew: the workers were dissatisfied with the progress of perestroika. They demanded that it move forward. They had great faith in him, but they criticized the slowness, and the things done only halfway. After four days of lively confrontations with the people and the leaders of Krasnoyarsk, Gorbachev drew the conclusions he needed to speed things up in his Moscow battle. The people had changed, he said, because "we have given politics back" to them. The right policy had been chosen. "The people are worried about the progress of the reform; they are not willing, and rightly so, to be satisfied with the way things are." The problems could not be solved through a "clean cut." Such an act would be "remote from serious politics, from the realities of life, and dangerous for its results." But, he added:

We must also reject with equal firmness the points of view of those people who are afraid of the democratization of society, the reform of the economy, cooperatives, the rehabilitation of the moral climate, and reflection on our past, and also the people who see all of this as a threat to socialism.[11]

The new social relations that were being introduced take time, Gorbachev continued in his speech to the Krasnoyarsk cadres: leasing lands to the farmers (as well as factories to partnerships), family and team contracts, and independent management for enterprises could not be achieved by decree. The workers had to get used to them. But there were things that had to be done right away. First of all, there had to be a rise in the standard of living of the people, a change in the quality of life for huge masses. This meant urgently getting to work on the problems of food, housing, consumer goods, health, education, and the environment. Gorbachev hereby announced an economic policy that would reroute huge quantities of resources toward social consumption.

When Gorbachev returned to Moscow, there were signs that something was happening in the political leadership. A sudden crisis quickly played itself out in the space of eight days. It would not be possible to reconstruct what happened in the second half of September until the future, but a careful study of its features uncovers enlightening details.[12] The July plenum had helped speed up the reform of the apparats, starting with the central apparat. This clearly implied a necessary redistribution of duties inside the Politburo and a modification in the role of the Secretariat. In fact, it was the premise for a *redde rationem* in the ruling group. But Gorbachev set about it without wanting to outwardly dramatize this revolution in the balances of power; he was performing a simple reshuffling of the cards without any trauma, a logical consequence of the reform of the apparats. This was when the unexpected happened. The conservative group dug in its heels and said no. Let's try to reconstruct the probable chain of events.

First of all, we know that on 21 September Shevardnadze had left Copenhagen for Washington without knowing that there was about to be a plenum. Otherwise, he would not have scheduled a series of meetings in New York that would take up the entire next week. We can deduce that at that moment the debate had not yet reached its dramatic peak. Another clue confirms this. Two days later, on 23 September, Andrei Gromyko held a meeting of the Presidium of the Supreme Soviet to approve a plan of operation "until March 1989," and to decide on the regular meeting of the Supreme Soviet, tentatively scheduled for 27 October.[13] It was Friday the twenty-third. On the same day, Gorbachev, accompanied by Aleksandr Yakovlev, held a meeting of the representatives of the mass media and gave a speech full of "signals." He said:

We realize that certain issues cannot be resolved unless they are faced in the old way, the way it used to be. What else can you do? This is the reality of life.

What did this mean? That Gorbachev was "forced" to do something he didn't want to do, and not only that. He had to do it "the old way," with a *coup de main*. Someone was trying "in the old way" to keep the new decisions from being enacted. Gorbachev made it as explicit as possible: the democratization of the inner life of the party "would not be easy":

> There are requests for resignations. Some of our comrades have experienced this as a drama. I instead think that it is a natural process. Yes, they have to go. But only the ones who are not willing to work under the new conditions, or who realize they do not have the strength.

Thus "resignations" were being announced. The verb in the past tense ("experienced this as a drama") indicated that the discussion had already led to concrete proposals for changes and that the resistance had suddenly grown very strong. Upon what was this dispute pivoting? Gorbachev said it openly:

> We are busy with the reform of the party apparatus. And we want to do it quickly. For that matter, the discussion has already taken place and the Politburo has already made its decision.[14]

But someone, and it's not difficult to guess who, intended to reargue what had already been decided on. In that moment the plenary meeting still had not been convened. In fact, the weekend was marked by a rapid succession of feverish consultations. On Sunday, 25 September, Andrei Gromyko was still in office.[15] In fact, on Monday *Pravda* reported that at the invitation of Kim Il Sung he would be going to North Korea "in the second half of October, in his capacity as president of the Presidium of the Supreme Soviet."[16] Perhaps this was a sign that Gromyko's fate still had not been influenced by the changes announced, but that it was threatened.

Between Monday and Tuesday one, or perhaps two, meetings of the Politburo settled the problem.[17] On those same days the Moscow military district was placed on alert. Airplanes and helicopters flew over the downtown area, an absolutely unusual sight in the capital. On Tuesday the Politburo decided to convene the plenum. Gorbachev may have delivered an ultimatum: either they would proceed according to the deadlines set by the Nineteenth Conference, or he would go on national television Tuesday night and openly denounce the existence of obstacles inside the party leadership. He responded to the latest "micromodel of a coup d'état" with a "counterattack." This may have been what he meant in his allusion to resolving certain issues "in the old way." On the same day, Tuesday the twenty-seventh, Shevardnadze spoke to the U.N. General Assembly, but that evening the dramatic news of his early return to Moscow was announced. His vote was needed. On Thursday the twenty-ninth, the foreign minister's plane landed in Moscow. On Friday the thirtieth, the defense minister, General Dmitri Yazov, came back to Moscow from India.

The plenum sanctioned the result of the most dramatic show of force yet to take place inside the new leadership. This time the clash was not between the old Brezhnevites and the new forces who had emerged after April 1985. Instead, it was a conflict inside the new leadership. Although Gromyko had been one of the last representatives of Brezhnevism, he had been the godfather of the March 1985 reversal; now he risked everything by siding with the conservatives. Maybe the rhythm of changes had exceeded his ability to absorb them.

But Gorbachev, as we have seen, did not want this outcome. He could not avoid becoming president in March 1989: the entire design of the institutional reform and the transfer of powers from the party to the state pivoted on this final outcome. He had no intention of becoming president ahead of time, in "the old way," but he seemed forced by the extreme danger of the moment. Faced by a jolt that would alter all the balances inside the party leadership, a "victory on points" was not enough. The party had to receive an unequivocal signal. Replacing Gromyko with a man from the renewal group would mean sacrificing the latter in the space of six months. But it was also impossible to have a "lukewarm" supporter of perestroika take Gromyko's place temporarily (and perhaps no one could be found who would be willing to do it). Finally, it would be risky to appoint an adversary. Therefore, Gorbachev had to move the clock ahead. He would become president immediately, even at the risk of alienating some of the populace.

The picture that emerged was the result of the greatest "reshuffling of the cards" that had taken place since Gorbachev had taken power. Two full members (Gromyko and Solomentsev) and two candidate members (Dolgikh and Demichev) left the Politburo. Anatoli Dobrynin left the Secretariat.[18] The six Central Committee commissions, through which the reform of the apparat would be carried out, were to be headed as follows: Vadim Medvedev (the only one to enter the circle of the "full members" of the Politburo) for ideology; Viktor Chebrikov for legal reform; Yegor Ligachev for farm policy (flanked by Viktor Nikonov); Nikolai Slyunkov for economic reform; Aleksandr Yakovlev for foreign policy; and Georgi Razumovsky for policy on cadres. Anatoli Lukyanov was promoted to candidate member of the Politburo, and he became first vice president of the Presidium of the Supreme Soviet. Aleksandra Biryukova became a candidate member of the Politburo and first deputy chairman of the Council of Ministers. The former interior minister, Aleksandr Vlasov, also became a candidate member of the Politburo and was appointed head of the government of the RSFSR.

Ligachev came out of this with a clear reduction in his duties. He was no longer the "number-two man," and he had no say in what went on in ideology. He was assigned a difficult and risky task: agricultural reform. Chebrikov lost the KGB, and with a subtle malice he was assigned the job of overseeing the work of reforming the legal system. In other words, he had to deal with respect for human rights, among other things. Vorotnikov moved on to duties that were more symbolic than powerful. It fell to Lev Zaikov, first secretary of Moscow, to nominate Gorbachev as president at the 1 October session of the Supreme Soviet. In Kremlin protocol this was always an important task, usually assigned to the most influential member of the Politburo after the general secretary. The person did not necessarily have to be "number two," but he clearly had a special role. In effect, the situation was still transitory and unstable. Once again Gorbachev had won, but he had to put together a new compromise, with concessions that were hardly insignificant. For example, Aleksandr Yakovlev had to abandon ideology, the nerve center, to withdraw into a role that did not overshadow the others. Ligachev, Chebrikov, and Vorotnikov had been demoted, but now Gorbachev had to come to terms with the "moderates," a group of at least four voting members of the Politburo who had definitely supported the reorganization, but took very cautious if not outright conservative positions: Zaikov, Slyunkov, Nikonov, and Shcherbitsky. Yet the reform group was now clearly the strongest, with five sure votes (Gorbachev, Yakovlev, Ryzhkov, Shevardnadze, and Medvedev), but it would be in the minority—seven to five— if the moderates shifted to the right.

October was spent in the feverish activity of the preparatory meetings of the Supreme Soviet, which had to approve the reform of the Constitution and the law on elections. But economic issues became more and more pressing. The food situation got worse. There was no clear policy to deal with it. In the middle of the month Gorbachev convened a large meeting of the heads of agroindustrial enterprises. Ligachev, who had just been appointed chairman of the Central Committee commission on farm policy, was absent. This consultation, which prepared for the agroindustrial plenum, focused the reformers' central ideas. Gorbachev said that it was time to recognize that the current "economic relations in the countryside do not stimulate farming." This was the true origin of the "people's passiveness," the fact that "in the kolkhozes and sovkhozes, the farmer has been separated from the means of production." There were no simple recipes, but an essential ingredient was leasing land to farm families. Where it had been experimented with, the results had been "exceptional." This experience had to be expanded as soon as possible, and in the meantime, a law should be passed on leasing that would clarify the rights of potential leasers. The instructions were clear, but Gorbachev accused the "vestiges of collectivist socialism" of preventing its application. The reasons were not mysterious: such a development would radically change the conditions of more than 20 million farm families and the relationship between city and country. It would be a social revolution as well as a political one. The entire management apparat would be swept away and made useless.

Numerous signs showed that the decisions of the Nineteenth Conference were being applied reluctantly. Everywhere there were attempts to distort its contents and reduce its innovative significance. The text of the new law on elections, subject to a "public consultation" that lasted a little more than one month, was a symbol and result of these contradictory aims.[19] The mechanism was extremely complex, and left many loopholes open for abuses. Of the 2,250 deputies of the Congress, 750 had to be elected directly by the plenums of the "social organizations," which were well known as conduits for the party's wishes. It was one of many tricks to keep the election under the party's strict control. However, there were many important innovations: a plurality of candidates, especially in the phase of the nominations by the rank-and-file organizations; a genuine election campaign, where candidates could publicize their programs in the media; a series of guarantees of public control over both the process of picking candidates and the correct functioning of the voting process. In the country's new political climate, these were all it took to ignite an extraordinary election campaign, unprecedented in the history of the Soviet Union.

In many areas the campaign upset the procedural red tape and the high-handed abuses by the apparats. Efforts to bridle and filter democratization were not just a conditioned reflex by the most conservative sectors. Even the progressive group—and Gorbachev himself—had evidently agreed to a cautious law, fearing that the growth of nationalistic drives could create uncontrollable situations. The enormous public participation in the Armenian movement proved in that same period that an entirely democratic election campaign would have a devastating effect on the party. In two Yerevan districts the supplementary elections to the Armenian Supreme Soviet (which took place at the beginning of October, still under the old election law) saw the dramatic defeat of party candidates.[20] The two candidates of the Nagorno-Karabakh Committee, Khatsik Stamboltsyan and Ashot Manutsyaryan, won by a landslide, 80 percent and 78 percent respectively. The elections were invalidated with the claim that there had been procedural irregularities, but Moscow got the message. Similar risks existed in Estonia, Latvia, and Lithuania. In the first two Baltic Republics, the "popular fronts" had already grown into mass movements with organizational forms making it easy to predict that, in the absence of procedural stratagems, they would be assured of absolute majorities in the republic's parliaments and send united, independent groups of deputies to the Congress. The progressives in the party had taken these risks into consideration and they were willing to run them. But they could not risk fracturing the country, which would mean both their own demise and the demise of perestroika.

The various, contrasting worries of the progressives and the conservatives thus walked the difficult path of cooperation. Now, however, it was in the presence of a new force that hadn't existed before: public opinion had grown strong, and was now endowed with legal tools that, in spite of their limits and their contradictions, proved extremely powerful. The unleashing of long-supressed energies was not limited to the non-Russian nationalities. An intellectual "club," the Moscow Tribune, was founded in the capital, and it intended to contribute to the development of perestroika from independent standpoints. Its promoters included Academicians Andrei Sakharov, Roald Sagdeyev, Yuri Karyakin, and Aleksandr Adamovich, along with a large group of other scientists and intellectuals who were leading figures of renewal.[21] Many were party members, and the initiative was agreed to in part by the Central Committee.[22] This was the end of "dissent" and the beginning of a public dialogue. Andrei Sakharov was elected to the Presidium of the Academy of Sciences with 234 votes for and 82 against—the same day on which he received authorization to visit the United States.[23]

Glasnost filled the newspaper pages and the television screens. The Soviet people learned that for long years the state's official budgets had been false. The Supreme Soviet approved a budget that would create a 36-billion-ruble deficit. For the first time inflation was not only acknowledged, but measured: 2 percent per year. Both figures were lower than reality, but this first approach to truth showed how serious the economic imbalances were. The government was for the first time attempting an economic policy maneuver based on "objective" criteria. But the entire economic structure was still virtually suspended in a void. Monetary policy, starting with the printing of paper money, was unheard of. Prices were still controlled by the ultracentrist policy of Stalinist planning. Fiscal policy was in the dark ages. The supply of money, the exact amount of which was unknown, was expanding more rapidly than the overall quantity of goods produced, leading to even sharper tensions between supply of and the demand for, consumer goods. Partly due to these "compelling" reasons, civilian savings deposits hit the amazing ceiling of 300 billion rubles. And these were just a few of the extreme difficulties in making the transition from the system of administrative command to a system regulated by economic laws.

The shifting of all enterprises over to "managerial and administrative autonomy" represented the first step toward the creation of a domestic market for the means of production.[24] The chief decision was for a strong move toward social consumption: two-thirds of government expenses would be used for the construction of houses and schools, and for health care and pensions. For the first time in the history of the USSR, the "b" sector (consumer goods) would surpass the "a" sector (the means of production) by a two-to-three ratio. The parasitical sectors would have to be cut without mercy: the banks and ministries would be prohibited from using emergency funds (over and above the limits of the law on state enterprises) to aid the twenty-four thousand enterprises (13 percent of the total) that operated at a chronic loss. These were courageous decisions that, nevertheless, most economists considered insufficient.

What was needed was a reform of the system of prices and the gradual abolition of the enormous cost of subsidized prices (108 billion rubles). But it was too dangerous to touch on these subjects. Without a strategy there was a risk of prices going haywire and consequent social tensions. In short, the October Supreme Soviet disclosed that the economic crisis was more serious and harder to control than had been thought in the previous two-year period.

And there was another gap being emphasized: politics was evolving more quickly than the economy. When the time came to ratify the decrees approved by the Presidium during the interval between the two regular sessions of the Supreme Soviet, another unprecedented fact was verified. Two decrees were approved by a majority. There were 13 votes against and 4 abstentions on the decree regulating demonstrations; 31 votes against and 26 abstentions on ukase no. 505, defining the powers of the Interior Ministry over "special troops" for maintaining public order. The latter decree was in practice only a formal legal sanctioning of regulations that had been in effect since 1918. But it contained a new element: in the event of serious public disorder, only the interior minister of the USSR would be qualified to make decisions. Local organizations ended up completely deprived of power. Whoever conceived of the ukase (which was approved in late July) predicted hard times ahead, in which the Moscow center could not count on the loyalty of the local police or even on the loyalty of local party leaders.

This prediction soon proved true. National issues posed a greater and greater threat. The opening provided by democratization released energies that had been suppressed for decades. The Moscow center had only one strategy: don't let all the problems come to the fore at the same time. The plan to modify the Constitution, which had been hurriedly drafted after the Nineteenth Conference, dealt only with the political reorganization of the leadership. The other "big issues" would be dealt with "in later stages of political restructuring." These included "the harmonization of relations between the union and the federated republics."[25] But this timetable was too slow to meet the pressing demands that had found free expression through the reform. The Estonian Republic turned the clock ahead. On Wednesday, 16 November, its Supreme Soviet voted overwhelmingly (250 to 7) to modify article 744 of the Estonian constitution and assume the right to reject or suspend the application of laws approved by the Supreme Soviet of the USSR. At the same time, an overwhelming majority also voted for a "declaration of sovereignty," which, if accepted, would mark the end of the Union of Soviet Socialist Republics as a unified state entity.

This turn of events became alarming from various perspectives. The pressure of the newly born "Popular Front" was at the origin of the Estonian decision, but the parliamentary vote showed that the entire Estonian party shared this line. Gorbachev reacted firmly. He called an emergency meeting of the Presidium of the Supreme Soviet and had the Estonian decision declared "contrary to the federal Constitution of the USSR." The position he so rapidly took was dictated by the need to anticipate analogous decisions by the Lithuanian and Latvian parliaments. At the same time, the Presidium announced an upcoming explanatory meeting, to which the representatives of the Estonian republic would be invited.[26] The Lithuanian party, brusquely called to order by Moscow, limited itself—amid public protests—to instituting an editorial committee for the new text of the republic's constitution and to approving three measures of high symbolic value: the adoption of the flag and of the national anthem from the "bourgeois" times, and the proclamation of Lithuanian as the official language of the republic.

Gorbachev, who was in New Delhi during this period, invited everyone to be calm and to enter peaceful discussions. But while everyone's eyes were focused on the Baltic Republics, a new fire was lit from the ashes of the clash between Armenia and Azerbaijan. The spark caught in Stepanakert, where yet another general strike was in progress, and spread to Yerevan, where thousands of people spilled into the squares. But this time something new happened: equally powerful anti-Armenian demonstrations took place in Baku and in other Azerbaijani cities. The delay and the uncertainty of the central powers gave the local mafias time to organize. The conflict spread like wildfire and turned into a tragedy of terrible proportions.

Gorbachev's plan—to proceed by steps over time—was threatened with ruin. The plenum on national issues, promised in February, was still far off. It would be impossible to hold it earlier: the subject matter was still "rough." Theory was clearly lagging behind, and had to catch up. The Soviet leader himself was not free of responsibility for this lag, nor was the entire ruling group. Moscow thus found itself forced to settle claims in various places and at various levels. Estonia was asking for "complete sovereignty" over its own resources, opposing itself to the union. By contrast, Armenia was demanding respect for its rights, which had been violated by the Azerbaijanis; Azerbaijan defended its ancestral claims to its own territorial borders, and rekindled religious hatred. These were qualitatively different drives, and could not be attributed to the same common denominator.

The people of the USSR were discovering democracy but, in the absence of proven political structures and of a "civic society" that could buffer the most immediate tensions, they could only recognize themselves as "nations" for the time being. The only instrument of mediation and unification—the party—was not up to the tasks it was facing—tasks that could no longer be solved through administrative command. In the separate realities and republics, the party was caught in a deadlock: either it embraced the individual claims completely or in part, or it would be dealt out of the movements. In either case, the local party was forced to enter into conflict with Moscow. When on the contrary it chose resolutely to stay with the center, then the leadership of the movement—initially made up of moderate national reformers who were looking for dialogue with the party—was forced to let through the more radical groups, not all of whom were always able to measure the effects of their choices in the general picture of the reform battle. They often set about "shooting at the Russian center," starting with the prevailing line. In some cases they were determined to explode all the balances. The lesson of Sumgait was that even the extremist conservative forces were interested in playing the "national card." The Gorbachev center therefore had to guard itself from both sides.

The crisis in the Caucasus, however, left no room for a political solution in the immediate present. Force had to be used to stop a massacre that was Sumgait many times over in size and in territory. Azerbaijanis were killing Armenians, and now Armenians were killing Azerbaijanis. Gorbachev had to declare a state of emergency in both republics. On the Baltic front, he reconvened the Presidium of the Supreme Soviet and recognized the existence of problems and the need to correct the policies of the past. But he criticized the Estonian leaders: "You have committed a theoretical mistake, a political mistake, and a practical mistake. Were your position to be accepted, it would radically compromise the whole unified structure of the country."[27]

The Estonian decision was formally invalidated, but a commitment was made not to close debate. Gorbachev did, however, set firm limits on future debate: everything could be held up for questioning except the country's unity. It had to be realized that democratization had not only brought to light "extremist positions," but also "positions extraneous to our values," in other words, enemy positions. The three Baltic presidents had to submit to the reprimand, but they issued a warning: autonomy was inevitable. The

Estonian Arndt Riuitel, the Lithuanian Antanas Barkauskas, and the Latvian Anatoli Gorbunov all insisted that if an adequate response to the public pressures were not found, it would no longer be possible to guarantee political control over the situation.

The Supreme Soviet that had to approve the constitutional reform thus met in an atmosphere of open political crisis. The night before, 28 November, the Soviet president convened a meeting of the Central Committee to ask for its approval of new concessions in an attempt to lower the "Baltic rebels'" pressures for autonomy. The debate was of an unprecedented liveliness and frankness, and concluded with the acceptance of a series of substantial amendments to the draft of constitutional changes.[28] The mediation succeeded: only five deputies voted no, while twenty-seven abstained. The new election law was unanimously approved.

No mediation was possible, however, in the Caucasus conflict. At the concluding session of the Supreme Soviet, Arkadi Volsky, the "prefect" of Nagorno-Karabakh, described a picture of outright civil war. The death toll of the two ethnic groups grew higher by the day. The official figure was more than 30 dead, with hundreds of wounded. In a double, overwhelming mass exodus, more than 230,000 people moved to Armenia, and 70,000 people moved to Azerbaijan. An emergency summit was held at the Kremlin on 1 December with the first secretaries, Vezirov and Arutyunyan. Two days later the USSR Council of Ministers issued a special resolution which in effect declared that a state of war existed in the two republics. Not even this decision was enough. The disorders continued in dozens of Azerbaijani and Armenian towns. Not even the terrible tragedy of the earthquake in Armenia, causing over 25,000 deaths and enormous destruction, would stem the Azerbaijanis' hatred. Gorbachev, who left New York upon hearing of the disaster, found a hostile climate in Armenia, the population of which had been martyred in the spirit and in the flesh, could not believe what was happening, and had lost all faith. The damages were huge, and difficult to repair. The army garrisoned the two republics, for no other way would guarantee the return to peaceful coexistence and normality.

The year that was coming to an end had been crucial to perestroika in every sense. Two political crises, one in March and the other in September, had been overcome. The party conference had sanctioned an extraordinary move toward the "rule-of-law state." Democratization had found its first legal bases and was moving toward an election campaign in the spring of 1989 that was unlike anything the Soviet people had ever experienced. Gorbachev would have many reasons to consider himself a winner, but he had just as many reasons to look toward the future with apprehension. The transition from the old to the new grew longer, creating new imbalances and growing tensions. The trust that had been built up among the masses now risked erosion through routine and the Soviet citizen's traditional distrust of power. There was no time to lose, otherwise the stranglehold of public disappointment and the revenge of the apparats could crush perestroika.

The final 1988 issue of *Moskovskiye Novosti* expressed this restlessness by publishing a dramatic open letter to Gorbachev signed by six party members, six intellectuals whom no one could accuse of being "avant-garde": Grigori Baklanov, writer and editor in chief of the magazine *Znamya*; Aleksandr Gelman, playwright, who was the first to react against Nina Andreyeva's letter; the writer Daniil Granin; the director Yelem Klimov; Academician Roald Sagdeyev; and Mikhail Ulyanov, president of the Theater Union and an actor at the Vakhtangov Theater. It was a declaration of faith, and at the same time, a cry of alarm. We will vote for you, Mikhail Sergeyevich, even if your name is not written on our ballots! We will vote for your policies. But be careful! Too many leaders who do not want perestroika "remain in their positions." The renewal of party jobs had been effected with "such instructions and tricks" that it could only produce a poor outcome. The renewal was blocked "not only by single conservatives, but by entire general staffs." Was their alarm excessive? The six men urged Gorbachev not to underestimate it. At the pace the enemies of perestroika were trying to impose on the country, "the party's objectives for the economy cannot be achieved."

EIGHTH CONVERSATION

THE NINETEENTH CONFERENCE; GORBACHEV'S TACTICS; THE NATIONAL QUESTION AND SEPARATIST MOVEMENTS; THE NEW CONSERVATIVE OFFENSIVE

•   •   •

G.C. Roy Aleksandrovich, was the Nineteenth Party Conference truly an historical event?

R.M. I'm convinced that there will be a lot of talk about it in our country for years to come. True, it wasn't a revolutionary change, yet it was one of the most important moments in these years, one that requires not only commentary, but particularly accurate study. Large sectors of the public participated in the preceding phase, including people who had remained outside the events in the first phases of perestroika. The "Theses" was an interesting document, but compromising. There was "socialist pluralism"; and a new law was introduced to establish the rotation of leaders. In other words, for the first time a mechanism was provided for the succession to positions of command. But the debates went far beyond these innovations and ended up involving every aspect of Soviet society.

G.C. Both you and I have used the word "compromise" a few times. Perestroika is a history of compromises.

R.M. In a certain sense, yes. In the spring of 1988 perestroika began to run into difficulties. Economic reform was blocked. National conflicts became more pronounced. The standard of living grew worse. The press carried more and more critical articles. But glasnost encountered serious resistance. There was a joke making the rounds: "It's gotten more interesting to read than to live." The election of delegates was too rushed. The time wasted in the clash over the Nina Andreyeva letter made it necessary to cut corners. But this time there was a real battle, often between two opposing platforms. Even the tens of thousands of letters that are traditionally sent to the congresses (and the conference, in a certain sense, could be compared to a congress) were not merely complaints or individual requests. In many cases they were about political proposals, transcending individual interests. This too was a sign of a growing politicization. And the people followed the proceedings with a totally unusual passion. If in the years of stagnation no one read the newspapers during the congresses, now people lined up at the newsstands.

Gorbachev's report was very interesting; it went well beyond what Gorbachev himself had said previously. This is why he couldn't raise other hopes and other fears (depending on the personal standpoints of whoever was listening to him). For example, his clear reference to the need to drastically reduce the apparats and entire departments in the party disturbed many people. The healthy self-criticism pervading his speech, his call for "purging" the party and the society, and his instructions to reexamine party history and the events of the 1930s and 1970s were all clear signs of Gorbachev's desire to continue on the chosen path.

G.C. Not everything in his speech appeared so convincing.

R.M. True. You can't agree with some of his formulations. I found some of his proposals incomprehensible. Let me give some examples. Gorbachev pointed to new economic priorities, in the social sense. There was talk about developing cooperatives and individual work activities. By this time there were many mixed enterprises backed by foreign capital. In the countryside more land was leased to both families and nonfamily groups. City dwellers were now given more land for their vegetable gardens. It became possible to lease or buy abandoned houses in the villages and cultivate the plots of land attached. Earlier prohibitions of individual handicrafts were eliminated. Now cooperation between kolkhozes was authorized, motivated by the creation of agroindustrial enterprises.

This whole list of "good" decisions, however, affected only about 10 percent of the economy. The remaining 90 percent was still subject to the old style of management, and it produced low-quality goods and services. In short, the causes for the lag in the Soviet economy were clear, yet a well-conceived comprehensive plan for a way out of the crisis could not get off the ground. In the past three months the national revenue had grown very slowly. "Acceleration" had turned into little more than a slogan. Gorbachev spoke about a 4.6 percent salary increase over a two-year period, but it can be definitely stated that most workers had experienced no increase in real income, and I emphasize real. The country had suffered a huge loss due to the Chernobyl disaster. In a two-year period the volume of imports and exports went down by 10 percent, and now if a Soviet woman had to buy two bad pairs of Soviet shoes rather than one good pair of Italian shoes, this was certainly no improvement. Huge amounts of money ended up in the pockets of people who ran illegal stills to make vodka, while commercial distribution plans were not carried out. Salaries increased nominally, but low-cost consumer goods disappeared from the stores. Everywhere there were shortages of milk and meat, as well as sugar.

G.C. There was no true economic "recovery," but the political situation also remained confusing.

R.M. Here you have to distinguish. The proposal for a clear division of tasks between the party organizations and the soviets was a good idea. The same must be said for the expansion of the soviets' powers to the territories in their jurisdiction. The power of the Council of Ministers had to increase correspondingly. Gorbachev promised a new election law and a modification of the Constitution that would establish the Congress of People's Deputies, a new political body that would meet once a year and whose members would elect a smaller Supreme Soviet than the current one, which in turn would become the lawmaking body. The president of the Supreme Soviet was invested with huge powers. This is how a Soviet form of presidency was outlined, where the president was also the general secretary of the party. The proposal left many delegates perplexed. It wasn't clear to everyone how the new system of relations between the party and the soviets would function at the local level—in the cities, provinces, and regions. In fact, according to Gorbachev's proposal, at every level the first secretary of the party would also head the corresponding soviet.

G.C. The most innovative proposals at the conference were often greeted by a reaction that could hardly be described as "calm."

R.M. The tension during the debates was unprecedented. More than 300 people signed up to speak. Only 60 ended up actually speaking, while another 150 spoke at committee meetings. After a few months the proceedings of the entire conference were published, including the texts of speeches that hadn't been given but had been handed in to the chairman. The debate made it possible to see more than dissent on single issues—it made the existence of "currents" of opinion in the party clearly visible.

If you were to draw a diagram, you could divide this phase into three different political groups. The first is made up of open enemies of perestroika, unmistakable conservatives who wanted the party and the country to go back to the way they had been. Who were they? Heads of ministries and districts, cadres who managed sectors of the Central Committee, and cultural administrators. All of them had immense power and influence. However, in general this group preferred not to expose itself by stepping into the debates. Not even criticism drove them into the open. The only one who spoke was Yuri Bondarev, in a speech that did not hide his hatred and fear of perestroika. But don't let their silence fool you. They will not give up without a fight, and they certainly suffer no lack of forces willing to fight.

The second and more numerous faction is made up of cadres who realize the need for perestroika and the impossibility of continuing to live and work the way people did in the past. But they wanted to effect the changes, which they considered necessary, with the usual systems of administration and command—in other words, without glasnost and democracy. They expressed intolerance of a press that was "too liberal"; they feared "excessive" mobilization of and action by young people and by large popular groups; they considered the reinvestigation of ideological stereotypes and the criticism of past crimes prejudicial to party authority. You cannot say in general that they were corrupt, but they were not capable of openly confronting positions, not even within the limits of what Gorbachev called "socialist pluralism." They were lacking in political flexibility; they were used to commanding, not to persuading. Many of the regional party leaders who spoke at the conference belonged to this group. Yegor Ligachev, secretary of the Central Committee and a member of the Politburo, proved himself to be the leading representative of this second group in his long, puritanical, and narrow-minded speech. He attacked his direct adversary, Boris Yeltsin, but he also issued a warning to Gorbachev, reminding him that he had helped elect him at the March 1985 plenum. In essence, he said: "Don't forget that we gave you the power. Therefore, don't go too far and don't pit yourself against us." These were warnings that a politician had to keep in mind, even if he didn't necessarily have to submit to them. Before the Twentieth Party Congress, Molotov, Malenkov, Kaganovich, and Voroshilov had done the same with Khrushchev, reminding him that without their help, he would not have become party leader.

Finally, the third group was made up of those who pushed for a development of perestroika in the areas of democracy, economics, and foreign policy. As we have seen, the leader of this group—to which most of the intellectuals among the delegates belonged—was Gorbachev himself. In many respects, the future of perestroika depended on the ability of this group to conduct the political struggle. But it could not win without the support of Gorbachev, Aleksandr Yakovlev, and other prominent leaders. You could be certain that the future would bring many bitter political battles between these different tendencies inside the party.

G.C. Allow me to clarify something. You claim that Gorbachev is the leader of the third group. Yet during the conference Gorbachev contradicted, interrupted, and even argued with the members of the third group: with Ulyanov, Baklanov, and Abalkin. He did this in a friendly way, without bitterness, almost as if he were inviting them not to force too much with their demands. I got the impression several times that Gorbachev was playing both sides against the middle. But Gorbachev could not be, on the outside at least, the "head" of this group. He had to "mediate"; otherwise he would be defeated. What do you think?

R.M. That is the soft spot. The conference clearly ended with an increase in Gorbachev's popularity. However, it is not difficult to make out the traces of the compromises that were reached. They allowed Gorbachev to take a step forward, but not as big a step as he needed. One of the compromises, and probably the hardest for Gorbachev, was the decision not to change the membership of the Central Committee. Thus, their political contents had evolved, but the balance of power remained unaltered. This would be sharply felt when the time came to carry out the political decisions made by the Nineteenth Conference. In short, the probabilities of perestroika being successful had grown, but so had the dangers along its way.

G.C. How would you evaluate the national question with respect to perestroika?

R.M. The national question is destined to become even more acute and to become a passage through which perestroika is forced. These problems are no less important than the economy, nor are they less felt by the population. The current crisis in Armenia arose over the autonomous region of Nagorno-Karabakh, which was inside Azerbaijani territory although the majority of the population was Armenian. For decades the Armenians in Nagorno-Karabakh were discriminated against. As soon as a glimmer of hope for political expression appeared, they issued a proclamation from a regional soviet requesting a shift to Armenian administration. Their request corresponded perfectly to the region's historical roots and ethnic composition. The first territorial subdivision of the Caucasus region, starting in the years 1920–21, included Nagorno-Karabakh within the Armenian Republic. At that time 91 percent of the inhabitants were Armenian, and only 4 percent were Azerbaijani. In 1923, for unexplained reasons, it was decided to transfer Nagorno-Karabakh to Azerbaijan.

Today the population is made up of about 75 percent Armenians and 20 percent Azerbaijanis. But the Armenians are subject to systematic discrimination. Every nationality is sensitive to discrimination, but the Armenians are particularly so. They were the first in the twentieth century to suffer a terrible genocide: the massacre in 1915–16 of one and a half million Armenians who lived in the areas under Turkish control. In the years 1919–20, tens, perhaps hundreds, of thousands more who lived in Nakhichevan were slaughtered with the help of Turkish troops. It's no secret that the Turks were aided in their assassinations by Azerbaijani nationalists, the notorious Musavatists. Peace reached the entire region only with the advent of Soviet power, but national tensions have stayed alive. The events of later years certainly didn't help calm things down.

G.C. The problem of Nagorno-Karabakh, however, is much older by far.

R.M. It goes back to the birth of Jesus Christ. In those times the Caucasus area had a "Great Armenia." Over a period of three to four centuries, the Armenians populated vast expanses of the region, including the present-day Nagorno-Karabakh. The Armenians were converted to Christianity at the beginning of the fourth century. Later the region was invaded first by the Seljuk Turks, and then by the Mongols. After this the Persians arrived. The only thing that changed were the feudal lords. In 1813 the principality of Karabakh was united with Russia after a long war with Persia. It is a very complex history—long, difficult, and often bloody. Yet one fact remained constant: Nagorno-Karabakh was inhabited predominantly by Armenians. None of its many conquerors ever succeeded in uprooting them from the land.

Azerbaijan is a country of the Muslim religion with another culture. Trying to impose it on the Armenians is completely unacceptable. But similar problems exist in other parts of the Caucasus. The Armenians have claims over Georgia. The autonomous republic of Abkhaz has claims over Georgia. Georgia, in its turn, has problems to settle with Armenia and Azerbaijan. At one time the majority of the population of Tbilisi, the capital of Georgia today, was Armenian. This resulted from the Armenian emigration after the genocide of 1915–16. At that time Russia was at war with Turkey, and the Armenians sought refuge in the Caucasus.

In February the leadership of the Armenian movement was still in moderate hands. In Moscow Gorbachev received the poet Silvia Kaputikyan and the journalist Zori Balayan, who were representing the Nagorno-Karabakh

Committee. Then events took a different turn. Up until that time the evolution of the situation seemed controllable. Gorbachev wanted to hear the proposals and the requests of the Armenian people from the actual representatives of public opinion. Their meeting lasted more than an hour, and it was preceded by an almost four-hour-long talk between the two Armenians and Aleksandr Yakovlev. It was on that occasion that there was talk for the first time of convening a special meeting of the Armenian Supreme Soviet. This request was completely legal.

For weeks in the streets of Yerevan there had been huge rallies, sometimes with as many as a million people—the majority of the adult population of the whole republic. A particular fact emerged here which is one of the advantages of a small republic. As was the case in ancient Greece, the birthplace of democracy, a small country could unite almost its entire population in its capital's squares, thereby effecting direct and at the same time representative democracy. We are not used to this. Armenia by contrast had experienced huge public demonstrations for a long time. Every year hundreds of thousands of people united in mourning at the monument in memory of the Armenian genocide.

I know that during the meeting Gorbachev asked for a suspension of the demonstrations, in other words, of the pressure on the center. I can understand that. I imagine that he had not been brought completely up to date on the situation. Settling the dispute in a short time was, objectively speaking, very difficult. Convening the Armenian Supreme Soviet—which did take place later—would have created a very difficult institutional precedent. The Armenian representatives agreed to Gorbachev's request, but they could only promise one month of "respite," to give Moscow enough time to grasp what was happening. However, all it took was that one talk to interrupt the strikes and demonstrations. In that transitory phase, compromise solutions may still have been possible. For example, the autonomous region could have been given the status of an autonomous republic, while keeping it inside the borders of Azerbaijan. The rights of an autonomous republic are better defined than the more vaguely described rights of an autonomous region. But Moscow was worried that such a gesture would give vent to a series of other claims, each of them different but analogous.

G.C. It was in this exact predicament that the Sumgait pogrom broke out.

R.M. A horrible tragedy that changed the entire psychological and political situation. Sumgait is a large industrial city (about 250,000 inhabitants, at least 20,000 of whom are Armenian) sixty kilometers from Baku. At ten o'clock in the evening on 28 February, organized gangs of armed Azerbaijanis got together. The hunt for Armenians began. There were already many deaths in the first hours. Information provided by Tass was very cloudy. It talks about thirty-one dead, without giving figures for the wounded. It talks about "criminal elements" and "different nationalities murdered." Many questions were raised immediately: where did so many "delinquents" and "common criminals" come from? And why not say right away that most of the murder victims were Armenian? It also said that the army had stepped in and that a curfew had been declared. But the information—which arrived late—raised uncontrollable rumors. Rather than calming the situation, it inflamed it.

It was obvious that most of the Armenians who lived in Azerbaijan did not believe the official news. The same held true in Armenia. Indignation greeted the decision to appoint the head of the Azerbaijani government, Seidov, to chair the committee of inquiry into the Sumgait events. Rumors and "open letters" spread in Armenia that in Sumgait there had been more than three hundred dead and a thousand wounded. The rumors proved to be stronger than the official reports. The press, however, said nothing. Journalists were forbidden access to Sumgait. The only sources of information were refugees from the city, many of whom were arriving in Nagorno-Karabakh, Yerevan, and Moscow. Tragically, not even Armenian television was able to provide its public with any information.

In order to understand what looked absurd from abroad, you have to keep in mind certain specific characteristics of the Soviet information system, inherited from our past. In reality, what is always essential to our information system is not so much the event being communicated as the commentary presented with it, and the specific "visual" angle from which it is proposed to the public. In this case, there was no "visual" angle elaborated by the capital. The press's silence represented Moscow's uncertainty. Today, months later, we still don't know what happened, who allowed it to happen, and why.

G.C. The national pushes were extremely powerful, but to me it seems overly simplistic to reduce it to terms of "nationalism." What do you think?

R.M. To scornfully call the Armenian movement "nationalistic," as part of the Soviet press still keeps doing, is completely unfair. The term is too generic, and it hides highly diverse realities. The Armenians showed a completely justified reaction to the discrimination they had been subject to. The same could be said, for very different, partly historical reasons, about the reactions in the Baltic Republics. There is definitely inflamed nationalism in all these places, but you need to make distinctions. Otherwise, it is impossible to adopt an appropriate policy line. Not all nationalisms are the same, nor can they be put on the same level. It was a serious mistake to equate Azerbaijani nationalism, which was aggressive and the cause of the Armenians' oppression, with the Armenian nationalism born from the revolt against long-standing injustices.

The immediate political situation evolved differently in the two republics. In Armenia it had been clear since the beginning of the year that the political standing of Karen Demirchyan, who had been in power since 1974, was threatened. Gorbachev was trying to replace him, but he ran into the resistance of the local apparat. Part of the populace saw this offensive from the center as a new threat to the republic's autonomy. But as far as I know, Demirchyan did not have a very good reputation among the Armenian intelligentsia. The renewal promoted by Moscow had not spread in Armenia at all, where the party apparat was still completely Brezhnevite, conservative, and corrupt. Demirchyan thus found himself in a situation of isolation. When the wave of the movement for Nagorno-Karabakh began, he was trapped between two fires. Opposing the people's demands would mean losing the residual support of the republic, but it would not necessarily mean earning back Moscow's support. Opposing Moscow would be equally dangerous. When Demirchyan tried to speak to the demonstrators, they booed him. Only his apparat defended him. Thus, his destiny was sealed.

In Azerbaijan the ruling group had been built by Aliyev, who had been ousted from the Politburo in October 1987. Bagirov was the man whom he had designated as his successor. Initially, there were no mass demonstrations in Azerbaijan, but Sumgait proved that the party apparat was unable to dominate the situation, and, as later investigations would show, had taken a "laissez-faire" attitude, at the very least. Bagirov also had to go. There were good reasons for the delay with which both retirements were decided upon. It is not easy to find political leaders who have sufficient authority to govern. The Brezhnev era had created immeasurable breakdowns almost everywhere. In Kazakhstan they had to send an "outside" cadre to replace Kunayev. In Uzbekistan the fall of Rashidov had started a chain reaction of changes at all levels that lasted for years. Uzmankhodzhayev, who had succeeded him as the republic's first secretary, was also arrested.

I wish to add that I do not agree with those who say that there is no "brotherhood of peoples" in the USSR. There was and there is cooperation among nations. There is a new historical and social community: the "Soviet people." All this is not a "myth." But it would be an unforgivable mistake to state, as Stalin and others did, that the national problem in the USSR had been resolved once and for all. We do not have the mechanisms to solve conflicts between nations. The friendship among populations does not exclude the rise of disputes when more than a hundred different nations, each with its own traditions, live side by side. In Muslim Azerbaijan they did not eat or produce pork, but this religious prohibition was also extended to Nagorno-Karabakh, where the majority were Christians. The Azerbaijanis could celebrate a marriage and party loudly in the streets on the day of mourning when the Armenians recalled the genocide. Nor should foreign influence be ignored. We have only mentioned it in connection with the Jewish question and, to an extent, the Baltic issue. But the turbulent activism of the Third World, especially the Muslim world, would be bound to influence the peoples of Soviet Central Asia. At least 10 million Azerbaijanis live in Iran. The political and religious changes in that country were obviously reflected in the behavior of the Azerbaijanis.

G.C. Doesn't it seem to you that the explosion of the national questions took the renewal group by surprise, starting with Gorbachev and Yakovlev?

R.M. As far as the surprise goes, I think that it's the result of a long estrangement of the political leadership as a whole from the actual problems of the country. Gorbachev himself has said several times that the problems he has run into during these years have proved to be more difficult than he thought they would be in 1985. This also holds true for the national question. As far as the threat to the unity of the Soviet Union is concerned, I would like to remind you of a conversation that took place in my presence during the Khrushchev era. A well-known member of the Central Committee said: "In Stalin's time the Communist movement was unified and all the parties obeyed Moscow. The diaspora began with Khrushchev." He was talking about the Italian Communist Party, which had already taken independent positions back then. But was "Stalin's unity" built on a sound foundation? Was the diaspora really caused by Khrushchev's decisions? The same thing could be said about the national questions. It is not in the least bit true that they were created by perestroika and by democratization. They had existed earlier. Sooner or later they would have emerged under any regime. And it was better to face them now, for the longer they lasted, the harder they would be to settle. Perestroika's supporters had reasons with which they could defend themselves. A more liberal regime made it easier to identify the problems and decide on them more quickly.

G.C. The decision by the Presidium of the Supreme Soviet described the Armenian request to modify the administrative borders of the two republics as "inadmissible." But the Constitution of the USSR provides for this possibility. Therefore, how could this request have been inadmissible?

R.M. In fact, the decision accepted all Nagorno-Karabakh's social demands: the possibility of picking up Armenian TV; textbooks in the Armenian language and an increase in the publication of Armenian literature; a return to teaching Armenian history at the Stepanakert Pedagogical Institute; restoration of the monuments of Armenian culture, and so on. You are correct in pointing out that the statement that a change in the borders of the republics was "inadmissible" contradicts the text and the spirit of the Constitution of the USSR. However, in actuality, a new situation was arising: Nagorno-Karabakh was now directly controlled by Moscow. The new regional government had been constituted by a Central Committee decision. Now the first secretary of the regional party was an Armenian, while the second secretary was a Russian (neither Armenian nor Azerbaijani). Baku's powers over the region were diminished *de facto*. I think that, sooner or later, it will be necessary to transfer Nagorno-Karabakh to Armenia.

Moscow's hesitation may certainly have been dictated partly by its concern not to raise conflicts with the 50 million Muslims living in the USSR. But here I would make a distinction. There are Kirghizes, Kazakhs, Uzbeks, Turkmen, and Azerbaijanis. There is evident religious activism. But in my opinion, religion is not the dominating factor. Furthermore, religion in Central Asia is much less "aggressive" than in Azerbaijan. Finally, the Azerbaijanis are mainly Shiite Muslims, while the other Muslims in the USSR are primarily Sunni, and therefore less subject to the "foreign" influences we've already spoken about.

G.C. Do you think there is a direct tie between the rise of the Armenian question and the raging growth of demands for autonomy—and separation—in the Baltic Republics?

R.M. I think that the events surrounding Nagorno-Karabakh had a huge influence on the entire country. However, I think they will lead mainly to eruptions of other conflicts in the Caucasus region. As far as the Baltic Republics are concerned, we are witnessing another dynamic, other problems, other characteristics, and another history. In Armenia no one, at least until the fall of that year, had raised the issue of the republic seceding from the USSR. In the Baltic, however, these demands had been strong ever since the beginning of the movement, and they were not at all marginal.

G.C. Nineteen eighty-eight ended after great battles, none of which was conclusive. The economic situation became not better, but worse. The political situation witnessed a certain erosion of Gorbachev's popularity. Should we be optimistic or pessimistic about the future of perestroika?

R.M. More than three years had gone by and perestroika still hadn't produced the results the people were expecting. There were changes, but there was no sign of the concrete changes that could be appreciated by ordinary people. I think that Gorbachev realized this. The initial enthusiasm was dying down. One of the reasons that drove the Soviet leader to push up the timetable for rotating the leaders may have been the idea that it was time to get rid of superficial hindrances in order to make the process more dynamic again. But making changes in the party's top leadership was just one of the issues. Many of the decisions made had not been carried out because they were dampened by the bureaucratic and administrative spirit rather than nourished by democracy. There was an urgent need to change leaders at every level. The old mentality still dominated, and posed obstacles in every direction.

The campaign to renew the party cadres began late, in a lackluster way, and in no way corresponded to real needs. There still had not been a "purge," or a sufficient influx of new energies and skills. Therefore, Gorbachev tried to speed up the process. In order to do this he needed to reinforce his own strongholds in the party leadership. He succeeded in part. A certain dynamism did not pick up until after the September plenum. I think that Gorbachev decided to make the trip to Krasnoyarsk in order to shake up the situation. In this way he was able to show the country the quantity of unresolved problems, and the party the absolute need to move more quickly.

The bureaucratic-administrative apparat suffers from a deadly inertia. Look at how the antialcohol campaign was run. Its unpopularity was clear from the outset, but it was made worse in every way possible: an exaggerated cutback in the places liquor could be sold; a sharp decrease in the production of both vodka and wine; the application of regulations in an indiscriminate way, without accounting for different traditions. In Moldavia and Georgia hundreds of thousands of acres of vineyard were destroyed. Aberrations. Nothing was offered in exchange. The stores stayed the same way they were before—empty. The cutback in liquor sales lowered the circulation of money in many areas. At the same time, illegal distilleries increased at a bewildering rate.

Let me give you another concrete case of an insidious offensive by the antiperestroika forces. Immediately after the Nineteenth Conference a new directive established a ceiling on the number of subscriptions—only five days after the beginning of the subscription campaign. This measure affected forty-five newspapers and magazines, including most of the ones that most actively supported perestroika. The excuse given was a paper shortage. Protests were vehement. Everyone understood the gist of the operation. Immediately after the September plenum Ryzhkov held a meeting of the Council of

Ministers and rescinded this regulation. The hundred thousand tons of extra paper had been "found." Once again someone had tried to take advantage of Gorbachev's absence—he was on vacation in those weeks—to stage an actual *coup de main*.

G.C. One of the most questionable decisions of the conference regarded the "double" role of the first secretary of the party and the president of the corresponding soviet. What do you think?

R.M. Actually, many people didn't like it. Many didn't understand why it was introduced, especially since it seemed to contradict indications for a clear separation of the party's functions from those of the state. I also think that there was not enough thought on this issue. However, this solution does have functional elements. Contrary to appearances, it could facilitate a cutback in the party's powers. If the first secretary of a city's party committee also became chairman of the city's soviet, he would no longer need the two parallel structures, the party and the soviet, that basically take care of the same things. One of the two would become superfluous. This could facilitate the simplification and the cutback of the apparats. In the second place, the first secretary was in this way made directly "responsible" for carrying out decisions that had been made. He used to issue directives from his party office, but he was not substantially responsible for their being enacted. Often the buck was passed. Finally, the presidency of the soviet became an expression, at least formally, of the will of the electors, and not of the party apparats' power groups. Thus, the president could act with greater independence. The new election law now allowed the electors to vote down a party boss if he proved unworthy. In this way, the electorate established relative control over the party. But I repeat, as a whole the mechanism should be reviewed, because it is quite general, and open to opposite interpretations.

My opinion of the double role of the general secretary of the party and the president of the Supreme Soviet is different. This confers a completely new position of strength on Gorbachev. He no longer depends on the vote of a body that is separated from public control, in other words, the party's Central Committee. He is elected by the Congress. He is elected for at least one year, and no one can depose him before the next session. Even if the plenum were to lose its confidence in him, he would remain in office as president of the Supreme Soviet. This line of reasoning, as you see, is not legal and institutional, but essentially political. Everyone understands that Gorbachev's role is decisive to the success of perestroika. His fate could not be left up to the will of the three or four hundred members of the Central Committee, many of whom were elected in Brezhnev's day. In other words, the decision on the double office consolidated his personal power, and given the situation, it was a good choice.

G.C. I understand your viewpoint, but many people fear that if for some reason, Gorbachev were forced to vacate his office, this immense concentration of power could also be used in an authoritarian way.

R.M. As long as Gorbachev is around, I think that the political reform is in no danger. However, it is clear that now a radical institutional reform must be achieved that defines a system of guarantees, including the respect of democratic rights for individuals and for bodies of public power. Even here there have been serious obstacles. The draft bill that was proclaimed two years ago still has not been enacted. There is still no law on the press, no law on the activities of the KGB. The democratization of our lives is behind schedule.

G.C. What provoked the "earthquake" at the September plenum?

R.M. At first glance the changes were surprising. In reality, if you analyze them in depth, they were the "logical consequence" of the party's Nineteenth Conference. I don't mean to imply that everything had been set up beforehand. On the contrary, I think that Gorbachev meant to accomplish his changes gradually. But in effect the men who were not on Gorbachev's "team" either left or were demoted. First, Gromyko could not remain head of the Presidium of the Supreme Soviet during such a decisive phase. The chairman of the commission for party control, Mikhail Solomentsev, one of the Brezhnevite old guard, was openly criticized during the conference. Ligachev was demoted from the number-two spot to the fourth or fifth position in the hierarchy. Even the importance of Viktor Chebrikov, former head of the KGB, was cut back. Now he was no longer the one to have that extremely powerful apparat directly at his disposal. But the importance of the KGB per se was also reduced. General Vladimir Kryuchkov, who took his place, managed the KGB's foreign affairs: espionage and counterespionage activities, not matters of "domestic control." This pointed to the wish to give the KGB different functions, which no longer had to do with ideological control. Kryuchkov had been one of Andropov's trusted men, and he followed him first in his diplomatic work, and then into party office.

But now I would like to respond to your question, and it's not easy to come up with a satisfactory answer. The events you speak of are very recent, and not everything is clear yet. We know for certain that during Gorbachev's vacation, from the end of August through most of September, there were very critical rumors about him in Moscow—the "usual criticisms" that had been fermenting for a while in the middle strata of the party, but that now were particularly fierce: Too much glasnost. Where will we end up? The reason why is clear: In those weeks the preparations for the reform of the Central Committee apparat proceeded at a rapid pace. When Gorbachev went away, he left precise instructions: we must quickly fulfill the commitments we made at the Nineteenth Conference. The design was clear and consisted of an original dialectic: reinforce the authority of the Gorbachev center and of Gorbachev himself, not to suppress glasnost and democratization but rather to free his hands in the fight against the apparats and to be able to accelerate the rotation of the cadres in the party's entire middle strata.

G.C. His design was clear to the "others" too, don't you think?

R.M. I think that Gorbachev's enemies were well aware of the risks that such a maneuver implied for their destiny. On the other hand, both one and the other witnessed the serious deterioration of the country's economy. Gorbachev realized that for the vast majority of the people, glasnost was not the primary issue. What mattered the most was what was in the stores, what there was to eat. And the food situation had definitely deteriorated, in part due to mysterious reasons. First sugar disappeared, and then the sweets and chocolates. Yet the candy factories were working at full capacity and more sugar was being produced than before. Some people said that this was due to hoarding by the illegal vodka distilleries, but I think that this wasn't the only reason.

Soap and laundry detergent also disappeared. The fact of the matter is that there is no security in the future. Everyone hoards imperishable foodstuffs. It's an old reflex in reaction to continued "deficits," which were now worsened by the uncertainties of the situation. Refrigerators, televisions, and washing machines also disappeared. It wasn't that fewer of them were being manufactured: they were being sold under the counter. All salespeople use state products as "private" goods for exchange. Moreover, there is a huge amount of money in circulation, and people are afraid of price increases. Thus, they immediately buy whatever they can. This exacerbates the imbalance between supply and demand. It also exacerbates the buyers' discontent.

It is completely logical that the "holders of power" would try to exploit this discontent to damage Gorbachev's authority and prestige. They knew that Gorbachev wasn't surrounded by a safety belt, a "second lineup" of leaders ready to "back him up." Figures like Aleksandr Yakovlev and Vadim

Medvedev, even though they were talented, did not have the overall qualities of political leaders. The only such men among the progressives were Razumovsky and two or three others. This is why it became indispensable to strengthen Gorbachev himself. The weak point of perestroika's adversaries was that not even they had a leader who could replace Gorbachev. This is probably why they had to accept the consequences of the September plenum, but this did not mean that they had abandoned the field.

CHAPTER 9

FOREIGN POLICY IN 1988: THE YEAR OF CHANGE; THE MOSCOW SUMMIT; OUT OF AFGHANISTAN

•   •   •

In the wake of the Washington summit, the year opened under good signs. Gorbachev and Reagan sent their best wishes to each other's peoples via television. These unprecedented courtesies symbolized a situation that had already changed. On 4 January a positive signal was sent. Shevardnadze flew to Kabul to speak with Najibullah. The American position still had not changed. Michael Armacost, the assistant secretary of state, was in Islamabad. He spoke with Zia ul-Haq and with the heads of the armed opposition, confirming to both that American military assistance would be stepped up. However, Moscow wanted to speed up the timetable, given the new round of negotiations between Pakistan and Afghanistan. It was a tough operation. The policy of "national reconciliation" proclaimed by Najibullah was limited to allowing 110,000 refugees to return. A coalition government truly representative of all the patriotic forces was, for the time being, not on the horizon.

Gorbachev had already given off signals of greater flexibility, announcing that the Soviet withdrawal could take place in less than thirteen months. But America was not willing to provide any preliminary guarantees, and Pakistan remained firm in its requests for an even earlier withdrawal. Thus, the withdrawal would become politically viable only if the Kabul government were able by itself to militarily withstand the guerrillas' pressures for a certain period of time. There was no doubt that this is exactly what was being discussed, both in Moscow and Kabul. However, the Soviet spokesman was publicly optimistic: "Now it's no longer a question of years but of months."[1] Shevardnadze himself emphasized that "the American side agrees to take the role of the guarantor, and accordingly to suspend aid to armed groups conducting military actions in Afghanistan."[2] Perhaps Shevardnadze had received guarantees from Washington, perhaps not, but the Kremlin intended to reassure Najibullah to get his consent. Dialogue with the Kabul regime was definitely carried out on these bases, and on these bases, Najibullah had given his consent.

In Washington the debate was still wide open regarding what stance to take. George Shultz affirmed that the U.S. administration would reserve the right to "ascertain, in the course of the withdrawal, whether further aid was necessary." This is different from what Armacost had told Islamabad, but it was still too vague to reassure Najibullah. A comment by *Pravda* specified that "the point to clarify is not the date the Soviet troops will begin withdrawal, but the date that American aid to the *dushmani* will end." After which, "if an agreement can be signed for 1 March, then the date to begin withdrawal can be set for 1 May."[3] The sixty days between signing the agreement and beginning withdrawal, already agreed to in Geneva by Afghanistan and Pakistan, constituted the period of time needed to give Islamabad a way to eliminate rebel bases on its own territory. But two months is not enough time to meet this need, even if you hypothesize a complete respect for the commitments made by Pakistan. Both sides pretended that they had already set into place many pieces of a mosaic while in reality they were still looking for them.

The analysis of all these details is important: it shows, in retrospect, that none of those conditions had actually been agreed to, and that Moscow was willing to accept vague and perfunctory assurances from the United States and Pakistan so long as it could open the way to withdrawal. Later events would prove this. The Soviet withdrawal would take place, but with a delay of a few months, and it would take place within a nine-month period, as agreed to in Geneva. Moscow conceded everything in order to get itself out of the Afghan trap once and for all. Washington, instead, would make no concessions, just to make the Kremlin pay the highest possible price for its 1979 mistake. Gorbachev was perfectly aware of this. He calculated the risks and the advantages. The risks were essentially tied to questions over the Kabul regime's actual ability to hold out for a certain period of time. The advantages—on both the national and the international level—were immeasurably greater. On 8 February the Soviet leader announced on TV that, in the event of an agreement at Geneva, the withdrawal would begin on 15 May. First, the Soviet troops would go even if a new coalition government had not yet been created in Afghanistan. In the second place, in the eventuality of attempts to destabilize the situation from abroad, "we might look for the cooperation of the United Nations Security Council." It would be up to the Afghans to decide on the rest. Gorbachev said, "If Afghanistan is independent, nonaligned, and neutral, we will be quite happy to have such a neighbor on our southern border." That "if" enclosed the irrevocable decision. The Kremlin had decide to pull out no matter what.

The decision can hardly have been "peaceful." Not everyone, in the Politburo or among the top-ranking military leaders, thought that the field should be surrendered before actual guarantees had been made by the American side. At least a part of the DPAP leadership stubbornly refused the idea of Soviet withdrawal and the renunciation of revolutionary and socialist objectives. Up until the last minute there were hesitations and clashes.[4] This was explicitly confirmed by Gorbachev's speech at the February plenum. He did not hide the break in continuity in foreign policy since April 1985. He disclosed that immediately after becoming general secretary, he had urged the Politburo to own up to the Afghan crisis "without mincing words," in order to "untie the main knots in that extremely difficult regional conflict." Now it emerged that "the possibility of a solution opened up after genuine national forces entered into play in Afghanistan, headed by Najibullah." In other words, Gorbachev disclosed that Moscow was trying to correct its error by defending the shift toward "national reconciliation," but that shift was impossible as long as Babrak Karmal remained in power. As far as the resistance in the Soviet Union was concerned, Gorbachev brought the ruling group back into line with the premises of the "new way of thinking":

> It is clear, comrades, that our participation in the Afghan conflict is a very complicated problem; it affects many aspects of the problems we are overcoming with perestroika, and it affects the way we are putting the new foreign policy into practice.[5]

The round of negotiations in Geneva, with Diego Cordovez mediating, thus opened under radically changed conditions. The Pakistani demands had been fully met: the withdrawal would take place in nine months, and in the first three months the most massive reduction would take place—half of the contingent. The only thing missing was the date it would start. Islamabad probably hadn't foreseen such compliancy. Now it was forced to forward another request: a transitional government had to be formed "beforehand." It was clear that Pakistan was trying to block a solution, or even to delay the beginning of the Soviet withdrawal. Their latest demand was completely exploitative, and moreover, it glaringly contradicted the thesis of Islamabad (and the Afghan leaders) that the Kabul government would not be able to resist a single day without the Soviet military presence. This "surprising" Pakistani shift was not independent of American influence.[6] The meetings in Washington between Shevardnadze, Reagan, and Shultz saw "a refusal on the American side . . . to participate in the political settlement . . . on the basis of the Geneva agreements."[7] The Kremlin replied to these developments, which it may have expected, in an even more surprising way. The Politburo examined the "variants" and concluded: "It is entirely possible to bring the Geneva processes to an end even without the American guarantees—for example, through a bilateral agreement between Afghanistan and Pakistan," with whom Moscow would sign an integrative document.[8] Now Washington issued a new proposal: a "symmetrical" suspension of Soviet military aid to Kabul and of American aid to the rebels. Moscow rejected it, stating that it placed a legitimate government, represented at the United Nations, on the same level as forces that had no international legal legitimacy.[9] But it pushed further in another direction. "What will happen if Pakistan, against common sense and against its own national interests, will not accept even a bilateral agreement?" Could the "Soviet policy decision on withdrawing the troops remain unchanged . . . based on a separate Soviet-Afghan agreement and in conditions advantageous to the USSR and to Afghanistan."[10]

Gorbachev "threatened" to leave, even by himself, even without guarantees, but in the time limits and in the ways he considered most opportune, collecting the entire international political dividend and leaving both Washington and Islamabad empty-handed. It was immediately clear that he wasn't bluffing. Shevardnadze flew to Kabul on 3–4 April. Two days later Gorbachev and Najibullah met in Tashkent to study the "different variants" of the withdrawal in the event of a Geneva failure. The dizzying acceleration of Moscow's initiative forced everyone to speed up the times. The United States and Pakistan agreed to participate in the agreement. The eight-point communiqué of the Tashkent meeting disclosed that Washington and Moscow had found a compromise solution and that President Najibullah had accepted it. Its contents were not made known. The president of Pakistan, Zia ul-Haq, confirmed that an agreement had been reached regarding military aid to the two sides who were fighting, but he made no appraisal of it. The only negative reaction came from Yunus Khales, one of the Peshawar leaders: "The agreement was not in our favor . . . we shall continue our 'Holy War.' "[11] Judging from these facts, at that moment the American administration had actually conceded something substantial to Moscow, and probably obtained Moscow's consent to the "symmetrical" suspension of military aid.

The agreement was signed in Geneva, while the whole world looked hopefully toward an end to the conflict. The Soviet withdrawal began, as agreed, on 15 May. But the only ones to respect the letter and spirit of the agreement were the Soviets. Still, 1988, starting with Afghanistan, saw extraordinary developments in Soviet foreign policy. Certainly, the elimination of the USSR's military presence outside of its own borders paved the way for Gorbachev's designs, starting with an acceleration of dialogue between the Russians and the Chinese. At the beginning of the year Gorbachev granted the first interview to the magazine *Liaovan*, in which he made explicit mention of the eventuality of a Soviet-Chinese summit, calling it a "logical development" of the ongoing improvement of relations between the two countries. This was an early hint of the Asian policy that the Soviet leader intended to develop, and which would enter a crucial stage in the next year, with the summit between Gorbachev and Deng Xiaoping.

But the primary focus was obviously on relations with the United States. The Washington summit had changed many things, but in Moscow no one dared to speak about the achievement of a shift toward détente. The first months of the year, to keep the hurried enthusiasms in check, actually saw a kind of cooling. The "See you in Moscow" with which the two leaders departed struggled to materialize. The Geneva negotiations on strategic nuclear arms ran into serious technical and political obstacles. Matters certainly weren't helped by small provocations, like two American ships discovered in Soviet territorial waters on the Black Sea, which risked causing a serious incident. The Soviet response was firm but contained. Moscow didn't go for the bait, maintaining that the incident had been planned by someone interested in embittering relations on the eve of George Shultz's arrival. Therefore, the talks between the U.S. secretary of state and the Soviet leader took place in a favorable climate.

It's quite true that in the two months after the Washington summit, "nothing significant happened," but steps were made toward a new summit.[12] For various reasons, both leaders were interested in developing dialogue. The reaction of international public opinion to the first steps taken was so positive that it melted Ronald Reagan's remaining doubts. Gorbachev, in his turn, had repeatedly emphasized the indissoluble bond between domestic perestroika and a new international strategy. The USSR needed dialogue vitally. Gorbachev wanted to renew the USSR, because abandoning isolationism was a prerequisite for introducing the country into the cultural, technological, and economic flow of the international market. Thus, starting with the concrete results of the negotiations, both Reagan and Gorbachev agreed on the utility of a grand "political spectacle" that would signal a change in climate to the world. The two foreign ministers agreed to see each other three more times, while the task forces moved on to drafting three protocols for the agreement on a 50 percent reduction in strategic nuclear weapons. When they departed, Shevardnadze said, "We are walking together down the road of a political dialogue that . . . proves the depth of the changes underway in Soviet-American relations."[13] But neither Shevardnadze's subsequent trip to Washington, nor Shultz's later trip to Moscow, would permit real progress. At the end of April, when the "summit" seemed almost definite, it was also clear that there would be no agreement on strategic weapons.

According to Shevardnadze, there was still "a lot of work to do" on the ABM Treaty.

The fourteenth U.S.-USSR summit, Gorbachev and Reagan's fourth, was thus largely a political spectacle. There would be no important agreements, but the Moscow meeting was destined to be a true watershed in relations between the two superpowers. Gorbachev would rather have had immediate, concrete results, and on the eve of the summit he did not hide his chagrin over the prospects of a meeting that would not allow him to attain anything specific. In fact, it would take another year, and a new president of the United States, before the threads of negotiation could be tied together again. It was logical that Gorbachev aimed at reaping the maximum benefit with a partner who had proved indispensable, and to a certain extent, also flexible. But the outcome of the Moscow summit had an extraordinary psychological effect on public opinion in both countries, both of which were ready to abandon the heavy stereotypes of "the enemy's image." When Gorbachev and Reagan met for the fourth time, they knew they were acting out widespread desires in the world that had been stimulated by their own actions.

The "Theses" of the Nineteenth Party Conference would reflect this new atmosphere by including in the sections devoted to foreign policy formulations that radically revised past ideas. Now Gorbachev could attribute to the "new concept of international relations" a series of steps that had been well received in the world, increasing the prestige and the trustworthiness of a Soviet Union that was no longer an "evil empire":

> The program to eliminate nuclear weapons in stages by the year 2000; a system of global security; the freedom to choose social systems; the balance of interests; the "common European home"; restructuring relations with Asia and with the Pacific Ocean; the doctrine of "adequate defense"; international economic security; the strengthening of national and regional security by reducing the number of weapons; willingness to negotiate a mutual reduction in foreign troops and bases in other countries' territories; the measures of trust; the idea of an immediate influence of scientific authority over international politics.[14]

There was a frank acknowledgment that

> Critical analysis of the past has shown that dogmatism and subjective approaches have also left their traces in our foreign policy . . . Once military parity was achieved, in the past the possibility of obtaining the security of the state through political means was not always pursued . . . with the result that we became involved in the arms race.

But the distinctive characteristic of the "Theses" was that "our foreign policy 'creed' is 'dialogue.' " Imperialism was still dangerous, however:

The influence of the contemporary world's reality and possible modifications of different objective factors, from which the danger of war is born, allow one to believe that the security of the state will be transferred more and more to the area of relations between military and political powers.

Any deterministic vision was abandoned. The opening of the USSR to the rest of the world was the way to know and, better yet, to let yourself be known. Did all of this help to avert the threat of war? Indubitably, the "Theses" replied, "the threat of war, with the participation of the superpowers, has been lowered."

The Conference on Organization only marginally touched on the party's foreign policy. On this front, resistances to change seemed either weaker or overwhelmed by the debate on domestic problems. Whatever the case, Gorbachev and Shevardnadze seemed free in their movements; no predicaments of any kind were noticeable in the months that followed, when the Soviet initiatives would move at a faster and faster pace. The first of these took place in mid-July, with the meeting of the political leadership of the Warsaw Pact in the Polish capital. In specific circles inside NATO, fears had not cooled that in a Europe without missiles the United States would find itself exposed to the Warsaw Pact's "overwhelming superiority" in conventional arms.

On several occasions Gorbachev had already expressed the Soviets' willingness to engage in an examination of conventional forces and armaments in Europe for the sake of reducing them. Now the waiting period was over. A long document from the Warsaw Pact proposed "immediate negotiations, already in 1988," a kind of "European Reykjavik." NATO was caught completely off guard, but it could not reject a proposal that it had pressed for by creating unrest over the other bloc's "superiority." Moreover, the Kremlin and its allies gave a detailed explanation of the mechanism for a true negotiation, whose first stage would consist of reaching an approximately balanced level of forces on the two sides. Secondly, to "eliminate the danger of a sudden attack, it proposed the creation of a belt or zone of a smaller armed presence, from which the most dangerous or most destabilizing conventional weapons would be withdrawn or reduced."

The third point reintroduced Gorbachev's 1987 proposal: "From the very start of negotiations, exchange comprehensive data on armaments and on military forces, simultaneously providing for systems of verification through on-site inspections." Thus, the field was cleared even as far as verification was concerned, which only yesterday had been the Kremlin's *bête noir*. The final point was destined to be rejected by the West: the inclusion of tactical nuclear weapons in the negotiations. Accepting this point would necessitate a revision of NATO's military doctrines, in particular the so-called flexible nuclear response. The Atlantic alliance was still not ready to take this step, but the Warsaw Pact intimated that this idea could be the object of parallel and relatively independent negotiations. With existing "asymmetries" thereby eliminated, they would move on to the reduction of armed forces: "approximately 25 percent, equivalent to 500,000 men." In the last part, the document specified that the negotiation should not replace the work of the European Security Conference, since "a close correlation exists between conventional disarmament in Europe and the further development of measures to increase security and mutual trust."

The October visits of the Italian premier, Ciriaco de Mita, and the West German chancellor, Helmut Kohl, to Moscow confirmed that Western Europe not only welcomed the progress in the American-Soviet dialogue, but intended to contribute to it through its own influence. Under the sign of a great easing of tensions, spaces were opened for economic cooperation that had previously been unthinkable. Economic perestroika and programs for making the ruble convertible provided glimpses of an immense, almost virgin market. An Italian credit line of more than 1 trillion lira and a German line of 3 billion marks were the calling cards with which European business was introduced to the Soviet market.

The Kremlin had filed the old "bipolar" rigidities away in the archives, but a multipolar world was the true dimension of the new phase of détente. Europe, which was becoming more and more united as a political entity, was on the way to becoming a crucial economic and political partner, as were Japan, China, and India. But a "dialoguing" Europe would also be an essential factor in the course of future strategic negotiations. Moscow realized that a real dialogue, mutually advantageous and without "cards up one's sleeves," would require a radical break with the mutual suspicions of the past. The negotiations on the reduction of conventional weapons thus became an essential test. Italy and Germany came to Moscow to say, in the name of Europe, that the Vienna "forum" could end, and they were ready to begin true negotiations.

After eroding the European wall in October, Gorbachev went to India in November for the second time. He issued a flood of new proposals on China, Japan, and South Korea, ranging from the creation of economic areas that would be under special jurisdiction, to the direct participation of the Chinese in the agricultural development of the Soviet Far East, to the start of a collective Asian process to reduce armaments and to build up trust. The great "Asian triangle," Moscow–Beijing–New Delhi, was becoming a reality. Rajiv Gandhi would fly to Beijing a few weeks after receiving encouragement and assurances from Gorbachev that the new Soviet policy would not damage the Moscow–New Delhi axis, while Gorbachev would relaunch the idea of a historical summit between Moscow and Beijing. The only "cold" response came from Japan. Shevardnadze's trip to Tokyo, however, allowed some steps forward in this area of the Kremlin's Asian strategy too, at the same time that contacts with Seoul were quickly intensifying.

The world observed this Soviet evolution-revolution, uncertain and still dubious, fascinated but suspicious. Many people still thought that what was happening was only a product of Gorbachev the man, or of the circumstances in which he found himself working. Others thought that it was only a remarkable display of fireworks to cover up the "background noises" of the dramatic problems that perestroika was uncovering on the domestic front. Still others maintained that it was a cover fire, essentially propagandistic, to hide the USSR's weakness—the acquired awareness that the competition between the two systems had been lost by socialism. In other words, Gorbachev's revolutionary policies were interpreted as a way to kill time while waiting for the "great comeback." According to this interpretation, the West ran the risk of "donating" to Gorbachev's USSR the time it needed to catch its breath.

But too many elements did not concur with a vision of this type. Ever since the Twenty-Seventh Party Congress, Gorbachev had clearly linked domestic perestroika and the "new way of thinking" in foreign policy, calling them "two sides of the same coin." In the next two years the evolution was extraordinary, and the inextricable bond between the reform of the country and opening toward the outside world became clear. Gorbachev had never hidden from the world the seriousness of his country's economic, political, and moral situation. He had no choice, since he had to use glasnost to break the inertia of stagnation. But having done that, he proved to the world that it wasn't a question of little tricks, but of a historical realization. For example, the world was bound by numerous interdependencies. Not only objective, determined by the immensity of the problems of development and the need to reexamine the very notion of progress, but also subjective, a result of power relations and the wearing out of old psychological models of behavior. Once the curtain of mutual fears had been broken, it was possible to see that "on the other side" there were partners ready to welcome the innovations and travel that part of the road that concerned them. It was no accident that many of the regional crises born over the previous fifteen years now moved toward solutions: from the situation in the Horn of Africa, where the withdrawal of Cuban troops from Angola had begun as part of a complex series of negotiations, to that in Cambodia, where substantial progress was made that would lead to the decision to withdraw Vietnamese troops, to the end of the war between Iran and Iraq, to Afghanistan.

These same events had a big influence on the Soviet ruling group. There was a clear sign of this at the end of July during the "scientific conference" for the Soviet diplomatic corps, convened to examine Soviet foreign policy in light of the party's Nineteenth Conference. Eduard Shevardnadze, who on this occasion proved that he was no longer just a brilliant executor, but also a creator, explained the foundations of a huge conceptual revolution, much deeper and more multilateral than the previous revolutions started by perestroika.

He declared, "Today we overcome the 'wreckage' from the time of stagnation, we are building a foreign policy that will exclude forever the possibility of discrepancies between our ideals and our behavior." When the foreign minister focused his analysis on the relationship between domestic policy and international policy, the idea that they were "two sides of the same coin" was reiterated. "The democratization of the country is a prerequisite and premise for a democratization of international relations." The study of recent history showed that "the deformations of our domestic life have influenced our foreign policy." Therefore, foreign policy could no longer be monopolized by closed groups who thought the Soviet Union was infallible. In the new conditions "the role of political methods increases in the search for security." This had to be stated in no uncertain terms, because "we have not completely exploited every chance to avoid the appearance of the 'Iron Curtain,' to limit the dimensions of the opposing positions, of the arms race." The revision went far beyond the Khrushchev doctrine of "peaceful coexistence." Now, Shevardnadze continued, "we renounce interpreting it as a particular form of class struggle," while he proclaimed that "the struggle between the two opposing systems no longer constitutes the determining tendency of the contemporary era."

Once again Shevardnadze faced the issue of domestic democracy. Now it was indispensable that democratic procedures be created to establish who would make the country's military decisions and how they would be made. "All the ministries that deal with military issues and military production must now be subject to the inspection of the elected bodies." It was time to put an end to "excessive secrecy." Now the fiery words that Gorbachev had uttered at the meeting of the Soviet diplomats in May 1986 emerged:

> The idea fixed in the thoughts and actions of certain strategists, according to which the USSR, by itself, can be as strong as any coalition of states opposed to it, is absolutely inconceivable. By following this idea we went clearly against national interests. [15]

Thus, the summit had clarified many problems regarding purposes, after having concluded a tense discussion that had lasted almost two years. But

263

what had been clear at the summit was not equally clear "moving down the ladder."

Six months later Shevardnadze would have to return to the subject in even more explicit terms, if that were possible, thereby disclosing the existence of resistance, misunderstandings, and obstacles. In an interview with *Moskovskiye Novosti* he would say, "It is not rare to find a lot of foot-dragging on decisions made by the political leadership when the time comes to apply them."[16] This was true of the Foreign Ministry, the Defense Ministry, and Gosplan. For example, "two years have gone by since we declared our willingness to publish the military budget . . . now we should communicate what we have done and what is left to do." Instead, there was still no data. The districts jealously hid their figures, from both the international and the Soviet public. If Gorbachev declared to the U.N. that there would be a unilateral reduction in troops, then he could not be credible before the world until he specified "what kind of tanks would be dismantled and on what schedule." If commitments were made in the area of human rights, then they had to be respected. Instead, Shevardnadze exclaimed, "it is no secret that in practice we still have the same lacunae in respecting international agreements." There had been improvements, but it was time to break with the "restrictive interpretations of a series of agreements." And to what extent had Soviet refusal of inspections blocked negotiations? "We were afraid . . . you would think they were threatening our national sovereignty, you would think these were tricks to interfere in our domestic affairs."

This was a lashing self-criticism. This speech was even more timely after Gorbachev, in New York, conferred a broad and central role to the U.N. as part of the détente process then underway and after the exceptional international solidarity that the whole world had demonstrated toward Armenia after it was struck by an earthquake. The foreign minister said, "The USSR has barely participated in the activities of the United Nations Office for International Aid in cases of calamities. . . . Now tragedy has knocked on our door and a hand has been extended to us. . . . What can we feel except shame for our old positions?"

This revision of theory could hardly avoid touching what was perhaps the most sensitive and complicated knot: the relations between the Soviet Union under perestroika and the other countries in the socialist "camp." One year earlier, at the Moscow meeting organized on the occasion of the seventieth anniversary of the October Revolution, Gorbachev had touched on the problems of opening the Communist world to other currents from the socialist world and from progressive forces. He had touched on them, but not faced them in depth, for the ground was fraught with obstacles.

The doctrine of limited sovereignty had been disavowed ever since the

Twenty-Seventh Congress, but its legacy was still alive and present in the countries of Eastern Europe. The Soviet ruling group had changed, but in Prague, Berlin, Bucharest, Budapest, and Sofia, ruling groups from the past were still in power. It was true that János Kádár had set Hungary on the road to experimenting with reform, and that the political atmosphere in Budapest was quite different from that in Prague and Berlin, for example. The ruling groups in Czechoslovakia and East Germany watched what was happening in Moscow with barely concealed suspicion. Gorbachev had many valid reasons for fearing, on the one hand, that domestic opponents would lend their intolerance to that of conservatives in the socialist countries. On the other hand, there was the risk that the conservative groups in countries in the "field" would be upset by waves of public discontent that could become uncontrollable, and would have negative repercussions on the balances in the Kremlin. The situations were highly diverse, from Jaruzelski's Poland, which was laboriously trying to find a path to political pluralism (with Moscow's tacit approval), to the other extreme represented by Nicolae Ceauşescu's Rumania, a tragic parody that had degenerated into the absolute power of the dictator's family.

Gorbachev could not and would not actively export his "recipe," and he declared this openly. He placed his faith in the power of facts and in exerting discreet and multilateral pressures, including economic pressure, to urge the allies to reform themselves as Moscow was doing. But he rejected entreaties to approve a new form of "limited sovereignty," although it was designed in accordance with the principles of reform. This explained, for example, the Soviet silence on the twentieth anniversary of the Prague Spring. An explicit condemnation of the intervention by five countries in the Warsaw Pact—which no one would defend in Moscow today—would have provoked a dramatic political crisis in Prague. Thus, the official sources limited themselves to cool, appropriate comments, but without emphasizing the past. However, contacts with allied countries continued at a fast pace. Gorbachev went to Warsaw in person as soon as the Nineteenth Conference ended. The new Hungarian leader, Károlyi Grosz, flew to Moscow. Nikolai Ryzhkov visited Prague, where the beginning of the year saw the first shake-up since Miloš Jakeš had taken power: a solution that did not settle the problems, but indicated that their existence had been noted. Nothing, or almost nothing, happened in Berlin or in Sofia.

Warsaw and Budapest were two Eastern capitals that forged ahead in political experimentation. The Hungarian multiparty system and Polish pluralism were not recipes that the Kremlin could follow, at least for the time being. But Moscow did not disavow the two attempts. At the same time there was a growing need for an ideological comparison of the different options.

The exchange of experiences took place at a "scientific conference" of ideologists from socialist countries that opened in Moscow on 7 October. Vadim Medvedev, the new head of ideology for the Soviet Communist Party, illustrated Soviet positions to the "cream" of Marxist-Leninist philosophers from Eastern Europe. His dramatically candid words rained down on a floor divided into two camps: the first amazed and restless, the second receptive to and hopeful about the novelties. Medvedev urged everyone to "reexamine" many current ideas about contemporary socialism. The dismantling of dogmatic approaches had to start with the realization that "even Lenin's positions underwent important evolutions in the passage from barracks communism to the NEP." Criticism of the Stalinist period could not be reduced to a matter of identifying "tactical errors," since "the substance of the distortions of socialism went deeper, and led to the abandonment of Lenin's concepts, and of the humanistic contents of socialism."

Medvedev said that people were "irresponsible" who "denied the socialist nature of our society" or "questioned the justness of the socialist choice."[17] But it was time to drop the suspicion that the "diversities" were a sign of "the abandonment of Marxist-Leninism and of internationalism." Moreover, objective self-study was essential, but it was no longer enough. Now it was time to focus on "the experience of humanity as a whole, including that part of the world that isn't socialist." This was the only way to learn the necessary lessons and acknowledge the technological underdevelopment of socialist society in recent decades. No less important, Medvedev maintained, was a "serious analysis of the practice of modern social democracy" that did not obscure the results it had obtained "in the defense of the social and democratic conquests of workers."

Equally "outdated," Medvedev concluded, was the representation of "socialism and capitalism developing along parallel lines, so to speak." Instead, "the roads of their development inevitably intersect; both systems cannot help but interact inside the same human civilization." Medvedev stated that "each of the two systems will continue to develop according to its own laws." But now it was necessary to clarify that "not only priorities of class exist," but that there were also "general human interests." The political reform that the USSR was preparing was a "historical attempt" to create a system of government that was "substantially new, based on a strong democratic system, but one in which the party maintained its guiding role," which "takes into account the real structure of society." The economic reform, in its turn, implied the acknowledgment that the "formal nationalization" of the means of production, abnormal centralism, and the suppression of autonomy could not be "the criteria by which socialist transformations are measured."

The process that had been triggered was "irreversible," and would "give new forms to the social ownership of the means of production, which in many respects had not even been glimpsed in recent decades." Cooperatives, individual initiatives, and the leasing of land to the farmers (but also of enterprises to the workers) would be essential components of a new way of planning, in which the market would be recognized as an "irreplaceable instrument for matching production and social demand." Accurately weighed though they may have been, these formulations allowed no misunderstandings as to the shapes of the transformations Gorbachev was planning. The Communist parties in power had in fact been faced by the need to acknowledge them. They were relatively free to reject them as a whole or in part. But the enthusiastic welcome that Prague and Warsaw gave Gorbachev proved that the public in the socialist countries had understood and approved, and that perestroika was no less popular in the East than in the West. The strategy of a "controlled chain reaction" seemed to be a winning card, at least for the moment, in the socialist countries. But many serious unknowns were in play. The speed of the reaction depended on many factors, not all of which could be controlled. The quality of the ruling groups in the countries concerned did not inspire optimism over their ability to confront the crisis with the necessary flexibility. The precariousness of the economic situation, different though it was from country to country, raised other questions regarding the amount of patience that should be expected of the respective populations.

Gorbachev had few options available. In effect, the strategy he adopted was both the most gradual and the least risky. He was also counting on the hypothesis that the United States and Western Europe were interested in "stability" rather than in fostering imbalances in Eastern Europe. This opinion appeared realistic. But Washington had no intention of easing its pressure on Moscow as far as Afghanistan was concerned. In August, as the agreements stipulated, half of the Soviet troops had already left the country. The guerrillas, as expected, stepped up their pressure on the Kabul government, thanks to military aid from the United States and Pakistan, which rather than being reduced became more massive. The Kremlin issued a series of diplomatic "warnings" that received no response. Foreign Minster Shevardnadze issued a warning to President Reagan in the course of a speech at the U.N. General Assembly, accusing Washington and Islamabad of not respecting the Geneva agreements. And at this point Moscow decided to suspend withdrawal of its troops. [18]

This was a tactical move, meant to shift international and American public opinion. It was also probably the result of a debate in the Soviet ruling group. Signing the Geneva agreement did not seem to raise any dissenting voices in Moscow, but now there was someone in the ruling group, among the military, who complained that the Soviet leadership had placed too much trust in the American administration.[19] However, this move proved to be counterproductive. First of all because it represented the Kremlin's giving in to the tactics of the Washington hawks, whose cause would be aided by a prolonged Soviet presence in Afghanistan. In the second place, when Moscow suspended the withdrawal, on the grounds that neither the United States nor Pakistan had honored the agreement, it too was breaking the agreement and losing all the advantages in image conferred on it by the withdrawal.

At the same time, in November and December it had become clearer that Moscow's diplomatic efforts were not producing any results.[20] Therefore, after a brief pause for reflection, the Kremlin decided that it had to get out of the "quagmire" with a new "unconventional" decision. The withdrawal would recommence in January and end once and for all on 15 February 1989, the final date set at Geneva. Gorbachev probably had to overcome more than a little resistance inside the DPAP, but he closed the chapter on Afghanistan, and won on both the domestic and international fronts.[21] No one could accuse Gorbachev's USSR of not having respected the pacts. No one in the Soviet Union could forget that Gorbachev brought his soldiers home.

The New York summit and the Soviet leader's speech to the United Nations sealed the year of change. Most of the problems were still waiting to be solved, but the world noticed that the first bricks of the new house had been cemented into place. Only one truly important agreement had been signed by the two powers during the previous year, in Washington. But 1988 was the year that saw the most marked changes. Mikhail Gorbachev chose to speak to the U.N. to describe a model of collective government for settling international conflicts, preempting earlier theoretical and political systems of cooperation. But he did not just bring winged words to New York. He announced another unilateral decision that amazed and moved people all over the world, as well as diplomats. The Soviet Union would reduce its army in a two-year period by half a million men, and it would dismantle 10,000 tanks, 8,500 pieces of artillery, and 800 airplanes: this was the greatest and most unique Christmas present one could imagine. Six divisions would be withdrawn from East Germany, Czechoslovakia, and Hungary. Others would be withdrawn from the Chinese border. Gorbachev specified that these were assault troops, which would be eliminated, along with their weapons, while the Soviet divisions that would remain in the territories of allied countries would be "reorganized" in such a way as to transform the entire military machine into a "clearly defensive" force.

The immensity of the decision—almost 10 percent of the Soviet armed forces would be affected—cannot be underestimated. No one, not even the U.S. administration, considered it a simple propagandistic gesture. International reaction was unanimously positive. Yet it was the philosophical context in which the new Soviet decision was announced that most struck the collective imagination. It was the idea, which was both logical and utopian, of "international government." It was the proposal to elevate the role of the United Nations to a new level, recognizing the need for a true supranational instrument, which "is indispensable" to steer "our common civilization" in the contemporary world. There was a profound truth that regulated this conclusion: today's problems could not be solved without "global coordination." A "new thinking" had to be born, because the modern world "is different from what it was at the beginning and during the middle of this century." It was different because nuclear arms had cast doubt not on the victory or defeat of a country, but on the survival of the human race. Different because people and nations burst onto the international scene with irrepressible needs and their own uniqueness, neither of which should be repressed, else the community of nations would be impoverished. Different because the development of science and technology had brought radical changes in the areas of economics, energy, the environment, information, agriculture, and relations between people. Different because the idea of progress itself had changed, along with the end of the illusion that it could be realized through linear developments.

The idea of global interdependence, presented for the first time at the Twenty-Seventh Congress, was expanded into an organic concept, which buried pretenses of authoritarian management of international relations, along with isolationist, autarchical visions of closed societies, impervious to foreign influence. This applied to everyone—also, and above all, to Gorbachev's USSR. The Soviet president's other warning also applied to everyone. We cannot stop at a dispute over the past. We have to confront and manage a contemporary situation where countries that are highly advanced, those that are underdeveloped, and those still in a preindustrial stage coexist and collide. World peace is tied to the ability to help the latter countries enter into a process of growth without being violent toward them. It is impossible, if not naive, to think these problems can be solved with methods from the past. Ultimately, such attempts would backfire, because the differences between peoples, nations, and cultures, far from being obstacles, could become factors of mutual enrichment.

Today we are in an absolutely original situation, in which "there are no longer omnipotent countries," and at the same time, there are increasingly strong "options for different values and defenses of different interests." There was no other way except to search for a balance based on "general human consensus" and "unity in diversity." In order to do this without any country renouncing its own values, the Soviet leader continued, it was necessary to "deideologize relations between states." And here Gorbachev proposed an absolutely unprecedented "synthesis" of the bourgeois revolution of 1789 and the socialist revolution of 1917. Both had changed the course of world events by their "exceptional impact." But to be inspired by one or the other today was not the key to solving contemporary problems. "We are faced by a different world and we must look for a different road for the future."

Was it realistic to set such broad goals? "I am convinced," Gorbachev replied, "that we are not losing contact with reality at all." He knew that the ability to grasp his arguments depended on the credibility of the "revolution" underway in his own country. This is why he confronted and frankly explained the difficulties of the task. We knew, he said, that we would make mistakes, that we would run into growing opposition and contradictions. But we were equally aware of the unavoidable need for reform. Now it has already left a lasting mark on the life of our country. To whoever in the West or at home doubted perestroika's possibilities of success, Gorbachev replied with the words that had allowed him to defeat the opposition on more than one occasion: "There is no alternative to perestroika." This was the strongest guarantee—and on close examination the only one—that the Soviet president could offer in his dialogue with the world. [22]

Ninth Conversation

• • •

R.M. With a certain surprise, I must say, I found myself among the forty "representatives of the Soviet intelligentsia"—writers, poets, artists, directors—who met Ronald Reagan at the Writers' House breakfast during the fourth summit meeting of the American president and Gorbachev. And I think that everyone who attended was convinced, once more, of the truth of the proverb "Better to see one than to hear a hundred." Soviet-American contacts had reached an unprecedented intensity. The year 1988 would add a fifth summit to the series, with George Bush as the president-elect and Reagan still in office. Shultz and Shevardnadze, in their turn, had achieved a record of at least twenty-five meetings. For the first time in history the two countries' defense secretaries met. Military experts on both sides had access to each other's formerly top-secret installations. This progress was even more remarkable when compared with the state of things in the 1979–85 period, when the United States refused to ratify the SALT II treaty and the USSR called off all negotiations.

G.C. These results were undeniable. However, I would say that we are still barely at the first steps of a change that could become a watershed in history, but that could also fall far short of being one. Many things are still open. There were reasons why it was not possible to sign an agreement on reducing strategic weapons by 50 percent. This would have been a truly radical step. But the United States and Reagan still would not make a decision that Gorbachev had already been ready to make in 1988.

R.M. The debate in the United States is still not over. I am not surprised that certain conservative American commentators still obstinately insist that a more quickly developing Soviet Union with a growing influence on international politics could represent a greater danger to capitalistic American interests and values than a socialist giant in slow decline. Luckily, most

271

Americans do not share these fears. It was already clear on the eve of the Moscow summit that the "maximum program" would not be achieved. And as proof that dialogue was still difficult, there was the risk on the eve of the summit that not even the "minimum program" would be realized. Yet judging from the conclusive document, moves forward had been made on many substantial issues: disarmament, regional questions, and bilateral relations. But I would say that the very fact that the two leaders were meeting was a crucial factor in the development of relations between the United States and the USSR. We were convinced that Gorbachev's visit to Washington in December 1987 had contributed greatly to an increase in the American people's trust of Gorbachev personally and of the USSR. Now we could see with our own eyes that Reagan's trip to Moscow had greatly changed, for the better, the Soviet people's ideas about the United States and its president.

G.C. The Washington and Moscow summits had a great psychological effect on public opinion in the two countries, although Geneva, and even more so Reykjavik, had been the setting for "true" discussions.

R.M. I think that summits in third countries are less useful than the ones held in the capitals of the two countries concerned. In Geneva and Reykjavik thousands of journalists had no choice but to describe Nancy and Raisa's toilettes. And the two leaders lacked the opportunity to meet more people and deal with anything other than the technical subject of disarmament. These circumstances proved to be anything but secondary or peripheral. Instead, the circumstances made it clear how obsolete the cold-war mentality had become. The fact that Reagan and Gorbachev had less time to deal with each other face-to-face in Washington and Moscow than in Geneva and Reykjavik did not make these negotiations any less productive. Moreover, the same highly complicated negotiation mechanisms had been perfected from meeting to meeting. Now two experienced "teams" were participating, and not just the two leaders.

G.C. Without taking away credit from either, I must underline, however, that different combined circumstances helped quite a bit. Of the two, Gorbachev was the one who pursued his goals with the most determination. But he also had good tactical and strategic reasons for doing so.

R.M. The personal success that both men achieved was undeniable. Reagan was on the verge of exiting the political scene. In a certain sense the Moscow summit was the last prominent act of his presidency. I don't think that this by itself had a decisive influence on the results of the later elections. However,

Ronald Reagan did conclude this phase brilliantly, and confirmed his place in the American conscience as one of the most popular and effective presidents in United States history. Gorbachev was still at the initial stage of his political career, and you could say that he was just at the beginning of the work of perestroika, which he thought of as a profound transformation of every aspect of Soviet society. A success for his foreign policy would be invaluable for facing an even more difficult domestic policy planted with unsuspected traps.

G.C. The dialogue was also a great duel before the eyes of the whole world—in different "rounds." Gorbachev won some of them hands down, such as Reykjavik. Some were ties. Reagan was in top form in Moscow. Once the surprise of the first talks was over, he proved to know how to adjust to an interlocutor who was certainly well prepared.

R.M. For now we know little about how the direct talks between the two leaders went. I think that it was anything but easy for Reagan to face Gorbachev, who, as you say, was well prepared, had the initiative in his hands, and was younger and more energetic. But with an outside audience, such as at Moscow University or the Writers' House, Reagan had no problems surpassing the other speakers. He was the one who on every occasion proved more flexible and better prepared, while the Soviets who were facing him proved incapable of dialogue with such an effective representative of another ideology and another system of values. This was not a question of exchanging kindnesses. It was a coherent and meaningful confrontation.

Reagan proceeded carefully, with speeches prepared by his staff in which nothing was neglected either in form or in content. I asked myself why the representatives of the Soviet intelligentsia didn't do the same. They all arrived at the talk with their pieces of paper, with speeches that lacked the originality and humor of the American president's. The president of the Filmmakers' Union began to speak—who knows why—about how difficult it is to make a film in the Soviet Union, as if this were an operative meeting with Soviet leaders. The president of the Artists' Union complained that Soviet painting was not very well known in the United States. The editor in chief of *Novy Mir* started to criticize private property, but later admitted that he did not know precisely what socialism was. The first secretary of the Writers' Union, in his feeble speech, actually compared Reagan and Gorbachev to Jesus Christ, since, he said, "God created the world and Reagan and Gorbachev have saved it." A truly unfortunate phrase that visibly embarrassed Ronald Reagan. For that matter, it was still too early to declare that our leaders had saved the world.

Reagan's speech was completely different. He paid great homage to Soviet culture, particularly to Russian culture, which through illustrious representatives like Kandinsky, Rostropovich, Stravinsky, and Dostoevsky had exerted an immense influence on American culture. He emphasized that in the United States they can admire our best ballerinas (who have stayed there) and can read Solzhenitsyn. He quoted Akhmatova and Gumilyov. He talked about how American democracy works, how even a simple actor could become president, and how having been an actor could help someone to be a president. In short, he gave a natural and charming speech, even if every now and then he took a glance at his notes. But he allowed himself to underline this with a polite and ironic remark: "Seeing as you, the representatives of the highest Soviet intelligentsia, are reading your speeches, I suppose it's all right for me too, the old American president."

At the end Anatoli Karpov acknowledged that the prize for the best speaker of the evening went to the guest. But this was not, in fact, an oratorical duel, but rather a particular ideological duel. Something similar had happened when Margaret Thatcher easily defeated three of our best political commentators in an interview that was broadcast to millions of Soviets. Reagan had done the same in a television interview that preceded his arrival in Moscow. I think that all of this was a result of our inability to conduct a truly pluralistic debate. We had lived in a closed society for too long. We have to learn to debate and argue with other ideologies and schools. This could only enrich us.

I remember that Reagan showed that he liked our proverbs. At his first meeting at the Kremlin he quoted one of them: "*Rodilsya—ne toropilsya*" ("It was born, it was in no hurry"). He was referring to the accord on Euromissiles and to the new relations between the United States and the USSR. But he used another Russian proverb that says, "*Yesli nachal rodit— nechevo godit*" ("Seeing that you've begun to give birth, then go ahead"). In other words, since the child has been conceived, its birth mustn't be delayed, because it would be dangerous for both mother and child. Under Krushchev détente didn't have time to be born; under Brezhnev it was born, but the child was weak and sickly, and soon died—making it more important today to take care that a healthy and strong child be born, ready to live a long life.

G.C. Nineteen eighty-eight was the year in which the end of the Soviet presence in Afghanistan was decided. We saw how Gorbachev gave the final acceleration at the February plenum. But also how, as Gorbachev himself disclosed, he had raised the question ever since the moment of his election as general secretary. The entire affair deserves a more thorough treatment.

The motives that led the Soviet leadership to military intervention at the end of 1979 are still mostly unknown. It is only recently, in the midst of the election campaign for the new Congress, that the candidate Boris Yeltsin disclosed that the decision had been made by four Politburo members unbeknown to the others, who were informed of it as a *fait accompli.* According to Yeltsin, the four were Brezhnev, Gromyko, Suslov, and Ustinov.

R.M. I've always tried to follow the Afghan events as closely as possible. I have my own theory about it, but I've never been able to substantiate it with all the necessary elements because of a lack of information. In Brezhnev's time no one in the USSR wrote about Afghanistan. From the Soviet press you might even get the idea that our troops were not engaged in combat. How much of the territory was controlled by government troops and how much by the enemy was unknown. The relatives of the soldiers who died there received the news with the words "died in fulfilling international duty." But this could have been anywhere, in Africa or on the border with China. Official figures on the dead and wounded were not known; it was easier to make a list of what you didn't know. Western observers were equally uninformed, including those who risked their lives by entering into Afghanistan as part of a guerrilla incursion. The country's domestic politics were also difficult to analyze because of the lack of information. In recent years the amount of news in the mass media began to increase, but so did the number of young men—hundreds of thousands—who did their military service in Afghanistan, came back, and got together in Afghan clubs where they told other people about their experiences there.

I had the chance to speak with a former paratrooper who took part in the intervention during the initial phase, and was actually among those who took Amin's presidential palace. From him I learned that at that moment Babrak Karmal stayed out of Kabul, and that his appeal to the Afghan people had been taped. Karmal arrived in Kabul, accompanied by special Soviet troops, only after the capital had been put under the iron-fisted control of our forces. I was also able to speak with a pilot who made regular bombing flights taking off from an airport located on Soviet territory. It was perfectly clear that the bombing did not just strike the combat forces, but that civilians died too. This information helped, but it wasn't enough to draw a complete picture. However, by assembling all the available elements I reached the following conclusions. In the first place, I am convinced that the main error took place when we proclaimed that the events of April 1978 were a popular revolution. On the contrary, it was a military "coup" staged in Kabul by a relatively small group of officers, most of whom had received their military training in Moscow.

G.C. Military and ideological training.

R.M. Exactly. Not even the most elementary factual circumstances, the real situation, were taken into account. Afghanistan was one of the poorest and most backward countries in the world. It was still a feudal country that had not yet experienced antifeudal peasant movements. About 90 percent of the population was made up of farmers. There was virtually no working class. A significant percentage of the population lived in prefeudal conditions, organized tribally, barely connected to the country's center. The vast area of the "free tribes" took up not just part of Afghan territory, but of Pakistani territory as well. The Muslim religion and traditions were quite strong. One should also add that Afghanistan has never been an ethnically homogeneous country. More than twenty different peoples lived there, belonging to different linguistic groups. The Afghans were the most numerous, but there were also Tadzhiks, Uzbeks, Turkmen, Kirghizes, and Kazakhs. One should also note that part of the Afghan population was made up of refugees of the previous century who had escaped from Central Asia during the time of the Russian conquests, and of refugees from this century who had escaped during the civil war that took place after the Bolsheviks took power.

As you know, until 1973 Afghanistan was a constitutional monarchy. Relations with the USSR had always been good, whether under King Zahir, or under his premier, Muhammad Daoud Khan, who deposed the king in 1973 and proclaimed the republic. The Afghan bourgeoisie was dissatisfied with the country's backwardness, and shared this feeling with the intelligentsia and many army officials. The first political parties were formed in the 1960s, including a small Communist Party made up of a few thousand members and divided into two bitterly opposed factions from the beginning: Khalq (People) and Parcham (Flag). Daoud was initially fairly tolerant of the Afghan Communists and of the military's procommunist sympathies. He even went so far as to offer them positions of responsibility in the government. But later on, in the mid-1970s, he engaged in repressive policies toward them. Then the two Communist Party factions joined forces temporarily to overthrow Daoud. Some people maintain that this was a defensive step to prevent the physical elimination of the party. Maybe. But in 1978 there was certainly not what is generally considered a revolutionary situation.

Partly for this reason, the new leaders should have acted with maximum caution and without accelerating events. Instead, those who took power in 1978 immediately made a series of grave mistakes (I don't know if there were already Soviet advisers in that phase), starting "revolutionary reforms" that had not been well studied. These included an agricultural reform that immediately unleashed hostility against the government from both the feudal lords and many of the peasants. You could not distribute the land to peasants who had never asked to have it, since they didn't consider it theirs. The "revolutionary" government also solicited the hatred of the urban bourgeoisie. Moreover, the Democratic Party of the Afghan People, which had just taken power, broke into the two previous factions again, and a bloody conflict ensued. The civil war began immediately, starting in the summer of 1978. Soviet helicopters pushed the first guerrilla formations out of Kabul, but they were not able to prevent the fighting between Communists. The first defeat was suffered by Parcham, and its leader, Babrak Karmal, was sent to Prague as the ambassador. Then the fight flared up between Taraki and Hafizullah Amin, in which Taraki was killed and Amin became a dictator with enormous power.* The Kabul prisons were filled with inmates. The guerrillas already controlled a good deal of the territory and they prepared to attack the capital.

G.C. There is the famous question of the Kabul government's requests for military aid, which Brezhnev in his time had used to justify the intervention.

R.M. The Afghan government had already asked the USSR for direct military assistance several times. I think that Amin also asked. At the end of 1979 the military situation was in fact very critical. The opposition was still very small and poorly armed, but it was stronger than before. At that point the USSR had three possible alternatives. First, it could let things follow their course and not intervene. America had made this choice with Iran, and Khomeini took power. After Vietnam there was probably no other way the United States could have acted. The second alternative was to directly intervene in support of Amin. The third alternative was to bring Karmal (i.e., Parcham) to power, forcing the party to unite under this flag. We know that the third option was chosen. We also know what the international impact of this choice was.

G.C. Many questions were raised in this regard. Is it possible that no one had weighed the risks of such a venture?

R.M. It was clearly a decision that was not only mistaken, but not even studied. Evidently, the experts, the specialists in Afghan issues, were not at

---

* In April 1978 the Democratic Party of the Afghan People (DPAP) took power in a military coup d'état, the so-called "April Revolution" that ousted Daoud. Nur Muhammed Taraki became the leader of Afghanistan. He remained in power until December 1979, when he was assassinated in a coup by another faction of the DPAP, which was under Amin's leadership at the time.

all equal to the task. The Soviet government was not able to assess the domestic and international consequences of this gesture. The country was considered too weak to react and the USSR too strong to run into difficulties. Some leaders may have thought that the national affinities of many Afghan minorities with the peoples of Soviet Central Asia would have made the job easier. An infinity of other factors were not taken into account, including the eventuality of foreign aid to the Afghan guerrillas.

G.C. Yet someone warned the Kremlin. *Literaturnaya Gazeta* published a letter from Academician Oleg Bogomolov, in which he disclosed that the Central Committee had received analyses compiled by the researchers at the Institute for the Economy of the International Socialist System urging against false steps in Afghanistan.

R.M. I think it was a rule of the Soviet government to ignore scientific opinions that did not correspond to the decisions it wanted to make. At that time Bogomolov was not even an academician. His institute dealt with other issues. Bogomolov himself disclosed that the studies he sent to the Central Committee in the mid-1970s did not specifically regard Afghanistan, but rather strategies toward Angola and Ethiopia. After unfortunate experiences in Egypt, Guinea, Ghana, and Indonesia, many Soviet scholars were convinced of the danger of implementing Soviet policies in unstable Third World regimes. The United States had also had to learn similar, bitter lessons. Bogomolov's note on the subject of Afghanistan wasn't sent until 20 January 1980, three weeks after Soviet troops had entered the country. However, its interpretations were correct: the intervention would create a hotbed of tensions, rouse the hostility of the Muslim world, weaken the Soviet position toward nonaligned movements, increase China's distrust, and seriously undermine relations with the West as a whole.

However, you must not forget that in 1979 there were other factors that greatly worried the Soviet Union and that helped push it toward the intervention in Afghanistan. The first was the sudden military and political rapprochement between China and the United States. In that year half a million Chinese soldiers entered Vietnamese territory to "punish" Hanoi and assist the criminal leaders of the Khmer Rouge. In those weeks the Soviet soldiers came as close as 500 meters to the Chinese border. Tensions ran high. I remember the reply of a Soviet diplomat when asked what the USSR would do if the United States and China were to enter into an actual military alliance: "The USSR would correct the balance on the other side." The Soviet strategists thought they could "surround" China, threatening it from the north, west, and south. This was the same line of reasoning the Americans followed when they got mixed up with Vietnam: they wanted to create a base against China, which at that time was considered the main enemy in the area of the Pacific Ocean and the Far East.

These circumstances have to be taken into consideration to analyze Soviet behavior. Then, as often happens, international developments moved in completely different directions. China did not become a military ally of the United States and Reagan ceased to be interested in the "China card." The entire Chinese situation changed radically and a slow rapprochement began between the USSR and China. The tensions between China and Vietnam also eased. Through great efforts the dialogue between the USSR and the United States gave off its first positive signals. And the entire situation in Afghanistan changed substantially. Four million Afghan refugees, most of whom fled to Pakistan, formed a huge reserve for the armed resistance. Another 4 or 5 million peasants took refuge in Kabul or in the other big Afghan cities. In other words, the entire domestic social picture changed. The DPAP strengthened its positions. It created a better organized army, which was aided by an efficient militia and secret police. At the same time, there was an improvement in the opposition's organizational abilities and an increase in armaments. In this situation the probability of military success by the regime, even in an intermediate period, became null. The Gorbachev leadership's decision to leave Afghanistan must be partly framed according to these considerations.

G.C. When Gorbachev accelerated the development of events, he gave the impression that he wanted to leave "at any cost." The Afghan crisis had become the only contradictory factor in the new Soviet foreign policy developed over the past three years. Prolonging it overshadowed the offensive by the "new way of thinking."

R.M. Not "at any cost." The decision to withdraw the troops had already been made, in my opinion, in 1985 or 1986. But the minimum conditions had to be created to carry it out. Above all it was necessary to strengthen Najibullah, both on a military-organizational and on a political level. The policy of national reconciliation also helped this, and it achieved some success. Once the Kremlin had completely abandoned its previous ideas, it aimed for a neutral Afghanistan, friendly and nonaligned. It could not afford to have a Lebanese-type situation on its southern borders.

G.C. You have to say that the United States and Pakistan did everything possible to prevent Gorbachev from paying the lowest price in withdrawing.

R.M. Gorbachev had also taken this eventuality into account. The Geneva accords were signed without the USSR having specific guarantees that the United States would respect the agreements. A certain margin of risk was calculated. But all of the risks of leaving were still less than those of staying. Once the Soviet troops had been withdrawn, the only reasonable solution was a compromise between the two sides of the combat. Without this, a long and bloody civil war would have to be prevented, a war that could lead to no favorable results for either side.

G.C. Now I would like us to turn to the 1988 "September crisis." I use this term because I am convinced that it was no less crucial a moment than the "March crisis."

R.M. Not everything that happened in September is clear to me. I can make out the mechanism of the events as a whole. Gorbachev realized that the situation was in danger of getting bogged down again, and the decisions to reform the central apparat were not keeping to the timetable. He pushed for an acceleration. The apparat, which still had immense power, exerted a huge resistance. The atmosphere of hostility toward Gorbachev grew rapidly in the apparat, among the members of the Central Committee, and in the KGB apparat. You can imagine that some of his adversaries tried to take advantage of this atmosphere. Gorbachev, who was aware of these moods, thus decided to take the initiative. He convened the Politburo and put forward a comprehensive proposal to redistribute jobs that would upset all the balances. Among other things he proposed the de facto elimination of the Secretariat of the Central Committee. This never became official. Formally, the Secretariat still exists, but it no longer meets. This meant that no one presided over it any longer—in other words, there was no longer a "number two." The proposal was made as an ultimatum, and even if resistances were manifested, it was approved. An emergency meeting of the Central Committee was convened that lasted only fifty minutes. There was an equally quick convening of the Supreme Soviet to elect Gorbachev as its president. In this way Gorbachev's personal power was substantially strengthened, and Ligachev was demoted to the third position, losing a good deal of his previous power.

G.C. Why do you say "third position"?

R.M. Because there was no longer a second position.

G.C. There are those who say that Zaikov now holds the second position.

R.M. I don't think so. Zaikov is also in the third position. However, he is not part of Gorbachev's "team." He is not an adversary, nor is he his first ally.

G.C. So you think that there is a "centrist" group that determined the balances in this phase?

R.M. Exactly. There is Gorbachev's group, strengthened after the September plenum. And there is a centrist group, to which Vadim Medvedev belongs.

G.C. Would you situate Medvedev in the center?

R.M. Yes. You must be careful. Aleksandr Yakovlev was shifted from ideology to international problems "in exchange" for the simultaneous removal of Ligachev from ideology. Medvedev was temporarily assigned to ideological issues to prevent Ligachev's defeat from becoming visible. Gorbachev gave him only a part of the ideological tasks, partly because Medvedev is an economist by training, not an ideologist. Their relations are good, but in my opinion they are not in complete agreement. Finally, there is a small group of right-wingers, some of whom were demoted. The greatest demotion was that of Ligachev, who now chairs the Central Committee's Commission for Agriculture.

G.C. And Chebrikov?

R.M. Chebrikov also ended up being demoted. Now he no longer directly controlled the KGB. I think the appointment of a "civilian" to the Defense Ministry was being prepared, but this was prevented by the earthquake in Armenia. It will happen, I think, in a later phase.

G.C. Do you think the September plenum was preceded by an actual attempt to bring together the different currents in the opposition?

R.M. Maybe not yet. Maybe there was a discourse of this type when the reform began. The opposition to Gorbachev was a real fact. It continued to lack organization and a leader. Gorbachev had to prevent it from uniting. To do this, he equipped himself with his own information system, his own secretariat, and his own personal guards. Now he had at his disposition independent information that allowed him to check up on what was happening in the fundamental nerve centers of the party and the state. The fact that various types of plots against him had been repeatedly hatched during his absence could not escape his attention, nor could the fact that the political climate changed every time he went on a mission abroad or even simply outside of Moscow. This is what probably prompted his decision to step up his timetable and build a sufficiently secure backup. As we have seen, his maneuver was only partly successful, and the balances in the Politburo remained transitory.

G.C. The interior minister was also a new man.

R.M. He was probably appointed on Gorbachev's direct instructions. I know Vadim Bakatin's political background well, and it contains clearly progressive tendencies. But his predecessor, Aleksandr Vlasov, was also promoted a grade, becoming president of the RSFSR Council of Ministers. It is common knowledge that Vlasov is very close to Gorbachev. They have known each other for a long time and share a friendly personal relationship. All of this is very important in a situation characterized by a sharpening of the economic crisis and growing public dissatisfaction. The year ended badly in this respect. The harvest was worse than that of the previous year, the food and consumer-goods "deficit" grew, and the USSR's situation on the international market worsened considerably. Some leaders might be tempted by demagoguery to take advantage of the circumstances against Gorbachev.

G.C. This was precisely one of the reasons for the spreading restlessness. The situation was very strange. Gorbachev's personal power had grown, as you said. Yet he was once again under a certain threat. The balances in the leadership, at least the way I see them, were such that the "centrist" group (including Zaikov, Slyunkov, Nikonov, and in my opinion Shcherbitsky) could decide the fate of every important decision. Frankly, Slyunkov's positions on economic reform, for example, don't strike me as very progressive. The same could be said about Nikonov. Zaikov did not fail to imply that he took a very, very "cautious" line. For example, 1989 opened with a harsh debate over agricultural reform. The "agricultural" plenum was postponed because of disagreement over the steps to be taken. Ligachev's stance on leasing land to the farmers was totally different from what Gorbachev had expressed. If the centrist group, which favored the September plenum's solution, tended toward the right, then Gorbachev's group could suddenly find itself in the minority.

R.M. True. This is why Gorbachev decided to become president immediately, at the same time transforming the office of the head of state into a body of real power, independent from the Politburo. The mechanism he built made the Supreme Soviet and the soviets stronger than the party.

G.C. However, people did not like the fact that Gorbachev was elected by the old Supreme Soviet, in the traditional way, rather than becoming president through the Congress. I myself heard many criticisms.

R.M. This is also true. But not everyone understands all of the nuances of the situation. For that matter, it was better for Gorbachev not to have everything clear. The fact that he placed agriculture and the economy in the hands of men who were not on his team represented, in my opinion, a deliberate choice. In this way, since things were really going badly, he could effect a new rotation at the opportune time, giving as his reason the inability of those men to confront the problems. When the first session of the new Congress took place, he would have more power to effect other changes in the leadership.

G.C. Yet there are indications that Gorbachev was experiencing difficulty confronting the situation. Until the Nineteenth Conference he made almost no "mistakes." All of his moves were made with the public mood in mind, and each move helped increase his popularity. Even in critical moments, when he was "up against the wall" (as in the Yeltsin case), he succeeded in turning the situation around to his own advantage. By contrast, after the Nineteenth Conference there were moments when he lost direction. Gorbachev's management of the crisis between Armenia and Azerbaijan, especially in the second half of the year, when he repeatedly stepped in in person, showed serious uncertainties and mistakes in judgment. In the second place, the economic maneuver he had imposed at the end of 1987 did not work, and got out of hand. Here the legacy of the past certainly played a part, as did his adversaries' boycotts. But this was predictable. If in 1987 salaries grew by a rate of 7 percent and work productivity by just 5 percent, this was the political responsibility of the current management and not of its predecessor. Another example: the new law on elections. This was a questionable step forward, but it was such an incongruent mess that it proved not only the strength of the adversaries, but also the uncertainty of the reformers.

R.M. I agree. Gorbachev made mistakes in this last phase. Even his trip to Armenia after the earthquake was not a good moment. The decision on Nagorno-Karabakh seems relatively good to me. Now Moscow administers the region in reality, but this decision should have been made back in the

283

spring of 1988. The delay aggravated the problem and caused others to follow. The fact is that when so much power is concentrated in one person, timely and wise management of many different problems becomes impossible. The perestroika process is extremely complex and everything converges on Gorbachev, including ideological questions. For example, Medvedev's appointment to ideology provoked open conflicts, from which Gorbachev then had to shield himself. Medvedev prohibited the publication of Orwell's novel *1984* in *Novy Mir*, leading to Sergei Zalygin's resignation. Then Zalygin came out on top and Orwell was published. But the prohibition of mentioning and publishing Solzhenitsyn proclaimed by Vadim Medvedev raised a wave of protests from the intellectuals.

Despite Gorbachev's mistakes and uncertainties in this last phase, a realistic assessment needs to be made. The Soviet leaders who preceded him were all much worse when it came to concentrating vast powers in their hands. This applies to Khrushchev, Brezhnev, Stalin, and Lenin. These are defects of the authoritarian system, but now the authoritarian system was needed to effect perestroika. This time, however, it is not directed against the people, but against the apparats and the bureaucracy. Without enormous personal power, Gorbachev could not overcome the resistance of the state, party, military, and industrial apparats. Do not forget that he also had to deal with the population's passivity. There was a clear crisis of confidence. The people were tired of words. Stalin did away with Lenin's legacy in the way we know. Khrushchev denounced Stalin. Brezhnev superseded Khrushchev. Gorbachev superseded Brezhnev. In the eyes of the great masses this looked like a continuous loss of political capital.

Not only the great masses suffered from this crisis of confidence—many intellectuals were caught up in it too. If there were free elections, maybe not even Gorbachev would win. The Central Committee did not want to risk losing, so it called itself a "social organization" and put all its leaders on the party list. Almost none of the party leaders had to face an election. Even narrow victories would have proven that there was a high rate of distrust toward the party.

The mechanism was built based on this fear, and was obviously anything but democratic. However, it did contain elements of democratization and held surprising possibilities in reserve. The Academy of Sciences could reject Sakharov, as it did, but thus suffered an irreparable blow to its authority. The new elections unveiled a veritable *Who's Who*. Public participation increased, even if there was still a lack of experience and of democratic traditions. In many situations conflicts arose between the political leaders and the citizens. Political, national, and social problems emerged at the same time. In Minsk the police dispersed a mass demonstration that demanded that Byelorussian be declared the official language of the republic. The Byelorussian leaders were against it because none of them knew the language very well. In the Baltic Republics, on the other hand, local leaders had sided with the people's demands that the rights of the local national majority be protected from incursions by Moscow.

G.C. The election law was also designed to prevent national movements from finding a virulent and immediate expression. Here Gorbachev's calculation was aimed at avoiding the separatist movements, or at least containing them and diluting them over time. But here you could see the overlapping of two different plans. One was Gorbachev's, to take a democratic step forward without risking the dissolution of the state—in other words, avoiding the risk, such as in the elections for the Estonian Supreme Soviet, that an overwhelming majority of deputies would be opposed to Moscow. The other plan was by Gorbachev's adversaries, to maintain strict apparat control over the entire process of selecting candidates. We know the results: 880 candidates for 750 positions in the "social organizations"; 2,091 candidates for 1,500 positions in the territorial and territorial-republican districts. In short, the law allowed tens of thousands of candidates to be nominated, but it contained a practically insurmountable system of obstacles.

R.M. True. I would add that the law is so complicated that most people find it incomprehensible. Moreover, it was made so quickly that there was no time to debate the draft bill, or to work on preparing for the elections, for candidates, etcetera. Yet I think we have to move forward in stages. And I think Gorbachev deliberately strove for the country to undergo a new and transitory experience. Later lessons could be drawn from it, and new political faces would emerge. This was the point to keep in mind. There was still a strong lack of true political leaders. For the moment there was just one man who could be even remotely compared to Gorbachev—Yeltsin—and Yeltsin realized this. When they asked him if, in the hypothetical case that there were alternative candidates for the office of secretary-general, he would declare his candidacy, he replied, "I probably would." There is certainly an element of demagoguery in this, because Yeltsin's skills are inferior to Gorbachev's, and he would not be able to manage the situation. But the fact remains. Napoleon guided an empire with a band of formidable marshals by his side. Such a situation still does not exist in the Soviet Union today.

G.C. Ryzhkov proved to be a brilliant marshal, especially during the tragic event of the earthquake.

R.M. Only in the last few months. In effect, he did win general favor in Armenia and in the rest of the country. His television appearances, day after day, seemed convincing. But take the example of Aleksandr Yakovlev. He is unquestionably a man of great culture and intelligence, and the most important "coauthor" of the "new way of thinking." But he is already old, and he's sick. He can lead one sector very well—ideology—but he couldn't lead the whole country. Vadim Medvedev would be even less capable of doing so. There is no other all-around leader who could keep a strong grasp on the situation. And at the same time, the task before us is immense. We need to build a new ideology to unite the supporters of perestroika. Gorbachev worked hard in this direction. He has already said things of great theoretical importance. When he proclaimed the need to give priority to "general human interests" rather than "class" interests, he was proposing a radical innovation. But all of this takes time and collective efforts to develop. People continued to talk in the name of Leninism, but we are already at another level of conceptual development. It is a change from every angle.

PART FOUR
1989

CHAPTER 10

THE LONG STRUGGLE OF PERESTROIKA

•　　　•　　　•

"This scenario was already written once—two hundred years ago!" This warning cry from Nikolai Shmelyov was not just an effective rhetorical device at the first session of the Congress of People's Deputies. Gorbachev's revolution from above was turning into a situation that was broadly "revolutionary."

In this chapter, written immediately after the Congress's first session, I am not attempting to analyze the situation in the first half of 1989. I am struck by the extremely rapid change in the country's domestic situation. The election campaign, which lasted almost five months, was a litmus test for modifications in the social mood. The trick of having 750 deputies elected by the "social organizations" was supposed to permit—in the plans of whoever wrote the law—an early control over one-third of the congress. In the territories, candidates for deputy were supposed to be filtered out by the complicated mechanism of preliminary assemblies, after which the candidates who emerged would be elected by universal suffrage. But an additional filter was introduced to step in at the last minute and eliminate candidates who might have slipped through the cracks—the "district electoral assemblies," made up of the "grand electors," whom it would be easy to select in a thousand different ways. Finally, a Congress that had already been strongly "preselected" was to elect from among its members the Supreme Soviet: the permanent parliament and the actual lawmaking body.

You cannot say that these "safeguards" did not work: they guaranteed the party a series of embankments and dikes. But the wave that was about to hit was much higher and more powerful than anyone had predicted. Boris Yeltsin's receipt of almost 6 million votes in Moscow was only one episode in the political upheaval that Gorbachev had consciously set in motion. The party apparat was forced to suffer dramatic defeats. The entire ruling groups in Leningrad, Kiev, and Moscow were rejected by the voters. Approximately thirty regional first secretaries were not elected. *Izvestia* talked about the "sensational" outcome in 168 districts, where although there were only one or two candidates, no one obtained an absolute majority when the votes were counted.

In the Baltic Republics the "popular fronts" won overwhelming majorities for their candidates. The local party leaders were also elected triumphally, in places like Estonia, if they had supported the claims of sovereignty expressed by the mass movements. Those who had opposed them won by a narrow margin or were voted down. It was no longer only a question of big cities. In the whole Russian Federal Republic, including the smaller provincial towns, the same tendencies were displayed. In the distant Far East the unknown Nanaian ethnologist, Yevdokia Gaer, would dramatically defeat the commander of the military region. Candidate member of the Politburo and first secretary of Leningrad, Yuri Solovyov, did not win election, even though he ran unopposed. By contrast, Politburo member Vitali Vorotnikov won in Voronezh, but after he had withdrawn from the territorial-republican district of Moscow, where he rightly feared the possible double competition of Boris Yeltsin and Andrei Sakharov. The list of examples goes on.

The electors had aimed their ballots with extraordinary precision. The conservatives were beaten wherever it was possible to run a true election campaign. Burning defeats were not only suffered everywhere by men in the apparat, but also by all of those who in some way stood out for their hostile stances toward glasnost and democratization. The example of the writer Yuri Bondarev applied to everyone. He was a candidate in a Volgograd district, and was beaten by a young functionary from the local Komsomol. The percentage of voter participation revealed the truth. Wherever people could debate more or less freely and voting was done in the new way, voter turnout ranged from 80 to 90 percent. The only places it was higher were in the Central Asian republics, in Azerbaijan, and in a few other regions, which reported a 96 to 97 percent turnout, as a result of old-style stuffing of the ballot boxes. It was obvious that in those republics the apparat had succeeded in almost completely quashing the law's innovative contents and electing its own hand-picked deputies. This became clear the moment the first session of the Congress began, when the delegations from those republics formed a noisy coalition against the minority of progressive deputies.

The political outcome was even more striking where the election campaign had been impeded by emergency situations. In Armenia, for example, the party resorted to every means, legal and illegal, to prevent the nomination of candidates from the Nagorno-Karabakh Committee—with the result that the voter turnout (we will never know whether the figures are "real") was only 71 percent, with an even lower 55 percent in Yerevan.

Mass politicization therefore exceeded all predictions of the apparats and of the reformers, who were expecting a more modest outcome. The first votes at the Congress, when the procedural battle began, showed immediately that a variable group of deputies, ranging in number from four hundred to eight hundred, followed an autonomous orientation and voted independently of the Presidium's instructions. This "variability" was the sign of a situation that was still extremely fluid, and the positions had not been consolidated. The political competition saw dozens of deputies ushered in by the vote. These were completely new, inexperienced faces, but because of this, they were not easily subordinated. In the debates, many of the deputies supported by the party, from the social organizations, disclosed extraordinarily independent judgment and the will to affirm the Congress's power. For the first time, many deputies brought with them a genuine public mandate, and had to respond to their electors. They knew they could not return home with their heads held high if they proved to be dominated by the party's decisions. Everything led one to believe that the first session of the Congress of People's Deputies was just the beginning of a complex process of maturation, differentiation, and consolidation of groups and tendencies that went far beyond groupings according to republic, territory, or nation.

Here I propose to point out the areas where action is needed.

The final months of 1988 and the first months of 1989 saw a serious worsening of the economic and social crises. The uncertainties and mistakes of the present compounded the legacy of the past. National revenue in the last quarter had grown an average of 3.6 percent a year—definitely below the plan's forecasts. The proclaimed effort to reroute choices in a social direction produced no results. There were some improvements in the area of construction, but the promise to give every Soviet family a home by the end of the century could not be achieved unless profound changes were made in organization and the management of production. The market for consumer goods and food was far below the minimum acceptable standard, and it grew worse from day to day.

The official figures signaling considerable increases in production were contradicted by day-to-day experience in every sector. The notorious *val* (gross production expressed in rubles) still ruled, offering fewer and fewer honest indicators. Enterprises and ministries fought with each other over their conflicting goals—the first fought for real autonomy, and the second fought to maintain their prerogatives. Both were allied in the misfortune of having to achieve the old plans, which were increasingly devoid of any real content. Entire categories of goods disappeared from production because they were no longer profitable for the enterprises. The prices of widely consumed goods increased uncontrollably. The plans were achieved—in rubles—but there were fewer goods for sale and they were more expensive. Salaries rose faster than the productivity of work, and the supply of money at families' disposal spread more quickly than the volume of goods and services that reached the "market." But a market, in the true sense of the word, still did not exist.

The industrial enterprises were now formally in the legal condition of *khozraschyot* (entrepreneurial autonomy), but they continued to have to fulfill state commissions, which often took up nearly all of their productive potential. Under these conditions, a market based on the means of production could not be formed. The enterprises themselves were obstructed by the bureaucracy, disliked by the public, subjected to the rackets of the underworld and the extortion of functionaries, and continuously threatened by crazy fiscal impositions and limitations of every sort.

The most serious problems continued to be in agriculture. It was disclosed that the Soviet government had to import approximately 30 billion rubles' worth of fruit and vegetables in three years. This burden was added to the almost 44 million tons of grain that had to be imported from Western farmers. "In many regions of the country," wrote *Pravda* in January, "farm production is not increasing: it's decreasing." For the first time it was disclosed that the Soviet government had a budget deficit. At first the official figure was 37 billion rubles. In June, Leonid Abalkin disclosed the true figure: more than 100 billion rubles. There were different causes for this imbalance, which was becoming even more serious at a disturbing rate. (The imbalance had existed at a more contained level in previous decades, but was hidden.) The main cause was the reduction in state income resulting from the drastic antialcohol campaign, which provoked a financial gap of about 30 billion rubles. But the consumption of alcohol had not, in fact, gone down. Millions of hectoliters of vodka were distilled illegally, and were at the origin of a colossal illegal market. Huge amounts of money accumulated in private hands, and powerful criminal bands arose that were mixed up with the mafias inside the distribution system. The mass media denounced an alarming spread of criminality, for which the interior minister provided the general statistical figure: up by 16.9 percent from 1988.

The government's valuable currency income—more than three-quarters of which derived from exporting oil and natural gas—was mowed down in the early 1980s by the sharp decrease in the international price of oil. This decrease led to the decision to decrease imports of consumer goods, food, medicine, and other types of prime necessities, further aggravating tensions between a growing demand, stimulated by families having more money available, and a diminishing supply. The "forced" savings piling up in the banks had already risen way above the dizzying mark of 300 billion rubles (without counting the sums "inside the mattress," which many Soviet economists assume was of similar proportions). In the judgment of economist Nikolai Shmelyov, to this you had to add the additional amount of 150 billion "hot" rubles, money that immediately sprouted up on the goods market in search of an outlet, often in vain. The official figure, which situated inflation at 2 percent per year, seemed much lower than reality.

In confronting this picture the central organizations for economic management appeared both powerless and stubbornly inclined to continue in their old habits. One example illustrates this. Despite the severe prohibitions of the Council of Ministers, the volume of state investments in unfinished works (mostly factories) rose to 13 billion rubles. The problems were thus clearly visible. But the identification of a solution was nowhere in sight— for political and ideological reasons, first of all, but also for reasons that we could call "cultural." Breaking the old mechanism of administrative control was difficult because of the resistance that its managers put in the way at every step. But even if it were possible to make such a break, it was still not clear which other mechanism could replace it.

One example can illustrate this. The most urgent issue was agriculture and food. A Central Committee plenum had been announced months before to come up with, Gorbachev would say, a "mediated concept," a "global approach." The continued postponements of the plenum (which would be convened in March) disclosed, however, that the shift to "new relations of production and property" in agriculture was not only doggedly blocked by the existing bureaucratic structures, in the center and in the provinces, but that too many problems were still undefined even in the minds of the most resolute reformers. The fact is that, as Gorbachev himself would admit, "We have very little experience in the system of setting prices. The same could be said about fiscal policy. For the time being, none of these aspects are regulated." Nor would they be after the March plenum, where radically different ideas clashed, and a compromise was reached that would not solve the problems.

Even the supporters of radical choices were forced to safeguard against the risks that insufficiently studied decisions could trigger. The most progressive experiments in farm production proved that the results could be extraordinary and could be achieved in a short time. This led to the request to actually abolish the plan's impositions and to allow farm enterprises to produce whatever they wanted and to sell when and where they pleased. But the inequalities between areas, republics, and farm enterprises were too great to ward off the implicit danger of shifting farm produce to a free market situation. There was too great a threat of dramatic shortages in the food supply of entire regions, which would cause an inevitable, though temporary, productive crisis and a huge increase in the prices of fruits and vegetables.

Thus, it was not easy to make quick and wise decisions, partly because of political obstacles. But time was running out, and the social crisis sharpened. The reform group was in the grip of a stranglehold that could suddenly tighten, joining political hostility and a growing discontent. While Gorbachev's international popularity experienced dramatic successes, as seen in his trips to Beijing, Bonn, and Paris, his prestige on the home front was quickly wearing thin. Among the progressive sectors of the widespread intelligentsia, a schizophrenic situation arose: there was a loss of confidence in the leader's will (or ability) to consistently follow the reform line, and the alarm of incumbent dangers, since in spite of everything, it was clear that Gorbachev was the last hope.

To paraphrase a famous remark by the Marquis de Custine, one must come to Russia to realize "what someone who can do everything cannot do." The thousand paradoxes of the situation included Gorbachev's personal role. He had immense power, on which limits had to be set. He showed that he realized this and wanted to proceed in this direction. Democratizing the country necessarily implied breaking the authoritarian mold. But he had to use the power he commanded—and even reinforce it—or else be defeated by powerful forces, opposed to each other and equally uncontrollable, which perestroika itself evoked and spurred into combat. The unification of the offices of general secretary of the party and president of the Supreme Soviet, which Gorbachev had wanted, outwardly reproposed past models. True, he had done this for different purposes: to maintain his grip on an extraordinarily difficult battle; to directly guide the shift of powers from the party to the state; to remove himself from the conditioning of the Central Committee, establishing the investiture of the "boss" by a new parliament elected by the people, whose sovereignty was superior to the party's. The Nineteenth Conference instituted the principle of succession, rigorously establishing a maximum of two consecutive terms for every office, including the top office. There should no longer be "lifetime" leaders. But at times Gorbachev was "forced" by his own strategy to emphasize the authoritarian side of himself and his role. Thus, the suspicion spread even among many of his supporters that he had imminent Bonapartist ambitions. To follow him in this operation unconditionally implied having complete faith not only in his "good intentions," but also in his strategy.

Therefore, the questions regarding Gorbachev's strategy during this phase became one of the crucial issues. The "rule-of-law socialist state," launched at the Nineteenth Conference, was in principle clearly a radical change, and may have been one of perestroika's most substantial conceptual "revisions." But between the fall of 1988 and the summer of 1989, this issue became the focus of a new compromise. The election law and the revisions of the

Constitution were studied to guarantee that the party's role not be jeopardized. For different reasons, which in this case were not conflicting, the ideas of the party's radical reform group and the ideas of the moderate conservative group converged on this point. The latter group, not to be confused with the extreme right-wing faction, fought for a "cosmetic-technocratic" perestroika, one that would not affect political power relations and the party's guiding role.

Gorbachev's team realized that the rule-of-law state implied a substantial revision of the party's role in society, but it was equally convinced that the party was, and for an entire historical phase would remain, the "only" unifying instrument that could guide the transformation process. The team clearly thought that "this party" could not do it; it would take a profound renewal, and glasnost had to be asserted as a means of permanent control over the party, while the party had to be stripped of its current governmental functions. Gorbachev thus sought to achieve a gentle shift, repeating the tactical moves he had perfected in the four preceding years.

But as the clash grew more bitter and the strategies grew clearer, Gorbachev had to realize that he could not win by staying shut up inside his palace. "The fate of perestroika is in the hands of the people," he said at the conclusion of the January 1987 plenum. After that he repeated his appeal to the people several times. Now, at the most critical moment, it seemed clear that the processes triggered had overtaken and upset all previous balances. The 26 March elections proved that glasnost had produced irreversible results. The "restitution of politics to the Soviet citizens" had set into motion a machine that moved independently of the demiurge's will. At the same time the party did not succeed in restructuring itself and fell out of step with the whirlwind politicization sweeping through the whole of Soviet society. Up to what point was Gorbachev able to confront the new conditions? For four years he had shown uncommon tactical and conceptual flexibility, clearly manifesting the evolution of his concepts. But this "moment of truth" could not be compared with the previous ones. Gorbachev would not have become general secretary if he had not been a product—atypical though he may be—of the very machine he aimed to change.

The signals that Gorbachev sent to the country in this phase were contradictory, now showing a genuine weariness in adapting to the new situation. The conceptual leap was now truly substantial, and the Soviet leader showed at times a serious blurring of his horizon and unusually slow reflexes. However, the significance of the outcome of the 26 March vote did not escape him, nor did the opportunity to utilize it. He recognized its "positivity," bluntly urging the party to "learn the necessary lessons." The sovereign voice of the people had spoken, affirming that it was not subject to higher judgment.

At the April plenum he dramatically forced 110 old members off the Central Committee: deadweight that had encumbered every decision for four years. This was a clear response to the popular vote. But the debate at the plenum proved that "those who remain" were no less hostile or worried than those who left. Gorbachev decided to publish the transcript of all the speeches "so that the party and the country will know." He bared his opponents, unveiling their weaknesses and their aggressions. At the same time, he reassured them by postponing the elections for the republican and regional soviets until the following spring: a new consultation with the voters too soon would have turned into a catastrophe for the local parties' ruling groups.

The other exceptionally important signal was the decision to broadcast live all the proceedings of the first session of the Congress of People's Deputies. It was a shrewd decision. No one knew better than Gorbachev the real power relations inside the assembly. Allowing it to proceed behind closed doors would have meant exposing himself to serious compromise. Showing all to millions of Soviets would be a way of forcing the conservatives to moderate their pressure and diminish their importance. This effect was obtained.

There were more reformers than even they themselves had realized. Their offensive, while uncertain and full of mistakes, forced the majority of deputies to meet defeat more than once in those fifteen fatal days. A formidable battle unraveled before a multitude of television viewers, who, after four years of glasnost, had become more astute. But Gorbachev's decision cut two ways. In his own way, once things were done, the Soviet leader confirmed that he knew the power relations better than any of the others, but he had not taken into account all of the new factors involved in the situation. In fact, he succeeded in achieving all his goals: to become the indisputable head of the country, beyond party control; to prove that no one, on the right or on the left, could do without his presence in the leadership of the country and of the party; to further weaken many conservative leaders, who were openly and repeatedly confronted by the perestroika deputies; finally, to involve the newly elected Congress in the responsibility for managing the crisis.

The party's power remained substantially intact, but now public pressure would have two different targets. Still, his victory would not help his "great dialogue" with the country. He had triumphed in the Congress, but before the eyes of his fellow citizens, he showed his limits—his own and those imposed by circumstance. The transformation of the Congress into an assembly called on to ratify decisions made by the party; the inversion of the agenda's logic, with the elections for the most important offices in the new parliament—including the Supreme Soviet—starting with a programmatic debate; the stubborn insistence with which he, conceding everything to the apparats, imposed the duplication of state and party functions on the assembly; the refusal to accept under any circumstances alternative candidates, even when this would not have posed any threat to those who had been nominated (epitomized in the extraordinary episode of Deputy Nikolai Obolensky nominating himself for president of the Supreme Soviet, a motion rejected by Gorbachev and by the Congress). All of these episodes fell like a burning rain of disappointment on the hopes of "outside" observers, who had been told—and this would be repeated in the final resolution—that the Congress of People's Deputies had assumed "the full powers of the state."

These hopes were certainly naive, and were themselves born of an inadequate assessment of actual power relations, resulting from the lack of democratic experience of the huge masses that were entering politics now for the first time. But now they too constituted a fact of reality, more powerful than in the whole previous history of Russia. As Igor Klyamkin wrote in *Moskovskiye Novosti*:

> To become a reformer, with the intention of making radical decisions, the candidate is forced to limit himself or herself to half-measures, to be skillful, to maneuver, to look for a consensus of a broad strata of public opinion through insignificant concessions, to make promises that cannot be kept, and, as a result, to lose popularity and authority.[1]

The drama was all in this contradiction, present since the beginning of perestroika, but that now became disruptive after four years of extraordinary changes, not all of which were positive. Faced by such conditions, the proud statement that "the party was the one to get perestroika started" was no longer enough, since there were now too many people demanding an explanation from the party for having led the country into the unprecedented crisis that was violently shaking it.

This crisis in the first half of 1989 carried indications of a downward spiral. The politicization of the masses in the most progressive areas of the country led to an increase in separatist movements. But to this alarming fact was added a new element, caused by the decline in the real standards of living of broad masses of the people: social revolt. The Fergana massacre in Uzbekistan, whose victims were Meskhet Turks, resulted from an explosive mix of elementary social claims, religious activism, and a subversive political Jacquerie made up of organized mafias, state powers, and party fringes. The Novy Uzen revolt in Kazakhstan showed even more clearly the social consequences of glasnost, even if everywhere—from Central Asia, to the Caucasus, to the Baltic—all the social and economic demands were triggered by national claims. The Novy Uzen Kazakhs rose up against the Caucasians, the Uzbeks against the Meskhet Turks, the Azerbaijanis against the Armenians, and the Georgians against the Abkhazes because they could not distinguish between the violation of their elementary needs and the violation of their traditions and their history. The Soviet Union was a container holding dozens of similar latent conflicts that were ready to explode. The economic reform itself would inevitably cause a new series of unprecedented social and territorial imbalances. From 12 to 15 million jobs would be "gotten rid of" by the end of the century as a result of the projected development of productive technology, adding to the already serious tensions in the labor market in areas with high rates of population growth.

Gorbachev had tried to avoid having to face the problems all at the same time. But the circumstances were imposing a different setting for the fight. And each of the episodes of national, social, or religious conflict became the occasion for organized attempts at subversion, "warnings" to the center to give up on its reform program. The Tbilisi drama was the clearest symptom, just as Sumgait had been at the beginning of 1988. Since then the death toll had reached and surpassed three hundred. These deaths were still far from the European cities in the USSR, in regions and republics where "life was worth less." But it would take much less blood in any of the cities on the Baltic, in any Ukrainian or Byelorussian square, to destabilize the situation beyond every limit that could be tolerated by the current political order.

The powerful grip squeezing the reform groups, inside and outside the party, kept increasing its pressure. Everything led one to predict that unless steel obstacles were set in the way, it could crush them along with the moderate conservatives. Having no leaders or alternative strategies, the latter were only worried about defending their own power, and blocking the necessary economic and political transformations. The return to a tranquil stagnation was not, in fact, a possible alternative. The economic and social conditions for this no longer existed. Questions could no longer be answered with paternalism or politics because the people had no more fear and no more patience. What is the possible alternative to the reform? asked Aleksandr Yakovlev, the man who perhaps more than anyone helped to found the "new thinking":

> We might not be able to create the new? We might be afraid of facing certain difficulties? Then destructive tendencies in the economic and political and moral sphere can reach levels that in a certain sense can no longer be corrected. Then there could be the threat not just of a return to the past, to the times of stagnation of the conscience, but rather an aggressive conservativism that will celebrate its victory. The Communists of a great party have to see and must understand this. [2]

That this was no exaggeration could be seen during the congress when Chervonopisky, an invalid from the war in Afghanistan, jumped up to the podium to unleash an offensive against Andrei Sakharov (and against Gorbachev) by uttering three watchwords that could not have better represented the alternative being prepared in the event of perestroika's defeat: "Power, Homeland, Communism." He spoke on behalf of an alliance among the dogmatists, the right wing of the apparat, and the pro-Russian, anti-Semitic, chauvinistic, and anti-Western tendencies that openly sought a consensus in the army. They were the modern Black Hundreds—Pamyat (to which writers like Rasputin and Belov more or less consciously lent an intellectual veneer), and the "Marxist-Leninist" model Nina Andreyeva. It would be the end of détente, a Tiananmen Square of shocking proportions. For the reform forces, for the enlightened leadership that in 1985 promoted a revolution "from above" because "there was no other way," the time to choose had come. It was only logical that the moment would come in which another revolution, "from below," would begin to stir. On 26 March we learned that the reform was in truth a mass movement representing sentiments that had remained alive in Soviet society. The desire for reform had been repressed, suffocated, blocked, subject to violence, and to paternalism, and had been restrained by the hypocritical belief that the people still had to "learn" democracy. This was why they were kept chained to the first step, awaiting the time that it was hoped would never come. This is the force the reformers can count on, if they wish to win. And with which they must not lose touch if they do not want to suffer a glaring defeat.

But there is also less time in which to decide. Now time must be measured in months, not in years. Can and will Gorbachev abruptly accelerate reform, toward the market, toward a definitive opening of the country, toward a confederation of autonomous states, and at the same time, toward a drastic reform of the political system, which shifts the center of power to the new parliament, and sanctions the separation of powers? We join Klyamkin in saying that "the next months will show the true dimensions of Gorbachev's personality." He was never the only actor in this great tragedy, whom all the world watches with bated breath. But he is the prime protagonist. And he cannot make a mistake. If he succeeds, and how can we not wish that, a completely new phase will begin, full of difficulties and sorrow, but also of new hope. If he does not succeed, his prophecy will still hold true: whoever comes after him, maybe not immediately, maybe after the interruption of an unspeakable tragedy, will have to do what Gorbachev could not. Perestroika is a long road.

CHAPTER 11

THE FINAL MONTHS OF 1989: CAN THE CENTER HOLD?

•   •   •

At this point the reader must already realize that some of the questions we raised have been answered in the months following the first session of the Congress of People's Deputies. These answers are partial, and embryonic, but they serve as important indicators of how the situation might evolve. Even as I deliver these final pages to the editor, the situation in the Soviet Union is developing rapidly, but the sequence of current events is so overwhelming that I cannot resist making a final attempt to update my chronicle. Still, I realize that by the time the book comes out, other crucial events might have already greatly altered the balance of power in the country as well as its political and social situation.

The second half of 1989 was one of the most turbulent and difficult phases in the four years of Gorbachev's rule. Public debate at the Supreme Soviet over the composition of the new government—most of which was televised—represented a clear proof of renewal. Never before had ministers been subject to such relentless scrutiny. This included even the heads of the most secret and inaccessible ministries, Politburo members, and the head of the KGB. The members of the new Supreme Soviet had been elected by a predominantly conservative Congress, but they demonstrated an ability to play politics that contradicted Yuri Afanasev's curt descriptions in his speech to the Congress.

Although the new Supreme Soviet could definitely be steered by the reformists, moderates, or conservatives in the party leadership, it could hardly be compared to a Stalinist-Brezhnevite assembly that would rubber-stamp the party's proposals. A majority rejected nine ministers, and voted down the nominee for first vice president, Vladimir Kalashnikov. Kalashnikov, the former first secretary of Volgograd, had delivered one of the most insidious and openly hostile attacks on the general secretary's line at the April plenum. While this episode may seem secondary, it was highly significant from a variety of viewpoints. First, it proved that the new body representing the will of the people could overrule a decision that had been made behind the closed doors of the Politburo and the Central Committee. Moreover, the decision to appoint Kalashnikov had heralded important consequences for the hierarchy of power in the top leadership. He was the new man being promoted by the conservatives and had been accepted by the reformers as part of a difficult compromise. His position in the new government would have placed him at the same level as Yuri Maslyukov: in other words, he was poised to become at least a candidate member of the Politburo as soon as the occasion arose. The Supreme Soviet's decision upset the pact and altered the balances within the party leadership. Gorbachev did not miss this opportunity. While he and Ryzhkov had defended and ultimately imposed some disputed candidates, they heeded the protests against Kalashnikov and others. The Supreme Soviet has made its decision? Then we must yield to its will.

This was not the only indication that Gorbachev was exploiting the new situation of "dual powers" to push the apparat conservatives into a corner. The second important episode was the Supreme Soviet's debate over the Baltic Republics' proposal for economic autonomy, which took place at the end of June. The proposal was clearly contrary to the existing Constitution, but turning it down would have sent a negative and dangerous signal to the Baltic peoples. Gorbachev was strongly opposed to the People's Congress making "hurried" decisions on constitutional reform. Thus, it was decided to confront the issue later on in a more systematic way, in light of the laws that were being drafted on ownership of land, autonomy of enterprises, civil liberties, etc. Yet in this case the Soviet leader supported a major exception. The Supreme Soviet formally authorized the Baltic Republics to take all the necessary steps to institute "entrepreneurial autonomy" beginning 1 January 1990.

Another significant development took place by means of a Supreme Soviet decision: the republics were authorized to hold elections for their own and the local soviets, "at the times and with the modalities they consider opportune." This was another sharp break with a pact approved by the Central Committee immediately after the damage suffered by the party in the 26 March elections. The apparats had been thrown into a panic by the popular vote. They reacted angrily by demanding, maybe even imposing, postponement of the fall 1989 local elections—set by the Nineteenth Conference—until spring 1990. In the meantime, a new election law could be passed that was even more restrictive than the current law (possibly reserving quotas for the party, like the Polish model) and that would prevent the formation of parliaments in the republics and regions that the party could not control.

Gorbachev agreed to this demand, well aware that many of the party organizations, which had already been upset by the first defeat and were obviously incapable of practicing politics under the new conditions, could not withstand a new set of elections. This compromise gave the apparats enough time to reorganize and prepare for the battle with a new set of mechanisms for narrowing down and selecting candidates. But it also worked well with the Soviet president's plans. Gorbachev, in fact, was aiming for both a development of the political reform and a transferral of power from the party committees to the local soviets, but in gradual and controlled ways. At the same time, he could present himself to the apparats as the "guarantor" of their safety, thereby strengthening his position as general secretary of the party. As he would say a few months later in Kiev, when he dismissed the last Brezhnevite dinosaur, Vladimir Shcherbitsky, "We will not abandon the party to scorn."

But Gorbachev, faced by the public pressure expressed by the Baltic deputies and the most resolute reformers, chose a route that was more flexible and more intricate. He granted the republics' parliaments the de facto freedom to approve separate election guidelines for the local soviets and to hold elections at different times. In this way, it became the responsibility of each of the party's ruling groups in the provinces to assess its own capacity to handle the situation. Whoever considered themselves ready to face a democratic trial was authorized to do so. Whoever wanted to take their time could do so. Whoever wanted to impose more restrictive election laws would have to accept full responsibility, and in the event of a defeat, pay the consequences. Gorbachev removed the protective shield of the center and applied the standard of "decentering the responsibilities." It was a telling move: the Soviet leader was quickly realizing that he could no longer support the demands of the most reactionary sectors of the apparat, nor could he accept the idea of a slow and gradual transformation of the party's role. The social processes were evolving too quickly, while the apparat lagged even further behind both politically and psychologically.

The inevitable consequence of these dramatic developments was a sudden acceleration of the struggle inside the party leadership. The April plenum (the entire proceedings of which had been published in *Pravda* at Gorbachev's insistence) had underlined the anguish of the apparats, which seems to have peaked at the end of June. Rumors circulated that a new plenum was forthcoming. This plenum did not take place, for the conflicts were too sharp. Gorbachev may have sensed the risk of an attack from the center; as he had after the April 1988 Nina Andreyeva affair, he avoided convening the ruling body in order not to risk a possible *coup de main* by "discontented majorities." But while the question of how to settle the conflicts in the party leadership was being decided on, the Kuzbass miners' strike erupted on 10 July. Once again, reality acted as a reminder that the political struggle could no longer

302

be carried on behind closed doors. In a matter of a few days, the strike spread from western Siberia to Donbass, from Vorkuta to Kazakhstan. The long-feared "social question" exploded in all its virulence. Gorbachev was caught off guard, as was the rest of the leadership, but his reaction was timely. Their form of protest was unacceptable, he said, but their demands were legitimate and justified. No efforts were made to repress the movement, and negotiations between the government and the miners were aimed at meeting the strikers' political and economic demands.

At the same time, the Soviet president turned necessity into a virtue and used the issue of the miners at the Central Committee. On 10 July he convened a broadened meeting in Moscow of almost all the plenum members, including the new party leaders from the provinces who had been elected after the Twenty-Seventh Congress but had not yet had a chance to attend a plenum. Once again the public was able to read the stenographer's report of the proceedings in *Pravda*. The vast majority of the speeches revealed the extent of the hostility of top-ranking party officials to the general secretary's policies. This time around there were speeches by many Politburo members who had remained silent during the session of the Congress of People's Deputies. The conservatives expressed themselves openly. Even Nikolai Ryzhkov, rightly considered a supporter of reform, gave a contradictory speech fraught with grave misgivings, and containing a surprising reprimand to Gorbachev to perform his role as general secretary more fully. Perhaps Ryzkhov had not switched sides, but a Moscow intelletual described his intervention as "a speech by someone who has not yet realized that he's shifted over to the opposition." This was a sign that the unity of the Politburo itself was substantially shaken. Ligachev made no secret about his positions. He actually opened with an obvious gesture to the military, making himself their spokesperson, defending their prestige and warning his countrymen not to lower their guard against foreign enemies. This was language from another time, an unmistakable sign that he was on the lookout for right-wing allies. To this he added a harsh criticism that socialist values had been "sold out," and he defended to the bitter end the party's guiding role in the state, thereby rejecting the shifting of power from the party to the Supreme Soviet—the new parliament—and from the party committees to the local soviets.

Gorbachev's reply on this occasion was severe. Faced by an unprecedented offensive, not only did he not retreat, but he went on the counterattack. Stopping this process was impossible and unthinkable. The cadres had only two possible choices: either to act in accordance with the country's demands, and therefore renew their ranks and enter the political struggle under the new conditions, or to go. He brusquely announced that new changes in the leadership would be necessary. The "team" that had launched perestroika in April 1985 no longer existed, and the Politburo's current membership could no longer meet the needs of the situation. It would take him two more months to keep this commitment, but Gorbachev would prove that he was not throwing words to the wind. There was a further sign that the Soviet leader was "correcting" his marching plans. In these same days he announced the decision to import 10 billion rubles' worth of consumer goods (equal to almost $16 billion worth at the official rate of exchange). Pressed by public malaise, Gorbachev seemed to perceive the need for emergency decisions, exactly as the "radical" economists had requested during the congressional debates. In fact, it was increasingly clear that even if the decisions that were approved broke clearly with the system of administrative command of the economy, the results would not be perceived by the population for another two or three years. In the meantime, the imbalances that arose during the transition provoked a loud public outcry.

A short time later the government announced another truly revolutionary decision originally proposed by the radical economists: to make cash purchases of grain that had "exceeded the plan" from the kolkhozes and sovkhozes. But this decision would not produce immediate results either, and Gorbachev wanted to give the party and the country a more immediate signal. Yuri Solovyov, a candidate member of the Politburo and the first secretary of Leningrad—Nina Andreyeva's "only candidate"—was dismissed from his post four months after he had been inexorably rejected by his constituents.

All of these signals were meant to satisfy the demands of the left and of public pressure "from below." But this was not enough to prevent a "radical" minority from deciding to stop postponing and to form an opposition group in the parliament in July. Approximately 400 deputies met at the Cinema House and founded the Interregional Group. Deputies with different orientations joined, but they were united in the conviction that it was time to move rapidly toward a showdown with the party apparat and to make radical decisions regarding the economy and politics. Their decisions were often contradictory, as could be seen in their two days of debates and when they elected their leaders. A five-member board of directors, and not Boris Yeltsin by himself, would guide the huge squad that had done battle in the Congress and in the first session of the Supreme Soviet. The five directors (Boris Yeltsin, Yuri Afanasev, Gavriil Popov, Andrei Sakharov, and Viktor Palm) represented the different "spirits" of this heterogeneous opposition in search of a unifying strategy. Their demands included a speedy reconvening of the Congress in early September. They could have legally imposed such a decision with 450 signatures (20 percent of the Congress's deputies), but their actual numbers totaled fewer than 400 deputies. Boris Yeltsin launched the idea of a special party congress before the year's end to elect a completely new Central Committee. A few weeks later Gorbachev's reply arrived: the party's Twenty-Eighth Congress would be moved ahead, but to the fall of 1990. A long-distance dialogue, with frequent skirmishes, was kept up between Gorbachev and the radicals. During the days at the Cinema House, to the surprise of the participants in this historical meeting, an appearance was made by Yevgeni Primakov, recently elevated to the chairmanship of the Supreme Soviet.

In the meantime, the Armenian and Azerbaijan republics were quickly sliding into civil war. Georgians and Abkhazes were killing each other, and the army had to intervene to prevent Georgians and the Southern Ossets from doing the same. Monstrous pogroms of Turkic Meskhetes took place in Uzbekistan. National and linguistic clashes broke out in Moldavia. Centrifugal forces were rapidly overwhelming the desperate attempts being made to consolidate and find political compromises.

In August the congressional commission chaired by Aleksandr Yakovlev made public its conclusions: the secret protocols attached to the Molotov-Ribbentrop pact actually existed. The Baltic Republics marked the fiftieth anniversary of one of Stalinism's darkest pages with massive public demonstrations, but in a climate different from those of bitter recrimination in the past. Contrary to the expectations of many, Moscow had proven its courage and its commitment to glasnost. The recognition of this historical truth brought one whole chapter to an honorable conclusion while it opened another: now the Latvian, Estonian, and Lithuanian peoples (as well as Bessarabia and part of the present-day Ukraine) had a legal claim for national independence. Gorbachev had no choice: Silence would mean contradicting the very bases of democratization and glasnost. Continued silence would lead to the grave risk of an even more dramatic split. The Kremlin reformers could not allow a change in the Soviet borders, but now they hoped to contain claims for independence through the broad autonomy they had been prepared to grant the three Baltic Republics. It was a step in the right direction, but the new democratic institutions—the Congress and the Supreme Soviet—did not have the necessary prestige or power to achieve the difficult task of bringing peace to the country.

The plenum on national problems took place in September. It had first been announced in early 1988, repeatedly postponed, and prepared amid almost two years of turmoil during which the national question literally exploded. The plenum would not have the last word on a subject that, in effect, was inextricably tied to other unresolved problems in the Soviet Union. For that matter, no one expected Gorbachev to be able to go beyond general indications of how, in the future, to solve the problems that flung peoples and nations against each other in a gravely ill country. On the whole, the party still did not have the tools—particularly the cultural tools—to grasp the full meaning of such a huge issue. An organic solution would imply deep changes in the status of the republics (in the Russian Federal Republic first of all), in the relations between the republics and the autonomous republics and regions (possibly even a surpassing of the "three-tiered hierarchy" that had produced such venomous results and that today revealed its true nature as an instrument of central power that aimed to divide in order to dominate). All of these issues would have to be dealt with in the massive reform of the country's Constitution that the People's Congress was in the process of drafting. Gorbachev's method was to search for a consensus among the national groups, which would not be easy to obtain without provoking further clashes, and perhaps tragedies, because the groups are all at different stages of national and cultural development, making different demands, and above all, contaminated by decades of mutual aggression. It was thus useless to expect miracles in the short term. The national question will remain on perestroika's agenda for years to come.

However, the September plenum had a surprise for many observers. The Soviet president, who was apparently facing difficulty on every front, succeeded in keeping his July promise. In one fell blow, three men were gone from the Politburo: the elderly Shcherbitsky, the last of the Brezhnevite old guard, and Viktor Chebrikov and Viktor Nikonov, two men from the "team" that had emerged at the party's helm after 1985. In one stroke Gorbachev was freed from the burden of three negative (or permanently uncertain) votes in the party's top decision-making body. At the same time, the new head of the KGB, Vladimir Kryuchkov, and the president of Gosplan, Yuri Maslyukov, were promoted to full membership, and Boris Pugo and Yevgeni Primakov became candidate members, creating the most conspicuous modification in the top leadership since the beginning of perestroika. This time the new men could in all likelihood be considered proreform, even if it would be hasty to call them all "Gorbachev's men." Even though men with a questionable commitment to radical change kept their positions, Gorbachev still succeeded in his intent to place a generally more trustworthy and less discredited team at the helm.

Other changes at the high and intermediate levels could be expected in the months to come. A new ruling class was now approaching the threshold of power, no longer waiting for an invitation through the traditional inner workings of the party. Instead, they were propelled upward by popular consensus, formed in the cross fire of an electoral battle that the old cadres were not even capable of attempting. Many of the new faces were party members, but their consciousness of their rights and power was immeasurably different from that of the old leaders. Gorbachev had to take this into account when he looked for solutions to the myriad organizational problems awaiting him. If it was indeed possible to solve the party's prestige problem, this could apparently be done by giving leadership roles to the men who had received the public consensus in the elections. But it would not be easy. The transition toward a new alignment of power, even if all were to go well, would take place in a nonlinear way amid thousands of skirmishes and battles. Moreover, individuals who could not be controlled by party logic were now a permanent presence. They had gained enough prestige and force to influence the course of events, and consequently they accepted huge responsibilities.

Gorbachev was the absolute protagonist of these events, but now he shared the burden of not being able to take one false step with Boris Yeltsin, Andrei Sakharov, Yuri Afanasev, and many, many more. Together they had to face not just a social and political crisis unprecedented in the country's history, not just the inertia and the distrust of a work force that now had to be persuaded to work, whose approval had to be won back in the hypothesis of reconstruction, but also the extremist and irrational movements, and the expectations of speedy solutions. And they had to respond to the moves made by powerful and unsuppressed adversaries who still occupied powerful positions throughout the bureaucracy, and moves made by fools who, like naive adventurers, always chose to express themselves during the difficult moments of transition between one society and another. It took Viktor Afanasev's last dramatic "mistake"—the publication of a report in an Italian newspaper packed with falsehoods regarding Yeltsin's trip to the United States—to convince the Politburo to replace the editor in chief of *Pravda*. His mistake was not so much in publishing a false report, as in not realizing that even if it were true, it would still increase Boris Yeltsin's popularity. This was a classic episode that recalled a famous saying by Mao Zedong, that reactionaries lift boulders above their heads to . . . let them crash to their feet.

The final months of 1989 marked a further political radicalization in every direction—not just on the left, but also on the right. There were now separatists inside the Communist Party as a result of the national movements. When in mid-January the vast majority of Lithuanian Communists decided to form a party independent of Moscow, the Central Committee was faced by a clear-cut choice: either to forcibly block the secession or to accept it as a *fait accompli*. Gorbachev was able to reject the first alternative with the support of a segment of the apparat, and he flew to Vilna to persuade the Lithuanian Communists to wait. But his undertaking proved impossible, and the Soviet leader was only able to get them to postpone for a few more months. In the same days, the Lithuanian Supreme Soviet proclaimed a multiparty system, on a collision course with the present Constitution of the

USSR. A similar declaration was approved by the Central Committee of the Estonian Communist Party. But the Communist diaspora was now being expressed in the form of currents, groups, and factions that openly entered the field. The establishment of the Interregional Group marked the birth of a left-wing opposition, both in the Congress and in the party. Its "parliamentary" forces decreased steadily, however, from almost 400 deputies at the end of July to 158 at the end of December. Internal divisions in the group, divergent strategies by its leaders, and outright errors of political judgment (such as the decision to declare a December strike in opposition to article 6 of the Constitution, granting the party the guiding role) certainly helped to weaken its role. The death of Andrei Sakharov heightened the crisis of the radical groups. But when he had brought the issue of single-party rule up for debate, it lost by only a few votes; the same vote in Congress showed almost 900 deputies in favor of a historical revision of the Constitution to take away the Communist Party's monopoly of power.

The first embryo of a Russian nationalist party, the Rossiya Club, was created in October. This organization was a right-wing faction of the Communist Party, founded by twenty-eight deputies who appealed to the Congress in openly Stalinistic terms. But their initiative was supported by magazines such as *Nash Sovremennik* and *Molodaya Gvardia*, as well as by newspapers like *Sovetskaya Rossia* and *Literaturnaya Rossia*. They were joined by organizations such as the Writers' Union of the RSFSR, the All-Union Foundation for Culture, and antiperestroika political movements such as the United Front of Russian Workers. These were the same forces that the first secretary of the Leningrad Party, Boris Ghidaspov, led in demonstrations at the end of November. They had clear supporters inside the Central Committee and among the bulging ranks of regional first secretaries who openly challenged the general secretary's policies. Thus, Gorbachev was faced by a new situation, lacking the only "tool for unification" he had at his disposition. It was an uncertain and resistant tool, but nevertheless the respository of much real power. Under these conditions the Soviet leader ran the risk of going to the party congress—which had been moved ahead to the fall of 1990—too weakened to be able to effect changes in the leadership in harmony with his policies.

Between December 1989 and January 1990, the Azerbaijan crisis deteriorated into open civil war, forcing Gorbachev to call for military intervention in Baku to prevent further pogroms against the Armenians, war between the two republics, and in all likelihood, the armed secession of Azerbaijan under the leadership of the Popular Front. As the Soviet Union entered the new decade, it was like a powder keg surrounded by crazed torchbearers. The country's economic situation was long past the point of collapse. Gorbachev's efforts to begin a radical shift toward economic reform between fall and summer was initially tolerated by the conservatives and then rejected. The reformer Leonid Abalkin, brought into the government to spearhead this move, was surrounded by moderates and procrastinators dominated by conservative pressures—men such as Nikolai Ryzhkov, the chairman of Gosplan, and Nikolai Slyunkov, head of the reform inside the Politburo. While the country plunged into chaos, the men directly responsible for the basic economic decisions were able to postpone until the following spring the discussion of the package of reform laws on property, rents, land, and finance. The instructions that Ryzkhov gave first to the Supreme Soviet and then to the Congress, on 13 December, indicated his stubborn wish to preserve for three more years a centralized economic system and to postpone until 1993 the shift to a "socialist market." Through Pavel Bunic the radicals would ask in vain that the reform be enacted starting 1 January 1990. The intermediate proposal by Abalkin (and by Gorbachev) to limit the preparatory period to one year, and effect the new norms at the end of 1991, would not be accepted either. The apparat proved deaf to every rational consideration. They had become the exponents of a reaction that pervaded the middle and upper strata of managerial and ministerial personnel: in the centers of administrative command, they had clearly understood that their power was irrevocably threatened by radical reform. Abalkin's dismay was visible when he clearly illustrated the situation at the end of three days of debate with more than fourteen hundred economic managers convened in Moscow in mid-November: "I was psychologically prepared for pressure from the radicals, from those who say we are moving too slowly, that we are talking about half-measures. What happened instead is that the pressure came only from the conservative forces." The problem had come to the fore. Tens of thousand of industrial managers realized that they did not have the required skills to face the market and competition. Tens of thousands of kolkhoz and sovkhoz managers saw themselves as feudal landowners. The 417 deputies from farm areas who during the first session of the Congress had approved a common appeal for moderate reform, now lined up behind Ligachev. They did not have an alternative strategy, and they had nothing more to propose to the country than the maintenance of the status quo. But they were united in their defense of their powers and their privileges. They worked, unconsciously, to make Nikolai Shmelyov's prophecy come true.

Chronology of Events
Mentioned in the Text

1917
February and October revolutions.

1917–21
Civil War.

1921
New Economic Policy (NEP) put into effect.

1924
Lenin dies.

1928
End of NEP; first five-year plan; beginning of collectivization of agriculture.

1934
Kirov murdered.

1936
Start of Great Terror and show trials of Old Bolsheviks.

1939
Molotov-Ribbentrop pact.

1940
Trostky murdered.

1941
22 June: Nazi troops invade USSR.

1941–45
Great Patriotic War.

1953
5 March: Stalin dies.

1956
Twentieth Party Congress: Khrushchev delivers "Secret Speech" on the crimes of Stalin.

1964
Brezhnev succeeds Khrushchev.

1979
Soviet military intervention in Afghanistan begins.

1982
Andropov succeeds Brezhnev.

1983
March: Ronald Reagan's "evil empire" speech.

November: United States deploys intermediate-range nuclear weapons in Europe.

1984
Chernenko succeeds Andropov.

1985
11 March: Gorbachev succeeds Chernenko.

6 August: Beginning of USSR unilateral moratorium on nuclear testing.

19–21 November: Geneva summit.

1986
Staging of Shatrov's play *The Dictatorship of the Conscience*.

26 February–6 March: Twentieth Party Congress.

26 April: Chernobyl disaster.

28 May: Announcement of two resolutions against unearned income.

30 August: Arrest of Nicholas Daniloff.

11–12 October: Reykjavik summit.

20 November: Afghanistan leader Babrak Karmal replaced by Najibullah.

17–18 December: Riots in Alma-Ata following Kunayev's forced retirement from Kazakhstan Central Committee.

19 December: Andrei Sakharov released from internal exile.

1987
Publication of Rybakov's novel *Children of the Arbat*, Akhmatova's poem *Requiem*; general distribution of Abuladze's film *Repentance*.

January: Plenum of the CPUS that opens the way to "democratization" of Soviet Society.

January: End of jamming of BBC and most other Western radio broadcasts.

1 January: New policies go into effect easing restrictions on travel, allowing certain sectors to directly manage exports, introducing salary reform, introducing Gospriyomka quality-control system.

13 January: Introduction of procedures allowing joint enterprises with Western and developing countries.

9 February: Talks with China on border dispute (first of their kind since 1979).

10–21 February: Release of 140 political prisoners.

26 February: End of unilateral Soviet moratorium on nuclear testing, after 569 days and after twenty-six nuclear tests carried out by United States.

1 May: Law permitting individual work activities in twenty-nine basic sectors goes into effect.

6 May: Demonstration of nationalist group Pamyat.

28 May: Mathias Rust lands in Red Square.

July: Series of protests by Crimean Tatars.

23 August: Demonstrations in Latvia, Lithuania, and Estonia on anniversary of Nazi-Soviet nonagression pact.

2 November: In major speech to mark the upcoming seventieth anniversary of the October revolution, Gorbachev praised Khrushchev, called guilt of

Stalin "unforgivable," and announced commissions to reexamine victims of Stalin's purges and to revise the history of the Communist Party of the Soviet Union.

7–10 December: Washington summit; signing of Intermediate-Range Nuclear Forces Treaty.

1988

Publication of Pasternak's *Dr. Zhivago*, Bulgakov's *Heart of a Dog*, Shalamov's *Kolyma Tales*, Grossman's *Life and Fate*, and Zamyatin's *We*.

1 January: Introduction of New Economic Mechanism: conversion of 60 percent of industrial enterprises to more autonomous system of self-management.

4 February: Rehabilitation of ten Old Bolsheviks (including Bukharin) convicted in show trial of 1938.

11 February: Nagorno-Karabakh regional soviet requests to become part of Armenian Republic; demonstrations in Armenia and Azerbaijan.

17–18 February: Boris Yeltsin removed from Politburo.

28 February: Sumgait massacre.

13 March: Publication of Nina Andreyeva article.

26 April: Gorbachev meets with Russian Orthodox Patriarch Pimen and admits mistakes in treatment of church.

15 May: Beginning of Soviet troop withdrawal from Afghanistan.

29 May–2 June: Moscow summit.

June: General strike in Nagorno-Karabakh; Memorial group requests monument to victims of Stalinism.

5–16 June: Celebratin of millennium of Russian Orthodox Church.

13 June: Rehabilitation of Zinoviev and Kamenev.

28 June–1 July: Nineteenth Party Organizational Conference (first since 1941) sets up framework for elections for new Congress of People's Deputies.

23 August: Demonstrations in Latvia, Lithuania, and Estonia on anniversary of Molotov-Ribbontrop pact.

26 August: Approval of resolution to grant leases of up to fifty years on farmland.

21 September: State of emergency declared in Nagorno-Karabakh; troops deployed.

October: Establishment of independence movements in all three Baltic Republics, with official sanctions of local party authorities.

1 October: Gorbachev becomes head of the Presidium of the Supreme Soviet.

7 December: Earthquake in Armenia.

1989
Publication of Orwell's *1984*.

February: Completion of Soviet troop withdrawal from Afghanistan.

26 March: Elections for Congress of People's Deputies.

9 April: Demonstration in Tbilisi, ending in violence by security forces.

25 May: First Congress of People's Deputies convenes; Gorbachev formally elected to new position of president of Supreme Soviet.

26 May: Deputies select members of new Supreme Soviet.

3 June: Supreme Soviet convenes.

July: Widespread miners' strikes.

17 July: New Council of Ministers takes office.

27–28 July: Formation of Interregional Group: independent grouping of about 400 deputies.

September: Azerbaijan establishes rail blockade of Armenia.

9 October: Supreme Soviet recognizes right to strike.

17 October: Readmission of Soviet society of psychiatrists to World Psychiatry Association.

12 December: Second Congress of People's Deputies convenes.

THE CHANGING COMPOSITION OF THE POLITBURO FROM 1976 TO 1988

1976

5 March: After the Twenty-Fifth Congress the full members of the Politburo are: Leonid Brezhnev, Yuri Andropov, Andrei Grechko (dies 26 April 1976), Viktor Grishin, Andrei Gromyko, Andrei Kirilenko, Aleksei Kosygin, Fyodor Kulakov, Dinmukhamed Kunayev, Kirill Mazurov, Arvid Pelshe, Nikolai Podgorny, Grigori Romanov, Mikhail Suslov, Dmitri Ustinov, Vladimir Shcherbitsky. The candidate members are: Geidar Aliyev (first secretary of Azerbaijan Central Committee), Pyotr Masherov, Boris Ponomaryov, Saraf Rashidov, Mikhail Solomentsev.

1977

May: Nikolai Podgorni leaves the Politburo.

October: Konstantin Chernenko (secretary of the Central Committee) and Vasili Kuznetsov (first vice president of the Presidium of the Supreme Soviet) become candidate members.

1978

17 July: Fyodor Kulakov dies.

November: Kirill Mazurov leaves the Politburo. Konstantin Chernenko is made a full member. Nikolai Tikhonov (first deputy chairman of the Council of Ministers) and Eduard Shevardnadze (first secretary of the Georgia Central Committee) become candidate members.

1979

27 November: Nikolai Tikhonov is promoted to full membership. Mikhail Gorbachev becomes a candidate member.

1980

October: Mikhail Gorbachev becomes a full member. Tikhon Kiselyov (first secretary of the Byelorussian Central Committee) becomes a candidate member. Pyotor Masherov dies in a car accident. Aleksei Kosygin resigns for health reasons and dies on 18 December.

1981

3 March: After the Twenty-Sixth Congress the full members are: Leonid Brezhnev, Yuri Andropov, Mikhail Gorbachev, Viktor Grishin, Andrei Gromyko, Andrei Kirilenko, Dinmukhamed Kunayev, Arvid Pelshe, Grigori Romanov, Mikhail Suslov, Nikolai Tikhonov, Dmitri Ustinov, Konstanin Chernenko, Vladimir Shcherbitsky. The candidate members are: Geidar Aliyev, Pyotor Demichev, Tikhon Kiselyov, Vasili Kuznetsov, Boris Ponomaryov, Saraf Rashidov, Mikhail Solomentsev, Eduard Shevardnadze.

1982

January: Mikhail Suslov dies.

May: Vladimir Dolgikh (Central Committee secretary) is promoted to candidate membership.

10 November: Leonid Brezhnev dies.

12 November: Yuri Andropov is elected general secretary of the Central Committee of the Communist Party.

22 November: Geidar Aliyev is promoted to full membership. Andrei Kirilenko leaves the Politburo.

1983

June: Vitali Vorotnikov (chairman of the RSFSR Council of Ministers) becomes a candidate member. In the following months Arvid Pelshe and Tikhon Kiselyov die, and Saraf Rashidov commits suicide.

December: Vitali Vorotnikov and Mikhail Solomentsev are promoted to full membership. Viktor Chebrikov (head of the KGB) becomes a candidate member.

1984

9 February: Yuri Andropov dies.

13 February: Konstantin Chernenko is elected general secretary of the Central Committee.

20 December: Dmitri Ustinov dies.

1985

10 March: Konstantin Chernenko dies.

11 March: Mikhail Gorbachev is elected general secretary of the Central Committee

April: Two Central Committee secretaries, Yegor Ligachev and Nikolai Ryzhkov, become full members. Segei Sokolov (minister of defense) is elected to candidate membership.

June: Grigori Romanov is retired. Eduard Shevardnadze (minister of foreign affairs) becomes a full member.

October: Nikolai Tikhonov retires. Nikolai Talyzin (first deputy chairman of the Council of Ministers and the chairman of Gosplan) beomes a candidate member.

1986

February: Viktor Grishin is retired. Boris Yeltsin becomes a candidate member, due to his position as first secretary of the Moscow Party Committee.

March: After the Twenty-Seventh Congress, the full members are: Mikhail Gorbachev (general secretary), Geidar Aliyev (first deputy chairman of the Council of Ministers), Vitali Vorotnikov (chairman of the RSFSR Council of Ministers), Andrei Gromyko (president of the Presidium of the Supreme Soviet), Lev Zaikov (secretary of the Central Committee), Dinmukhamed Kunayev, Yegor Ligachev, Nikolai Ryzhkov (chairman of the Council of Ministers), Mikhail Solomentsev, Viktor Chebrikov, Eduard Shevardnadze, Vladimir Shcherbitsky. The candidate members are: Pyotr Demichev, Vladimir Dolgikh, Boris Yeltsin, Nikolai Slyunkov (first secretary of the Byelorussian Central Committee), Sergei Sokolov, Yuri Solovyov (first secretary of the Leningrad Party Committee), Nikolai Talyzin.

1987

January: Dinmukhamed Kunayev is retired. Aleksandr Yakovlev (Central Committee secretary) becomes a candidate member.

June: Nikolai Slyunkov (Central Committee secretary), Aleksandr Yakovlev, and Viktor Nikonov (Central Committee secretary) become full members. Sergei Sokolov leaves the Politburo.

October: Geidar Aliyev is retired.

1988

February: Yuri Maslyukov (first deputy chairman of the Council of Ministers and chairman of Gosplan) and Georgi Razumovsky (Central Committee secretary) become candidate members. Boris Yeltsin leaves the Politburo.

June: On the eve of the Nineteenth Conference on Party Organization, the full members of the Politburo are: Mikhail Gorbachev, Vitali Vorotnikov, Andrei Gromyko, Lev Zaikov (first secretary of the Moscow Party Committee), Yegor Ligachev, Viktor Nikonov, Nikolai Ryzhkov, Nikolai Slyunkov, Mikhail Solomentsev, Viktor Chebrikov, Eduard Shevardnadze, Vladimir Shcherbitsky, Aleksandr Yakovlev. The candidate members are: Pyotr Demichev, Vladimir Dolgikh, Yuri Maslyukov, Georgi Razumovsky, Yuri Solovyov, Nikolai Talyzin (deputy chairman of the Council of Ministers), Dmitri Yazov.

30 September: The plenum retires Andrei Gromyko, Mikhail Solomentsev, Pyotr Demichev, and Vladimir Dolgikh.

1 October: The Supreme Soviet appoints Mikhail Gorbachev as president of the Presidium. At this point the full members of the Politburo are: Mikhail Gorbachev (general secretary of the Central Committee and president of the Presidium of the Supreme Soviet), Vitali Vorotnikov (president of the Presidium of the RSFSR Supreme Soviet), Lev Zaikov, Yegor Ligachev (chairman of the Central Committee commission on agriculture), Viktor Nikonov, Nikolai Ryzhkov, Nikolai Slyunkov (chairman of the Central Committee commission on economic reform), Viktor Chebrikov (chairman of the Central Committee commission on legal reform), Eduard Shevardnadze, Vladimir Shcherbitsky, Aleksandr Yakovlev (chairman of the Central Committee commission on international affairs), Vadim Medvedev (chairman of the Central Committee commission on ideological issues). The candidate members are: Yuri Maslyukov, Georgi Razumovsky (chairman of the Central Committee commission on organizational issues and on the cadres), Yuri Solovyov, Nikolai Talyzin, Dmitri Yazov, Anatoli Lukyanov (first vice president of the Presidium of the Supreme Soviet), Aleksandr Vlasov (chairman of the RSFSR Council of Ministers), Aleksandra Biryukova (first deputy chairman of the Council of Ministers).

Notes

Preface

1. *Voprosy Ekonomiki*, 1989, no. 2. This article is based on the conclusions given before the delegates to the Twenty-Second Conference on Organization of the Perm Party, 16 December 1988.

Chapter 1: *1986: From the Twenty-Seventh Party Congress to the Eighth Writers' Congress*

1. From 25 February to 6 March 1986.
2. Gorbachev's election was opposed up until the last minute inside the Politburo; it was probably decided by a single vote. The elderly Gromyko was in charge of presenting and guaranteeing Gorbachev's candidacy before the Central Committee.
3. *Pravda*, 26 February 1986.
4. *Pravda*, 15 March 1986.
5. The "sovkhozes" are the state agricultural enterprises. The "kolkhozes" are cooperative farms. In reality, the forced collectivization of the countryside almost completely eliminated any differences between the two forms of agricultural property and between the two types of production they represented.
6. "Prodnalog," i.e., tax in kind. It was approved by the All-Russian Central Executive Committee on 21 March 1921. Faced by the growing peasant resistance, the Bolsheviks decided to replace the requisition of surpluses with a graduated tax in kind, calculated according to percentages of the actual harvest. This provision was completed by a law that granted the right of free trade for surpluses "within the limits of local economic exchange."
7. *Literaturnaya Gazeta*, 1986, no. 16.
8. *Pravda*, 25 April 1986.
9. *Pravda*, 15 May 1986.
10. See chapter 2 and the Second Conversation.
11. *Sovetskaya Kultura*, 20 May 1986.
12. *Pravda*, 19 May 1986.
13. *Pravda*, 2 June 1986.
14. *Pravda*, 15 June 1986.
15. The Fifth Filmmakers' Congress took place from 13 to 15 May 1986. See also the First Conversation.
16. *Pravda*, 20 June 1986.
17. *L'Unità*, 7 October 1986.
18. *Pravda*, 13 February 1986.

19. Gosplan is the State Planning Committee.
20. *L'Unità*, 7 October 1986.
21. *Molodaya Gvardia* is a monthly magazine, the organ of the Central Komsomol Committee, the organization of Soviet Communist youth.
22. Zhdanovian, i.e., Zhdanov's.

CHAPTER 2: *FROM JUNE TO DECEMBER 1986: PREPARING THE REFORM*

1. *Pravda*, 19 June 1986.
2. *Pravda*, 17 June 1986.
3. *Moskovskiye Novosti*, 1986, no. 27.
4. *Pravda*, 18 July 1986.
5. *L'Unità*, 24 July 1986.
6. *L'Unità*, 24 July 1986.
7. *L'Unità*, 24 July 1986.
8. *Moskovskaya Pravda*, 10 August 1986.
9. *Pravda*, 16 August 1986.
10. *Sovetskaya Kultura*, 10 August 1986.
11. *Pravda*, 28 August 1986.
12. *Pravda*, 20 September 1986.
13. *Pravda*, 1 October 1986.
14. *Izvestia*, 26 September 1986.
15. *Pravda*, 31 October 1986.
16. *Pravda*, 7 November 1986.
17. Gospriyomka was authorized to reject manufactured products that did not meet specific standards. See also the Second Conversation.
18. *Pravda*, 20 November 1986.
19. *Moskovskiye Novosti*, 1986, no. 50.
20. *Pravda*, 27 December 1986.

CHAPTER 3: *FOREIGN POLICY IN 1986*

1. *Pravda*, 16 January 1986.
2. *Pravda*, 26 February 1986.
3. *Pravda*, 21 February 1986.
4. *L'Unità*, 23 March 1986.
5. *L'Unità*, 28 March 1986.
6. *L'Unità*, 30 March 1986.
7. *Pravda*, 21 April 1986.
8. *Pravda*, 21 May 1986.
9. *New York Times*, 29 May 1986.
10. *Pravda*, 10 July 1986.
11. *L'Unità*, 16 July 1986.
12. *International Herald Tribune*, 19 August 1986.
13. *Pravda*, 9 September 1986.
14. *L'Unità*, 8 October 1986.
15. *L'Unità*, 14 October 1986.
16. *Pravda*, 11 November 1986.
17. *Pravda*, 14 November 1986.
18. *L'Unità*, 29 November 1986.

1. *L'Unità*, 2 January 1987.
2. *Pravda*, 4 January 1987.
3. *Pravda*, 8 January 1987.
4. *L'Unita*, 24 January 1987.
5. *Il Giornale*, 23 January 1987.
6. *Pravda*, 20 January 1987.
7. *Moskovskiye Novosti*, 1987, no. 4.
8. The reconstruction of events proposed to the reader is partially based on later official disclosures, but also on numerous direct and indirect comments that appeared in the Soviet press, and on sources and versions gathered by the author and compared, wherever possible, with an available counterpart.
9. *L'Unità*, 30 January 1987.
10. *Pravda*, 28 January 1987.
11. *Pravda*, 23 January 1987.
12. Indirect disclosures were made to the press by Mikhail Ulyanov (*Sovetskaya Kultura*, 10 February 1987) and Yegor Yakovlev (*Moskovskiye Novosti*, 1987, no. 7).
13. All excerpts from Gorbachev's speech to the plenum are taken from *Pravda*, 28 January 1987.
14. *Pravda*, 29 January 1987.
15. *Pravda*, 29 January 1987.
16. *Novoye Vremya*, 1987, no. 4.
17. *Moskovskiye Novosti*, 1987, no. 6.
18 *Pravda*, 13 February 1987.
19. *Pravda*, 14 February 1987.
20. *Novy Mir*, 1987, no. 2.
21. *Novy Mir*, 1987, no. 6.
22. *Pravda*, 22 June 1987.
23. Tass, 12 February 1987.
24. *Oktyabr*, 1987, no. 4.
25. *Izvestia*, 5 June 1987.
26. *Moskovskiye Novosti*, 1987, no. 11.
27. *Le Monde*, 11 February 1987.
28. Quotations and the summary are the result of an interview by the author with Vasilev in October 1987, and of an analysis of numerous Pamyat documents.
29. In the interview cited, Vasilev boasted that in Moscow alone he had at his disposal "at least 25,000 activists." This statement is obviously to be taken cautiously, but other less biased sources verify that in that period Pamyat had at its disposal two hundred "full-time officials" who traveled throughout the country to make converts.
30. *Sovetskaya Kultura*, 21 March 1987.
31. *Sotsialisticheskaya Industria*, 24 May 1987.
32. *Pravda*, 7 January 1987.
33. Tass, 14 March 1987.
34. Tass, 10 March 1987.
35. *Pravda*, 16 March 1987.
36. *Pravda*, 6 March 1987.
37. The meeting took place on 17 March 1987. Long excerpts from Sergei Mikhalkov's address and from debates on the floor were published in *Literaturnaya Rossia*, 1987, no. 13.
38. *Kommunist*, no. 6, 1987.
39. *Pravda*, 6 April 1987.

40. *L'Unità*, 7 April 1987.
41. *Pravda*, 17 April 1987.

Chapter 5: *The June and October Plenums*

1. Tass, 12 June 1987.
2. *Pravda*, 26 June 1987.
3. *Sovetskaya Latvia*; quoted in *La Stampa*, 28 June 1987.
4. *La Repubblica*, 1 July 1987.
5. *Ogonyok*, 1987, no. 26.
6. *L'Unità*, 4 July 1987.
7. *Le Monde*, 8 July 1987.
8. *L'Unità*, 1 July 1987.
9. *Izvestia*, 8 July 1987; article by Yevgenia Maksimova and I. Martkovich. *La Repubblica*, 12–13 July 1987.
10. *Kommunist*, 1987, no. 9.
11. *Sovetskaya Kultura*, 7 July 1987.
12. The meeting took place on 9 July 1987. Tass would report it on 14 July 1987.
13. *Molodaya Gvardia*, 1987, no. 7.
14. *Sovetskaya Kultura*, 25 July 1987.
15. *Ogonyok*, no. 30, July 1987.
16. *Pravda*, 30 July 1987.
17. The television news program "Vremya." 30 July 1987.
18. *L'Unità*, 25 July 1987.
19. *Pravda*, 7 August 1987.
20. *Moskovskiye Novosti*, 1987, no. 33.
21. *Pravda*, 21 August 1987.
22. Tass, 23 August 1987.
23. *Le Monde*, 22–23 August 1987.
24. Tass, 26 July 1987.
25. *Pravda*, 15 July 1987.
26. *Le Monde*, 23 September 1987.
27. *Kommunist*, 1987, no. 11.
28. *Pravda*, 11 September 1987.
29. *Le Monde*, 17 September 1987.
30. *Pravda*, 17 September 1987.
31. *L'Unità*, 22 September 1987. The *New York Times* correspondent also heard rumors regarding this episode. *International Herald Tribune*, 24 September 1987.
32. *Znamya*, 1987, no. 9. The magazine *Don* had published Mozhayev's novel in installments in issues 1–3, 1987.
33. Briefing at the Foreign Ministry, 24 September 1987.
34. *Pravda*, 28 September, 1987.
35. *Ogonyok*, 1987, no. 40; *L'Unità*, 5 October 1987.
36. *Sovetskaya Rossia*, 4 October 1987.
37. *Literaturnaya Gazeta*, 1987, no. 40.
38. Tass, 2 October 1987.
39. *L'Unità*, 19 October 1987.
40. *Izvestia TsK KPSS*, 1989, no. 2. The stenographer's report for the October 1988 plenum was published eighteen months later, a few days after Boris Yeltsin's triumphant election as a deputy to the Congress with over 5 million votes in the district of Moscow. A complete

analysis of this document would go outside the limits of this study. Here I would only like to emphasize my doubts about the "completeness" of the published stenographer's report. The first of Yeltsin's two interventions seems confused and convoluted. His gesture of dissent was accompanied, it is true, by his request to resign, but it represents no real danger to the stability of the ruling group. In this version, the reactions of Gorbachev and numerous other members of the Central Committee seem exaggerated. Leaks made to the press a few days after the plenum (and different versions of Yeltsin's speech that circulated later) indicate a much more explicit attack on Ligachev. Moreover, some of the speeches make explicit reference to previous discussions, which may have taken place in the Politburo, or perhaps in the Central Committee, that could explain such a dramatic outcome, which is otherwise incomprehensible. The writer personally has some proof that the minutes are incomplete. According to a reliable source, Yeltsin's second intervention was followed by a kind of insurrection among the members of the plenum, more than ninety of whom asked to speak. There is not a trace of all this in the "stenographer's report."

41. See the previous note. In the text published by *Izvestia TsK KPSS*, Gorbachev's conclusion insinuates a last effort to "dedramatize" the episode, going so far as to leave the road open to Yeltsin should he wish to "reenter" the Politburo in the future in a leadership role. This would actually happen shortly after, when he was appointed vice president of the State Committee on Construction, with ministerial rank.

42. *Le Monde*, 3 November 1987.

43. *L'Unità*, 4 November 1987.

44. *Moskovskaya Pravda*, 6 November 1987.

45. *Pravda*, 3 November 1987.

46. *Pravda, Moskovskaya Pravda*, and *Sovetskaya Rossia*, 3 November 1987.

47. *Moskovskiye Novosti*, 1987, no. 47.

48. *Sovetskaya Rossia*, 24 November 1987.

49. *L'Unità*, 22 November 1987.

50. *L'Unità*, 27 December 1987.

51. XXVII Sezd KPSS. *Stenograficheski Otchyot*, vol. I (Moscow, 1986), pp. 624–25.

CHAPTER 6: *FOREIGN POLICY IN 1987*

1. *L'Unità*, 2 January 1987.

2. Tass, 1 January 1987.

3. *Le Monde*, 17 January 1987.

4. *L'Unità*, 5 February 1987.

5. *L'Unità*, 17 February 1987.

6. Tass, 26 February 1987.

7. Tass, 28 February 1987.

8. *L'Unità*, 5 March 1987.

9. *Pravda*, 17 March 1987.

10. Tass, 17 March 1987.

11. *L'Unità*, 19 March 1987.

12. Tass, 13 April 1987.

13. *L'Unità*, 28 May 1987. This was Gorbachev's second interview with a Western Communist newspaper. The first was in February 1986 with *L'Humanité*.

14. *L'Unità*, 22 July 1987.

15. *Corriere della Sera*, 28 August 1987.

16. *La Repubblica*, 8 September 1987.

17. *Pravda*, 17 September 1987.
18. *L'Unità*, 28 October 1987.
19. Tass, 13 November 1987.
20. *L'Unità*, 5 December 1987.
21. *L'Unità*, 12 December 1987.
22. *L'Unità*, 5 November 1987.

CHAPTER 7: *1988: A YEAR OF LESSONS*

1. *L'Unità*, 8 January 1988.
2. *Pravda*, 13 January 1988.
3. *Pravda*, 19 February 1988.
4. *Izvestia*, 9 January 1988.
5. Tass, 23 February 1988.
6. Tass, 25 February 1988.
7. Tass, 26 February 1988.
8. *L'Unità*, 1 March 1988.
9. Tass, 4 March 1988.
10. In a conversation with Alessandro Natta, general secretary of the Italian Communist Party, on a 29 March 1988 visit to Moscow.
11. *Moskovskiye Novosti*, 9 March 1988.
12. *Sovetskaya Karabakh*, 18 March 1988.
13. Article 112 establishes that the Supreme Court of the USSR can be convened either on the initiative of its Presidium, on the request of one-third of the deputies in its two houses, or "on the request of a federal republic."
14. *Pravda*, 21 March 1988.
15. *L'Unità*, 23 March 1988.
16. *Pravda*, 24 March 1988.
17. "It would seem as if we were ashamed to say that the Russian proletariat, whom the Trotskyites treated as if they were backward and uncultured, were the ones who achieved, in Lenin's words, 'three Russian revolutions,' and that the Slavic people were at the vanguard of the fight against fascism." The following statement epitomizes the article's anti-Semitic allusions: "It is well known that Marx defined entire nations as 'counterrevolutionary' at specific stages in their histories (nations, not classes or strata), calling for a decisive fight against them, even if he maintained a friendly rapport with many of their progressive elements. On the basis of a class approach, he was not ashamed to make destructive judgments about a series of nationalities, including the one which he himself belonged to." *Sovetskaya Rossia*, 13 March 1988.
18. Lidia Timashuk was both protagonist and instrument when she wrote an accusatory letter that inaugurated the "doctors' plot" shortly before Stalin's death. She received the Order of Lenin for her denunciations. In a unique and perhaps not entirely accidental coincidence, in all three cases a woman was "used" to unleash an offensive for the sake of "values" and the establishment.
19. Aleksandr Andreyevich Prokhanov (born 26 November 1938) is the editor of *Sovetskaya Literatura*, a magazine published in foreign languages for foreign readers. He wrote war novels, particularly about the war in Afghanistan, such as *Derevo v Tsentre Kabula* (*A Tree in the Center of Kabul*) of 1982, and *Tam, v Afganistane* (*Over There, in Afghanistan*) of 1988. His views on the political and literary debate had been expressed in numerous articles, often published in *Literaturnaya Rossia* (for example, "Kultura: Khram a ne Strelbishche," ["Culture: A Temple, Not a Shooting Gallery"] 1988, no. 4). His ideology

is characterized by his praise of the mission of the Russian people, the defense of Stalin, and explicit anti-Semitism.

20. According to Michel Tatu (see: *Problems of Communism*, no. 3, May-August 1988), the working intermediary of this contact might have been Vladimir Denisov, head of the Science and Education Department at *Sovetskaya Rossia*. Tatu informs us that Denisov was a correspondent for the paper in Tomsk (and Kemerovo) between 1978 and 1982, and had to have a close working relationship with the first secretary of the Tomsk party. Ligachev held that job until 1983.

21. I have had the opportunity to read the typescript that Andreyeva sent to the newspaper. Next to the signature, "Andreyeva Nina Nikolayevna, member of the Communist Party of the Soviet Union since 1966, candidate in Technical Sciences," an anonymous hand wrote "7 September 1987," presumably to register the date the letter was received.

22. A comparison of the text published in *Sovetskaya Rossia* with the original shows that only about five pages remained of the latter. The rest was considerably reworked, with entire sections disappearing, while others were added (see my "Storia Segreta del Manifesto Anti-Gorbaciov," *L'Unità*, 23 May 1988). In an interview that I later published, Ms. Andreyeva confirmed that the paper had "retouched" her text a bit, but that "the substance remained" (*L'Unità*, 25 June 1988).

23. The Leningrad Party Committee's secretary for ideology at that time, Aleksandr Yaki-movich Dekterov, claimed that "not even the Leningrad correspondent's office (for *Sovetskaya Rossia*) was notified of the publication of Andreyeva's letter. They protested too. We found out about it by reading the letter on 13 March." (See *L'Unità*, 25 June 1988).

24. Nina Andreyeva had been expelled from the party in 1978, together with her husband Aleksandr Klushin, who taught philosophy at the same school. At that time Klushin was vice chairman of the school's party committee. They were dismissed after it was discovered they had written several anonymous letters against their colleagues. Andreyeva confirmed the circumstances but claimed that her motives were noble: "I was accused because I spoke against the abuses of power and illegality." She added: "But I was readmitted shortly thereafter when the party's Central Committee for Control stepped in. It was 1980. The sentence was completely repealed. So the record states that I have been a member without interruption since 1966." Dekterov stated instead that Moscow stepped in to help them "by using legal cavils." According to another source, Andreyeva and Klushin were absolved because of procedural irregularities committed in the course of the party investigation. It seems that the investigators had a lab test made of the anonymous letters (which, as it turned out, had been written on Andreyeva's typewriter) without obtaining the necessary authorization.

25. Several Western correspondents in Moscow received information to this effect. I myself heard this from reliable sources.

26. The reconstruction of these events by Robert Kaiser of the *Washington Post* coincides with several of my own sources.

27. Some editors were excluded, such as Yegor Yakovlev (*Moskovskiye Novosti*) and Vitali Korotich (*Ogonyok*).

28. For the most part, this version matches Robert Kaiser's report.

29. Yuri Karyakin, who was in Leningrad on 25 March for a public conference, was told that Yuri Solovyov, first secretary of the party and a candidate member of the Politburo, had personally phoned Andreyeva to congratulate her. By contrast, the secretary for ideology, Dekterov, would strongly deny these rumors (see *L'Unità*, 25 June 1988).

30. Robert Kaiser quoted an anonymous newspaper editor who disclosed the existence of a confidential note from Tass that "authorized" the publication of the article in the provincial newspapers. Another source claimed instead that Tass had given the explicit instruction to publish the article. In any event, the existence of Tass's first directive is proven by a

second directive, dated 29 March 1988, whose text was quoted by Pavel Demidov (*Zhurnalist*, 1988, no. 5): "Regarding the newspapers' questions about reprinting Nina Andreyeva's article, we hereby communicate that this question must be decided in accordance with the local party authorities." The historian Yuri Afanasev would write in *Pravda* that "more than thirty of the party's regional committees" had obeyed the directive (26 July 1988). But an editorial comment in a footnote stated that "this information cannot be confirmed." The most accurate information on the subject was provided by Demidov. The article was reprinted in *Gorkovskaya Pravda* (Gorky), *Uralski Rabochi* (Sverdlovsk), *Voroshilovskaya Pravda* (Voroshilovgrad), *Vercherni Donetsk* (Donetsk), and *Novgorodskaya Pravda* (Novgorod). But there were also rebellions. *Tambovskaya Pravda* attacked Nina Andreyeva on 2 April, i.e., before *Pravda*'s solemn reply. Moreover, Demidov announced that the newspaper of the Byelorussian Komsomol, *Znamya Yunosti*, had refused to publish Ms. Andreyeva. Finally, none of the republics' newspapers carried the article, by contrast with its April 2 publication in *Neues Deutschland* (the newspaper of the East German Communist Party).

31. Aleksandr Gelman is the director of IMEMO (Institut Mirovoi Ekonomiki i Mezhdunarodnykh Otnosheni; Institute of the World Economy and International Relations) at the USSR's Academy of Sciences. He is considered very close to Aleksandr Yakovlev. His report would be published in *Sovetskaya Kultura* only after Yakovlev's response in *Pravda*.

32. Robert Kaiser maintains that Gorbachev actually intended to leave the meeting after calling for a vote of confidence, and await the verdict at his dacha. But this circumstance has been denied by other sources, and seems highly improbable.

33. This was the first step in disciplinary procedures against a party member, on the basis of article 9 of the bylaws.

34. *Pravda*, 7 April 1988.

35. Andreyeva would verify that she had been invited to speak at the KGB's Leningrad school, adding, however, that it had been a debate with four "opponents" (see *L'Unità*, 25 June 1988). After her letter was published, she had spoken in public at the Karl Marx Cultural House at a conference organized by the Lenin Neighborhood Party Committee. According to my sources, Andreyeva said that she had spoken to Ligachev in person. Someone in the audience asked, "Why didn't you speak to Gorbachev?" Andreyeva replied, "I thought that Ligachev would understand my intentions better." However, in the interview mentioned, Andreyeva answered a specific question by categorically denying that she had spoken directly to Ligachev. She also denied Solovyov's phone call: "I did not receive any phone call from Solovyov. I have not had any contact with the party. I didn't need to."

36. The quotation marks around "letter to the editor" were in his text, put there evidently to emphasize that the reader was well aware that it was much more than that.

37. The speech to the Uzbek party rank and file was delivered on 8 April, but would be circulated by Tass on the ninth and published in *Pravda* on the tenth.

38. Tass did not announce these meetings until 20 April 1988, in a news brief, when the game was already over.

39. *L'Unità*, 22 April 1988.

40. Yakovlev was placed in charge of the media and television.

41. *Komsomolskaya Pravda*, 21 April 1988. This was a letter from a Leningrad youth, Ruslan Kozlov, that describes what happened in the city after the appearance of Nina Andreyeva's letter. His version was in sharp contrast to the description by Aleksandr Dekterov.

42. *L'Unità*, 22 April 1988.

43. *Pravda*, 11 May 1988. The meeting was held on 7 May.

44. The exception for a third term, which was still contained in the "Theses," would be rejected by the Nineteenth Conference.

45. *Pravda*, 10 June 1988.

46. Both were forced into retirement, at the same time, for "health reasons."
47. Tass, 22 June 1988.
48. Tass, 27 June 1988.

CHAPTER 8: *THE NINETEENTH PARTY CONFERENCE*

1. On 28 October 1988, *Moskovskiye Novosti* disclosed the arrests of Izmail Dzhabbarov (a candidate member of the Central Committee) and Nazir Radzhabov, the first secretary of Samarkand "in the past few days." Inamzhon Uzmankhodzhayev, the former Uzbek first secretary, and Akil Salimov, the former chairman of the Uzbek Supreme Soviet, were handcuffed along with them. Other arrests followed after a few weeks.
2. *Izvestia TsK KPSS* (1989, no. 2) would publish the stenographer's minutes of the October 1987 plenum during the election campaign, in a step clearly designed to "cut down to size" the popular candidate Boris Yeltsin.
3. He himself disclosed this in an interview with the television service of the Novosti agency that had been prepared for the foreign press and taped the day before he was allowed to speak at the plenary assembly.
4. The September 1988 plenum would force both Solomentsev and Gromyko into retirement. Ligachev and Chebrikov would have their powers reduced.
5. All of the quotes from the Nineteenth Conference are taken from *Pravda* on 29 and 30 June and 1 and 2 July 1988.
6. *Pravda*, 25 July 1988.
7. This highly debatable formula contained two "spirits." The idea of granting direct representation to the "social organizations" was motivated, sincere only in part, by the people's "lack of democratic experience." In the situation of a single party, the social organizations should represent a part of the pluralism of social interests. On the other hand, as would be concretely verified during the election campaign, the existing social organizations were still dominated by corporative bureaucracies who were very protective of their privileges. Consequently, almost everywhere the plenums of these organizations would suppress democratic and innovative drives. The "bureaucratic" spirit, as the conservatives intended it, would get the best. The apparats were able to use this filter to choose candidates of their own liking.
8. The "Theses" also provided for the eventuality of a third term in exceptional circumstances.
9. *Pravda*, 14 July 1988. The meeting took place on 11 July 1988.
10. *Pravda*, 30 July 1988.
11. *Pravda*, 17 September 1988.
12. The reconstruction that follows is a factual synopsis, but it is also an analysis of different news items provided to the author by reliable Soviet sources that complement, and sometimes correct, the official information.
13. *Pravda*, 24 September 1988.
14. *Pravda*, 25 September 1988. One of the participants later reported that the Soviet leader appeared very tense. At the end of the speech he said (but this sentence did not appear in *Pravda*'s 25 September report), "I would also like to know your opinion, but today, unfortunately, we don't have time to enter into a discussion." The *Pravda* text, however, concluded with an unusual expression, "*Vsevo vam dobrovo.*" This ending could be translated as "Best wishes," confirming that this was a "communiqué" and not a debate.
15. In other words, he meant to ward off the blow by letting everyone know that he still held his position and he meant to keep it.
16. *Pravda*, 16 September 1988.
17. There would be no official communication of this meeting.

18. Dobrynin was appointed as foreign-policy advisor to the president. There is no reason to think his leaving was the result of political conflicts.
19. *Pravda* and *Izvestia*, 23 October 1988.
20. The republic's foreign minister, Anatoli Mitrcian, and its interior minister, Husik Arutyunyan.
21. Roald Sagdeyev was the director of the Institute for Astronomic Research until mid-1988.
22. The initiative received the discreet sponsorship of Aleksandr Yakovlev and other high-ranking Central Committee functionaries.
23. Tass, 21 October 1988.
24. I would propose this translation of the word *khozraschyot*, which means literally "economic calculation," but corresponds to nothing in Western economic terminology.
25. *Pravda*, 11 November 1988.
26. Tass, 17 November, 1988.
27. Speech of 26 November 1988, broadcast in its entirety on Soviet TV on 27 November 1988.
28. The amendments were explained by Razumovsky after the meetings of the Commission on Legislative Proposals for the soviet's two branches. The republics gained the right to make recourse directly to the Committee on Constitutional Control (a new body). Furthermore, the central parliament had to have the endorsement of the parliament of the republic concerned when it wanted to declare a state of emergency. The republic's soviets could issue public referendums on issues that were within their competence. Finally, a resolution was voted on regarding "successive acts for the political reform of the state structure" that constituted a formal commitment to face the "second stage," which had to define the distribution of jurisdiction between the union and the republics.

CHAPTER 9: *FOREIGN POLICY IN 1988*

1. Statement by the spokesman for the foreign minister, Yuri Alekseyev, Tass, 7 January 1988.
2. Interview with the official Afghan agency Bakhtar, taken from Tass, 7 January 1988.
3. *Pravda*, 11 January 1988.
4. A significant detail shows that the text of Gorbachev's television statement had been prepared at the last minute. On the evening of 8 February, the "Vremya" news program went on the air ten minutes late, an unprecedented occurrence.
5. *Pravda*, 15 February 1988.
6. Tass, 3 March 1988.
7. Tass, 30 March 1988. The Politburo communiqué was published on the same day.
8. Tass, 2 April 1988.
9. At the beginning of 1989, when the Soviet withdrawal was almost complete, the USSR would make the American proposal its own. But Washington was no longer willing to put it into practice.
10. Tass, 2 April 1988.
11. *L'Unità*, 8 April 1988.
12. Statement to Tass by Viktor Karpov, 20 February 1989.
13. Tass, 24 February 1988.
14. This and all subsequent quotes from the "Theses" are taken from *Pravda*, 28 May 1988.
15. See chapter 3. The text of Gorbachev's speech was not published by the Soviet press. The newspapers gave only a concise report of the meeting that had taken place and of the fact that Gorbachev spoke.
16. Taken from *L'Unità*, 22 December 1988.

17. He was in clear disagreement with the historian Yuri Afanasev, who had denied the socialist nature of Soviet society in *Pravda*, 22 July 1988. He was also in disagreement with many opinions expressed in the Soviet press in recent months.

18. The announcement was made on 4 November by the deputy minister of foreign affairs, Aleksandr Bessmertnykh. *Pravda*, 5 November 1988.

19. In this period I heard reports from a reliable source that there had been at least two meetings of the Politburo to deal with the question of whether or not to suspend the withdrawal.

20. The ambassador to Kabul, Yuli Vorontsov, had several meetings, in Islamabad and Teheran, with the Pakistani and Iranian governments (Vorontsov was still deputy minister of foreign affairs despite his appointment as ambassador to Kabul). But it was known that there were secret meetings between emissaries of the Soviet government and the heads of the armed opposition—up to the time the official announcement was made in December that Vorontsov would meet a guerrilla delegation in Saudia Arabia. No results were produced by a surprise visit by Vorontsov to Rome, to meet with King Zahir. Vorontsov offered the exiled king broad guarantees in the event that he returned to his homeland.

21. The political commentator for *Izvestia*, Aleksandr Bovin, returning from a long trip to Afghanistan, wrote, "Many of those with whom I spoke down there do not completely believe, do not want to and cannot believe, that the Soviet soldiers will go, that they are going." *Izvestia*, 23 December 1988.

22. Quotes from Gorbachev's speech to the U.N. are taken from *Pravda*, 8 December 1988.

CHAPTER 10: *THE LONG STRUGGLE OF PERESTROIKA*

1. *Moskovskiye Novosti*, 1989, no. 27.
2. *Voprosy Ekonomiki*, 1989, no. 2.

INDEX

Armenia (*cont.*)
  interdependence concept and, 60–61,
    156
  Krasnoyarsk radar station issue, 155
  medium-range missiles agreement, 58,
    59, 66, 151–52, 154, 159–60
  military's attitude toward Gorbachev's
    policies, 165–68
  nongovernmental initiatives, 63
  nuclear disarmament proposal, 58,
    59–60
  nuclear test moratorium, 58–59, 61,
    62, 65, 68, 150, 151
  nuclear test negotiations, 156
  Pershing IA issue, 155
  political popularity of, 160
  public discussion of, 69–70
  Reykjavik summit, 65–66, 72–73, 148
  SDI issue, 59, 64, 157, 159–60, 161
  Shultz-Shevardnadze negotiations
    (April, 1987), 152–53
  strategic weapons, proposed fifty per-
    cent reduction, 258–59, 271–72
  unilateral Soviet initiatives, 268–69
  Washington summit, 156, 157–61,
    164–65
art, 215–16
Arutyunyan, 224, 236
Askarov, Asanbai, 88
Askoldov, Aleksandr, 132, 215
Astafev, Viktor, 18, 176
Aukhadev, Kenes, 88
Azerbaijan, 290; *see also* Nagorno-
    Karabakh problem

Babak, Mikhail, 132
Bagirov, Kyamran, 199, 246
Bakatin, Vadim, 282
Baklanov, Grigori, 12, 17, 18, 19, 24,
    122, 183, 237
Baklanov, Oleg, 184
Balayan, Zori, 185–86, 243
Baltic Republics: *see* Estonia; Latvia;
    Lithuania
Barkauskas, Antanas, 236
Baruzdin, Sergei, 19
Batenin, Gen. Geli, 151
Begun, Iosif, 85, 87

Bek, Aleksandr, 87, 98
Belov, Vasili, 16, 20, 176
Belyayev, Albert, 19, 97, 115
Berggolts, Olga, 96
Beria, Lavrenti, 101,102
Berkhin, Viktor, 77–78
Berlinguer, Enrico, 163
Bessmertnykh, Aleksandr, 152, 159
Biryukova, Aleksandra, 4, 229
Blyukher, Vasili, 105
Bodyguard (Gai), 213
Bogomolov, Oleg, 199, 278
Bogoraz, Larisa, 87
Boiko, Viktor, 88
Bondarchuk, Sergei, 13, 14
Bondarev, Yuri, 16, 17, 20, 89, 220,
    222, 241, 290
Bonner, Yelena, 34–35, 92, 93, 168
Borzunov, Sergei, 89
Bovin, Aleksandr, 70, 82, 127
Brest Litovsk peace, 83
Brest Peace (Shatrov), 83
Brezhnev, Leonid I., 45, 49, 55, 70–71,
    93, 94, 106, 166, 168, 275, 277,
    284
Brezhnev, Yuri, 23
Brezhnev clan, campaign against, 23, 27,
    88
Brief Encounters (film), 15
"bring suit" against public officials, right
    to, 112
"brotherhood of peoples" in USSR, 246
Brushstrokes for a Portrait of Lenin (film),
    15
budget deficit, 292
Bukharin, Nikolai, 99, 106, 107, 128,
    183, 210
Bukovsky, Vladimir, 85, 169
Bulgakov, Mikhail, 32
Bulgaria, xi, 161, 162
Bunic, Pavel, 309
bureaucracy of the ministries, campaign
    against, 27–28, 78–79, 81
Burlatsky, Fyodor, 5
Buryatsky, Boris, 27
Bush, George, 271
Bykov, Vasili, 12, 84
By Right of Memory (Tvardovsky), 96

Moscow Forum, 150–51
"new thinking," 68–72, 150, 152, 256
perestroika and, 156–57, 258, 262,
    263
public discussion of, 69
public opinion, diplomacy of, 61–62,
    64–65
radical change from the past, 259–60,
    263
ruling groups affected by policy
    changes, 263–64
socialist countries, relations with,
    161–63, 264–67
United Nations and, 264, 269
United States, relations with, 61–62,
    65, 150, 152–53, 254, 258–59,
    271–74
see also Afghanistan policy; arms
    control
France, 64, 73
Frolov, Ivan, 196
Further, Even Further . . . (Shatrov), 183
Fyodorov, Vasili, 116

Gaer, Yevdokia, 290
Gai, David, 213
Gamzatov, Razul, 224
Garage (Ryazanov), 96
Gdlyan, Telman, 220
Gelman, Aleksandr, 193, 199, 237
general secretary of the party and presi-
    dent of the Supreme Soviet, dou-
    ble role of, 250–51
Genscher, Hans-Dietrich, 64
Georgia, 29, 184, 243
Gerasimov, Gennadi, 78, 85, 120, 152,
    155
German, Aleksei, 15
German, Yuri, 212
Germany, East, xi, 265
Germany, West, 261
Ghidaspov, Boris, 308
Gladki, Ivan, 31
glasnost, ix
    Chernobyl catastrophe and, 7
    criticism from conservative press,
        115–18
    Gorbachev's endorsements, 11–12

opposition to, 12
social vitality due to, 77–78
taboo subjects made public in media,
    7–8, 113–15
see also historical reexamination; Sta-
    linism, debate on
Glasnost (magazine), 87, 113, 118, 124,
    171
Glazunov, Ilya, 216
Godfather (Puzo), 213
Goncharenko, Boris, 88
Gonzales, Felipe, 62
Gorbachev, Mikhail S., ix, x, 90
    Afghanistan policy, 63, 67, 70,
        148–50, 153–54, 254, 255, 256,
        257, 268, 274, 279–80
    agriculture policy, 225, 230–31
    alcoholism problem, approach to, 11
    alternatives to, lack of, 285–86
    Asian strategy, 66–67, 261–62
    authoritarian system, management of,
        283–84
    bodyguard, 208
    Central Committee meeting (July,
        1989), 303–4
    Central Committee Plenums:
        June, 1986, 8, 22
        January, 1987, 77, 78–82
        June, 1987, 109–12
        October, 1987, 124, 125
        February, 1988, 183–84, 201–4,
            256
        July, 1988, 225–26
        September, 1988, 227–30
        April, 1989, 296
    Chernobyl catastrophe, 6
    Chinese–Soviet relations, 257–58
    Congress of People's Deputies:
        elections for, 295
        proceedings, 296–97
    conservative offensives:
        March, 1988, 192–96
        September, 1988, 227–30, 280–83
        July, 1989, 303–4
    conventional arms control, 260,
        268–69
    coup against, possible, 208
    crisis of confidence in, 294–95
    cultural world, policy on, 17–18

337

Polyakov, Yuri, 123
Ponomaryov, Boris, 3, 63, 107
Popov, Filipp, 220
Popov, Gavriil, 130, 181, 304
Prague Spring, twentieth anniversary of, 265
Pravda, 6, 7, 9, 10, 23, 24, 28, 36, 77, 88, 93, 116, 117, 123, 132, 152, 174, 182, 188, 191, 193, 194, 199, 207, 221, 255, 292
Press Khronika, 171
price reforms, 233
Primakov, Yevgeni, 192, 224, 305, 306
Pristavkin, Anatoli, 96
profitable ventures, government opposition to, 51–52
Prokhanov, Aleksandr, 191
Proskurin, Pyotr, 89
prostitution, 113
Pugo, Boris, 306
Puzo, Mario, 213
Pyadyshev, Boris, 123, 158
Pyatakov, Grigori, 99, 106, 200, 210

Qaddafi, Muammar, 62
quality control programs, 30–31, 52–53, 83

Rabotnitsa, 176
Radek, Karl, 99, 200, 210
Raikin, Arkadi, 37
Rashidov, Saraf, 33, 55
Raskolnikov, Fyodor, 105, 113
Rasputin, Valentin, 18, 20, 176
Razumovsky, Georgi, 4, 7, 90, 184, 185, 196, 197, 209, 220, 229
Reagan, Ronald, 148, 254, 258, 271, 279
    Afghanistan policy, 256
    arms control policy, 58, 65, 66, 73, 157, 159, 160
    Moscow summit, 259, 272–74
    Reykjavik summit, 65
    Washington summit, 160
Referendum, 171
rehabilitations of Stalin's victims, 99–107, 128, 131–32, 146–47, 183, 200, 210

religious rights, 78
Repentance (film), 15, 29, 78, 95
Requiem (Akhmatova), 84, 86
Reykjavik summit (1986), 65–66, 72–73, 148
Riuitel, Arndt, 236
river diversion plans, 7, 26, 46–47
rock music, 216
Romanov, Grigori, 3, 56
Romm, M., 176
Rossiya Club, 308
rule-of-law socialist state, 172–73, 198, 294–95
Rumania, xi–xii, 161–62, 265
Russian nationalism, 86–87, 308
Russian Revolution, 38
Rust, Mathias, 90, 91
Ryazanov, Eldar, 96
Rybakov, Anatoli, 18, 87, 96, 190
Rykov, Aleksei, 106
Ryzhkov, Nikolai, 9, 22, 61, 110, 196, 249–50, 265, 285–86, 301, 303, 309

Sad Detective Story (Astafev), 18
Sagdeyev, Roald, 232, 237
Saikin, Valeri, 86
Sakharov, Andrei, 87, 299
    Academy of Sciences, election to, 232, 284
    death, 308
    Interregional Group, 304
    interviews with media, 118
    liberation, 34–36, 92–93
    Moscow Forum, 150
    SDI, criticism of, 159
salary reform, 47–49, 83
Samsonov, Aleksandr, 88
savings, "forced," 292–93
Schlesinger, Arthur, Jr., 161
second economy, 42, 43–45
    individual work activities, 31–32, 49–52
Secretariat of the Central Committee, changes in, 3–4
Seidov, 245
Sellers, Michael, 61
Selskaya Zhizn, 174

Selyunin, Vasili, 83, 213
separatist movements, xiv, 234, 235–36,
    248, 285, 297, 307–8
  legitimate claims of, 305
shabashniki (unlicensed construction
    companies), 49
Shafarevich, Igor, 213
Shakhnazarov, Georgi, 72
Shalamov, Varlaam, 212
Shatrov, Mikhail, 15, 32–33, 83, 99,
    183, 190, 199
Shcharansky, Anatoli, 168
Shcherbin, Boris, 6
Shcherbitsky, Vladimir, 41, 116, 193,
    302, 306
Shevardnadze, Eduard, 29, 56, 66, 152,
    196, 260
  Afghanistan policy, 67, 149, 254, 256,
    257, 267
  arms control, 157–58, 166
  "conceptual revolution" in foreign pol-
    icy, 263–64
  conservative offensive (Sept., 1988),
    227, 228–29
  Foreign Minister, appointment as, 63,
    71
  Japan visit, 262
  U.S.–Soviet relations, 258–59
Shkolnikov, Aleksei, 31
Shmelyov, Nikolai, 84, 199, 289, 293
Shultz, George, 61, 152–53, 157, 196,
    255, 256
Shvernik, Nikolai, 104
Silver Wedding (Shatrov), 99
Simonov, Konstantin, 212
Simonov, Yevgeni, 84
Slutsky, Boris, 96, 212
Slyunkov, Nikolai, 3, 109, 111, 196,
    229, 282, 309
Sobesednik, 176
social consumption, policy on, 227,
    232–33, 304
socialist countries, Soviet relations with,
    161–63, 264–67
social revolts of 1989, 297–98, 305
Sofronov, Anatoli, 19, 33, 97
Sokolov, Marshal Sergei, 90–91
Sokolov criminal investigation, 27

Solomentsev, Mikhail, 193, 221, 229,
    251
Solovyov, Yuri, 3, 23, 290, 304
Sorokin, Pitirim, 205
Sovetskaya Kultura, 7, 19, 26, 97, 114,
    115, 116, 121, 174–75, 214
Sovetskaya Rossia, 123, 174, 189, 191,
    195, 196–97, 207, 308
Soviet Encyclopedia, 78
Stalin, Iosif, 5n, 54, 95, 101–2, 144–45,
    168, 208, 284
Stalinism, debate on, 113
  collectivization issue, 108
  conservative position, 114–22,
    145–46, 189, 194–95
  Gorbachev's condemnations, 127–28
  media's role, 213–14
  novels and films, 29–30, 87–88,
    95–97
  in Poland, 120
  rehabilitations of Stalin's victims,
    99–107, 128, 131–32, 146–47,
    183, 200, 210
Stamboltsyan, Khatsik, 231
state enterprises:
  autonomy for, 109–11
  bureaucracy of the ministries, cam-
    paign against, 27–28, 78–79, 81
Story of Asiya Klyachiana Who Loved
    Without Getting Married (film),
    215
Strategic Defense Initiative (SDI), 59, 64,
    73, 93, 151, 156, 157, 159–60,
    161
Sukalo, Viktor, 116
Sukharev, Aleksandr, 85
Sumgait massacre, 186–87, 209, 244–45
Supreme Court of the USSR, 183
Supreme Soviet:
  elections for, 223, 296–97
  proceedings following election,
    300–302
Suslov, Mikhail, 45, 212, 275
Sychev, Vyacheslav, 152

Talyzin, Nikolai, 65
Taraki, Nur Muhammed, 277
Tarkovsky, Andrei, 14, 35, 146

Yakunin, Gleb, 87
Yampolsky, Boris, 212
Yarin, Veniamin, 222
Yashin, Aleksandr, 212
Yazov, Gen. Dmitri, 91, 168,
  229
Yefremov, Oleg, 199
Yegorov, Aleksandr, 105
Yeltsin, Boris, 23, 24, 27, 123, 182,
  184, 275, 307
  as alternative to Gorbachev, 285
  commercial sector corruption, attacks
    on, 135–37
  election victory, 289
  Gorbachev, relations with, 140
  Gosstroi appointment, 130
  Interregional Group, 304
  limitchiki episode, 138–39
  Nineteenth Party Conference, 220–21,
    222
  Pamyat and, 86, 141–42
  party leaders' privileges, attacks on,
    135, 139–40
  popularity of, 143
  see also Yeltsin affair
Yeltsin affair:
  as conflict between party factions,
    133–34
  dismissal from Moscow party, 124–27,
    128–30
  Gorbachev's reaction to Yeltsin's
    speech, 140–41
  media coverage, 144

protests against dismissal, 130–31,
    142–43
  speech criticizing progress of pere-
    stroika, 124–25
  Yeltsin's personal qualities and,
    134–35
Yevtushenko, Yevgeni, 18, 84, 97
Yezhov, Nikolai, 102

Zagladin, Vadim, 125
Zahir Shah, Muhammad, 153, 276
Zaikov, Lev, 3, 23, 90, 131, 196, 224,
  230, 280–81, 283
Zakharov, Gennadi, 65
Zakharov, Vasili, 25
Zalygin, Sergei, 12, 17, 19, 24, 84, 284
Zamyatin, Leonid, 64
Zamyatin, Yevgeni, 212
Zaslavskaya, Tatyana, 199
Zatvornitsky, Vladimir, 131
Zhdanov, Yuri, 122, 213
Zhemchuzhina, Polina, 100
Zhigulin, Anatoli, 96
Zhivkov, Todor, 162
Zhukov, Marshal Georgi, 100
Zia ul-Haq, Muhammad, 254, 257
Zinoviev, Aleksandr, xv, 85, 128
Zinoviev, Grigori, 99, 106, 200, 210
Znamya, 19, 32, 97–98, 132, 175, 176,
  183, 212, 213
Znaniye-Sila, 20
Zoshchenko, Mikhail, 17
Zvezda, 176

346

About the Authors

Ousted from the Soviet Communist Party in the late sixties, ROY MEDVEDEV is now a leading figure in Soviet life, and plays a key role as a member of the new Supreme Soviet. He is also the author of a major biography of Stalin, *Let History Judge*, and is now widely published in Russia as well as in the West.

GIULIETTO CHIESA is the Moscow correspondent for the Italian paper *l'Unità* and the author of several books on the Soviet Union, including a previous work with Roy Medvedev. He is spending this year as a fellow at the Woodrow Wilson Center in Washington.